MOUNTAINEERING LITERATURE

MOUNTAINEERING LITERATURE

A Bibliography of Material Published in English

by

Jill Neate

CICERONE PRESS
MILNTHORPE

MOUNTAINBOOKS
SEATTLE

First published as *Mountaineering and its Literature*
1978 © W. R. Neate
Revised and extended as *Mountaineering Literature – A Bibliography*
1986 © Jill (W. R.) Neate
Published by Cicerone Press, Milnthorpe, Cumbria, England

Printed in Scotland by Holmes McDougall Ltd. Edinburgh

ISBN 0-902363-82-4

Published in North America by Mountainbooks,
Box 25589, Seattle, Washington 98125, USA

ISBN 0-938567-05-5

CONTENTS

INTRODUCTION

Facing page:
Eigerwand, Switzerland

PREFACE TO SECOND EDITION

Nearly ten years have passed since I completed the draft of the first edition which has established itself as a standard reference work worldwide. Since then the Alpine Club have published the catalogue of the books in their library and Yoshimi Yakushi has published the much enlarged second edition of his prized catalogue of Himalayan literature. There has also appeared an elegant tribute to Francis Farquhar's contribution to the field of mountaineering literature. To each of these publications, as well as to personal contacts at home and abroad, this new edition is greatly indebted, both as to form and content.

A practicable definition of a 'mountaineering book' continues to elude me. However guidelines were necessary and, as well as books with an obvious mountaineering content, my intention has been to include items which seem to me to be of 'practical use, pleasure and historical interest' to climbers. This is perhaps a little wide but not as open-ended as including everything likely to appear in booksellers' catalogues of books on mountaineering and mountain travel. Certain specific categories of books omitted are mentioned in the Explanatory Notes.

There was mention in the first edition of the non-availability of English-language literature on mountaineering in the Andes and mountaineering by Japanese climbers, now possibly the most numerous and enthusiastic in the world. As regards the latter the position has ameliorated slightly as Japanese publications increasingly include short summaries in English. As to the Andes very little has been published in English during the intervening years, compared with the output in French, German, Italian and Spanish. Being interested, I have prepared a full-length reference book on mountaineering in the Andes, comprising concise accounts of the geography and climbing history of each range and group; an annotated index of peaks and routes climbed; and an annotated bibliography of some 2,000 books and articles in English, French, German, Italian and Spanish. Although this particular project is now being finalized for publication shortly, I shall be very glad to hear any time from any Andes enthusiasts, with whom I am not already in touch.

Over the years mountain fiction has grown to be a fully-fledged offspring of mountaineering literature encompassing now some 300-400 titles, according to one's definition of it. Much of the original research was done in the 1940s by J. Monroe Thorington, then President of the American Alpine Club and a distinguished mountain historian. More recently an article by George Pokorny and a paper I gave in September 1981 at a 'Sporting Fictions' workshop at the University of Birmingham have served to stimulate interest in this branch of the literature. The staple of this mass of fiction is the mountain/mountaineering-backed thriller. If there is a climbing fiction genre at all it is the big-wall climb, typified by the North Face of the Eiger, which has been used as a setting several times.

Mountaineering literature, like mountaineering, is still developing and, like the sport, has its polemics. It has become fashionable to write in a style which uses a great deal of crude vernacular, particularly in fiction and drama. Oscar Wilde declared that there is no such thing as a moral or immoral book, only books well written, or badly written and it is only with the quality of writing that I am presently concerned. Some years ago there was a furore over the article 'Hands' by an American climber Anne Marie Rizzi, which contained one line of expletive. Stylistically, I consider it to be an excellent example of how the technique should be used, whereas constant repetition for effect is self-defeating, as witness Alexander Pope in his *Essay On Criticism:*

> 'While expletives their feeble aid do join,
> And ten low words oft creep in one dull line.'

Authors would do well to bear this in mind before committing themselves to paper. After all, that most over-worked adjective 'nice' is also a four-letter word.

A further point in the matter of writing, about which commentators have complained over the years, is the all too frequent banality of mountaineers' jokes. Stephen Leacock's article on 'Humour' in the *Encyclopaedia Britannica* (14th ed.vol.XI,p.885) makes the point that 'the highest range of humour is that which turns on the depiction of human character', and in this category he cites the *Tartarin* novels among others; whereas the burlesque of books such as *Rum Doodle* is of a lower order. To return to another eighteenth century writer, the Earl of Chesterfield has the following to say, in *Letters To His Son:*

> 'Every company is differently circumstanced and has its peculiar cant and jargon; which may give occasion to wit and mirth within that circle, but would seem flat and insipid in any other.'

A popular pastime is the compiling of lists of 'The 100 best . . .' kind. On a serious level such lists can have little validity. So far, I believe, there has not been a full-length study in depth of the whole field of mountaineering literature (in English at any rate), although more than one attempt has been made to assemble the data, for example in the doctoral thesis, *A Study of the Literature Of the Mountains and Of Mountain Climbing Written In English,* by Robert Bates. I am reminded of the story of the man who wished to acquire a collection of Alpine books. He began with Leslie Stephen's *Playground of Europe* and tried each succeeding volume by its standard. His library remained a collection of one volume (until it was doubled by the addition of Schuster's *Peaks and Pleasant Pastures).* The book on my pedestal is Whymper's *Scrambles,* which is unique, in the near perfection of its construction, moving as it does between Mont Blanc and the Matterhorn, the Alpha and Omega of the Alps. It is the mountaineering book which most nearly fulfills the quality of epic, i.e. that it should be one action; an entire action with just and regular progress from origin to consummation; and a great action with far-reaching consequences. Even without the tragedy, which raises it epically to even greater heights, it is incomparable.

Many people have contributed to the improvement of this bibliography but a special vote of thanks is due to John Pollock, of Seattle, originally in his capacity as Director of Publishing at The Mountaineers, and subsequently as friend and proprietor of Mountain Books, Seattle. Nearer home, close friend Audrey Salkeld has given unstintingly of her expertise as always.

One of the ills of modern times is the problem of information retrieval. Fortunately it is also the age of the computer, now the only practicable means of updating and indexing the mass of data on such a relatively small subject as mountaineering. Coupled with computerized typesetting it is to be hoped that it will prove economically viable to publish much more in specialized fields such as bibliography in the future.

JILL NEATE

Keswick, Cumbria.
1986

EXPLANATORY NOTES

Subject to a few exceptions the works listed are restricted to books and pamphlets published in English, either originally or in translation. Some of the foreign language publications included, especially those in Japanese, have only short summaries and/or captions in English. By and large books on the following subjects are excluded: rambling, hiking, backpacking, mountain countryside, camping, caving, skiing, polar travel, geography, geology, mountain flora and fauna, vulcanology. Generally speaking, offprints from journals and magazines are excluded. A few which have appeared in publications not usually accessible to climbers have been included.

Indexes

The short title index lists every item in the bibliography except journals and bibliographies. The general index replaces the subject and mountain indexes of the first edition. Novels, short stories, drama and poetry are not indexed as to content.

References and Sources

The following are the principal references and sources consulted:

Alpine Club, Library Catalogue (v. 1, 1982)
Alpine Journal
American Alpine Club, Library working list (1973)
American Alpine Journal
Bates, Study of the literature of the mountains
Booksellers' catalogues (from U.K., U.S.A., Italy, Germany)
Bridge, Rock-climbing in the British Isles, 1894-1970: a bibliography of guidebooks
British National Bibliography
Campbell, Bibliography of mountains and mountaineering in Africa
Cox, Classics in the literature of mountaineering
Cumulated Fiction Index (vols. for 1945-78)
Encyclopædia Britannica (14th ed.)
Fell & Rock Climbing Club, Library Catalogue (and supplements)
Himalayan Journal
Krawczyk, Mountaineering [bibliography]
Library association, Readers' guide to books on mountaineering
Meckly, Bibliography of privately printed books
Montagnier, Bibliography of the ascents of Mont Blanc
National Library of Scotland, Shelf Catalogue of the Lloyd Collection
Read, Mountaineering, the literature in English
Yakushi, Catalogue of Himalayan literature (2nd ed.)

Paperbacks

The following list gives the names of paperback editions mentioned in the text with the publisher's name in parentheses:

Aldine (Dent)
Arrow (Hutchinson)
Consul (World Distributors)
Corgi (Transworld Publications)
Coronet (Hodder & Stoughton)
Dragon (Granada)
Four Square (Landsborough Pub)
Fontana (Collins)
Guild (Cambridge University Press)
Mayflower (Granada)
New English Library (New English Lib.)
Paladin (Granada)
Pan (Heinemann)
Panther (Granada)
Pelican (Penguin Books)
Penguin (Penguin Books)
Piccolo (Pan Books)
Puffin (Penguin Books)
Sphere (Thompson Publications)

Reference Numbering System

The reference numbering is alpha-numerical. In the main body of entries capital letters are used, according to the initial letter of authors' surnames; in the subsidiary sections the following conventions are used: Q = Climbers' Guidebooks; X = Fiction; j = Journals & Periodicals; b = Bibliographies; a = addenda.

Principal Abbreviations Used

A.A.C.	American Alpine Club
A.C.	Alpine Club
A.e.g.	All edges gilt
B.C.A.	Book Club Associates
Bibl.	Bibliography
B.J.	Black Jacket
C.C.	Climbers' Club
Cm.	Centimetre
Col.	Colour
C.U.P.	Cambridge University Press
Ed.	Edition
Fold.	Folding
F.M.C.I.	Federation of Mountaineering Clubs of Ireland
F.R.C.C.	Fell and Rock Climbing Club of the English Lake District
Illus	Illustration
Ldn	London
M.	Metre
N.d.	No date
N.p.	No place
N.Y.	New York City
O.U.P.	Oxford University Press
Pkt	Pocket
Ptg	Printing (impression)
Rev.	Revised
R.P.	Reprint
R.U.	Readers' Union
S.F.	San Francisco
S.M.C.	Scottish Mountaineering Club
S.M.T.	Scottish Mountaineering Trust
T.B.C.	Travel Book Club
T.e.g.	Top edges gilt
Trans.	Translated
Univ.	University
Var. pag.	Various pagination
Yak.	Yakushi
4to	Quarto
8vo	Octavo

Official abbreviations used for the States of the U.S.A.

These have been used more easily to identify the place of publication.

CA	California
CO	Colorado
CT	Connecticut
IA	Iowa
ID	Idaho
IL	Illinois
MA	Massachusetts
ME	Maine
MI	Michigan
MN	Minnesota
MT	Montana
NH	New Hampshire
NJ	New Jersey
NV	Nevada
NY	New York
OH	Ohio
OK	Oklahoma
OR	Oregon
PA	Pennsylvania
RI	Rhode Island
SC	South Carolina
TX	Texas
UT	Utah
VA	Virginia
VT	Vermont
WI	Wisconsin
WV	West Virginia
WY	Wyoming

Climbers' Guidebooks

This sub-section generally contains only modern guidebooks, certain historical items by, for example, Ball, Conway, Coolidge, Packe and Haskett Smith being included in the main listing.

THE BIBLIOGRAPHY

Facing page:
Quarry climbing at Trowbarrow, North Lancashire

A

A01. ABRAHAM, Ashley Perry (1876-1951)
Rock-climbing in Skye. Ldn: Longmans, 1908. xxii, 330p, 31 plates, illus, map (in pkt). 24cm.
Third part of the classic Jones-Abraham trilogy. The author was a mountain photographer who, with his brother George and O. G. Jones, was largely responsible for the development and popularization of rock-climbing in the Lake District and other parts of the British Isles.

A02. ABRAHAM, George Dixon (1872-1965)
British mountain climbs. Ldn: Mills & Boon, 1909. xvi, 448p, 18 plates, illus. 18cm. Some early copies were box-bound. R.P., 1923, 1932, 1937, 1945, 1948.
His second most important work. Basically a guidebook but readable as a history. Abraham, a mountain photographer, pioneered many rock-climbs in the Lake District, often with his brother and O. G. Jones. He also climbed in the Alps and other parts of Britain.

A03. ABRAHAM, G. D.
The complete mountaineer. Ldn: Methuen, 1907/N.Y.: Doubleday, 1908. xvi, 493p, 75 plates, illus. 23cm. R.P., 1908.
—3rd rev. ed. Methuen, 1923.
Omnibus instructional work; virtually a distillation of all his writings.

A04. ABRAHAM, G. D.
First steps to climbing. Ldn: Mills & Boon, 1923. 126p, 24 plates, illus. 19cm.
—U.S. ed. N.Y.: McBride, 1925.

A05. ABRAHAM, G. D.
Modern mountaineering. Ldn: Methuen, 1933. x, 198p, 16 plates, illus. 20cm.
—2nd ed. 1945.
—3rd rev. ed. 1948.

A06. ABRAHAM, G. D.
Mountain adventures at home and abroad. Ldn: Methuen/N.Y.: Doubleday Page, 1910. x, 308p, 26 plates, illus. 23 cm. U.S. title-page shows only 'Mountain Adventures'. R.P., 1910.
Personal and other adventures.

A07. ABRAHAM, G. D.
On Alpine heights and British crags. Boston: Houghton Mifflin, 1916/Ldn: Methuen, 1919. xi, 307p, 24 plates, illus. 23cm. U.K. ed. was delayed by World War I.
Climbing reminiscences and other topics.

A08. ABRAHAM, G. D.
Rock-climbing in North Wales. Keswick: G. P. Abraham, 1906. xxii, 394p, 30 plates, illus. 24cm.
His most important work, being the second part of the classic Jones-Abraham rock-climbing trilogy.

A09. ABRAHAM, G. D.
Swiss mountain climbs. Ldn: Mills & Boon, 1911. xvi, 423p, 24 plates, illus. 18cm. Some early copies were box-bound.
Similar to his *British mountain climbs* but never as successful.

A10. ACADEMIC ALPINE CLUB OF KYOTO
Ascent of Noshaq: the Japanese Pamir expedition, 1960. Tokyo: Asahi-Newspaper, 1961. var. pag., plates (some col), illus, map. 26cm. In Japanese with English summary. Yak. j. 244.
First ascent from Afghan side.

A11. ACADEMIC ALPINE CLUB OF KYOTO
Chogolisa: Japanese Chogolisa 1958 Expedition (by ...). Tokyo: Asahi-Newspaper, 1959. 138p, illus. (some col), maps. 26cm. In Japanese with English summary. Yak. j. 243.
First ascent. Karakoram.

A12. ACADEMIC ALPINE CLUB OF KYOTO
Saltoro Kangri: Japan-Pakistan Joint Expedition, 1962. Tokyo: Asahi-Newspaper, 1964. var. pag., illus, 2 maps. 26cm. In Japanese with English summary. Yak. j. 245.
First ascent; first half of book is a photo-album.

A13. ACADEMIC ALPINE CLUB OF KYOTO

Yalung Kang. Tokyo: Asahi-Newspaper, 1975. var. pag., illus. (some col), maps 26cm. In Japanese with English summary. Yak. j. 246.
First ascent of Yalung Kang (Kanchenjunga West, 8505m); first half of book is a photo-album.

A14. [ADAMS, William Henry Davenport]

Alpine adventure: or, Narratives of travel and research in the Alps, by the author of 'The Mediterranean Illustrated', . . .Ldn: Nelson, 1878. 237p, illus. 19cm.
—Rev. ed. entitled *Alpine climbing: narratives of recent ascents of Mont Blanc, the Matterhorn, the Jungfrau, and other lofty summits of the Alps.*
The author wrote numerous books for young adults.

A15. [ADAMS, W. H. D.]

Mountains and mountain climbing: records of adventure and enterprise among the famous mountains of the world, by the author of 'The Mediterranean Illustrated', . . .Ldn: Nelson, 1883. 415p, illus. 20cm.
Includes Norway, Teneriffe, Mauritius, Chimborazo, Hawaii.

A16. AGNEW, Crispin Hamlyn, of Lochnaw yr

Army East Greenland Expedition, 1968. Expedition report by . . .and others. [Glasgow]: The Expedition, [1968?]. iv, 56p, illus, maps. 30cm.

A17. AGNEW, C. H.

Joint Services Expedition to Chilean Patagonia, 1972-73. General report by . . .Expedition Trust Committee, 1974. ix, 70p, fold. plate, illus, map, bibl. 30cm.

A18. AHLMANN, Hans Wilhelmsson

Land of ice and fire. Trans. from the Swedish by Klares & Herbert Lewes. Ldn: Kegan Paul Trench Trubner, 1938. xi, 271p, plates, illus, map. 23cm.
Iceland: an account of the author's exploration of the great Vatnajökull ice-field, including a traverse.

A19. AHLUWALIA, Hari Pal Singh

Eternal Himalaya. New Delhi: Interprint, 1982. 216p, illus, maps. 31cm.
His experiences in the Himalaya and a short history of exploration in the area; together with a reprint (pp. 69-208) of George Francis White's book, *Views in Himalaya.*

A20. AHLUWALIA, H. P. S.

Faces of Everest. New Delhi: Vikas, 1978. xxiv, 238p, illus, map. 28cm.
Climbing history to autumn, 1977.

A21. AHLUWALIA, H. P. S.

Higher than Everest: memoirs of a mountaineer. Delhi: Vikas, 1973. ix, 188p, illus, map. 23cm. R.P.., 1973.
—2nd rev. ed. 1974. R.P., 1975.
—4th rev. ed. Bombay, 1975. viii, 186p.
—Adapted for children as *Climbing Everest.* Delhi: Vikas, 1976. 72p, plates, illus. 21cm.
Ahluwalia, an Indian soldier, reached the summit of Everest during the 1965 expedition; he also recounts his experiences in the Indo-Pakistan war.

A22. AIREY, Alan F

Irish hill days. Manchester: Open Air Pub, [1937]. 47p, fold. map. 18cm.
Reminiscences; usable as a guidebook.

A23. AITKEN, Samuel

Among the Alps: a narrative of personal experiences. Illustrations by Vittorio Sella. Northwood, Middx: The Author, 1900. xvi, 119p, 73 plates, illus. 29 × 39cm.
This sumptuous volume was designed as a Christmas present for the author's friends and illustrated with many of Sella's finest Alpine photographs.

A24. ALACK, Frank

Guide aspiring. Edited by J. Halket Millar. Auckland: Oswald-Sealy, [1963]. 229p, 8 plates, illus. 23cm.
Autobiography of New Zealand guide from the Austrian Tyrol, who climbed between the wars.

A25. ALCOCK, Sir Rutherford

The capital of the tycoon: narrative of a three year's residence in Japan. Ldn: Longmans, 1863.

—U.S. ed. N.Y.: Harper, 1877.
Includes account of his ascent of Fujiyama in 1860, the first by a European.

A26. ALEITH, R. C.
Bergsteigen: basic rock climbing. N.Y.: Scribner's, 1975.
Based on the Arizona Mountaineering Club training handbook.

A27. [ALLAN, Alastair]
Anglo-Danish mountain survey in East Greenland: preliminary report.
Cambridge: The expedition, 1969. 9p, plate, map. 30cm.
Watkins Mountains expedition, 1969.

A28. ALLEN, Charles
A mountain in Tibet: the search for Mount Kailas and the sources of the great rivers of India. Ldn: Deutsch, 1982. 2-255p, illus. 25cm.
The author, a radio & TV documentarist, born in India, has trekked and climbed extensively in the Himalaya.

A29. ALLEN, Dan H.
Don't die on the mountain. New Hampshire Chapter of the Appalachian Mountain Club, 1972. 27p. Softbound.
Survival guide.

A30. ALLEN, John
Manchester Karakoram Expedition, 1968: report. Edited by . . .[Manchester]:
The Expedition, [1969?]. 21p, fold. plate, illus, map, bibl. 25cm.

A31. ALLEN, J.
Manchester Nepalese Expedition, 1970. Report, written by members of the expedition; edited by . . .Manchester: The Expedition, [1971]. 25p, fold. plate, illus, map, bibl. 26cm.

A32. [ALPINE CLUB]
Peaks, passes and glaciers: a series of excursions by members of the Alpine Club. Edited by John Ball. Ldn: Longmans, 1859. xvi, 514p, 8 col. plates, illus, 9 maps. 22cm.
—2nd, 3rd & 4th ed. 1859, with corrections. The first edition is distinguished from later editions by a different vignette on the title-page, 23 wood-cuts in place of 24 later, the gilt illustration on the front cover narrow (44mm) and the slope at 60° instead of 45° on the others.
—5th ed. 1869. Traveller's 'Knapsack' ed. xvi, 328p. 18cm.
One of the most famous titles in mountaineering literature, this series of pieces by members of the Alpine Club led directly to the commencement of the *Alpine Journal* in 1863.

A33. [ALPINE CLUB]
Narratives selected from 'Peaks, passes and glaciers'. Edited with introduction and notes by George Wherry. Cambridge: University Press, 1910. [6], 156p, maps. 18cm.
Six chapters from the first series.

A34. [ALPINE CLUB]
Peaks, passes and glaciers: being excursions by members of the ALpine Club. Second series. Edited by Edward Shirley Kennedy. Ldn: Longmans, 1862. 2v. plates, illus, maps. 22cm.

A35. [ALPINE CLUB]
Peaks, passes and glaciers. Selected and annotated by E. H. Blakeney. Ldn: Dent, 1926. xxxxviii, 317p. 18cm. (Everyman's Library series)
—Another ed. Heron Books. With new intro. by W. A. Chislett.
Selection from first and second series.

A36. [ALPINE CLUB]
Peaks, passes and glaciers: by members of the Alpine Club. Third series. Edited by A. E. Field and Sydney Spencer. Ldn: Methuen, 1932. xii, 307p, 16 plates, illus. 23cm. Bound with or without gilt block on front cover.
Selection from volumes 1-5 of the *Alpine Journal.*

A37. [ALPINE CLUB]
Peaks, passes and glaciers. Selections from the *Alpine Journal* compiled and introduced by Walt Unsworth. Ldn: Allen Lane/Seattle: Mountaineers, 1981. 284p, plates, illus. 24cm.
Articles spanning the period from Whymper to John Harlin.
—Penguin paperback, 1982.

A38. ALPINE CLUB
Treasures of the Alpine club: rare books and pictures. Ldn: Alpine Club, 1982. 27p, illus.
Exhibition catalogue.

A39. ALPINE CLUB OF CANADA
The Alpine Club of Canada in Jasper National Park, Alberta, 1926: photographs. [Vancouver]: Canadian National Railways, [1926?]. Vol. of illus. 27 × 34cm.
Photo-album with explanatory captions.

A40. AMENT, Patrick Oliver (b.1951)
Master of rock: the biography of John Gill. Boulder: Alpine House, 1977. vi, 197p, illus. 27cm.
John Gill is renowned for his bouldering prowess and mental approach to rock-climbing. Many illustrations.

A41. AMENT, P. O.
Rock Wise: reflections, safety and technique in rock climbing. Boulder: 1978. 169p, illus. 21cm.

A42. AMENT, P. O.
Swaramandal. Boulder: Vitaar Pub, [1973]. viii, 133p, illus. (some col). 22cm. Softback.
Stylish descriptions of Colorado rock-climbs by well-known American climber.

A43. AMERY, Leopold Charles Maurice Stennett (1873-1955)
Days of fresh air: being reminiscences of outdoor life. Ldn: Jarrolds, 1939. 320p, 47 plates, illus. 22cm.
Memoirs of a leading British politician who was President of the Alpine Club, 1944-6.

A44. AMERY, L. C. M. S.
In the rain and the sun: a sequel to 'Days of fresh air'. Ldn: Hutchinson, 1946. 251p, 33 plates, illus. 22cm.
Further memoirs of leading British politician-mountaineer.

A45. AMPLEFORTH COLLEGE
Ampleforth College Himalayan Expedition, 1977: report. Ampleforth, Yorks: Ampleforth College, [1978]. 49p, plates, illus, maps. 21cm.

A46. ANDERSEN, Johannes c.
Jubilee history of South Canterbury. Auckland: Whitcombe & Tombs, 1916. xv, 775p, illus, maps. 26cm.
Includes the first attempt to compile a first ascents list of the central Southern Alps.

A47. ANDERSON, Eustace (1819-89)
Chamouni and Mont Blanc: a visit to the valley and an ascent of the mountain in the autumn of 1855. Ldn: Cornish, 1856. vi, 113p, 2 col. plates (1 fold), illus. 18cm.
Late example of pre-'Golden Age' Alpine literature. By this date travellers no longer 'abstained from everything likely to produce concussion of the air' or, when a companion jumped a crevasse without a rope, rebuked him for 'the impropriety of his conduct in thus endangering his life'. The author is best remembered for his attempts on the Schreckhorn in 1857. His Alpine career ended many years before his death.

A48. ANDERSON, E. H.
Liverpool Institute Mountaineering Club Iceland Expedition, 1975: official report. By ...[and others]. Liverpool: [The Expedition], 1975. 44 leaves, plates, illus, col. maps. 35cm.

A49. ANDERSON, John & MORSE, Stearns
The book of the White Mountains. N.Y.: Minton Balch, 1930. 300p.

A50. ANDERSON, J. R. L.
High mountains and cold seas: a biography of H. W. Tilman. Ldn: Gollancz/Seattle: Mountaineers, 1980. 366p, 28 plates, illus, maps, bibl. 24cm.
Tilman was one of the leading twentieth century exponents of rugged lightweight exploration. In later life he took up ocean sailing.

A51. ANDERSON, J. R. L.
The Ulysses factor: the exploring instinct in man. Ldn: Hodder/N.Y.: Harcourt Brace Jovanovich, 1970. 352p, plates, illus, bibl. 23cm.
Includes chapters on Maurice Herzog, Shipton and Tilman.

A52. ANDERSON, Warwick
To the untouched mountain: the New Zealand conquest of Molamenging, Tibet. Wellington: Reed, 1983. 242p, 12 col. plates, illus, maps.
Molamenging (7703m) is adjacent to Xixabangma and was the world's third highest unclimbed peak.

A53. ANHALZER, Jorge & NAVARRETE, Ramiro
Por Los Andes Del Ecuador. Quito: Ediciones Campo Abierto, 1983. 3-171p, col. illus. 30cm. Text in Spanish, English and German.
Finely illustrated descriptions of the most interesting peaks.

A54. ANKLESARIA, Russi D.
Himalchal, the story of an Himalayan adventure. Calcutta: E. N. Kanga, Navroz Printing Works, 1942. 154p, illus.
Seven Indian mountaineers led by Jal Bapasola attempted Kanchenjunga and Pandim, and climbed Guicha peak, Sikkim Himalaya. Not in Yakushi.

A55. ANNAN, Noel Gilroy, Lord Annan
Leslie Stephen: his thought and character in relation to his time. Ldn: MacGibbon & Kee, 1951. x, 342p, 8 plates, illus. 23cm.
Biography of one of the most famous of Victorian mountaineers.

A56. ANNAN, N. G.
Leslie Stephen: the godless Victorian. Ldn: Weidenfeld & Nicolson, 1984. xvi, 432p, plates, illus. 24cm.
Partly biography, partly a study of Victorian thought and its origins.

A57. [ANONYMOUS]
The ascent of Pieterboth Mountain, Mauritius, 13 October 1864. Mauritius: E. Dupuy & P. Dubois, printers, 1864. 15p, plates, illus. 13cm.

A58. [ANONYMOUS]
The peasants of Chamouni: containing an attempt to reach the summit of Mont Blanc, and a delineation of the scenery among the Alps. Ldn: Baldwin Cradock & Joy, 1823. 164p, plates, illus. 15cm.
—2nd ed. 1826.
Includes the story of the Hamel accident. This little book inspired Albert Smith, who made his own ascent in 1851.

A59. ARCHER, Clement Hugh
Climbs in Japan and Korea: a photographic record and guide. [N.p.]: The Author, [1936]. xi, 221p, illus, maps. 27cm. Typed and bound by the author.

A60. ARMSTRONG, Betsy & WILLIAMS, Knox
The avalanche book. Golden: Fulcrum, 1986. [iii], 231p.

A61. ARMSTRONG, Patrica Kay
Summits of the soul: a collection of mountaineering poems. Compiled and edited by . . .[Naperville: Naperville Sun, 1978]. viii, 66p, illus. 23cm.
Poems mostly reprinted from *Summit* magazine.

A62. ARPS, Louisa Ward
High country names: Rocky Mountain National Park. By . . .and Elinor Eppich Kingery. Denver: Colorado Mountain Club, 1966. ?p, illus, maps.

A63. ARUNDALE, George S.
Mount Everest: its spiritual attainment. Wheaton, IL: Theosophical Press, 1933. 197p.

A64. [ASAHI-NEWSPAPER]
The magnificence of the Himalayas. Compiled by . . .Tokyo: Asahi-Newspaper, 1978. 219, viip, illus, (mostly col), maps, 26cm. In Japanese with English summary. Yak. j. 23.
Photo-album of 136 high peaks and 'Coping with high peaks in the Himalayas' by Kyûya Fukata.

A65. ASHBURNER, John
Cambridge Hindu-Kush Expedition, 1966: report. By . . ., Henry Edmundson & Paul Newby. [Cambridge]; the Expedition, [1967]. 66p, plates (2 fold.), illus, maps. 25cm. Yak. A. 101.

A66. ASHENDEN (pseud. Sidney Edward Payn Nowill)
The mountains of my life: journeys in Turkey and the Alps. Ldn: Blackwood, 1954. xii, 212p, 28 plates, illus. 25cm.
Climbing reminiscences.

A67. ASSOCIATION OF BRITISH MEMBERS OF THE SWISS ALPINE CLUB

Inauguration of the Cabane Britannia, on the Klein Allalinhorne, Saas Fee, August 17th, 1912. And obituary notices and portrait of Clinton Dent. Ldn: A.B.M.S.A.C., 1913. [2], 54p, 14 plates, illus, port. 22cm.
The Britannia hut is the only mountain refuge in the Alps built entirely by money raised by British climbers. Clinton Dent was the first president of the Association, 1909-12.

A68. ASSOCIATION OF BRITISH MEMBERS OF THE SWISS ALPINE CLUB

Mountaineering handbook: a complete and practical guide for beginner or expert. Published for the . . .Ldn: Paternoster Press, 1950. 168p, illus. 19cm.

A69. ASSOCIATION OF BRITISH MEMBERS OF THE SWISS ALPINE CLUB

The technique of Alpine mountaineering. Publication of the Uto Section of the S[wiss] A[lpine] C[lub]. English edition adapted by members of the . . .Trans. by E. A. M. Wedderburn. [Ldn: A.B.M.S.A.C., 1935]. 74p, illus. 16cm. From the original: *Technique d'alpinism* by Emile Kern (Uto Section, 1929).

A70. ATA-ULLAH, Mohammad (1903-77)

Citizen of two worlds. N.Y.: Harper, 1960. xii, 285p, illus.
Autobiography of Pakistani soldier, doctor and climber who accompanied the American and Italian K2 expeditions in 1953 and 1954.

A71. ATKESON, Ray

The Cascade Range. Portland: Belding, 1969. [viii], 191p, illus. [4to].
Spectacular colour illustrations.

A72. ATKINS, Henry Martin (c.1818-42)

Ascent to the summit of Mont Blanc on the 22nd and 23rd of August, 1837. Ldn: Calkin & Budd, 1838. 51p, 6 plates, illus. 23cm.
—Reissued in 1842 with an account of his funeral.
Atkins made the 24th ascent of Mont Blanc.

A73. ATWATER, Montgomery M.

The avalanche hunters. Introduction by Lowell Thomas. Philadelphia: Macrae Smith, 1968. [xix], 235p, illus., bibl. 25cm.
The author was with the U.S. Forest Service at an avalanche research centre.

A74. ATWOOD, Wallace W.

The Rocky Mountains. N.Y.: Vanguard Press, 1945. 324p, 16 plates (1 fold.), illus, maps. 24cm. (American Mountain series, 3)

A75. AULDJO, John Richardson (1805-86)

Narrative of an ascent to the summit of Mont Blanc, on the 8th and 9th August, 1827. Ldn: Printed for Longmans, 1828. xii, 120p, 20 plates, illus, map. 33cm. Grey boards, paper label.
—2nd ed. 1830. xii, 148p, 19 plates, illus, 3 col. maps. 22cm.
—3rd ed. 1856. xii, 119p, illus. 18cm. (Traveller's Library series, 100). Includes annotated list of ascents of Mont Blanc.
—4th ed. 1867. Reprint of 3rd ed.
—Facsimile of first edition. Bologna: Libreria Alpina, 1972. Numbered edition of 220 copies.
Auldjo made the 19th ascent of Mont Blanc. His book was the first to popularize Mont Blanc and its influence persisted until the 1850s and the 'Golden Age' of mountaineering.

A76. AUSTIN, Cecil K.

On mountain climbing for professional men. Boston: Heath, 1907. 35p, illus. [8vo]. Reprinted from the *Boston Medical & Surgical Journal,* v. 156, no. 25, June 20, 1907, pp. 799-808.

A77. AUSTRALIAN ANDEAN EXPEDITION, 1969

Report. [Sydney: Concord Printing for the Expedition, 1970]. 32p, illus, map. 25cm.
First ascents in the Pumasillo group, Cordillera Vilcabamba, Peru.

A78. AZEMA, Marc Antonin
The conquest of Fitzroy. Trans. from the French by Katherine Chorley & Nea Morin. Ldn: Deutsch/Fairlawn: Essential Books, 1957. 237p, 12 plates, illus, maps. 22cm. From the original: *La conquête du Fitzroy* (Paris: Flammarion, 1954)
First ascent of this very severe Patagonian rock spire.

B

B01. BADÉ, William Frederic
Life and letters of John Muir. Boston: Houghton Mifflin, 1923-4. 2v. ports. 21cm.
Mountain and nature lover Muir was largely responsible for the establishment of Yosemite and other areas as national parks.

B02. BAGLEY, Arthur L.
Holiday rambles in the English Lake District. Ldn: Skeffington, [c. 1925]. 211p, 12 plates, illus. 20cm.
—2nd ed. 1936 celebrating the 50th anniversary of Haskett Smith's ascent of Napes Needle.
Hillwalking and easy climbs.

B03. BAGLEY, A. L.
Holiday rambles in North Wales. Ldn: Skeffington, [1920]. viii, 203p, 16 plates (1 fold), illus. 20cm.
Hillwalking and easy climbs.

B04. BAGLEY, A. L.
Walks and scrambles in the Highlands. Ldn: Skeffington, 1914. viii, 204p, 12 plates, illus. 20cm.
Hillwalking and easy climbs.

B05. BAILEY, Adrian
Lakeland rock: classic climbs with Chris Bonington. Ldn: Weidenfeld & Nicolson, 1985. 144p, illus (some col). 22cm.
Book of television series.

B06. BAILEY, Frederick Marshman (1882-1967)
No passport to Tibet. Ldn: Hart-Davis, 1957. 294p, plates, illus, maps. 23cm.
Account of his six-month journey with H. T. Morshead in 1913, during which they discovered Gyala Peri. Bailey was a soldier, Sikkim political officer and explorer.

B07. [BAINBRIDGE, W.]
Alpine lyrics. Ldn: Longmans, 1854. vii, 308p, 18cm.
Poems.

B08. BAINES, Jack
Hong Kong Mountaineering Club Expedition to the Snow Mountains of New Guinea, 1972. [Report], narrative section ...by Jack Baines. Hong Kong: The Expedition, [1973]. 27p, illus, maps. 26cm.
Third ascent of Carstenz Peak.

B09. BAKER, Ernest Albert
The British highlands with rope and rucksack. Ldn: Witherby, 1933. 236p, 11 plates, illus. 22cm.
—Facsimile reprint. Wakefield: E.P. Ltd, 1973. With new introduction by A. H. Griffin.
Baker was a contemporary of the Abraham Brothers with whom he climbed on occasions. He was also one of the party who made the first ascent of the Ben Nuis Chimney on Arran in 1901, a route not repeated for over fifty years.

B10. BAKER, E. A.
The Highlands with rope and rucksack. Ldn: Witherby, 1923. 253p, 19 plates, illus. 23cm.
Climbing in Scotland.

B11. BAKER, E. A.
Moors, crags and caves of the High Peak and the neighbourhood. Manchester: Heywood, [1903]. 207p, 43 plates, illus, 2 fold. maps. 23cm.
Pioneer rock-climbing on the outcrops of the Derbyshire Peak District. His most important and sought-after book.

B12. BAKER, E. A.
On foot in the Highlands. Glasgow: Maclehose, 1932.
—2nd ed. 1933. 204p, illus, bibl.

B13. BAKER, E. A. & ROSS, Francis E. (Editors)
The voice of the mountains. Ldn: Routledge, [1905]. xxii, 294p, 17cm.
—1st reprint with corrections, [1906].
—3rd reprint, [1913].
Well-known anthology.

B14. BAKER, George Percival (1856-1951)
Mountaineering memories of the past. Ldn: The Author, 1942. 38p, 4 plates, illus. 22cm.
—2nd ed. Ldn: The Author, 1951. 62p, 111 plates, illus. 22cm.
Chiefly material derived from his articles in the *Alpine Journal.* Baker was a wealthy British climber whose expeditions included Ararat, the Caucasus, and the Canadian Rockies, where he climbed with Collie.

B15. BAKER, Noeline
Surveyor in New Zealand, 1857-96. [J. H. Baker's diary edited by his daughter] Christchurch: Whitcombe & Tombs, 1932.
Baker was Samuel Butler's friend and co-discoverer of the Whitcombe Pass.

B16. BALCH, Edwin Swift (1856-1927)
Mount McKinley and mountain climbers' proofs. Philadelphia: Campion, 1914. 142p. 27cm.
An attempt to resolve the conflicting claims to the first ascent, using evidence later proved to be false. Balch was a founder member of the A.A.C. and climbed in the western and eastern Alps in the late nineteenth century.

B17. BALDWIN, John
Exploring the Coast Mountains on skis: a guide to over 150 ski touring trips. Vancouver: The Author, 1983. 144p, 12 plates, illus, maps. Softback.

B18. BALL, Benjamin Lincoln
Three days on the White Mountains: being the perilous adventure of Dr. B. L. Ball on Mount Washington during October 25, 26 and 27, 1855. Written by himself. Boston: N. Noyes, 1856. 72p.

BALL, John (1818-89)
[The Alpine guide. Basically this consists of three parts — Western, Central and Eastern Alps. In 1873 the whole thing was also issued in ten sections. See Nos. B19.-B32. below.]

B19. BALL, J.
Bernese Alps. Ldn: Longmans, 1873. [4], 144p, 3 maps. 18cm.
—New ed. 1875.

B20. BALL, J.
Central Alps. Ldn: Longmans, 1864. xx, 502p.
—2nd ed. 1866
—3rd ed. 1870. xx, 521p, R.P., 1873, 1876, 1882.
—Part I of revised edition, 1907. General editor A. V. Valentine-Richards. xxviii, 326p.
—Part II of revised edition 1911. General editor George Broke. xx, 432p.

B21. BALL, J.
Central Tyrol. Ldn: Longmans, 1873. [2], 139-314p, 3 maps. 18cm.
—New ed. 1878.

B22. BALL, J.
Eastern Alps. Ldn: Longmans, 1868. xxiv, 639p, 8 maps. 18cm.
—New ed. 1869. R.P., 1870?
—New ed. 1874. xxiv, 639p. R.P., 1879.

B23. BALL, J.
East Switzerland. Ldn: Longmans, 1873. [2], 347-489p, 5 maps. 18cm.
—Another ed. 1876.

B24. BALL, J.
Introduction to the 'Alpine Guide'. Ldn: Longmans, 1864. First appearance as a separate publication, being previously included in the Western Alps 1863 edition.
—Another ed. 1873. cxxxp. 18cm.
—Another ed. 1875.
—New edition 1899. Prepared on behalf of the Alpine Club by W. A. B. Coolidge, entitled *Hints and notes practical and scientific for travellers in the Alps being a revision of the general introduction to the 'Alpine Guide'.* clxivp. 18cm.

B25. BALL, J.
North Switzerland. Ldn: Longmans, 1873. [4], 145-244p, 2 maps. 18cm.

B26. BALL, J.
North Tyrol, Bavarian and Salzburg Alps. Ldn: Longmans, 1873. [4], 138p, 3 maps. 18cm.

B27. BALL, J.
The Pass of St. Gotthard. Ldn: Longmans, 1873. [4], 245-346p, 2 maps. 18cm.

B28. BALL, J.
Pennine Alps. Ldn: Longmans, 1873. [4], 181-378p, 4 maps. 18cm.
—New ed. 1875.
—New ed. 1878.

B29. BALL, J.
South Tyrol and Venetian or Dolomite Alps. Ldn: Longmans, 1873. [2], 399-529p. 18cm.
—New ed. 1876. 399-534p.

B30. BALL, J.
South western Alps. Ldn: Longmans, 1873. [4], 180p, 6 maps. 18cm.

B31. BALL, J.
Styrian, Carnic and Julian Alps. Ldn: Longmans, 1873. 315-393p & 530-602p, 3 maps. 18cm.
—New ed. 1876.

B32. BALL, J.
Western Alps. Ldn: Longmans, 1863. cxliv, 377p.
—2nd ed. 1866.
—3rd ed. 1870. xxiv, 404p. R.P., 1873.
—New edition 1898. Reconstructed and revised on behalf of the Alpine Club by W. A. B. Coolidge. lii, 612p. 19cm.

B33. BAND, George C.
Road to Rakaposhi. Ldn: Hodder, 1955. 192p, 31 plates, illus, maps. 20cm.
—T.B.C. ed. 1955.
Attempt on Rakaposhi (7788m) by a British climber who was on the 1953 Everest expedition and who climbed Kanchenjunga with Joe Brown in 1955.

B34. BANKS, Michael Edward Borg (b.1922)
Commando climber. Ldn: Dent, 1955. xiv, 240p, 17 plates, illus. 22cm.
—Abridged ed. entitled *Snow commando.* Ldn: Burke, 1961.
Biography of British marine commando and mountaineer. His activities have included expeditions to Greenland and the ascent of Rakaposhi.

B35. BANKS, M. E. B.
Greenland. Newton Abbot: David & Charles, 1975. 208p, illus, map, bibl. 23cm.
Concise introduction to this fascinating land and its early exploration.

B36. BANKS, M. E. B.
High Arctic: the story of the British North Greenland Expedition. With four chapters by Angus Erskine. Ldn: Dent, 1957. xii, 276p, plates, illus, maps. 22cm.
The expedition made a 800-mile crossing of the ice-cap and some new ascents in the Barth Mountains.

B37. BANKS, M. E. B.
Mountaineering for beginners. By . . .with drawings by Toby Buchan. Ldn: Seeley Service, 1977. 92p, illus. 23cm.
—U.S. ed. entitled *Mountain climbing for beginners.* Edited for American readers by Andy Kaufmann. N.Y.: Stein & Day, 1978. 96p.

B38. BANKS, M. E. B.
Rakaposhi. Ldn: Secker & Warburg, 1959/N.Y.: A. S. Barnes, 1960. 238p, 19 plates, illus. 22cm.
Account of 1956 attempt and first ascent in 1958 with Tom Patey.

B39. BARBE-BAKER, R. S.
The lasting victories. By . . .[and others]. Ldn: 1948.
Reference to Everest; not in Yakushi.

B40. BARBIER, Andrew
Leicester Polytechnic Students Greenland Expedition, 1972. Kûgosuatsiaq, Søndre Sermilik, southern Greenland: [the official report]. Edited by . . .Leicester: City of Leicester Polytechnic, 1973. v, 159p, plates, illus, maps, bibl. 30cm.

B41. BARFORD, John Edward Quintus (1914-47) (Editor)
Climbing in Britain. Harmondsworth, Middx: Penguin Books, 1946. 160p, plates, illus. 18cm. Pelican paperback.
This instructional book was prepared for the newly formed British Mountaineering Council and helped to popularize climbing after World War II. Barford was killed in the Alps.

B42. BARKER, Ralph
The last blue mountain. Ldn: Chatto & Windus, 1959. 212p, 23 plates, illus. 23cm.
—U.S. ed. N.Y.: Doubleday, 1960. 210p, 8 plates.
—Another ed. Ldn: Diadem/Seattle: Mountaineers, 1979. Softback.
This account of the tragic 1957 Haramosh expedition was prepared from expedition diaries and discussions with the survivors.

B43. BARKER, R.
One man's jungle: a biography of F. Spencer Chapman, D.S.O. Ldn: Chatto & Windus, 1975. x, 374p, plates, illus. 23cm.
Chapman's adventurous life included polar exploration, jungle warfare and mountaineering, for which he is usually remembered by his ascent of the remote peak Chomolhari (7315m).

B44. BARNES, Albert Henry
Our greatest mountain and alpine regions of wonder. Tacoma, WA: The Author, [1911]. 69p, illus. 28cm. Softback. (National Park Art series) Mt. Rainier.
Photo-album, some hand tinted.

B45. BARR, Patricia
A curious life for a lady: the story of Isabella Bird, a remarkable Victorian traveller. N.Y.: Doubleday, 1970. 347p, illus, maps. 21cm.
Biography. Isabella Bird is best known through her own account of her adventures in Colorado (Longs Peak) but she also travelled alone in Tibet, and in China.

B46. BARROW, John (1808-98)
Expeditions on the glaciers: including an ascent of Mont Blanc, Monte Rosa, Col du Géant, and Mont Buet, by a private of the Thirty-eight Artists, and member of the Alpine Club. Ldn: E. & F. N. Spon, 1864. [6], 122p, plate, illus. 20cm.
The author was Keeper of Records at the Admiralty, with a special interest in arctic exploration. On retirement he involved himself in mountaineering and the Volunteer movement, rising to Lt. Col., 5th Volunteer Battalion of the Rifle Brigade.

B47. BARROW, J.
Mountain ascents in Westmoreland and Cumberland. Ldn: Sampson Low, 1886. viii, 208p, 2 plates, illus, fold. map. 20 cm.
—Rev. enlarged ed. 1888.
Describes the delights of hillwalking in Victorian England.

B48. BARRY, John
The great climbing adventure: Sparkford: Oxford Illustrated Press, 1985. [4], 251p, col. plates, illus. 23cm. U.S. ed. entitled *The great climbing game.*
His climbs in New Zealand, the Alps, Britain, Nepal and Alaska.

B49. BARRY, Martin (1802-55)
Ascent to the summit of Mont Blanc, 16th-18th of 9th month (Septr), 1834. Ldn: [The Author, 1835]. 40p, 2 plates, illus. 23cm. Title pages vary, 'Septr' being either in upper or lower case letters.
—2nd ed. Edinburgh: Blackwood, 1836. ii [viii], 119p, 2 col. plates, illus. 24cm Variation of title, i.e. *Ascent to the summit of Mont Blanc in 1834.* This edition revised and presented as two lectures. Large folding panorama of Mont Blanc.

B50. BARRY, R. G.
Mountain weather and climate. 1981.

B51. BARTLE, Jim
Parque Nacional Huascarán. Ankash, Peru/Healdsburg, U.S.A.: The Author?, 1985. 40p, col. illus, 3 maps. 28 × 22cm. English and Spanish text. Photo-album of Cordillera Blanca, Peru.

B52. BARTLETT, Richard A.
Great surveys of the American west. Norman: Univ. Press Oklahoma, 1962.
—Another ed. 1966.

B53. BARTOL, C. A.
Pictures of Europe: framed in ideas. —2nd ed. Boston: Crosby Nichols, 1856. 407p. 21cm.
Contains as an appendix I. S. Talbot's account of his ascent of Mont Blanc in 1854. This was the third ascent by an American.

B54. BARTON, Bob & WRIGHT, Blyth
'A chance in a million?': Scottish avalanches. Edinburgh: S.M.T., 1985. [vi], 119p.

B55. BASTERFIELD, George
Mountain lure. Kendal: Titus Wilson, 1947. [12], 166p, 6 plates, illus. 22cm.
Essays and verses.

B56. BASTERFIELD, G.
Songs of a cragsman. Published by G. R. Speaker for the Fell and Rock Climbing Club of the English Lake District (London Section), 1930. 27p. 26cm.

B57. BASTERFIELD, G.
Songs of a cragsman: twelve songs of the hills. Words and music by . . .Musical editor, Oliver Knapton. Barrow-in-Furness, Lancs: The Author, 1935. 27p. 26cm.

B58. BATES, Robert G. Hicks
Five miles high: the story of an attack on the second highest mountain in the world by members of the first American Karakoram expedition. [By . . .and others.] N.Y.: Dodd Mead, 1939. xiv, 381p, 29 plates, illus, 3 maps. 23cm. The U.S. edition has fewer plates but more illustrations overall.
—U.K. ed. Ldn: Hale, 1940. 319p, 31 plates, illus. 22cm.
This expedition set the standards for American Himalayan mountaineering; and the book is counted as one of the classics of American climbing literature.

B59. BATES, R. G. H.
A study of the literature of the mountains and of mountain climbing written in English. (Doctoral Dissertation series, University of Pennsylvania, 1950. Publication No. 2093.) Ann Arbor, MI: University Microfilms International, [published on demand]. 233, 14p, bibl. 22cm. Softback. Authorized facsimile.
Follows the literature chronologically through the history of mountaineering, but is not easy to consult, having no chapter or section layout, and no index.

B60. BAUER, Paul (b.1896)
Himalayan campaign: the German attack on Kanchenjunga. The second [sic] highest mountain in the world. Trans. [from the German] by Sumner Austin. Oxford: Blackwell, 1937. xviii, 174p, 64 plates, illus, maps. 23cm. From the original: *Im Kampf um den Himalaja* (Munich: Knorr & Hirth, 1931) and *Um den Kantsch* (Munich: Knorr & Hirth, 1933)
Account of the 1929 and 1931 German attempts, written by the leader of both expeditions.

B61. BAUER, P.
Himalayan quest. The German expeditions to Siniolchum [sic] and Nanga Parbat. Edited by . . .Trans. from the German by E. G. Hall. Ldn: Nicholson & Watson, 1938. xxvi, 150p, 96 plates, illus, maps. 26cm. From the original: *Auf Kundfahrt im Himalaja* (Munich: Knorr & Hirth, 1937)
Account of the 1937 attempt on Nanga Parbat. Bauer flew out after an ice avalanche had engulfed sixteen members of the expedition.

B62. BAUER, P.
Kanchenjunga challenge. Ldn: Kimber, 1955. 202p, 12 plates, illus. 24cm. From the original: *Kampf um den Himalaja* (Munich: Knorr & Hirth, 1952)
Largely a rewrite of *Himalayan campaign.*

B63. BAUER, P.
The siege of Nanga Parbat, 1856-1953. Trans. from the German by R. W. Rickmers. Ldn: Hart-Davis, 1956. 211p, 21 plates, illus. 22cm. From the original: *Das Ringen um den Nanga Parbat* (Munich: Süddeutscher Verlag, 1955)
History up to first ascent.

B64. BAUGHAN, Blanche Edith
Mt. Egmont. Auckland: Whitcombe & Tombs, 1929. 75p, illus. 17cm.
A volcano on North Island, New Zealand. A popular venue for climbers and skiers.

B65. BAUGHAN, B. E.
Snow kings of the Southern Alps. Christchurch: Whitcombe & Tombs, ?. 51p, illus. 21cm.

B66. BAUME, Louis Charles
Sivalaya: explorations of the 8000-metre peaks of the Himalaya. Reading: Gastons-West Col, 1978. 316p, illus, maps, bibl. 24cm.
—Softback ed. Seattle: Mountaineers/Vancouver: Douglas & McIntyre, 1979. 340p, illus, maps, bibl. 22cm.
Synopses of all expeditions pertaining to the fourteen peaks over 8000 metres.

B67. BEAN. Paul
The roof of the world: the report of the 1975 North of England Himalayas Expedition. Stockton: The Expedition, 1975. [28p], illus, maps. 30cm.
Hindu Kush and East Kulu.

B68. BEAN, P.
North of England Himalayan Expedition 1977: a return to the roof of the world and the story of a Himalayan trilogy. [Stockton]: The Expedition, 1977. 31p, illus, maps. 30cm.

B69. BECHTOLD, Fritz
Nanga Parbat adventure. A Himalayan expedition. Trans. from the German by H. E. G. Tyndale. Ldn: Murray, 1935/N.Y.: Dutton, 1936. xx, 93p, 80 plates, illus, maps. 26cm. R.P., 1935 twice, 1938. From the original: *Deutsche am Nanga Parbat. Der Angriff 1934.* (Munich: Bruckmann, 1935)
Account of the disastrous second German expedition on which four climbers and six porters died.

B70. BECKETT, J. Angus
Iceland adventure: double traverse of Vatnajökull by the Cambridge expedition. Ldn: Witherby, 1934. 197p, illus.

B71. BECKETT, T. Naylor (b.1908)
Mountains of Erewhon. Wellington: Reed, 1978. [xi], 154p, illus, maps. 24cm.
History of the exploration and development of climbing in the 1930s, in which the author participated, in the area from the Two Thumb Range through D'Archiac and Arrowsmith to the Potts River, one of the finest climbing regions of South Island, New Zealand.

B72. BECKEY, Fred W. (b.1923)
The Cascades. Portland: Graphic Arts, 1982. 128p, col. plates, illus, maps. [4to].
Beckey is a leading American mountaineer particularly associated with exploration in the Cascades. He has also made some outstanding climbs in Canada.

B73. BECKEY, F. W.
Challenge of the North Cascades. Seattle: Mountaineers/Vancouver: Mountain Craft, 1969. v-xvi, 280p, illus. 21cm.
—Softback ed. Seattle: Mountaineers, 1977.
Accounts of his ascents spanning over thirty years; a classic.

B74. BECKEY, F. W.
Mountains of North America: the great peaks and ranges of the continent. S.F.: Sierra Club, 1982. 256p, col. illus. 23 × 31cm.
—Another ed. N.Y.: Bonanza Books, 1982. 288p, col. illus.
—Another ed. 1984
Profiles 35 famous peaks in text and full colour photographs.

B75. [BEETHAM, George]
The first ascent of Mount Ruapehu, New Zealand, and a holiday jaunt to Mounts Ruapehu, Tongariro and Ngauruhoe. Ldn: The Author, 1926. 40p, 2 plates, illus. 22cm.
Ascents of volcanoes in North Island.

B76. BELCHER, Paul
City University-Brunel University Kishtwar Himalaya Expedition 1978. Report ..., written by Paul Belcher; appendices by Anthony Wheaton. [N.p.]: The Expedition, [1979]. 54p, plates, illus, map. 31cm.

B77. BELL, Sir Charles Alfred

Tibet, past and present. Oxford: Clarendon Press, 1924. xiv, 326p, illus, 2 maps. 22cm.
—Cheaper ed. O.U.P., 1927 xiv, 326p, illus, maps. 22cm.
—Reprinted. Oxford: Clarendon press, 1968. 340p, plates, illus, 2 maps.
—Another reprint. Taiwan: Ch'eng Wen, 1971.
A history of Tibet, its land and peoples, from the 15th century.

B78. BELL, Gertrude Margaret Lowthian (1868-1926)

The letters of Gertrude Bell. Selected and edited by Lady Bell. Ldn: Benn, 1927. 2v., plates, illus, maps. 25cm.
—U.S. ed. Boni & Liveright, 1927. 2v.
—Another ed. in one volume.
—Penguin paperback, 1939. 2v.
—Selected letters. Penguin paperback, 1953.
Before developing her career as a traveller, archaeologist and writer, Gertrude Bell had a brief Alpine career, which is usually associated with a long letter she wrote home recounting her dramatic attempt and retreat on the north-east face of the Finsteraarhorn in 1902.

B79. BELL, James Horst Brunnerman (1896-1976)

British hills and mountains. By . . ., E. F. Bozman and J. Fairfax Blakeborough. Ldn: Batsford/N.Y.: Scribner's, 1940. viii, 120p, 67 plates, illus, maps. 22cm.
—2nd rev. ed. 1943. R.P., 1944.
—3rd rev. ed. 1950.
General survey.

B80. BELL, J. H. B.

A progress in mountaineering: Scottish hills to Alpine peaks. Ldn: Oliver & Boyd, 1950. xii, 424p, 24 plates, illus, maps. 22cm.
A mixture of instruction and reminiscence in which he stresses the importance of Scottish winter climbing as preparation for the Alps. Bell was one of the best and most influential Scottish all-round climbers from the 1920s onwards.

B81. BELL, William (1924?-48)

Mountains beneath the horizon. Edited with an introduction by J. Heath-Stubbs. Ldn: Faber, 1950. 73p, plates, port. 24cm.
Poems. This promising young Ulster poet died in an accident on the Matterhorn.

B82. BELLOC, Joseph Hilaire Peter (1870-1953)

The path to Rome. Ldn: Allen, 1902. xv, 448p, plate, illus. 20cm.
—Another ed. Ldn: Nelson, [1910].
This well-known account of poet-essayist Belloc's walking holiday contains some famous passages about the Alps, including his attempt to cross a pass in a blizzard, dressed only in light summer clothes.

B83. BELLOC, J. H. P.

The Pyrenees. Ldn: Methuen, 1909. xi, 340p, plates (some fold), illus, maps. 24cm. R.P., 1910?
—2nd ed. 1916.
—3rd rev. ed. 1923.
—4th ed. 1928.
For many years, following Charles Packe's guidebook, this book was the best introduction to the range.

B84. [BELLOWS, William]

Zermatt and the Matterhorn. By W. B. Gloucester: The Author, 1925. 19p, plates, illus. 20cm.
The author describes a traverse of the Matterhorn, the 'mountain of my longing'.

B85. BENNET, Donald

Scottish mountain climbs. Ldn: Batsford, 1979. 192p, illus. 26 × 19cm.
General guide to selected Scottish mountains, featuring rock, snow and ice climbing, walking and ski-mountaineering; well illustrated.

B86. BENSON, Claude Ernest (-1932)

British mountaineering. Ldn: Routledge/N.Y.: Dutton, 1909. xii, 224p, illus. 19cm. Two different versions of this have been seen: (i) dark green patterned cloth; gilt-blocked design on front cover; gilt-blocked spine; rounded corners; 4pp advertisements at end. (ii) light green plain cloth; cover illustration and lettering in

black; less blocking on spine and lacking the word 'Illustrated'; square corners; no advertisement pages.
—2nd rev. ed. Ldn: Routledge, 1914.

B87. BENSON, C. E.
Crag and hound in Lakeland. Ldn: Hurst & Blackett, 1902. xvi, 313p, 28 plates, illus. 23cm.
Mixture of rock-climbing and fox-hunting.

B88. BENSON, C. E.
Mountaineering ventures. Ldn: T. C. & E. C. Jack, [1928]. 224p, illus. 21cm.
The Matterhorn story, etc. retold.

B89. BENT, Newell Jr.
Jungle giants. Norwood: The Author, 1936. 253p, illus.
Includes ascent of Kilimanjaro.

B90. BENUZZI, Felice (b.1910)
No picnic on Mount Kenya. Ldn: Kimber, 1952. 231p, 2 plates, illus. 23cm. R.P., 1952 three times, 1953.
—U.S. ed. N.Y.: Dutton, 1953. viii, 239p. 22cm. Also 2nd ptg.
—R.U. ed. 1953.
—Paperback. Kimber, 1955.
—Concise ed. Ldn: Longman, 1960. ix, 181p, 17cm.
—New ed. Kimber, 1974.
—New English Library paperback, 1976.
Classic mountaineering adventure. Benuzzi was an Italian diplomat, climber and international swimmer in a prisoner-of-war camp in East Africa. With two companions he broke out to make a remarkable attempt to climb Mount Kenya, with only makeshift equipment and hoarded rations.

B91. BERE, Rennie M.
The way to the Mountains of the Moon. Ldn: Barker, 1966. xii, 147p, 16 plates, illus, maps. 23cm.
The author's exhaustive knowledge of the Ruwenzori, as well as his expertise as a naturalist, enhances this climbing narrative.

B92. BERNHARD, Oscar
First aid to the injured, with special reference to accidents occurring in the mountains: a handbook for guides, climbers and travellers. Trans. from the German by Michael G. Foster. Samaden: Tanner, 1896. viii, 136p, illus. 18cm.
—2nd ed. Ldn: Fisher Unwin, 1900.
First book in English dealing with mountain accidents.

B93. BERNBAUM, Edwin
The way to Shambhala; a search for the mythical kingdom beyond the Himalayas. Garden City, NY: Anchor Books, 1980. 316p, illus, bibl.
Useful source book on Himalayan symbolism and myth, by a scholar-mountaineer.

B94. BERNSTEIN, Jeremy
Ascent: of the invention of mountain climbing and its practice. N.Y.: Random House, 1965. x, 124p, illus. [8vo].
The author is an American professor of physics.

B95. BERNSTEIN, J.
Mountain passages. Lincoln: Univ. Nebraska Press, 1979. ix, 278p, illus, maps. 22cm.
Reminiscences of climbing around Chamonix, Alpine guides, essay on Yvon Chouinard, etc.; a collection of previously published articles.

B96. BERRISFORD, A. B.
55-60 years of mountaineering in South Africa. [South Africa]: The Author, 1980. 114p. 25cm.
Reminiscences of his climbing since 1918, including 300 peaks and 120 first ascents. He was awarded the Gold Badge of the Mountain Club of South Africa in 1937.

B97. BERTRAM, Antony
To the mountains. With decorations by J. W. Power. Ldn: Knopf, 1929. xiii, 269p, plates, illus. 20cm.
Second half deals with climbing in the eastern Alps and in the Pyrenees.

B98. BETTEMBOURG, Georges (-1983) & BRAME, Michael
The white death. Seattle: Reymond, 1981. 310p, illus. 26cm.
Broad Peak, Kanchenjunga, Kusum Kanguru, Everest and Nuptse, with

Boardman, Scott and Tasker. Bettembourg was killed in a fall near Chamonix while crystal hunting.

B99. BHANJA, K. C.

Darjeeling at a glance: a handbook, both descriptive and historical of Darjeeling and Sikkim, with thrilling accounts of Everest and Kanchenjunga expeditions by land and air. Darjeeling: Oxford Book & Stationery, 1941. 144p, illus. 18cm.
—5th ed. 1947. 168p, illus. 19cm.

B100. BHANJA, K. C.

Kinchen-Everest: embodying in brief thrilling accounts of Everest & Kichenjunga expeditions by land and air. Darjeeling: The Author, 1942. 32p. 19cm. Paper covers. Not in Yakushi.

B101. BHANJA, K. C.

Lure of the Himalaya: embodying accounts of Mount Everest expeditions by land and air. Darjeeling: Gilbert, 1944. 255p, illus. 18cm.

B102. BHANJA, K. C.

Mystic Tibet and the Himalaya. Darjeeling: Oxford Book & Stationery, 1948. x, 306p, illus. 17cm.

B103. BHANJA, K. C.

Wonders of Darjeeling and the Sikkim Himalaya: accounts all authentic. Darjeeling: The Author, 1943. 163p. 18cm.
—2nd ed. Darjeeling: Gilbert, 1945. 198p, illus. 17cm.

B104. BHATTACHARJYA, Bidypati

Mountain sickness. Bristol: John Wright/Baltimore: Williams & Wilkins, 1964. 58p, plates, illus, bibl. 23cm.
Written by an Indian soldier-doctor. Summarizes the physiology of mountain sickness.

B105. BICKWELL, Peter

British hills and mountains. Ldn: Collins, 1947. 48p, 8 col. plates, illus. 23cm. (Britain in Pictures series)

B106. BINGHAM, Hiram

Inca land: exploration in the highlands of Peru. Boston: Houghton Mifflin, 1922. xvii, 365p, plates, illus, maps, bibl. 24cm.
Account of journeys from 1909-15. Includes ascent of Coropuna, near Arequipa, and exploration in the Vilcabamba which resulted in the discovery of the Inca city of Machu Picchu.

B107. BINGLEY, William

A tour round North Wales, performed during the summer of 1798 ...E. Williams, 1800. 2v., col. plates, illus, music. 22cm.
—Enlarged ed. entitled *North Wales, including its scenery, antiquities, customs ...delineated from two excursions ...during the summers of 1798 and 1801.* Ldn: Longmans, 1804. 2v., plates, illus, fold. col. map. 24cm.
—2nd ed. of *North Wales.* Ldn: Longmans, 1814. xxiv, 532p, plates, illus, fold. col. map. 22cm.
—'3rd' ed. entitled *Excursions in North Wales* with corrections and additions made during excursions in 1838 by W. R. Bingley. Ldn: Longmans, 1839. xxxi, 355p, fold. map. 24cm.
The Rev. William Bingley and his friend the Rev. Peter Williams were botanists who made a number of mountain expeditions in Snowdonia. Their most famous exploit, the first recorded rock-climb in Britain, was their ascent, in 1798, of the East Terrace of Clogwyn du'r Arddu, one of the most impressive cliffs in Britain.

B108. BIRD, Isabella [also known as Isabella Bird Bishop]

A lady's life in the Rocky Mountains. Ldn: 1879.
—U.S. ed. N.Y.: Putnam's, 1879-80 (?). xii, 296p + 4p. 19cm.
—3rd ed. 1880.
—Another ed. Ldn: Murray, 1910.
—Another ed. Norman, OK, 1960. Introduction by Daniel J. Boorstin. xxiii, 252p. 19cm. Also 2nd & 3rd ptgs.
—Facsim of 3rd ed. with into. by Pat Barr. Ldn: Virago, 1982. xxii, 296p, 8 plates, illus. 20cm.
During a sojourn in a log cabin in Colorado, this adventurous Victorian traveller, who later visited Tibet and China, made various excursions including an ascent of Longs Peak in 1873.

B109. BIRKETT, T. William
Lakeland's greatest pioneers: 100 years of rock climbing. Ldn: Hale, 1983. 192p, plates, illus. 23cm.
Written by the climber-son of one of the Lake District's great pioneer rock-climbers.

B110. BLACK, Charles E. D.
A memoir on the Indian surveys, 1875-1890. Ldn: Arnold, 1891. vi, 411p, illus, map. [4 to].
Himalayan background information.

B111. BLACKSHAW, Alan
Mountaineering: from hillwalking to alpine climbing. Harmondsworth, Middx: Penguin, 1965. 542p, illus, bibl. 18cm. Softback.
—Reprint with revisions, 1968.
—Hardback ed. Ldn: Kaye & Ward, 1968.
—3rd rev. ed. Penguin, 1970.
—Rev. ed. 1973.
—Rev. ed. 1975.
Standard British instruction manual approved by the B.M.C. and M.C. of S.

B112. BLAIKIE, Thomas (1750-1837?)
Diary of a Scotch gardener at the French Court at the end of the eighteenth century. Edited with an introduction by Francis Birrell. Ldn: Routledge, 1931. xii, 256p, plates, illus. 23cm.
In 1775 Blaikie made a nine-month botannical tour of the Jura and Chamonix Alps. In addition to a detailed account of several climbs made with Dr. Paccard, his book records the most remarkable series of Alpine expeditions by a British traveller of the eighteenth century.

B113. BLAKENEY, Edward Henry
Alpine poems. Winchester: Printed at the Author's private press, 1929. 38 leaves. 22cm. 60 numbered copies.

B114. BLANCHARD, Smoke
Walking up and down in the world: memories of a mountain rambler. S.F.: Sierra Club, 1985. [xvii], 299p, plates, illus, maps.
The author is an American mountaineer, guide, trek leader and raconteur. This is his account of a lifetime of adventure on peaks and trails around the world — McKinley, Logan, Hood, Sierra Nevada, Japan, etc.

B115. BLASHFORD-SNELL, John & BALLANTINE, Alastair (Editors)
Expeditions: the expert's way. Ldn: Faber, 1977. 256p, illus.
Contributions by ten distinguished authors; mountaineering section by Malcolm Slesser, medical notes by Peter Steele.

B116. BLAUROCK, Carl
A climber's climber: on the trail with Carl Blaurock. Evergreen: Cordillera, 1984. 84p, illus, maps.
Well illustrated account of his early ascents in Colorado and Wyoming.

B117. BLUM, Arlene
Annapurna, a woman's place. S.F.: Sierra Club, 1980/Ldn: Granada, 1981. xiv, 256p, 8 col. plates, illus. 26cm.
—Softback ed.
Account of the 1978 all-women expedition which resulted in one ascent and the loss of the second summit assault pair.

B118. BOARDMAN, Peter (1950-82)
Nottingham University Hindu Kush Expedition 1972. [Nottingham]: The Expedition, [1973?]. 37p, plates, illus, maps. 23cm.

B119. BOARDMAN, P.
Sacred summits: a climber's year. Ldn: Hodder/Seattle: Mountaineers, 1982. 264p, 24 col. plates, illus, maps. 24cm.
Includes Carstenz, New Guinea; Kanchenjunga; and Gaurisankar. Boardman was a good writer as well as a fine climber; he died attempting the north-east ridge of Everest.

B120. BOARDMAN, P.
The shining mountain: two men on Changabang's west wall. By ...with material by Joe Tasker. Ldn: Hodder, 1978. 192p, 16 plates (some col), illus. 24cm.
—Similar ed. Wembley: Leisure Circle, 1978.
—Arrow paperback, 1980.
This book received a literary prize. It recounts the Alpine-style ascent of the formidable west face, one of the most remarkable climbs in the Himalaya by a light-weight expedition. Boardman and Tasker disappeared on the north-east ridge of Everest in 1982.

B121. BODDAM-WHETHAM, J. W.
Roraima and British Guiana. Ldn: Hurst & Blackett, 1879.

B122. BOELL, Jacques
High heaven. Trans. from the French by Dilys Owen. Ldn: Elek, 1947. 126p, 32 plates, illus. 22cm.
Climbing in the Dauphiné Alps.

B123. BOHN, David
Glacier Bay: the land and the silence. S.F.: Sierra Club, [c.1967]. 165p, plates (some col), illus, maps, bibl. 35cm.
History, topography, mountains, glaciers and wildlife of Glacier Bay National Monument, Alaska. The author's own mountaineering experiences are given in diary form.

B124. BONATTI, Walter (b.1930)
The great days. Trans. [from the Italian] by Geoffrey Sutton. Ldn: Gollancz, 1974. 189p, 32 plates, illus. 23cm. R.P., 1976 (3rd), 1978.
Autobiography. Takes up the story after the retreat from the Central Pillar of Frêney.

B125. BONATTI, W.
Magic of Mont Blanc. Ldn: Gollancz, 1985. 208p, 200 col. plates, illus. 29cm.
High quality photographs of all the principal peaks of the Mont Blanc range.

B126. BONATTI, W.
On the heights. Trans. from the Italian by Lovett F. Edwards. Ldn: Hart-Davis, 1964. 248p, 16 plates, illus. 23cm.
—Softback ed. Diadem, 1979.
Autobiography of a leading Italian climber, whose solo ascent of the South-west Pillar of the Dru in 1955 was one of the most remarkable feats of Alpine mountaineering. His climbs include Himalaya and Patagonia. He was one of the three survivors of the disaster on the Central Pillar of Frêney in 1961.

B127. BONINGTON, Christian John Storey (b.1934)
Annapurna South Face. Ldn: Cassell/N.Y.: McGraw Hill, 1971. x, 334p, 48 col. plates, illus. 24cm. R.P., 1971, 1972.
—B.C.A. ed. Identical to original.
—Penguin paperback, 1973.
First ascent. The expedition's success was marred by the death of Ian Clough in an ice avalanche almost at the end of the descent.

B128. BONINGTON, C. J. S.
Changabang. By ...[and others]. Ldn: Heinemann, 1975. [x], 118p, 4 col. plates, illus. 26cm.
—U.S. ed. N.Y.: Oxford, 1976. 118p, illus (some col). 25cm.
First ascent of this Garhwal peak via Shipton's Col and the east ridge.

B129. BONINGTON, C. J. S.
Everest South-west Face. Ldn: Hodder, 1973. 352p, 56 plates (some col), illus, fold. map. 24cm.
—U.S. ed. entitled *The ultimate challenge.* N.Y.: Stein & Day, 1973. 352p.
—Penguin paperback, 1975. R.P., 1976.
Unsuccessful attempt in 1972.

B130. BONINGTON, C. J. S.
Everest the hard way. Ldn: Hodder, 1976. 239p, 80 col. plates, illus. 27cm. R.P., 1977, 1980.
—U.S. ed. Smaller and with only 64 plates. N.Y.: Random House, 1976.
—Arrow paperback, 1977.
—Children's ed. Harlow: Longman, 1980. 46p, illus (some col), map. 20cm.
Successful ascent of the south-west face; cameraman Mick Burke disappeared near the summit.

B131. BONINGTON, C. J. S. & CLARKE, Charles
Everest the unclimbed ridge. Ldn: Hodder, 1983. 132p, 64 col. plates, illus. 25cm.
Attempt on the last unclimbed ridge, the north-east. Boardman and Tasker disappeared near the second pinnacle in a final attempt to complete the climb.

B132. BONINGTON, C. J. S.
I chose to climb. Ldn: Gollancz, 1966. 208p, 40 plates, illus. 23cm. R.P., 1985.
—Large print ed. Leicester: Ulverscroft, 1985.
Autobiography. His first notable climb was in 1953 in Scotland. Includes British climbs; Alpine — first British ascent of the Eigerwand; Himalaya; and the Central Tower of Paine in Patagonia.

B133. BONINGTON, C. J. S.
Kongur, China's elusive summit. Ldn: Hodder, 1982. 224p, 58 col. plates, illus. 25cm.
Expeditions in 1980 and 1981.

B.134 BONINGTON, C. J. S.
The next horizon: autobiography II. Ldn: Gollancz, 1973. 304p, 56 plates (some col), illus. 24cm. R.P., 1976.
—Arrow paperback, 1975. R.P., 1978.

B135. BONINGTON, C. J. S.
Quest for adventure. Ldn: Hodder, 1981. 448p, illus (some col), maps. 28cm.
Includes section on mountaineering.

B136. BONNEY, Thomas George (1833-1923)
The alpine regions of Switzerland and the neighbouring countries: a pedestrian's notes on their physical features, scenery and natural history. With illustrations by E. Whymper. Cambridge: Deighton Bell/Ldn: Bell & Daldy, 1868. xvi, 351p, 5 plates, illus. 22-24cm.
The Rev. Bonney, geologist and A.C. President 1881-3, travelled and climbed extensively in the Alps for over fifty years. He collaborated with Elijah Walton, writing the supporting text for a series of illustrated folios of mountain scenery.

B137. BONNEY, T. G.
The building of the Alps. Ldn/N.Y.: Fisher Unwin, 1912. 384p, 32 plates, illus. 23cm. R.P., 1913.
Popular geology.

B138. BONNEY, T. G.
Memories of a long life. Cambridge: Metcalfe for the Author, 1921. 112, viip, 23cm.
Includes chapter on climbing.

B139. BONNEY, T. G.
Outline sketches in the high Alps of Dauphiné. Ldn: Longmans, 1865. xvi, 52p, 14 plates, illus, map. 26cm.
Account of climbing holidays, 1862-4, illustrated by many of his own simple but attractive mountain sketches.

B140. BONYTHON, C. Warren
Walking the Flinders Ranges. ?: Rigby Pub, [1973]. 231p.
Australia.

B141. BORTHWICK, Alistair
Always a little further. Ldn: Faber, 1939. 276p. 21cm.
—New ed. Stirling: Mackay, 1947. x, 221p. 19cm.
—3rd ed. Glasgow: T. Smith, 1969. viii, 221p.
—4th ed. Ldn: Diadem, 1983. vii, 221p, 8 plates.
Classic tales of climbing and outdoor life in Scotland in the 1930s, written by a well-known Scottish journalist, broadcaster and climber.

B142. BOURRIT, Marc-Theodore (1739-1819)
A relation of a journey to the glaciers in the Dutchy of Savoy. Trans. from the French of . . .by Cha. & Fred Davy. Norwich: R. Beatniffe, 1775. xxi, 264p, 19cm. From the original: *Description des Glacières . . .du Duché de Savoie.* (Geneva, 1773)
—2nd ed. Beatniffe, 1776. [52], xxii, 268p.
—Another ed. Ldn: G. Robinson, 1776.
—Another ed. Dublin: R. Cross 1786? xx, [8], xviii, 222p. 16cm.
Bourrit was a Swiss painter, traveller and writer who failed in his attempts to climb Mont Blanc, to his great chagrin. For a biographical sketch see De Beer, *Escape to Switzerland.*

B143. BOUSTEAD, Sir Hugh
Wind of morning. Ldn: Chatto & Windus, 1971. 240p, illus, 4 maps. 22cm.
Autobiography, including his climbs in the Alps and participation in the 1933 Everest expedition.

B144. BOWIE, Nan
Mick Bowie: the Hermitage years. Wellington: Reed, 1969. 196p, 16 plates, illus. 22cm. Also 2nd ptg.
Biography of Mount Cook guide, written by his wife. The Hermitage is a famous mountain hostelry and base for climbing Mount Cook, New Zealand.

B145. BOWKER, Tom
Mountain Lakeland. Ldn: Hale, 1984. 224p, illus, bibl. 23cm.
Routes, descriptions, reminiscences and anecdotes, appropriate to each area described.

B146. BOWLES, Samuel
Colorado: its parks and mountains. Springfield, MA: Sam Bowles & Co., 1869.
—Another ed. (presumably the same book?) entitled *A summer vacation in the parks and mountains of Colorado: Switzerland of America.* Bowles & American News, 1869. 166p.
Account of a journey in 1868, with interesting comments on mountain scenery. He made a couple of tourist ascents, mainly on horseback.

B147. BOWMAN, Isiah
The Andes of southern Peru: geographical reconnaissance along the seventy-third meridian. N.Y.: H. Holt for the American Geographical Society, 1916. [xi], 336p, plates (some fold. col), illus, maps. 26cm.
—2nd ed. N.Y.: Greenwood Press/Ldn: Constable, 1920.
The 73rd meridian passes through the Cordillera Vilcabamba.

B148. BOYD, William Harland (Editor)
A climb through history: from Caliente to Mount Whitney in 1889. Richardson, TX: Habilah Press, 1973. [viii], 49p, 14 plates, illus, 3 maps. 24cm. Edition of 800 copies.
Collection of 16 articles.

B149. BOZMAN, Ernest Franklin (1895-1968) (Editor)
Mountain essays by famous climbers. Ldn: Dent, 1928. vi, 256p. 16cm.
(Kings Treasuries of Literature series)
—Rev. ed. with additional extract from Smythe's *Kamet conquered.*
Anthology.

B150. BRAHAM, Trevor
Himalayan odyssey. Ldn: Allen & Unwin, 1974. 234p, 24 plates, illus, maps. 25cm.
The final 700 copies were softbound and marketed by Diadem in 1978.
Well-written, authoritative memoirs, by a former editor of the *Himalayan Journal* with thirty years' experience of exploring and climbing throughout the Himalaya, Karakoram and Hindu Kush.

B151. BRAND, Charles
Journal of a voyage to Peru: a passage across the Cordillera of the Andes, in the winter of 1827, performed on foot in the snow; and a journey across the pampas. Ldn: Colbourn, 1828. xix, 364p, plates, illus. 23cm. Boards, paper label. Issued with four uncoloured aquatints by the author but some copies have an extra plate at p. 326. (Sabin 7388; Abbey, *Travel* 724)
Brand was a Lieutenant in the Royal Navy. His account of his adventurous journey is extremely scarce. He crossed the Andes in the region of Aconcagua.

B152. BRASHER, Christopher
Sportsmen of our time. Ldn: Gollancz, 1962. 144p, 16 plates, illus. 21cm.
Chapter on Joe Brown.

B153. BRENDEL, Walter & ZINK, Roman A.
High altitude physiology and medicine. N.Y. & Berlin: Springer Verlag, 1982. 316p.
Collection of 49 papers presented at a 1980 symposium in Germany, by European, South American and Asian contributors, and others. Sixteen sections relate directly to mountaineering and high altitude illnesses.

B154. BRETT, David
High level: the Alps from end to end. Ldn: Gollancz, 1983. [6], 207p, 16 plates, illus, sketch maps. 23cm.
Solo 600-mile traverse through the Alps from the Dauphiné to the Gross Glockner.

B155. BREWER, William Henry (1828-?)
Rocky Mountain letters, 1869: a journal of an early geological expedition to the Colorado Rockies. Edited and annotated by Edmund B. Rogers. Denver: Colorado Mountain Club, 1930. 52p. 23cm. Softback.
Detailed letters to his wife about his mountaineering activities with Josiah

Whitney's expedition to ascertain the altitude of the mountains of central Colorado.

B156. BREWER, W. H.

Up and down California in 1860-1864: the journal of William H. Brewer. Edited by Francis P. Farquhar. New Haven: Yale Univ. Press, 1930. xxx, 601p, 32 plates, illus, fold. map. 24 cm.
—Another ed. Berkeley: Univ. California Press, 1949. xxv, 583p.
—Another ed, 1974.
Brewer was the field leader of Josiah Whitney's First Geological Survey of California, one of his team being Clarence King. His daily journal and letters home, which form the basis of this classic book, are an important record of early mountain travel in California.

B157. BREWSTER, Edwin Tenney

Life and letters of Josiah Dwight Whitney. Boston: Houghton Mifflin, 1909.
Whitney was head of the California Survey.

B158. BRIDGE, George

The mountains of England and Wales: tables of mountains of two thousand feet and more in altitude. Photographs by W. A. Poucher; maps by George Bridge. Goring, Reading: Gaston's Alpine Books, West Col Productions, 1973. 199p, illus, maps. 22cm.

B159. BRIDGE, L. D. ['Bill']

Mountain search and rescue organisation. Tararua Tramping Club, 1948. 48p, illus. 18cm.
—Rev. & greatly enlarged ed. entitled *Mountain search and rescue in New Zealand.* Federation of Mountain Clubs of New Zealand, 1961. 225p, 8 plates, illus, maps. 19cm.

B160. BRIDGE, L. D.

Safe climbing. Edited by . . .for the Tararua Tramping Club. Wellington: Reed, 1947.

B161. BRIDGE, Raymond

Climbing: a guide to mountaineering. 402p, illus.
U.S. manual.

B162. BRIDGES, T. C. & TILTMAN, H. H.

More heroes of modern adventure. 1929. vi, 266p, illus. [8vo]. R.P., 1931 (twice), 1932.
Chapter on Everest by Bruce. Not in Yakushi.

B163. BRIGGS, Raymond

First up Everest. [Illustrations by . . .] Text by Showell Styles. Ldn: Hamilton, 1969. [40p], illus (some col). 21cm.
—U.S. ed. N.Y.: Coward-McCann, 1969. 38p, illus. 21cm.
Account of the first ascent for young readers.

B164. BRITISH BARNAJ HIMALAYAN EXPEDITION, 1977

Expedition report. [Reading?]: The expedition, [1978?]. [20p], maps. 30cm.

B165. BRITISH HOGGAR MOUNTAINS AND BILMA SANDS EXPEDITION, 1976

Technical report. The Expedition, 1977. 69p, plates, illus, maps, bibl. 29cm.

B166. BRITISH JANNU EXPEDITION, 1978

[*Report*]. The Expedition, 1978. 11 leaves, map. 29cm.

B167. BRITISH NEPALESE ARMY ANNAPURNA EXPEDITION, 1970

The ascent of Annapurna, 20th May 1970. Army Mountaineering Association, [1970?]. 5 leaves, plate, maps. 33cm.

B168. BRITISH NORTH EAST GREENLAND EXPEDITION, 1980

Exercise Icy Mountains VI: report. The Expedition, [1980?]. 28p, map.
Exploration in the Hochstetters Forland area.

B169. BRITISH SOUTH AMERICA MOUNTAINEERING (CLIMBING) EXPEDITION, 1976/77

[*Report*]. [Sheffield]: The Expedition, [1977]. 37 leaves, plate, maps. 30cm.

Patagonia; Cordillera Huayhuash, Peru; Cordillera Real, Bolivia. With descriptions of 16 routes, most of which were first ascents.

B170. BROCKEDON, William (1787-1854)

Illustrations of the passes of the Alps, by which Italy communicates with France, Switzerland and Germany. Ldn: The Author, 1827-9. 2v., 109 plates, illus, maps. 30cm. Published in book form in quarto and folio; but see notes below about sizes. The plates consist of: one double-page engraved general map, 12 other engraved maps, 12 engraved vignette titles, and 84 steel engraved plates of views. Each group of 7 plates is accompanied by a map of the route, a vignette title and descriptive letterpress.
—2nd ed. Ldn: Charles Tilt & Thomas Warde, 1836. 2v., [92, 104p?], 96 plates, 13 maps. [4to]
—Another ed. Ldn: Henry G. Bohn, [1877]. 2v. 109 plates. 28cm.
N.B.: This work was originally published during 1827-9 in 12 parts. The original drawings were all by Brockedon and were sold in 1837 for 500 guineas. The following editions were offered for sale by the author:
Imperial 8vo at 10 guineas
Royal 4to proofs at 15 guineas
Royal 4to proofs on India paper at 20 guineas
Imperial 4to before the letters at 30 guineas
Ditto with etchings at 40 guineas
Colombier folio with etchings at 60 guineas
Brockedon was primarily a painter of historical subjects who exhibited during the period 1812-37. He made his first tour in the Alps in 1824 for the purpose of investigating Hannibal's route and later assisted in the preparation of Murray's Swiss guidebook. In the course of his researches he traversed the Alps fifty-eight times, crossing more than forty different passes.

B171. BROCKEDON, W.

Journals of excursions in the Alps: the Pennine, Graian, Cottian, Rhetian, Lepontian and Bernese. Ldn: James Duncan, 1833. xvi, 376p, fold. map. 21cm. Boards, paper label.
—3rd ed. 1845.
Account of his travels in 1824 and 1825.

B172. BROKE, Horatio George (1861-1932)

With sack and stock in Alaska. Ldn: Longmans, 1891. xi, 158p, 2 fold. col. plates, illus, maps. 21cm.
Account of his attempt on Mt. St. Elias in 1888. Broke was a British diplomat and A.C. member, who later took Holy Orders. He climbed extensively in the Alps, and edited part of Ball's *Alpine guide.*

B173. BRONGERSMA, Leo Daniel & VENEMA, G. F.

To the mountains of the stars. Trans. from the Dutch by Alan G. Readett. Ldn: Hodder, 1962. xvi, 318p, 48 plates (some col.), illus, maps. 23cm. From the original: *Hett witte Hart van Nieuw-Guinea* (Amsterdam: Scheltens & Giltay, 1960)
—U.S. ed. N.Y.: Doubleday, 1963. 318p, illus. 23cm.
Account of chiefly scientific expedition to the Antares Mountains of the Nassau range of New Guinea.

B174. BROOK, Elaine & DONNELLY, Julie

The windhorse. Ldn: Cape, 1986. iv, 224p, illus. 22cm.
Climbing in Nepal.

B175. BROOKS, Alfred Hulse

Mountain exploration in Alaska. N.Y.: A.A.C., 1914. 23p, illus, maps. 35cm. (Alpina Americana series, 3)

B176. BROUGHTON, Geoffrey

Climbing Everest. An anthology selected and edited by . . .from the writings of the climbers themselves. Illustrated by W. Heaton Cooper and Howard Somervell. Ldn: O.U.P., 1960. 149 p, illus. 20cm.
—2nd ed. 1963. 158p, illus, maps. 19cm.

B177. BROWER, David Ross (Editor)

Manual of ski mountaineering. Berkeley: Univ. California Press, 1942. 135p, illus.
—2nd ed. 1947. [xxiv], 200p, illus.
—3rd rev. ed. S.F.: Sierra Club, 1962.
—Softback ed. 1969.

B178. BROWER, Kenneth (Editor)
Earth and great weather: the Brooks Range. Photographs by Pete Martin [and others]: with selections from Lois Crisler et al. N.Y.: McCall [for Friends of the Earth], [c.1971]. 188p, col. illus. 36cm.
—Another ed. Seabury Press.
Alaska.

B179. BROWN, Hamish M. & MACMILLAN, Jas.
Eye to the hills: poems. Kinghorn: Petticur, 1982. 32p.
Poems about Scottish mountains.

B180. BROWN, H. M.
Hamish's Groats End walk: one man and his dog on a hill route through Britain and Ireland. Ldn: Gollancz, 1981. [xvii], 301p, plates, illus, maps. 24cm.

B181. BROWN, H. M.
Hamish's mountain walk: the first traverse of all the Scottish Munros in one journey, Ldn: Gollancz, 1978. 359p, plates, illus, maps, bibl. 24cm.
—Paladin paperback, 1980,
Basically a 'Munro' is a separate mountain top of at least 3000 feet, according to a classification system initiated in 1891 by Hugh Munro.

B182. BROWN, H. M.
Poems of the Scottish hills. An anthology selected by . . .Aberdeen: University Press, 1982. 196p, illus.

B183. BROWN, H. M. & BERRY, Martyn (Editors)
Speak to the hills: an anthology of twentieth century British and Irish mountain poetry. Aberdeen: University Press, 1985. xxix, 530p, illus. 24cm.
A fine new anthology.

B184. BROWN, H. M.
Time, gentlemen: some collected poems. Aberdeen: University Press, 1983. 10, 124p, illus.
Poems with a mountain flavour.

B185. BROWN, Joe (b.1930)
The hard years: an autobiography. Ldn: Gollancz, 1967. 256p, 33 plates, illus. 23cm. R.P., 1967, 1969, 1972, 1974, 1980.
—Penguin paperback, 1975.
Memoirs of a famous climber who led the resurgence of British rock-climbing in the 1950s, often in partnership with Don Whillans, pioneering many new climbs of exceptional severity. He also made some notable ascents in the Alps, together with first ascents of Kanchenjunga and the Muztagh Tower.

B186. BROWN, Percy
Tours in Sikkim and the Darjeeling district. Calcutta: W. Newman & C., 1917. 136p, illus, map. [8vo].
—2nd ed. 1922. xiii, 136p, plates (some fold), illus, map. 19cm.
—3rd rev. ed. 1934 with additions by Joan Townend. xvi, 223p, illus, map. 19cm.
—4th ed. 1944.
Well-known handbook for travellers in Sikkim.

B187. BROWN, Robert L.
Holy Cross: the mountain and the city. Caldwell, ID: Caxton Printers, 1970.
Holy Cross is a peak in Colorado, named after a snow formation on its flanks.

B188. BROWN, Thomas Graham (1882-1965)
Brenva. Ldn: Dent, 1944. xvi, 228p, 73 plates, illus, map. 22cm. R.P., 1945.
Brown was a British scientist, climber and mountain historian. Starting late in life he climbed extensively in the Alps and also further afield. The planning and execution of three new route on the Brenva face of Mont Blanc most notable among his many achievements.

B189. BROWN, T. G. & DE BEER, G. R.
The first ascent of Mont Blanc. Published on the occasion of the Centenary of the Alpine Club. Ldn/N.Y.: O.U.P., 1957. x, 460p, 16 plates, illus, maps, bibl. 23cm.
This scholarly examination of the controversy surrounding the first ascent proved Dr. Paccard's claims beyond doubt and provided a definitive history of the early ascents of Mont Blanc.

B190. [BROWN, T. G.]
Thomas Graham Brown. Edinburgh: National Library of Scotland, 1982. 19p, illus, facsims, ports. 25cm.
Catalogue of exhibition to mark the centenary of his birth. All Graham Brown's Alpine collection was given to the Library.

B191. BROWNE, Belmore (1880-1954)
The conquest of Mount McKinley: the story of three expeditions through the Alaskan wilderness to Mount McKinley, North America's highest and most inaccessible mountain. Appendix by Herschel C. Parker. N.Y.: Putnam's, 1913. xviii, 381p, 64 plates, illus, fold. map. 23cm.
—2nd ed. with introduction by Bradford Washburn. Boston: Houghton Mifflin, 1956. xxxii, 381p.
Expeditions in 1910 and 1912, the latter foiled by bad weather within a few metres of the summit. Browne was instrumental in disproving Dr. Cook's claim to have climbed the peak.

B192. BROWNE, George Forrest (1833-1930)
The recollections of a bishop. Ldn: Smith Elder, 1915. xi, 427p, plates, illus. 23cm.
Includes interesting mountaineering reminiscences by a past president of the A.C.

B193. BROWNE, J. D. H.
Ten scenes in the last ascent of Mont Blanc including 5 views from the summit. Dedicated to nine guides of Chamonix by . . .Ldn: Thos McLean, 1853. 13p, col. plates, illus. 56cm.
—Facsimile reprint, 1980.
Narrative of his ascent (42nd) on 8 July 1852: reprinted in *Stories from Switzerland,* Ldn, 1853.

B194. BROWNING, Oscar (1837-1923)
Memories of sixty years at Eton, Cambridge and elsewhere. Ldn: Lane, 1910. xii, 364p, illus, ports.
—2nd ed. 1910.
Browning was an historian and writer and member of the A.C. His book has many notes on Alpine climbing, including a search for the legendary Mont Iseran in 1860 with J. J. Cowell. He gave up climbing in 1878.

B195. BROWNING, Peter
Place names of the Sierra Nevada: from Abbot to Zumwalt. Berkeley: Wilderness Press, [1986]. 253p, 4 plates, illus, 2 maps. 23cm.
The author had access to Francis Farquhar's extensive revision notes.

B196. BRUCE, Hon. Charles Granville (1866-1939)
The assault on Mount Everest 1922. By . . .and other members of the expedition. Ldn: Arnold/N.Y.: Longmans, 1923. xii, 339p, 33 plates, 2 fold. maps. 26cm. R.P., 1924.
Bruce led this second Everest expedition.

B197. BRUCE, C. G.
Himalayan wanderer. Ldn: Maclehose, 1934. [viii], 309p, 16 plates. 23cm.
Reminiscences of his climbing and exploration, including the 'Alps from end to end' with Conway. Bruce, who served in the Indian Army, made numerous private climbing expeditions in the Himalaya, accompanied Conway in the Karakoram, and Mummery on Nanga Parbat, as well as leading the 1922 and 1924 Everest expeditions. A.C. President, 1923-5.

B198. BRUCE, C. G.
Kulu and Lahoul. Ldn: Arnold, 1914. xii, 308p, 24 plates, illus, map. 23cm.
Account of six months' climbing and exploration in 1912.

B199. BRUCE, C. G.
Twenty years in the Himalaya. Ldn: Arnold, 1910. xvi, 335p, 29 plates, illus, map. 21cm.
His experiences exploring, climbing and travelling in Sikkim, Nepal, Kumaon, Garhwal, Baltistan, Chitral, etc.

B200. BRUNNING, Carl K.
Rock-climbing and mountaineering. Manchester: Open Air Publications, [1936]. 108p, illus. 19cm.
—New ed. Ldn: Faber, 1946. 87p. R.P., 1946.

Instructional book written by a journalist who also edited the short-lived *British Mountaineering Journal* in the 1930s.

B201. BRYANT, Leslie Vickery ['Dan'] (1905-57)
New Zealanders and Everest. Wellington: Reed, 1953. 48p, illus. 22cm.
Bryant was a New Zealander who climbed extensively in New Zealand, Switzerland, Canada and the Himalaya, accompanying Shipton on the 1935 Everest reconnaissance.

B202. BRYCE, James, Viscount Bryce (1838-1922)
Memories of travel. Ldn: Macmillan, 1923. xiv, 300p. 23cm.
Includes climbing reminiscences, particularly the Tatras in 1878. Bryce, historian, statesman and A.C. President 1899-1901, was a great traveller but he died before being able to commit all his experiences to paper. Mount Bryce in the Canadian Rockies is named after him.

B203. BRYCE, J.
Transcaucasia and Ararat: being notes of a vacation tour in the autumn of 1876. Ldn: Macmillan, 1877. x, 420p, plates, illus, map. 20cm. R.P., 1877, 1878.
—4th rev. ed. 1896.
Includes the third ascent of Ararat in south-east Turkey.

B204. BRYSON, Sandy
Search dog training. [U.S.A.], 1984.

B205. BUCHAN, John, 1st Baron Tweedsmuir (1875-1940)
Great hours in sport. Ldn: Nelson. 1921. 288p, plates, illus, map. 22cm. (John Buchan's annual)
Includes 'Mont Blanc by a new way' by Geoffrey Winthrop Young.

B206. BUCHAN, J.
The last secrets: the final mysteries of exploration. Ldn: Nelson, 1923. 303p, plates, illus, maps. 19cm. R.P., 1923.
—Edinburgh Library ed. 1925. 303p. R.P., 1926, 1927, 1931.
Chapters on Ruwenzori, McKinley, Everest, New Guinea, etc.

B207. BUELER, William M.
Mountains of the world: a handbook for climbers and hikers. Tokyo & Rutland, VT: Tuttle/Ldn: Prentice-Hall, 1970. 279p, 43 maps (some fold). 18cm.
—Another ed. Seattle: Mountaineers, 1978.
Narrative guide to many areas and peaks; strongest on the ranges of the U.S.A.

B208. BUELER, W. M.
Roof of the Rockies: a history of mountaineering in Colorado. Boulder: Pruett, 1974. viii, 200p, illus, maps. 23cm.
Includes copious extracts from original accounts of historic climbs.

B209. BUELER, W. M.
The Teton controversy: who first climbed the Grand? Winona, MN: The Author, 1980. [2], 30p, illus. 23cm. Card covers.
Did the participants in the disputed 1872 ascent reach the summit of Grand Teton, highest in the range?

B210. BUHL, Hermann (1924-57)
Nanga Parbat pilgrimage. Trans. [from the German] by Hugh Merrick. Ldn: Hodder, 1956. 360p, 17 plates, illus. 23cm. From the original: *Achttausend drüben und drunter* (Munich: Nymphenburger, 1954)
—U.S. ed. entitled *Lonely challenge.* N.Y.: Dutton, 1956.
—Softback ed. Hodder, 1981.
—Penguin paperback, 1982.
Buhl was an Austrian climber who accomplished many very severe Alpine climbs. His solo ascent of Nanga Parbat, from the final camp, ranks as one of the most outstanding feats in climbing history. He fell to his death on Chogolisa, while descending in mist with Kurt Diemberger.

B211. BULWER, James Redford
Extracts from my journal. Norwich: The Author, 1853. 56p, 4 plates, illus. 24cm. Printed for private circulation only. In some references the author's name is given as BULWEN.
The bulk of the extract refers to his two attempts on Mont Blanc in 1852.

B212. BUNTING, James
Climbing. Ldn: Macmillan, 1973. 92p, illus, map. 23cm. (Leisure guide series)

B213. BURDSALL, Richard Lloyd (1895-1953) & EMMONS, Arthur Brewster 3rd (1910-62)

Men against the clouds: the conquest of Minya Konka. By ...with contributions by Terris Moore and Jack Theodore Young. N.Y.: Harper/Ldn: Bodley Head, 1935. xvi, 292p, 31 plates, illus, maps. 23cm. R.P., 1935.
—Reissued with new material and photographs by Terris Moore. Seattle: Mountaineers, 1980. 272p. Softback.
This Chinese peak (24,892 ft) at the extreme eastern end of the Himalaya was climbed by a small American party in 1932 and was the second highest peak ever climbed at that date. It remained the highest peak climbed by Americans until 1958. Burdsall later died of exposure descending Aconcagua.

B214. BURGESS, Alan & PALMER, Jim

Everest the ultimate challenge. Toronto: Gen. Publishing/Ldn: Hodder/N.Y.: Beaufort Books, 1983. 214p, col. illus, maps.
Successful but tragic 1982 Canadian expedition.

B215. BURGESS, Michael

Hong Kong Mountaineering Expedition to Lamjung Himal, Spring 1974.
Hong Kong: The expedition, [1974]. 39p, plates, illus, map.

B216. BURLINGHAM, Frederick

The ascent of the Matterhorn with a cinema camera. Illustrated programme of West End Cinema, London, 1913. 12p, illus. 25cm.

B217. BURLINGHAM, F.

How to become an alpinist. By ...*(The man who cinematographed the Matterhorn).* xii, 218p, 32 plates, illus. 20cm.
Includes a good selection of photographs of early climbers; good chapter on early women climbers.

B218. BURMAN, José

A peak to climb: the story of South African mountaineering. Published under the auspices of the Mountain Club of South Africa. Cape Town: C. Struik, 1966. xii, 175p, plates, illus, maps. 24cm. Limited edition of 1200 numbered copies of which the first 75 copies are leather bound de luxe.
—Another ed. Beverley Hills, 1967.
The only overall account of the history of climbing in South Africa. The book was commissioned as a contribution to the 75th anniversary celebrations of the Mountain Club of South Africa.

B219. BURPEE, Laurence Johnston

Among the Canadian Alps. N.Y.: Lane, 1914/Ldn: Lane, 1915. 239p, 35 plates, illus, 6 maps. 23cm.
Travel book with mountaineering sections.

B220. BURRARD, Sir Sidney Gerald

Exploration in Tibet and neighbouring regions, 1865-1879; 1879-1892. Dehra Dun: Trigonometrical Survey, Survey of India, 1915. x, 213p; xii, 214-411p, 12 + 12 charts (in pkt). 33cm.
Records of exploration in the Himalaya and Tibet by the Pundits — Nain Singh, Kishen Singh, Hari Ram, Lala, Kinthup, Rinzin Namgyal, and others.

B221. BURRARD, S. G. & HAYDEN, H. H. (-1923)

A sketch of the geography and geology of the Himalaya mountains and Tibet. Calcutta: Superintendent, Government Printing, 1907-8. xvi, 308, vip, illus, maps. 30cm.
—Rev. ed. by Burrard and A. M. Heron. Delhi: Geological Survey, Government of India, 1932-3. xx, 360, lviiip, illus, maps. 30cm.
Covers: the high peaks of Asia; the principal mountain ranges of Asia; the glaciers and rivers of the Himalaya and Tibet; the geology of the Himalaya.

B222. BUSK, Sir Douglas

The delectable mountains. Ldn: Hodder, 1946. xii, 274p, 37 plates, illus, 4 fold. maps. 23cm. R.P., 1947.
British diplomat's climbing reminiscences. Includes Pyrenees, Alps, U.S. Rockies, Persia.

B223. BUSK, D.
The fountain of the sun: unfinished journeys in Ethiopia and the Ruwenzori. Ldn: Parrish, 1957. 240p, 33 plates (some col), illus, maps. 23cm.
Travels in Ethiopia and climbing on the Ruwenzori, with an appendix on the mountains of Ethiopia.

B224. BUTLER, Samuel (1835-1902)
A first year in Canterbury Settlement. Ldn: Longmans, 1863.
—2nd ed. Ldn, 1914. Edited by R. A. Streatfeild. With other early essays.
—Another ed. Auckland: Blackwood & Janet Paul, 1964. Edited by A. C. Brassington & P. B. Maling.
Butler's letters home describing his life and explorations as a sheep farmer in New Zealand. He explored the headwaters of the Rangitata and later incorporated his experiences in his novel, *Erewhon.*

B225. BUTTERFIELD, Irvine
The high mountains of Britain and Ireland. Ldn: Diadem, 1985. 288p, illus. 24cm.
Well illustrated, informative guide to the peaks over 3000 feet.

B226. BYLES, Marie Beuzville
By cargo boat and mountain: the unconventional experiences of a woman on tramp round the world. Ldn: Seeley Service, 1931. 315p, 16 plates, illus. 22cm.
—U.S. ed. Philadelphia: Lippincot, n.d.
Includes climbs in Norway, Canada and New Zealand. The author was an Australian lawyer.

B227. BYNE, Eric (1911-69) & SUTTON, Geoffrey
High Peak: the story of walking and climbing in the Peak District. Ldn: Secker & Warburg, 1966. 256p, 25 plates, illus. 23cm.
Byne was a British climber who made a major contribution to climbers' guidebooks to the gritstone outcrops of the Peak District of Derbyshire. The book highlights the part played by gritstone training in post-war achievements in rock-climbing.

C

C01. CALVERT, Harry
Smythe's mountains: the climbs of F. S. Smythe. Ldn: Gollancz, 1985. 223p, plates, illus. 24cm.

C02. CAMBRIDGE HINDU-KUSH EXPEDITION, 1976
Preliminary report. Cambridge: The Expedition, [1976]. 13p, map. 30cm.

C03. [CAMBRIDGE UNIVERSITY]
Cambridge Colombian Expedition, 1959: general report. Cambridge: Foster & Jagg, 1959. 23p, illus, map.
Sierra Nevada de Cocuy, Colombia.

C04. [CAMBRIDGE UNIVERSITY]
Report of the glaciological party of the Cambridge Colombian Expedition, 1959 to the Sierra Nevada de Cocuy. [Cambridge]: 28p, 2 maps.

C05. CAMERON, Ian
Mountains of the gods: the Himalaya and the mountains of Central Asia. Ldn. Century, 1984. 248p, illus (some col), maps. 27cm.
Natural history, exploration and climbing. Published in association with the Royal Geographical Society.

C06. CAMERON, I.
To the farthest ends of the earth: 150 years of world exploration; the history of the Royal Geographical Society, 1830-1980. Ldn: Macdonald, 1980. 288p, col. plates, illus, maps. 26cm.

C07. CAMPBELL, John Robert (1826/7-97)
How to see Norway. Ldn: Longmans, 1871. viii, 84p, plates, illus, map. 19cm.
A revised version of his papers published in the *Alpine Journal* (vols. 4 & 5), being accounts of several seasons' climbing and exploring. Campbell's Alpine career was negligible.

C08. CAMPBELL-KELLY, Ben
A Patagonia handbook: Cerro Stanhardt 1974/75: the report of the 1974 Patagonian Mountaineering Expedition.

Compiled by ...with assistance from Brian Wyvill. Manchester: The Expedition, 1975. 30 leaves, plates, illus, maps. 30cm.
Fitzroy-Cerro Torre group.

C09. CAMBRIDGE WEST GREENLAND GLACIOLOGICAL EXPEDITION, 1958

General report. 1958.
On the west coast members climbed a number of peaks in the Sukkertoppen Ice-cap district.

C10. [CANADIAN PACIFIC RAILWAY]

A famous mountaineer in the Canadian Rockies. ?: C.P.R. Co., 1902. 24p, illus. [8vo].
Prettily illustrated advertisement, giving an account of Whymper's climbing in 1901.

C11. CANDLER, Edmund

On the edge of the world. Ldn: Cassell, 1919. vii, 278p, plates, illus, map. 22cm.
Includes a trip round Nanga Parbat.

C12. CAPPON, Massimo

Rock and ice climbing: the history, practice and techniques. Ldn: Orbis, 1983. 160p, illus (some col), bibl. 31cm.
An Italian book on climbing in the Alps but does not deal with the most recent developments.

C13. CARL, Louis & PETIT, Joseph

Mountains in the desert. N.Y.: Doubleday, 1954. 318p.
Exploration in the Tefedest Range of the central Sahara.

C14. CARLISLE MOUNTAINEERING CLUB

Kishtwar 77 Expedition report. 76p, illus, maps.
Attempt on Sickle Moon and ascent of unnamed 20,970 ft. peak.

C15. CARR, Herbert Reginald Culling

The Irvine diaries: Andrew Irvine and the enigma of Everest 1924. Reading: Gastons-West Col, 1979. 143p, illus. 22cm.
Irvine disappeared with Mallory on Everest in 1924.

C16. CARR, H. R. C.

The mountains of Snowdonia: in history, the sciences, literature and sport. By ...and others. Edited by ...and George A. Lister. Ldn: Bodley Head, 1925. xx, 405p, 29 plates (some col), illus, maps (some fold). 23cm.
—2nd rev. ed. Ldn: Crosby Lockwood, 1948. xiv, 312p.
Herbert Carr was prominent in Welsh climbing in the 1920s and was the author of the first Climbers' Club guidebook to Snowdon and Beddgelert district.

C17. CARSON, Russell L.

Peaks and people of the Adirondacks. Garden City, NY: 1928. 269p. [8vo]. Published under the auspices of the Adirondack Mountain Club.
Describes 46 peaks over 4000 ft and many first ascents.

C18. CARTWRIGHT, J. E.

Royal Air Force Greenland Expedition, 1975: report on the R.A.F. expedition to Søndre Sermilik Fjord in south-west Greenland, 10th June-8th July, 1975. By ...expedition leader. [R.A.F.M.A.], 1976. 63p, illus, maps. 29cm.

C19. CASEWIT, Curtis W.

The mountain world. N.Y.: Random House, 1976. 249p, illus (some col).
General survey.

C20. CASEWIT, C. W. & POWNALL, Dick

The mountaineering handbook, an invitation to climbing. Philadelphia: Lippincott, 1968. 222p, illus. 2nd, 3rd, 4th ptgs.

C21. CASSIN, Riccardo (b.1909)

Fifty years of alpinism. Ldn: Diadem/Seattle: Mountaineers, 1981. 207p, 90 plates, illus, 7 maps. 23cm.
Italian Cassin is one of the finest twentieth century mountaineers. His Alpine conquests included two fine Dolomite ascents and the Walker Spur on the Grandes Jorasses. He has also led important expeditions to the Himalaya, Mt. KcKinley, and Peru.

C22. CELBA, K. & STRAKA, B.

High Tatras. Preface by F. Krontil, text by J. Simko. Prague, 1953. N. pag., mostly gravure plates with captions in Czech and English. 30cm.

C23. CHANDEKAR, A. R.

The god that did not fail: expedition to Hanuman (19,930 ft), May-June, 1966. Bombay: Giri-Vihar, [1966]. [48p], plates, illus, map. 24cm.

C24. CENTRAL COUNCIL OF PHYSICAL RECREATION

Safety on mountains. By the staff of Plas y Brenin, the Snowdonia National Recreation Centre. Illustrated by Gordon F. Mansell.
—Reprinted. Ldn: C.C.P.R., 1961. 41p, illus. 16cm.
—3rd ed. 1962. 40p, illus. 15cm.
—Rev. ed. by John Jackson. Manchester: B.M.C., 1975. 48p, illus.
Standard British mountain safety booklet; regularly revised and reprinted.

C25. CHAPIN, Frederick Hastings (-1900)

Land of the cliff-dwellers. Boston: Appalachian Mountain Club, 1892. ix, 188p, 64 plates, illus, 3 maps. 19cm.
Includes climbs and explorations in the San Juan Mountains of southern Colorado.

C26. CHAPIN, F. H.

Mountaineering in Colorado: the peaks about Estes Park. Boston: Appalachian Mountain Club, 1889. 168p, plates, illus. 21cm.
—2nd ed. 1890.
—U.K. ed. Ldn: Sampson Low, 1890. Same as 2nd U.S. ed.
This was the first publication issued by the Appalachian Mountain Club and it describes early exploration and climbs in the vicinity of Longs Peak. The author climbed in the Alps in the late nineteenth century and was one of the first Americans to apply Alpine experience to the mountains of the United States.

C27. CHAPMAN, Frederick Spencer (1907-71)

Helvellyn to Himalaya: including an account of the first ascent of Chomolhari. Ldn: Chatto & Windus/N.Y.: Harper, 1940. xvi, 285p, 48 plates, illus, map. 23cm.
—T.B.C. ed. 1941.
—Reissued with another book as *Memoirs of a mountaineer.* Ldn: Chatto & Windus, 1945.
—Reprint Society ed. of *Memoirs.* 1945. R.P., 1951.
—Another ed. Gloucester: Alan Sutton, 1984.
Chapman led an adventurous life which included mountaineering. Chomolhari was his most important climb.

C28. CHAPMAN, F. S.

Lhasa, the holy city. Ldn: Chatto & Windus, 1938. xiv, 342p, plates (1 fold, some col), illus, map. 25cm.
—Reissued as part of *Memoirs of a mountaineer.* Chatto, 1945.
—Reprint Society ed. of *Memoirs.* 1945. R.P., 1951.
—Another ed. Gloucester: Alan Sutton, 1984.
Account of his trip with an official mission, 1936-7.

C29. CHAPMAN, F. S.

Lightest Africa. Ldn: Chatto & Windus, 1955. 288p, 38 plates (mostly col), illus. 22cm.
Account of a 17,000 mile journey from Cape Town through Africa with visits to the Drakensberg and mountains of East Africa, including an ascent of Kilimanjaro.

C30. CHAPMAN, F. S.

Living dangerously. Ldn: Chatto & Windus in association with Outward Bound Trust, 1953. 190p, plates, illus, maps. 21cm.
—U.S. ed. N.Y.: Harper Row, 1953. 253p, illus, maps. 22cm.
—T.B.C. ed.
Includes climbing and trekking experiences — Iceland, Greenland, Malaya, Chomolhari.

C31. CHAPMAN, F. S.

Northern lights: the official account of the British Arctic Air-route Expedition, 1930-1931. Ldn: Chatto & Windus, 1932. R.P., 1932, 1933.
—4th ptg (1st cheap ed.). xvi, 264p, 32 plates, illus, map. 26cm.
Greenland.

C32. CHAPMAN, F. S.
Watkins' last expedition. Published by Chatto & Windus in association with Wm. Heinemann. Ldn: Vanguard, 1953. 244p. 19cm. (Vanguard Library ed)
George H. (Gino) Watkins (1907-32) was a good climber who became a driving force in arctic exploration. He discovered the highest mountains in Greenland, now named after him. In 1932 he returned to Greenland but was drowned in a kayak accident.

C33. CHAPPELL, Kingsley
Wander with me in Switzerland. Ldn: Alvin Redman, 1956. 214p, 15 plates, illus. 23cm.
Narrative guide to the beauties of the Alps — walks, scrambles, lesser climbs, anecdotes.

C34. CHASE, Charles H.
Alpine climbers. Ldn: S.P.C.K. [1888?]. 63p. 16cm.
A series of religious addresses, suggested by climbing incidents.

C35. CHASE, Evelyn Hyman
Mountain climber: George B. Bayley, 1840-1894. Palo Alto, CA: Pacific Books, 1981. 173p, illus. 23cm.
Climbing in California. Biography of George Bayley, described by Francis Farquhar as one of the most remarkable climbers of his time. The author married one of Bayley's grandsons.

C36. CHEADLE, Walter Butler
Cheadle's journal of a trip across Canada, 1862-1863. Edmonton: Hurtig, 1971.
Cheadle accompanied Viscount Milton in an adventurous journey across Canada, starting from Quebec. The young men were the first tourists to cross the Rockies by the Yellowhead Pass.

C37. CHERRY-GARRARD, Apsley
The worst journey in the world: Antartic, 1910-13. 1922. 2v.
—2nd ed. 1923. Small corrections, omission of some plates.
—Braille ed. 1924.
—Reissued 1929.
—Single volume edition. Ldn: Chatto & Windus, 1937. lxiv, 585p, plates (some fold), illus, maps. 23cm.
—Penguin paperback, 1937. 2v. R.P., 1937 (twice), 1938.
—Penguin paperback, 1985.
Includes the second ascent of Mount Erebus in 1912, from the north. Members of the expedition spent two weeks on the mountain carrying out survey work.

C38. [CHINA]
Another ascent of the world's highest peak – Qomolangma. Peking: Foreign Languages Press, 1975. 120p, illus (mostly col). 26cm. Softback. Yak. C. 97.
Photo-album of 1975 Chinese ascent via North Face.

C39. [CHINA]
Conquering the father of the icy mountains. Peking: Foreign Languages Press, [1957]. N. pag., chiefly illus. 27 × 18cm. Yak. C. 90.
Photo-album of Sino-Soviet expedition to Muztagh Ata in 1956.

C40. [CHINA]
Glaciers in China. Shanghai: Shanghai Scientific & Technical Publishers, 1980. 177p, illus (mostly col), map. 30cm. Yak. C. 99.
Photo-album. Four sections — life of glaciers; distribution of glaciers in China; resources in glacier areas; expeditions and research.

C41. [CHINA]
High mountain peaks in China: newly opened to foreigners. Tokyo-Newspaper Publishing Bureau of Japan/People's Sports Publishing House of China, 1981. 151p Japanese text + 45p English text, illus (many col). 26cm. Softback. Yak. j. 424.

C42. [CHINA]
Mountaineering in China. Peking: Foreign Languages Press, 1965. [Compiled by the People's Physical Culture Publishing House.] 95p, illus (some col). 26cm. Softback. Yak. C. 91.

C43. [CHINA]
Photographic record of the Mount Jolmo Lungma Scientific Expedition (1966-68).

Peking: Science Press, 1977. 113p, illus (some col). 30cm. Yak. C. 96.
Account of the Tibet Scientific Expedition of the Chinese Academy of Sciences.

C44. [CHINA]
Photographic record of the Mount Shisha Pangma Scientific Expedition. Peking: Science Press, 1966. 90p, illus (some col). 29cm. Yak. C. 92.
Includes the first ascent of Shisha Pangma (8013m) in 1964.

C45. [CHINA]
Planting the five-star flag on Mt. Tomur. Peking: Foreign Languages Press, 1979. 104p, illus (mostly col). 26cm. Softback. Yak C. 98.
Tian-Shan; Mt. Tomur is called Pik Pobeda by the Russians.

C46. [CHINA]
The Tian-Shan Mountains. Edited by the Sinkiang People's Publishing House. Peking: China International Bookstore, 1980. 216p, col. illus. 26 × 23cm. English captions and explanatory notes. Yak. a. 56.
Photo-album.

C47. CHORLEY, Katherine Campbell, Baroness Chorley (née Hopkinson)
Hills and highways. Decorated with wood-engravings by Margaret Pilkington. Ldn: Dent, 1928. [xiv], 232p, illus. 19cm.
Delightful essays on climbing, Lake District, Alps.

C48. CHORLEY, K.
Manchester made them. 1950.
Interesting memoirs of the Hopkinson family by daughter of Edward Hopkinson. The four Hopkinson brothers were prominent among the pioneers of British rock-climbing. They also climbed in the Alps but in 1898 John and three of his children were killed climbing at Arolla, after which his brothers never climbed again.

C49. CHOUINARD, Yvon
Chouinard equipment. By . . ., Tom Frost and Doug Robinson. Santa Barbara, CA: Sandollar Press, [1972]. 72p, illus. 28cm.
A commercial catalogue in which Chouinard aired his views about the ethics and style of modern climbing.

C50. CHOUINARD, Y.
Climbing ice. S.F.: Sierra Club Books, 1978. 192p, illus. 28cm.
—U.K. ed. Ldn: Hodder, 1979. R.P. 1981.
—Large print ed. 1981.

C51. CLARK, Hilary
Two boots and a polybag. Wolverhampton: Clark & Howard, 1984. 212p, illus, maps. 21cm.
Reminiscences of climbing from 1934 onwards.

C52. CLARK, Jane Inglis
Pictures and memories. Edinburgh: Moray Press, 1938. 91p, 48 plates (many col), illus. 25cm.
Reminiscences of family life in Scotland, including climbing. The Charles Inglis Clark Hut on Ben Nevis was built in memory of her son killed in World War I.

C53. CLARK, Leonard
The marching wind. N.Y.: Funk & Wagnalls, 1954. xvi, 368p, illus, 5 maps.
—U.K. ed. Ldn: Hutchinson, 1955. 347p, plates, illus. 24cm.
Deals with exploration in 1949 of the Amne Machin (23,490 ft) range, once thought to be possibly higher than Everest. Useful descriptions of little known region.

C54. CLARK, Ronald William (b.1916)
The Alps. Ldn: Weidenfeld & Nicolson/N.Y.: Knopf, 1973. 288p, illus (some col). 26cm.
General survey by a well-known British writer and mountain historian.

C55. CLARK, R. W.
Come climbing with me. Illustrated by T. K. Beck. Ldn: Muller, 1955. 160p, illus. 19cm.
Young adult book.

C56. CLARK, R. W.
The day the rope broke: the story of a great Victorian tragedy. Ldn/N.Y.: Secker & Warburg, 1965. 221p, 4 plates, illus, bibl. 23cm.
Examination of the Matterhorn disaster.

C57. CLARK, R. W.
The early Alpine guides. Ldn: Phoenix, 1949/N.Y.: Scribner's, 1950. 208p, 32 plates, illus. 22cm.
Biographical sketches of the guides who led the mountaineers of the 'Golden age'.

C58. CLARK, R. W.
An eccentric in the Alps: the story of the Rev. W. A. B. Coolidge. Ldn: Museum Press, 1959. 224p, 17 plates, illus. 23cm.
Coolidge was an American who spent most of his life in Europe. He climbed with his aunt Meta Brevoort and his dog Tschingel for many years. He was a leading figure in climbing circles, with tremendous knowledge of the history of mountaineering, but was extremely quarrelsome.

C59. CLARK, R. W.
Great moments in mountaineering. Illustrated by Thomas K. Beck. Ldn: Phoenix House/N.Y.: Roy Publications, 1956. 128p, illus. 19cm.
Written for young adults. Includes the Alps, Clarence King on Mt. Tyndall, Hudson Stuck on McKinley, and Miss Du Faur on Mt. Cook.

C60. CLARK, R. W.
Instructions to young ramblers. Ldn: Museum Press, 1958. 128p, illus. 23cm.
Includes fell-walking, weather lore, etc.

C61. CLARK, R. W.
Men, myths and mountains. N.Y.: Crowell, 1976/Ldn: Weidenfeld & Nicolson, 1977. viii, 292p, illus, maps, bibl.
Fine historical survey of mountaineering.

C62. CLARK, R. W. & PYATT, E. C.
Mountaineering in Britain. A history from the earliest times to the present day. Ldn: Phoenix, 1957. 288p, 73 plates, illus, bibl. 25cm.
Excellent reference book.

C63. CLARK, R. W.
A picture history of mountaineering. Ldn: Hulton Press/N.Y.: Macmillan, 1956. 17p text + 137p illus. 29cm.
Fine collection of historical photographs.

C64. CLARK, R. W.
Six great mountaineers. Ldn: Hamilton, 1956. 203p, 6 plates, illus. 19cm.
For young adults.

C65. CLARK, R. W.
The splendid hills: the life and photographs of Vittorio Sella, 1859-1943. Ldn: Phoenix, 1948. x, 35p, 79 plates, illus. 30cm.
Biographical sketch plus many examples of the work of one of the greatest mountain photographers. Sella worked on the Alps, Caucasus, Mt. St. Elias, Ruwenzori, Himalaya and Karakoram.

C66. CLARK, R. W.
The true book about mountaineering. Illustrated by F. Stocks May. Ldn: Muller, [1957]. 143, illus. 20cm.
For young adults.

C67. CLARK, R. W.
The Victorian mountaineers. Ldn: Batsford, 1953. 232p, 31 plates, illus. 23cm.
History of the leading British climbers, from Forbes to Conway, in Britain and the Alps.

C68. CLARK, Simon
The Puma's Claw. Ldn: Hutchinson/Boston: Little Brown, 1959. 223p, 17 plates, illus, maps. 22cm. R.P., 1959.
—Identical Adventurers Club ed.
Cambridge University expedition to Pumasillo, Cordillera Vilcabamba, Peru.

C69. CLARKE, Arthur B.
Rock climbing. Illustrations by Ian A. R. Price. Ldn: Barrie & Jenkins, 1979. 123p, illus. 25cm. (Starter series)

C70. CLARKE, Charles (b.1944)
Everest. Ldn: Sackett & Marshall, 1978. [3-62p], col. illus. 33cm. (Epic Adventure series)
Chiefly pictorial account of ascent of the south-west face; by the medical officer of the British Everest Expedition, 1975.

C71. CLARKE, C.
Mountain medicine and physiology: proceedings of a symposium for

mountaineers, expedition doctors and physiologists: sponsored by the Alpine Club [Cover title]. Edited by ...[and others]. Ldn: Alpine Club, 1975. 143p, illus, bibl. 21cm.

C72. CLARKE, C. & SALKELD, Audrey (Editors)
Lightweight expeditions to the great ranges: proceedings of a symposium for mountaineers and expedition organisers sponsored by the Alpine Club (Plas y Brenin, 10 March 1984). Ldn: Alpine Club, 1984. [6], 90p, group port. 21cm.

C73. CLARKE, James Mitchell
The life and adventures of John Muir. San Diego: Word Shop Inc., 1979/S.F.: Sierra Club Books, 1980 x, 326p, illus. 26cm.
Scottish-born Muir was a great nature-lover and is best known for his association with the Sierra Nevada range and Yosemite in California.

C74. CLARKSON, J.
Junior Mountaineering Club of Scotland's expedition to East Greenland, 1961: general report. 1962.
Members made first ascents of 24 unnamed peaks in the southern sector of the Staunings Alps.

C75. CLEARE, John S. (b.1936)
Collins guide to mountains and mountaineering. Ldn: Collins, 1979. 208p, illus (some col), maps. 31cm.
—U.S. ed, entitled *World guide to mountains and mountaineering.*
Mountaineering atlas by a British climber and outstanding mountain photographer. Covers only selected areas.

C76. CLEARE, J. S.
Mountaineering. Poole, Dorset: Blandford Press, 1980. 169p, illus (some col), bibl. 20cm. (Blandford Colour series)
General survey.

C77. CLEARE, J. S.
Mountains. Ldn: Macmillan/N.Y.: Crown Pub., 1975. 256p, illus (some col), maps, bibl. 24cm.
—Softback ed. 1979.
Highlights of world mountaineering, his own climbs and photographs.

C78. CLEARE, J. S. & COLLOMB, R. G.
Sea cliff climbing in Britain. Ldn: Constable, 1973. 189p, illus, maps. 25cm.

C79. CLEMENTI, Mrs Cecil
Through British Guiana to the summit of Roraima. Ldn: Fisher Unwin, 1920. 236p, plates (1 fold), illus, map. 20cm.
—U.S. ed. N.Y.: Dutton, n.d.

C80. CLIFF, P.
Mountain navigation. The author, 1978.
—2nd ed. Leicester: Cordee, 1980. 54p, illus, maps. 21cm.

C81. CLINCH, Nicholas B. (b.1930)
A walk in the sky: climbing Hidden Peak, Seattle: Mountaineers, 1983. xii, 214p, illus. 23cm.
Karakoram — the only American first ascent of a 8000-metre peak. The expedition was led by the author who is a well-known American climber and past president of the A.A.C.

C82. CLISSOLD, Frederick
Narrative of an ascent to the summit of Mont Blanc, August 18, 1822: with an appendix upon the sensations experienced at great elevations. Ldn: Rivingtons & Cochran, 1823. [4], 56p, 22cm.
Account of the fifteenth ascent.

C83. CLYDE, Norman (1885-1972)
Close ups of the High Sierra.
—2nd rev. ed. Edited by Walt Wheelock. Glendale: La Siesta Press, 1976. 79p.

C84. CLYDE, N.
El Picacho del Diablo: the conquest of Lower California's highest peak, 1932 and 1937. By ... Introduction and biblography by John W. Robinson. Photographs by Nathan Clark. Los Angeles: Dawson's Book Shop, 1975. 96p, illus. 22cm. Edition of 500 copies. (Baja California Travels series, 36)
Ascent of difficult Mexican rock peak.

C85. CLYDE, N.
Norman Clyde of the Sierra Nevada: rambles through the Range of Light. 29 essays on the mountains by ...Foreward by Francis Farquhar, prologue by Jules

Eichorn, and a long letter from Smoke Blanchard. S.F.: Scrimshaw Press, 1971. [2], 179p, illus. 24cm. Edition of 3000 copies, of which 500 were hand-bound by Earle Gray.
Clyde, originally a schoolmaster, was a mountain nomad, carrying his home on his back. He made more than 100 first ascents in the Sierra Nevada, mostly alone.

C86. CLYDESDALE, Marquess of Douglas and Clydesdale & M'INTYRE, D. F.

The pilots' book of Everest. Edinburgh: Wm. Hodge & Co., 1936. xvi, 209p, 33 plates, illus, 4 maps. 24cm.
Account of the 1933 Houston-Mount Everest aerial survey expedition and flight over the summit.

C87. COBHAM, Sir A.

Tight corners: tales of adventure on land, sea and in the air. 1940. 265p, illus, maps.
—T.B.C. ed. 1941.
Includes chapter, 'Caught in an Everest blizzard' by J. L. Longland.

C88. COLE, S. A. C. [Mrs Henry Warwick Cole]

A lady's tour round Monte Rosa: with visits to the Italian valleys of Anzasca, Mantalone, Camasco, Sesia, Lys, Challant, Aosta, and Cogne, in a series of excursions in the years 1850-56-58. Ldn: Longmans, 1859. xii, 402p, 4 col. plates, illus, map. 22cm.
Mrs Cole was the wife of A.C. member Henry Warwick Cole whom she accompanied on the tours described in her book, which was illustrated by George Barnard (c.1807-90). Barnard was one of the first Alpine artists to draw mountains with any degree of accuracy, and also one of the earliest members of the A.C. to travel widely in the Alps.

C89. COLE, Terrance

The Sourdough Expedition: stories of the pioneer Alaskans who climbed Mount McKinley in 1910. Anchorage: Alaska Northwest, 1985. 64p, plates, illus, map.
Includes first-hand accounts by and interviews with the participants. Their climb was the first ascent of the lower North peak.

C90. COLEMAN, Arthur Philemon (1852-1939)

The Canadian Rockies: new and old trails. N.Y.: Scribner's/Toronto: Frowde/Ldn: Fisher Unwin, 1911. 384p, 31 plates, illus, 4 maps (some fold, some col). 23cm.
One of the most interesting accounts of Canadian mountain exploration and climbing in the 1880s. Coleman was a Canadian geologist who devoted three summers to searching for Mts. Brown and Hooker. With his brother and the Rev. George Kinney, Coleman was the first to approach Mt. Robson.

C91. COLEMAN, A. P.

Glaciers of the Rockies and Selkirks: with notes on five great glaciers of the Canadian National Parks by A. O. Wheeler.
—2nd ed. Ottawa: Department of Interior, 1921. 36p.

C92. COLEMAN, Edmund Thomas (1823/4-92)

Scenes from snow-fields: being illustrations of the upper ice world of Mont Blanc from sketches made on the spot in the years 1855, 1856, 1857, 1858; with historical and descriptive remarks . . .; the views lithographed . . .by Vincent Brooks. Ldn: Longmans, 1859. viii, 47p, 12 col. plates, illus. 57cm.
—Facsimile reprint. Bologna: Libreria Alpina, 1984. 47 × 32cm.
One of the rarest and most valuable of all mountaineering books. Coleman an original A.C. member, was one of the earliest painters of the high Alps, and was a regular contributor to the Alpine Club's winter art exhibitions. He ascended Mont Blanc twice and gives an account of a typical ascent, two attempts by the St. Gervais route (Bosses du Dromédaire), and his passage of the Col de Miage and ascent of Dôme (Aiguille) de Miage.

C93. COLERIDGE, Gilbert

Some and sundry. Ldn: Constable, 1931. 276p, port. 21cm.
Contains good descriptions of climbing in Skye and the Lake District, plus Mont Blanc.

C94. COLLIE, John Norman (1859-1942)

Climbing on the Himalaya and other mountain ranges. Edinburgh: Douglas, 1902. xii, 315p, 18 plates, illus, 3 fold. maps. 23cm.

Collie is one of the best loved figures in British mountaineering history. A.C. President, 1920-2. He is particularly remembered for his pioneer work in Skye and the Canadian Rockies. He accompanied Mummery to Nanga Parbat in 1895, and his book contains a full account of that unfortunate expedition.

C95. COLLINS, Francis Arnold

Mountain climbing. N.Y.: Century/Toronto: Goodchild, 1923/Ldn: John Long, [1924?]. vi, 314p, 15 plates, illus. 20cm.

General reference book.

C96. COLLOMB, Robin Gabriel (b.1930?)

Alpine points of view: or, Contemporary scenes from the Alps, including some observations and opinions of an itinerant alpinist. Ldn: Spearman, 1961. 239p, illus. 23cm.

The author is well-known as a mountain artist and publisher of mountaineering literature, principally Alpine guidebooks.

C97. COLLOMB, R. G.

A dictionary of mountaineering. Ldn: Blackie, 1957. 175p, illus. 20cm.

C98. CONS, G. J.

The challenge of Everest. An introductory reader to 'Climbing Mount Everest', the official sound film record of the 1933 expedition. 1934.

C99. CONWAY, William Martin, Baron Conway of Allington (1856-1937)

Aconcagua and Tierra del Fuego: a book of climbing, travel and exploration. Ldn: Cassell, 1902. xii, 252p, 19 plates, illus, fold. map. 23cm.

After a quick ascent of Aconcagua, Conway attempted Sarmiento in Tierra del Fuego. This mountain resisted many attempts to reach its twin peaks, which were not climbed for another fifty years. This expedition marked the end of Conway's career as a serious mountaineer. His principal occupation in life, other than that of mountain exploration, was that of art connoisseur. He was A.C. President, 1902-4.

C100. CONWAY, W. M.

The Alps. Described by . . .Painted by A. D. McCormick. Ldn: A. & C. Black, 1904. x, 294p, 70 col. plates, illus. 23cm. Also large paper edition limited to 300 numbered copies, signed by the publishers.

—Cheap ed. with illustrations from photographs by L. Edna Walter. Ldn: Black, 1910. viii, 294p.

—Another ed. 1914?

General description of the Alps and Alpine life.

C101. CONWAY, W. M.

The Alps from end to end. With 100 full page illustrations by A. D. McCormick [and a chapter by W. A. B. Coolidge]. Ldn: Constable, 1895. xii, 403p, 100 plates, illus. 25cm. Also 100 numbered copies on thick paper, bound in half vellum. R.P., 1895 three times.

—Cheap ed. 1900. viii, 300p. R.P., 1904, 1905.

—Shilling Library series. Ldn: Nelson, [1910].

—Travellers Library ed. Ldn: Cape, 1933.

A famous high-level traverse of the Alps in 1894, from Monte Viso to the Gross Glockner.

C102. CONWAY, W. M.

The Bolivian Andes. A record of climbing and exploration in the Cordillera Real in the years 1898 and 1900. Ldn & N.Y: Harper, 1901. ix, 403p, 55 plates, illus, bibl. 23cm.

The first major climbing expedition to the area. Conway's party made the first ascent of the south (highest) peak of Illimani (6402m) at the southern end of the range, and just failed to reach the summit of Ancohuma (6430m) at the northern end. They also prepared the first topographic survey of the range.

C103. CONWAY, W. M.

Climbing and exploration in the Karakoram-Himalayas: with 300

illustrations by A. D. McCormick and maps. Ldn: Fisher Unwin, 1894. xxviii, 709p, illus, fold. map. 26cm. Plus volume of scientific reports and maps. vii, 127p, frontis, 2 fold. maps (in pkt). Also limited edition of 150 copies of which 125 were for sale, numbered and signed by Conway and McCormick, with duplicate proofs on Japan silk tissue. 2v. (4v incl. reports & maps)
—U.S. ed. N.Y.: Appletons, 1894. Same as single volume U.K. Edition.

C104. CONWAY, W. M.
Episodes in a varied life, by Lord Conway of Allington. Ldn: Country Life, 1932. viii, 276p, plates, illus. 23cm.

C105. CONWAY, W. M.
The first crossing of Spitsbergen: being an account of an inland journey of exploration and survey, with descriptions of several mountain ascents. With contributions by J. W. Gregory [and others]. Ldn: Dent/N.Y.: Scribner's, 1897. xii, 371p, 8 col. plates, illus, 2 fold. maps. 25cm.

C106. CONWAY W. M.
Mountain memories: a pilgrimage of romance. Ldn: Cassell/N.Y.: Funk & Wagnalls, 1920. [x], 282p, 16 plates, illus. 25cm.
—Abridged ed. entitled *The autobiography of a mountain climber.* Ldn: Cape, 1933. (Travellers Library, 195)
Retrospective account of his climbing career.

C107. CONWAY W. M.
No man's land: a history of Spitsbergen from its discovery in 1596 to the beginning of the scientific exploration of the country. Cambridge: University Press, 1906. xii, 377p, plates, illus, map, bibl. 25cm.

C108. CONWAY, W. M.
With ski and sledge over arctic glaciers. Ldn: Dent, 1898. 235p, 14 plates (1 fold. col), illus, map. 21cm.
Sequel to his book *The first crossing of Spitsbergen.*

C109. CONWAY, W. M.
Zermatt pocket-book: a guide-book to the Pennine Alps, from the Simplon to Arolla; intended for the use of mountaineers. Ldn: E. Stanford, 1881. [4], 140p. 14cm.
The progenitor of all modern Alpine guidebooks.

CONWAY & COOLIDGE'S CLIMBERS' GUIDES
(A set of 15 volumes covering the western and central Alps.)

C110. CONWAY & COOLIDGE CLIMBERS' GUIDE
The Adula Alps. By W. A. B. Coolidge. Ldn: Fisher Unwin, 1983. xx, 192p. 13cm.

C111. CONWAY & COOLIDGE CLIMBERS' GUIDE
The Alps of the Bernina. By E. L. Strutt. Ldn: Fisher Unwin, 1910. 2v. 13cm.

C112. CONWAY & COOLIDGE CLIMBERS' GUIDE
The Bernese Oberland: (i) From the Gemmi to the Mönchjoch. By G. Hasler. Ldn: Fisher Unwin, 1902. xviii, 164p. 13cm.
—2nd ed. Part I. 1909.
—2nd ed. Part II. 1910.

C113. CONWAY & COOLIDGE CLIMBERS' GUIDE
The Bernese Oberland: (ii) From the Mönchjoch to the Grimsel. By W. A. B. Coolidge. Ldn: Fisher Unwin, 1904. xxx, 196p. 13cm.

C114. CONWAY & COOLIDGE CLIMBERS' GUIDE
The Bernese Oberland: (iii) Dent de Morcles to the Gemmi. By H. Dübi. Ldn: Fisher Unwin, 1907. xxiv, 136p. 13cm.

C115. CONWAY & COOLIDGE CLIMBERS' GUIDE
The Bernese Oberland: (iv) Grimsel to the Uri Rothstock. By H. Dübi. Ldn: Fisher Unwin, 1908. 2v. 13cm.

C116. CONWAY & COOLIDGE CLIMBERS' GUIDE

The central Alps of the Dauphiny. By W. A. B. Coolidge, H. Duhamel and F. Perrin. Ldn: Fisher Unwin, 1892. xx, 248p. 13cm.
—2nd rev. ed. 17cm.

C117. CONWAY & COOLIDGE CLIMBERS' GUIDE

The chain of Mont Blanc. By Louis Kurz. Ldn: Fisher Unwin, 1892. xxx, 143p. 13cm.

C118. CONWAY & COOLIDGE CLIMBERS' GUIDE

Climbers' guide to the central Pennine Alps. By W. M. Conway. Ldn: Fisher Unwin, 1890. viii, 156p. 13cm.

C119. CONWAY & COOLIDGE CLIMBERS' GUIDE

Climbers' guide to the eastern Pennine Alps. By W. M. Conway. Ldn: Fisher Unwin, 1891. xii, 152p. 13cm.

C120. CONWAY & COOLIDGE CLIMBERS' GUIDE

The Lepontine Alps. By W. M. Conway and W. A. B. Coolidge. Ldn: Fisher Unwin, 1892. xx, 106p. 13cm.

C121. CONWAY & COOLIDGE CLIMBERS' GUIDE

The mountains of Cogne. By G. Yeld and W. A. B. Coolidge. Ldn: Fisher Unwin, 1893. xvi, 176p. 13cm.

C122. CONWAY & COOLIDGE CLIMBERS' GUIDE

The range of the Tödi. By W. A. B. Coolidge. Ldn: Fisher Unwin, 1894. xxxii, 167p. 13cm.

C123. COOK, Frederick A. (1865-1940)

To the top of the continent: discovery, exploration and adventure in sub-arctic Alaska. The first ascent of Mt. McKinley, 1903-1906. N.Y.: Doubleday Page/Ldn: Hodder, 1908. xxiv, 321p, 47 plates, illus, maps. 24cm.
Dr Cook claimed to have made the first ascent of McKinley but this was later proved to be false.

C124. COOK, Hartley Kemball

Over the hills and far away: three centuries of holidays. [Compiled by ...] Ldn: Allen & Unwin, 1947. 263p, plates, illus, bibl. 21cm.
Chapters on the Lake District, Switzerland and the Alps, winter holidays.

C125. COOLIDGE, William Augustus Brevoort (1850-1926)

The alpine career (1868-1914) of Frederick Gardiner described by his friend W. A. B. Coolidge. [Woolton]: [Mrs Gardiner], 1920. 75p, port, bibl. 23cm. Limited edition of 50 copies.
Frederick Gardiner (1850-1919) was a Liverpool shipowner. He was a keen advocate of climbing in Britain and of guideless Alpine climbing. His guideless ascents (e.g. Écrins, Meije) were outstanding for the time.

C126. COOLIDGE, W. A. B.

Alpine studies. Ldn: Longmans, 1912. xiv, 307p, 16 plates, illus. 24cm.
Accounts of some of his climbs and miscellaneous pieces. Coolidge was an American anglophile, mountaineer and mountain historian. He edited the *Alpine Journal* and revised part of Ball's *Alpine guide,* apart from writing innumerable books and articles on mountain matters. His literary style is generally extremely dull but his works are invaluable for detail and accuracy.

C127. COOLIDGE, W. A. B.

The Alps in nature and history. Ldn: Methuen/N.Y.: Dutton, 1908. xx, 440p, 20 plates, illus, maps. 23cm.
His most readable book.

C128. COOLIDGE, W. A. B.

Climbs in the Alps made in the years 1865 to 1900. Ldn: The Author, [1900]. 23p. 21cm. Limited edition of 100 numbered copies.

C129. COOLIDGE, W. A. B.

Swiss travel and Swiss guide books. Ldn: Longmans, 1889. xi, 336p, bibl. 20cm.

C130. COOLIDGE, W. A. B.

Walks and excursions in the valley of Grindlewald. Grindlewald: Luf, 1900. 64p, illus, map. 17cm.
—3rd ed. 1929.

C131. COOPER, W. Heaton
The hills of Lakeland. Ldn: Warne, 1938. iii-xviii, 126p, 52 plates (some col), illus. 25cm.
—2nd ed. 1946.
—3rd ed. Frank Peters Publishing, 1984.
Climbing-orientated description by a well-known Lakeland artist and illustrator of climbers' guidebooks.

C132. COP, Jaka
The world among the summits: the Julian Alps. Ljubljana: Drzavna Zalozba Slovenije, 1962. 233p, illus.
Fine photo-album; short introduction in English.

C133. COPELAND, Fanny S. (c.1872-?)
Beautiful mountains: in the Jugoslav Alps. Split: Jugoslav Bureau, [1931 or 1935?]. 120p, illus. 26cm.
Written by a Scottish climber who spent forty years in Jugoslavia, including the Nazi occupation. She established a record by climbing Triglav at the age of eighty-six.

C134. CORBETT, Edmund V.
Great true mountain stories. Ldn: Arco, 1957. x, 213p. 23cm.
—Rev. ed. 1958.
Anthology.

C135. COVERLEY-PRICE, Victor (b.1901)
An artist among mountains. Ldn: Hale, 1957. 231p, 33 plates, illus. 23cm.
Climbing reminiscences (Britain, Alps, North and South America) written by a British climber-diplomat, illustrated by his own paintings.

C136. COXE, Henry (pseud. John Millard)
The traveller's guide in Switzerland . . .and a narrative of the various attempts to ascend Mont Blanc. Ldn: Printed for Sherwood Neely & Jones, 1816. xxxvi, 210p. 15cm. May also be copies with coloured plate.

C137. COXE, William (1747-1828)
Travels in Switzerland in a series of letters to William Melmoth. Ldn: Cadell, 1789. 3v., plates, illus, maps. 22cm.
—2nd ed. 1791. 3v. Title variation, viz: *Travels in Switzerland and in the country of the Grisons: in a series of letters to William Melmoth.*
—3rd ed. with maps and views from drawings by J. Smith. Printed for J. Edwards, 1796. 2v. [4to].
—4th ed. 1801.
The Rev. Coxe was an historian who travelled much in Europe in his capacity of tutor, and later published accounts of his journeys. His book (which in fact is the 3rd edition of an earlier work entitled *Sketches of the natural, civil and political state of Swisserland* (1779) contains interesting references to early attempts and ascents of Mont Blanc, updated through the editions. The 1801 edition was considered by Coolidge to be the best.

C138. CRABB, Edmund William
The challenge of the summit: stories of mountains and men. Ldn: Paternoster Press, [1957]. 152p, 16 plates, illus. 19cm.

C139. CRAIG, Robert
Storm and sorrow. Seattle: Mountaineers with A.A.C., 1977. xiv, 171p, 16 col. plates, illus, maps. 21cm. Softback.
—2nd ed. N.Y.: Simon & Schuster, 1977. 223p, 4 col. plates, illus. 24cm.
—Rev. ed. N.Y.: Simon & Schuster/Ldn: Gollancz, 1981.
Account of the 1974 international climbing meet in the Pamirs, when a number of climbers died.

C140. CRANE, Nicholas & Richard
Bicycles up Kilimanjaro. Ldn: Oxford, 1985. 185p, col. illus, maps.
Fund-raising for charity.

C141. CRANE, R. & Adrian
Running the Himalayas. Dunton Green: New English Library, 1984. 129p, 32 plates, illus, maps (endpapers).
The brothers ran the length of the Himalayas to raise funds for charity.

C142. CRANFIELD, Ingrid
The challengers: British and Commonwealth adventure since 1945. Ldn: Weidenfeld & Nicolson, 1976. xvii, 297p, plates, illus. 23cm.
Section on mountaineering.

C143. CRANFIELD, I.
Skiing down Everest: and other crazy adventures. Ldn: Severn, 1983. 208p, illus. Includes some mountaineering.

C144. CRAWFORD, Lucy
The history of the White Mountains, from the first settlement of Upper Coos and Pequaket. By Lucy, wife of Ethan Allen Crawford, Esq. White Hills: [Printed by F. A. & A. F. Gerrish], 1846.
—Modern reprint? 208p, illus.
Classic of early White Mountains literature. E. A. Crawford was a legendary figure in the White Mountains and a pioneer on Mt. Washington.

C145. CREMER, R. W.
Mount Everest and other poems. The Author, 1923. 59p.

C146. CREW, Peter
Encyclopaedic dictionary of mountaineering. Ldn: Constable, 1968. 140p, 16 plates, illus. 23cm.
—U.S. ed. Harrisburg: Stackpole, 1969.

C147. CROSS, Rosell Theodore
My mountains. Boston: Stratford & Co., 1921. 261p. [Small 8vo].
His appreciation of living, camping and climbing in the Rockies.

C148. CROUCHER, Norman
High hopes. Ldn: Hodder, 1976. 160p, 8 plates, illus. 21cm.
—Large print ed. Leicester: Ulverscroft, 1979.
Mountaineering by physically handicapped person.

C149. CROUCHER, N.
A man and his mountains. Kingswood, Surrey: Kaye & Ward, 1984. v, 217p, col. illus. 24cm.
Climbing around the world by a disabled person.

C150. CROUCHER, N.
Norman Croucher Peruvian Andes Expedition, 1978: report. The Expedition, [1979]. [16p], illus, bibl. 21cm.

C151. CROUCHER, N.
Shin kicking champion. Ldn: Barrie & Jenkins, 1971. 239p, port. 22cm.
Biography and early climbs of a man who lost both legs in an accident.

C152. CROUTER, George
Colorado's highest ...the majestic fourteeners. Edited by Carl Skiff. Silverton, CO: Sundance Pictorial, 1977. 144p (mostly col. illus). 30cm.
Fine photo-album of general interest.

C153. CROWLEY, Edward Alexander [Aleister]
The spirit of solitude: an autohagiography, subsequently re-antichristened The Confessions of Aleister Crowley. Ldn: Mandrake Press, 1929. 3v., plates, illus. 29cm.
—2nd ed. 1930 entitled *The confessions of Aleister Crowley.*
—New ed. edited by John Symonds and Kenneth Grant, entitled *The confessions of Aleister Crowley: an autobiography.* Ldn: Cape/N.Y.: Bantam Books, 1969. 1058p.
—Another ed. N. Y.: Hill & Wang, 1970. 960p.
Self-styled 'The Great Beast', Crowley, who dabbled in black magic, was possibly the most extrordinary figure in the history of mountaineering. He climbed in the Alps and led expeditions to K2 (1902) and Kanchenjunga (1905).

C154. CROZIER, Anita (Editor)
Beyond the southern lakes: the exploration of W. G. Grave. Wellington: Reed, 1950. 124p, plates, illus, map (endpapers). 23cm.
The letters and diaries of W. G. Grave edited by his daughter. Grave was active in the Milford Sound area of south-west New Zealand, attempted Mt. Tutuko and discovered the Grave-Talbot Pass.

C155. CUNNINGHAM, Alexander
Ladak: physical, statistical and historical: with notices of the surrounding countries. Ldn: Allen, 1854. xiv, 485p, plates (some col), illus, map. 27cm.
—Reprinted. New Delhi: Sagar Publ., 1970.
Account of the author's travels in 1846-8. His writings, together with those of his companions Strachey and Thomson, were of considerable help to their successors.

C156. CUNNINGHAM, Carus Dunlop (1856-96) & ABNEY, Sir William de Wyveleslie (1843-1921)

The pioneers of the Alps. Ldn: Sampson Low, 1887. xii, 287p, 24 plates, illus (chiefly ports). 33cm. Also large paper (41cm) edition of 50 copies numbered and signed by Cunningham.
—2nd ed. Sampson Low, 1888. viii, 180p, 23 plates, illus. 30cm.
—U.S. ed. Boston: Estes & Lauriat, 1888. 28cm. Same as 2nd U.K. ed.
Biographical sketches of the great early Alpine guides, illustrated with Abney's superb photographic portraits. Cunningham was an early advocate of Scottish winter climbing. Abney contributed to the development of photographic chemistry, about which he wrote several books.

C157. CUNNINGHAM, C. D. & ABNEY, W. de W.

A facsimile of Christian Almer's 'Führerbuch', 1856-94. Reproduced under the superintendence of ...With an introduction and a photo-gravure of Christian Almer. Ldn: Sampson Low Marston, 1896. [4], xxxii, 261p, plate, port. 20cm. Originally meant to be a limited edition of 200 copies. Only 68 were sold after which the plates were destroyed. This publication caused a furore in Alpine circles, which is why the book was withdrawn from sale. For a full account of the episode see Clark, *Eccentric in the Alps.*

C158. CURRAN, James (b.1943)

Trango, the nameless tower. Sheffield: Dark Peak, 1978. 175p, illus (some col). 25cm.
First ascent in 1976 of nameless 20,500 ft peak in the Trango Tower group, Karakoram. The author is a British climber, film cameraman and lecturer in art and design.

D

D01. DAFFERN, Tony

Avalanche safety for skiers and climbers. Seattle: Alpenbooks/Calgary: Diadem, 1983. 172p, illus.

D02. DAINELLI, Giotto

Buddhists and glaciers of western Tibet. Ldn: Kegan Paul Trench Trubner, 1933. xiii, 304p, plates, illus, map. 26cm. From the original: *Il mio viaggio nel Tibet occidentale.* (Milan: Mondadori, 1932)
In 1930 Dainelli and his companion spent two months in the Karakoram, principally making a geological and botannical survey of the whole of the Siachen glacier. He was also with de Filippi's great 1913-14 Karakoram expedition.

D03. [DANISH-ENGLISH EAST GREENLAND EXPEDITION]

Ingolffjeld Sydvaeg. Dansk-Engelok Østgrønlands-ekspedition, juli-august 1973. Herlev, Denmark, 1973. 109p litho, illus, 4 maps. [4to]. 250 numbered copies. In Danish with 40p English text.

D04. DARVILL, Fred T. Jr.

Mountaineering medicine. Mt. Vernon, WA: Skagit Mountain Rescue Unit, [1065]. 36p,
—4th ed. 1969.
—7th ed. 1975. 48p.
Specialized first-aid handbook, written by an American doctor.

D05. DAUNT, Achilles

Crag, glacier and avalanche: narratives of daring and disaster. Ldn: Nelson, 1889. 212p, 12 plates. 18cm. R.P., 1894.

D06. DAVIDSON, Art

Minus 148°: the winter ascent of Mt. McKinley. N.Y.: W. W. Norton, 1969. 218p, 16 plates. 23cm.
—U.K. ed. entitled *The coldest climb.* Ldn: Bodley Head, 1970.
—Enlarged ed. Seattle: Cloudcap, 1986. 242p.

D07. DAVIES, Joseph Sangar (-1900)

Dolomite strongholds: the last untrodden Alpine peaks. An account of ascents of the Croda di Lago, the Little and Great Zinnen, the Cinque Torri, the Fünffingerspitze and the Langkofel. Ldn: Bell, 1894. xii, 176p, 10 plates, illus, col. map. 20cm. Also a limited edition of 500 copies?
—2nd ed. Bell, 1896. Smaller format and with different gilt block on front cover.

Rather exaggerated accounts of fairly unremarkable climbs. The reviewer in the *Alpine Journal* noted with some satisfaction that the book had been advertised by one magazine under the heading of 'Fiction'.

D08. DAVIS, J.

Rope and rucksack. By ...[and others]. 1969.
Australian instructional book, including climbing, caving and canoeing.

D09. DEACOCK, Antonia

No purdah in Padam. The story of the Women's Overland Himalayan Expedition, 1958. Ldn: Harrap, 1960. 206p, 11 plates, illus, map. 22cm.
Three women travelled overland to India, trekked 300 miles from Manali to Ladakh, and made the first ascent of Biwi Giri (18,700 ft).

D10. DE BEER, Dora H.

Yunnan-1938: an account of a journey in south-west China. [Oxford]: Privately published, 1971. 88p, illus, 2 maps. Softback.
Includes two attempts on Satsito, the snowy mountain of Li-Kiang.

D11. DE BEER, Sir Gavin Rylands (1899-1972)

Alps and elephants: Hannibal's march. Illustrated by Audrey Weber. Ldn Bles, 1955/N.Y.: Dutton, 1956. xv, 123p, plates, illus, fold. map. 19cm. Also 2nd ptg.
Opinions differ as to the pass used by Hannibal to cross the Alps. De Beer was an authority on the history of travel in the Swiss Alps.

D12. DE BEER, G. R.

Alps and men: pages from forgotten diaries of travellers and tourists in Switzerland. Ldn: Arnold, 1932. 256p, 16 plates, illus, ports. 23cm.

D13. DE BEER, G. R.

Early travellers in the Alps. Ldn: Sidgwick & Jackson, 1930. xx, 204p, 40 plates, illus, maps. 23cm.
—New ed. 1966.
—U.S. ed. N.Y.: October House, 1967.
Alpine travel, 16th-18th centuries.

D14. DE BEER, G. R.

Escape to Switzerland. Harmondsworth, Middx: Penguin Books, 1945. 159p, music, bibl. 18cm. Softback.
Essays and Alpine travellers' tales from the past.

D15. DE BEER, G. R.

Speaking of Switzerland. Ldn: Eyre & Spottiswoode, 1952. 216p, col. plates, illus, bibl. 23cm. (New Alpine library)
Incorporates material from *Escape to Switzerland.*

D16. DE BEER, G. R.

Travellers in Switzerland. O.U.P., 1949. xviii, 584p, 23 plates, illus. 23cm.
Guide to the literature of travel in Switzerland arranged in chronological, topographical and alphabetical lists.

D17. DENMAN, Earl L.

Alone to Everest. Ldn: Collins/N.Y.: Coward-McCann, 1954. 255p, 7 plates, illus, maps. 22cm.
—Abridged Fontana paperback, 1956. Excludes most of the African section.
Canadian Denman travelled in disguise through Tibet with a few native companions and made a solo attempt on Everest from the north. The first half of the book recounts his ascents of all the remote Virunga Mountains in central Africa.

D18. DENNISON, L. R.

Devil Mountain. N.Y.: Hastings House, 1942. xv, 271p, plates, illus. 21cm.
A search for gold around the Auyantepui massif in the Venezuelan jungle.

D19. DENT, Clinton Thomas (1850-1912)

Above the snow line: mountaineering sketches between 1870 and 1880. With 2 engravings by Edward Whymper and an illustration by Percy MacQuoid. Ldn: Longmans, 1885. xiv, 327p, 3 plates, illus. 20cm.
The author was a leading figure in mountaineering in the late nineteenth century. The book describes, among other things, his first ascent of the Aiguille du Dru, at his 19th attempt.

D20. DENT, C. T.
Mountaineering. By ..., with contributions by W. M. Conway [and others]. Ldn: Longmans, 1892. xx, 439p, 13 plates, illus. 20cm. Also large paper edition of 250 numbered copies; xxii, 481p. 26cm.
—2nd ptg, 1892.
—3rd ed. with contributions by J. Bryce [and others]. Longmans, 1900. xx, 464p. 20cm. R.P., 1901.
Dent's didactic genius blossomed in this omnibus work, the first of its kind, complemented by H. G. Willink's irresistible drawings.

D21. DESIO, Ardito (b.1898)
Ascent of K2: second highest peak in the world. Trans. [from the Italian] by David Moore. Ldn: Elek Books, 1955. 239p, 24 plates, illus. 23cm. Abridged from the original: *La conquista del K2* (Milan: Garzanti, 1955).
—U.S. ed. entitled *Victory over K2.* N.Y.: McGraw-Hill, 1956. ix, 273p, 24 plates.
Italian geologist Desio climbed widely and led numerous expeditions, chiefly this first ascent of K2.

D22. DESMAISON, René
Total alpinism. Trans. [from the French] by Jane Taylor. Ldn/N.Y.: Granada, 1982. [6], 202p, 16 plates, illus. 24cm. From the originals: *La montagne à mains nues* (Flamarion, 1971) and *342 heures dans les Grandes Jorasses* (Flammarion, 1973).
Autobiography of a leading and often controversial French climber.

D23. DIAS, John (1928-64)
The Everest adventure: story of the second Indian expedition. Delhi: Ministry of Information & Broadcasting (Publications Division), 1965. 63p, plates (some col), illus. 29cm.
Dias, an Indian soldier, led this 1962 expedition. He had previously participated in climbs on Kamet, Cho Oyu and Nanda Devi. He died of leukaemia.

D24. DICKINSON, Leo
Filming the impossible. Ldn: Cape, 1982. 256p, col. illus. 26cm.
Memoirs of leading adventure sport cameraman. Includes Eigerwand, Cerro Torre, Matterhorn North Face in winter, Dhaulagiri, Everest, Patagonia ice-cap.

D25. DIEFFENBACH, Ernest (1811?-55)
Travels in New Zealand. Ldn, 1843.
Dr. Dieffenbach, a naturalist employed by the New Zealand Company, and a seaman, James Heberley, in December 1839 defied Maori *tapu* and made the first ascent of Mount Egmont, North Island.

D26. DIEMBERGER, Kurt (b.1932)
Summits and secrets. Trans. [from the German] by Hugh Merrick. Ldn: Allen & Unwin, 1971. 344p, 56p plates, illus, maps. 24cm.
—Reprinted. Leicester: Cordee, 1976
—Softback ed. Ldn: Hodder, 1983. 344p.
Autobiographical collection of pieces about his early life, great Alpine climbs and Himalayan expeditions, by a leading Austrian mountaineer, who made the first ascent of Broad Peak in the Karakoram. Includes details of the death of Hermann Buhl on Chogolisa.

D27. DILTZ-SILER, Barbara
Understanding avalanches: how to foil the white death. Signpost Pub, [1977]. 32p, illus, bibl.

D28. DINGLE, Graeme & HILLARY, Peter
First across the roof of the world: the first-ever traverse of the Himalayas — 5000 kilometres from Sikkim to Pakistan. Ldn & Auckand: Hodder, 1982. 232p, illus (chiefly col). 26cm. Also 2nd ptg.
—Softback ed. 1984.
Account of a 10-month continuously high-altitude route by two New Zealand climbers: superb illustrations.

D29. DINGLE, G.
Two against the Alps. Christchurch: Whitcombe & Tombs, 1972. 153p, illus. 23cm.
First winter traverse of the Southern Alps of New Zealand.

D30. DINGLE, G.
Wall of shadows: Jannu the New Zealand adventure. Auckland & Ldn: Hodder,

1976. 177p, 24 plates (mostly col), illus. 24cm.
Attempt on the very severe north face.

D31. DISLEY, John
Tackle climbing this way. Ldn: Stanley Paul, 1959. 127p, 17 plates, illus, maps. 20cm. R.P., 1961.
—Softback ed. 1968.
—Rev. ed. 1977

D32. DITTERT, René (1911-83)
Forerunners to Everest: the story of the two Swiss expeditions of 1952. By . . ., Gabriel Chevalley and Raymond Lambert. English version by Malcolm Barnes. Ldn: Allen & Unwin, 1954/N.Y.: Harper, [1954]. 256p, 25 plates, illus, maps. 22cm. From the original: *Avant-Premières à l'Everest.* (Paris: Arthaud, 1953).
—Panther paperback, 1956.
These Swiss expeditions paved the way for the British success in 1953. Dittert reached the South Col during the first expedition.

D33. DIXON, Christopher Michael
Rock-climbing. Ldn: Niblick Publishing for Educational Productions, 1958. 48p, illus. 14 × 21cm. Card covers. (Know the Game series)
—2nd ed. Wakefield: E.P. Pub. Co., 1968.
—3rd ed. 1972.
—New ed. by Dennis Kemp. Wakefield: E.P. Pub. Co., 1975.

D34. DOCHARTY, William McKnight
A selection of some 900 British and Irish mountain tops. Compiled and arranged by . . .Edinburgh: Darien Press for the Author, 1954. 124p, 9 fold. plates. 25cm.
List of mountains. Memento private edition.

D35. DOCHARTY, W. M.
Supplement to a selection of some 900 British and Irish mountain tops: and a selection of 1000 tops under 2500 feet. Compiled and arranged by . . .Edinburgh: Darien Press for the Author, 1962. 2v., 259p, plates. 25cm.

D36. DODDERIDGE, M.
Man on the Matterhorn. Edited by . . .from Edward Whymper's *Scrambles amongst the Alps.* Ldn: Murray, 1940. [8], 135p, illus, map. 17cm.

D37. DONOUGHUE, Carol
Everest. Compiled by . . .Ldn: Jackdaw Publications, 1975. 10 leaves (9 fold.), illus. 35 × 23cm. (Jackdaw series, 128)
Wallet containing 10 reproduction documents and accompanying explanations; for children.

D38. DOUGHTY, Joseph Henry (1889-1936)
Hill-writings of J. H. Doughty. Collected by H. M. Kelly. Manchester: Rucksack Club, 1937. xx, 150p, 2 plates, ports. 22cm.
Selected essays and other pieces by an English schoolmaster and climber whose example did much to improve the literary qualities of mountaineering club journals. A minor classic.

D39. DOUGLAS, John Scott
Summits of adventure: the story of famous mountain climbs and mountain climbers. N.Y.: ?, 1954/Ldn: Muller, 1955. xii, 227p, 16 plates, illus. 21cm.
Good of its type.

D40. DOUGLAS, John Sholto, 8th Marquis of Queensbury
The spirit of the Matterhorn. Ldn: Watts, [1881]. 30p. 22cm.
Poem with prefatory essay.

D41. DOUGLAS, William Orville
Beyond the high Himalaya. N.Y.: Doubleday, 1952/Ldn: Gollancz, 1953. 352p, illus (some col), maps. 22cm.
Travels in Kashmir, Gilgit, Hunza, Afghanistan.

D42. DOUGLAS, W. O.
Exploring the Himalaya. N.Y.: Random House, 1958. 177p, illus. 21cm. (World Landmark Books, W-36)
Miscellany of Himalayan exploration, Sherpa customs, Yeti, etc; written for young adults.

D43. DOUGLAS, W. O.
Of men and mountains. N.Y.: Harper, 1950/Ldn: Gollancz, 1951. xiv, 338p, map (end papers). 23cm.
Outdoor life in the Cascades.

D44. DOUGLAS-HAMILTON, James
Roof of the world: man's first flight over Everest. Edinburgh: Mainstream, 1983. 192p, illus, maps. 25cm.
The author's father was chief pilot on the 1933 flights. The book contains much original material and many previously unpublished photographs.

D45. DOWLING, Philip (b.1929)
The mountaineers: famous climbers in Canada. Edmonton: Hurtig, 1979. 3-258p, illus. 23cm.
Biographical sketches, with accounts of their most famous climbs, written by a past president of the Alpine Club of Canada. Includes Charles Fay, Val Fynn, Phil Munday, Conrad Kain and others.

D46. DOWNER, Arthur Cleveland (1846-1943)
Mountaineering ballads. Ldn: C. Murray, [1905]. 47p. 12 × 15cm.
The author was a clergyman and climber.

D47. DOWNIE, R. A.
All about Arran. 1937.
—Another ed. 1948.
Includes climbing and scrambling.

D48. DRAKE, Samuel Adams
The heart of the White Mountains: their legend and scenery. Illustrations by W. Hamilton Gibson. Ldn & N.Y., 1882. xii, 318p, illus, 3 maps. [4to].

D49. DRASDO, Harold (b.1930)
Education and the mountain centres. Llanwrst: Tyddyn Gabriel, 1972. 38p. 22cm.
—2nd enlarged ed. 1973. 65p.
—Rev. ed. 1979 entitled *Education and the mountain experience.*
Polemical work by British climber and outdoor pursuits administrator; well-known writer of guidebooks, essays and articles on mountaineering.

D50. DREW, Frederic
The Jummoo and Kashmir territories: a geographical account. Ldn: Stanford, 1875. xv, 568p, plates (some fold. col), illus, maps (1 in pkt). 25cm.
—2nd ed. entitled *The northern barrier of India.* Ldn: Stanford, 1877. xii, 336p, plates (2 fold.), illus, maps. 21cm.
—Another ed. Delhi: Oriental Publishers, 1971. xv, 568p. 22cm.
—Another ed. Graz: Akademische Druck-u-Verlagsanstalt, 1974. 584p.
—Another ed. Delhi: Cosmo Pub., 1976.
The author travelled extensively from 1862 to 1871 in the outlying parts of Kashmir. He was one of the first to suggest the formation of a Himalayan club.

D51. DUBIN, Marc S.
Greece on foot: mountain treks, island trails. Seattle: Mountaineers, 1986. 240p, maps.

D52. DUDLEY, Ernest
Rangi: Highland rescue dog. Ldn: Harvill Press, 1970. 126p, 16 plates, illus. 22cm.
Rangi was the first search dog trained by Hamish MacInnes.

→ **D53 DU FAUR, Freda (-1935)**
The conquest of Mount Cook and other climbs: an account of four seasons' mountaineering on the Southern Alps of New Zealand. Ldn: Allen & Unwin/N.Y.: Scribner's, 1915. 250p, 40 plates, illus. 27cm.
—Another ed. 1937?
—Facsimile reprint. Christchurch: Capper Press, 1977. Edition of 1000 copies.
Miss Du Faur was an Australian who made many notable climbs during the years 1909-13, in particular the first traverse of the summit ridge of Mount Cook. It is doubtful whether she ever climbed again. She spent most of the rest of her life in England, but died in Australia.

→ **D54. DUNDAS, Anne**
Beneath African glaciers: the humours, tragedies and demands of an East African Government station. Ldn: Wetherby, 1924. 238p, plates, illus. 23cm.
Includes an attempt in 1921 on the highest point of Kilimanjaro.

D55. DUNN, Robert

The shameless diary of an explorer. N.Y.: Outing Pub, 1907. viii, 297p, plates, illus, 2 fold. maps. 19cm.
American journalist Dunn tells a very good story of the first and only complete trip around Mt. McKinley in 1903 with Dr. Cook.

D56. DUNSHEATH, Joyce (1902-76) & BAILLIE, Eleanor

Afghan quest: the story of their Abinger Afghanistan expedition 1960. Ldn: Harrap, 1961. 239p, 8 plates, illus. 22cm.
Includes an attempt on Mir Samir (19,880 ft) in the Hindu Kush.

D57. DUNSHEATH, J.

Guest of the Soviets: Moscow and the Caucasus 1957. Ldn: Constable, 1959. viii, 183p, 7 plates, illus, map. 23cm.
Ascent of Elbrus and travels in Suanetia, Georgia.

D58. DUNSHEATH, J.

Mountains and memsahibs. By the members of the Abinger Himalayan Expedition 1956. Ldn: Constable, 1958. x, 198p, 9 plates, illus. 22cm.
Kulu area. The Bara Shigri glacier was explored and mapped. Deo Tibba and other peaks were climbed.

D59. DURAND, Sir Algernon George Arnold

The making of a frontier: five years' experiences and adventures in Gilgit, Hunza, Nagar, Chitral and the Eastern Hindu-Kush. Ldn: Murray, 1899. xvi, 298p, plates (1 fold. col), illus, maps. 23cm.
—2nd ed. 1900.
—Another ed. Nelson, [c.1900]. Pocket edition.
—Reprinted. Graz: Akademische Druck-u-Verlagsanstalt, 1974. 350p, 37 plates, map.
Classic travel book about the Nanga Parbat region. 1888-89.

D60. DURHAM, William Edward (1857-1921)

Summer holidays in the Alps, 1898-1914. Ldn: Fisher Unwin, 1916. 207p, 48 plates, illus. 28cm.
The Rev. Durham climbed extensively in the western Alps. He was killed in a rock-climbing accident on Tryfan, North Wales.

D61. DUTTON, E. A. T.

Kenya Mountain. Ldn: Cape, 1929. xvi, 219p, 56 plates, illus, fold. map. 27cm.
—2nd rev. ed. (minor corrections only). Cape, 1930.
This handsome book is still the classic work on Mount Kenya.

D62. DVORAK, Karel

Vilem Hèckel. Prague, 1982. 224p, illus. [4to]. Summary and captions in English, French, German and Russian.
Finely illustrated tribute to this celebrated Czechoslovakian photographer and alpinist.

D63. DYOTT, G. M.

On the trail of the unknown: in the wilds of Ecuador and the Amazon. 1926.
Sangay, Tungurahua.

D64. DYRENFURTH, Günter Oskar

To the third pole: the history of the high Himalaya. With contributions by Erwin Schneider. Trans. from the German by Hugh Merrick. Ldn: Laurie, 1955. xxx, 233p, 48 plates, illus. 26cm. From the original: *Zum Dritten Pol: Die Achttausender der Erde.* (Munich: Nymphenburger, 1952)
History of attempts on the 8000-metre peaks written by a German-Swiss mountaineer who led the 1930 international Kanchenjunga expedition, among others.

E

E01. EARLE, John

The springs of enchantment: climbing and exploration in Patagonia. Ldn: Hodder, 1981. 191p, 16 plates, illus. 23cm.
Expeditions with Eric Shipton and others to Mount Burney and the Darwin Range, Tierra del Fuego.

E02. EASTON, John

An unfrequented highway: through Sikkim and Tibet to Chumolaori. Ldn: Scholartis Press, 1928/N.Y.: Knopf, 1929. xii, 133p, 16 plates, illus. 26cm. Limited edition of 960 copies.

Account of a journey from Darjeeling to Phari Dzong and Chomolhari in 1923.

E03. EATON, Walter Prichard

Skyline camps; a notebook of a wanderer over Northwestern Rockies, Cascade Mountains and Crater Lake. ?: Wilde, 1924. 245p, 17 plates, illus.

E04. EBERHARDT, Perry & SCHMUCK, Philip

The Fourteeners: Colorado's great mountains. Chicago: Sage Swallow Press, 1970. 128p, illus, maps. 28cm. Softback. Description of 58 Colorado peaks, with useful information.

E05. EBERLI, Henry

An English mountaineer: A. W. Moore. Whitby; Whitby Gazette?, 1919. 40p. 17cm. Reprinted from the *Whitby Gazette,* Sept. 5, 12, 19, 26.

E06. ECKENSTEIN, Oscar Johannes Ludwig (1859-1921) & LORRIA, August (Editors)

The Alpine portfolio: the Pennine Alps from the Simplon to the Great St. Bernard. [The Editors, 1889]. 33p, 100 plates, illus. 42cm. A set of individually mounted photographs by Vittorio Sella, Mrs Le Blond, W. F. Donkin and others, with an introductory text.

Eckenstein and Lorria climbed together in the 1880s.

E07. ECKENSTEIN, O. J. L.

The Karakorams and Kashmir: an account of a journey. Ldn: Fisher Unwin, 1896. xvi, 253p. 20cm.

A rather dull account of his experiences after breaking away from Conway's famous expedition. Later he organized his own expedition to K2, one of his companions being the notorious Aleister Crowley. By profession an engineer, Eckenstein's main contribution to climbing was in the field of equipment design.

E08. EDHOLM, O. G. & BACHARACH, A. L.

Exploration medicine: being a practical guide for those going on expeditions. Bristol: John Wright & Sons, 1965. xvi, 410p, illus. 23cm.

E09. EDWARDS, Amelia Blandford (1831-92)

Untrodden peaks and unfrequented valleys: a midsummer ramble in the Dolomites. Ldn: Longmans, 1873. xxvi, 385p, 8 plates, illus, fold. map. 24cm. Green cloth, bevelled edges, gilt decoration on front.

—Another ed. Leipzig: Tauchnitz, 1873. 302p. 23cm.

—2nd. U.K. ed., entitled *Midsummer ramble in the Dolomites.* Ldn: Boutledge, 1889. 389p, 9 plates, illus, map. 24cm. Pictorial cover.

—Another ed. Ldn: Routledge, 1890. 389p. Apparently issued under both titles.

—Another ed. Ldn: Routledge, 1893. xxvi, 389p, Decor. cloth.

—3rd ed. Ldn: Routledge, [189?]. xxvi, 389p, 9 plates. 23cm. Apparently issued under both titles.

—U.S. ed. entitled *Midsummer ramble in the Dolomites.* N.Y.: Dutton, 1898?

—4th U.K. ed. Ldn: Routledge, 1898. Pictorial cover.

Miss Edwards was an English writer, novelist and Egyptologist. After her visit to Egypt in 1873 she devoted herself to Egyptology, being convinced that only scientific research could preserve the antiquities of the country. She helped to form the Egypt Exploration Fund and in 1877 published what was probably her best book, *A thousand miles up the Nile.*

E10. EGELER, Cornelis Geoffrey

The untrodden Andes: climbing adventures in the Cordillera Blanca, Peru. By . . .in co-operation with T. de Booy. Trans. From the Dutch by W. E. James. Ldn: Faber, 1955. 203p, 32 plates, illus, maps. 22cm. From the original: *Naar onbestegen Andes toppen* (Amsterdam: Scheltens & Giltay, 1953)

—U.S. ed. entitled *Challenge of the Andes.* N.Y.: David McKay, 1955.

First ascent in 1952 of Nevado Huantsán (6395m) and other peaks in the Cordillera Blanca, Peru.

E11. EGGLER, Albert
The Everest-Lhotse adventure. Trans. [from the German] by Hugh Merrick. Ldn: Allen & Unwin, 1957. 224p, 25 plates, illus, maps. 23cm. From the original: *Gipfel über den Wolken* (Berne: Hallweg, 1956)
Swiss ascent of Everest and first ascent of Lhotse.

E12. EICHLER, Arturo
Ecuador: snow peaks and jungles. N.Y.: Crowell, 1955. 165p. From the original: *Nieve y selva en Ecuador* (Guayaquil: Edit. Bruno Moritz, 1950)
—Bilingual ed. Quito, 1970.
Descriptions of his own and historical first ascents, and summaries of mountain ascents in Ecuador.

E13. EICHORN, Arthur Francis
The Mt. Shasta story: being a concise history of the famous California mountain. Mount Shasta Herald, Mount Shasta, 1957. 112p, illus. 21cm.
Shasta is an isolated volcano in northern Califorina. It has five glaciers, as well as a few vents and geysers, and was first climbed in 1854.

E14. EISELIN, Max
The ascent of Dhaulagiri. Trans. from the German by E. Noel Bownam. Ldn: O.U.P., 1961. xii, 159p, 29 plates (some col), illus. 23cm. From the original: *Erfolg am Dhaulagiri* (Zurich: Orell Füssli, 1960)
The last Nepal 8000-metre peak to be climbed.

E15. ELTON, Oliver
C. E. Montague: a memoir. Ldn: Chatto & Windus, 1929. xiii, 335p, plates, illus. 23cm.
Biography of the author of famous mountaineering short stories. He also included climbing episodes in his novels.

E16. ELWOOD, Harold (Editor)
The Queen's University Expedition to the Taurus Mountains, 1969; report. Belfast: Q.U. of Belfast, 1970. 96p, illus, fold. map. 22cm.
Includes outlines of previous expeditions and basic information on Turkey and its mountains.

E17. ENGEL, Claire Eliane (-1977)
A history of mountaineering in the Alps. Ldn: Allen & Unwin/N.Y.: Scribner's, 1950. 296p, 24 plates, illus. 25cm.

E18. ENGEL, C. E.
Mountaineering in the Alps: an historical survey. Ldn:Allen & Unwin, 1971. 318p, 24 plates, illus. 24cm.
A completely revised version of her *History of mountaineering in the Alps;* very readable.

E19. ENGEL, C. E.
Mont Blanc. An anthology compiled by . . .Ldn: Allen & Unwin/Chicago: Rand McNally, 1965. 232p, 48 plates, illus. 25cm. From the original: *Mont Blanc* (Paris: Editions d'Art et d'Histoire, 1965)

E20. ENGEL, C. E.
They came to the hills. Ldn: Allen & Unwin, 1952. 276p, 17 plates, illus. 23cm.
Biographical sketches, mostly of nineteenth century climbers.

E21. ENOCK, C. Reginald
Andes and the Amazon: Life and travel in Peru. Ldn: Fisher Unwin, 1907. 379p, 59 plates, illus. 23cm.
—2nd ed. 1908.
Enock was possibly the first European to penetrate the Cordillera Blanca. He made a hazardous crossing of the snow-covered Abra Villón (c.5200m) from Huaraz to Huari; and later made the first attempt on Huascarán, from the west, being turned back at c.5100m by large crevasses.

E22. ENRIQUEZ, C. M.
Kinabalu, the haunted mountain of Borneo: an account of its ascent, its people, flora and fauna. Ldn, 1927. 199p, illus, map. 23cm.
Kinabalu is the highest mountain in Malaysia. This horseshoe-shaped peak has an extensive summit plateau from which rise many pinnacles and knobs. The sides of the mountain rise precipitously out of the tropical rain forest.

E23. ERSKINE, Angus B.
Royal Navy Ellesmere Island Expedition, 1972. Expedition report by . . . [Dunfermline]: The Expedition, [1972]. 1v., illus, maps. 30cm.

E24. ESCARRA, Jean (1885-1955)
Himalayan assault: the French Himalayan Expedition, 1936. [By ..., Henry de Ségogne and others.] Trans. [from the French] by Nea E. Morin. Ldn: Methuen, 1938. xvi, 204p, 48 plates, illus. 23cm.
From the original: *Karakoram: Expedition française à l'Himalaya 1936* (Paris: Flammarion, 1938)
Attempt on Gasherbrum 1 (Hidden Peak).

E25. ETHERTON, Percy Thomas
The last strongholds: a pen-picture of the great range of Himalayan mountains and the lands adjacent to them. Ldn: Jarrolds, 1934. 297p, illus. 24cm.
Lt. Col. Etherton travelled widely in the Himalayan regions and was for a time British Consul at Kashgar (as was Eric Shipton in later years). Etherton also helped to organize the Houston Flight over Everest expedition in 1933.

E26. EVANS, Sir Robert Charles (b.1918)
Eye on Everest: a sketch book from the great Everest expedition. Ldn: Dobson, 1955. 123p, illus. 26cm.
Delightful book for children by the deputy leader of the 1953 expedition. Evans was one of the first pair ever to reach the south summit.

E27. EVANS, R. C.
Kanchenjunga: the untrodden peak. Ldn: Hodder, 1956. xx, 187p, 37 plates (some col), illus. 23cm.
—U.S. ed. entitled *Kanchenjunga climbed.* N.Y.: Dutton, 1957. Fewer plates.
—T.B.C. ed. 1962.
First ascent; an account by the leader of the expedition.

E28. EVANS, R. C.
On climbing. Ldn: Museum Press, 1956. 191p, 32 plates, illus. 24cm.
—U.S. ed. Woodstock: Countryman Press, [1955].
Mixture of instruction and reminiscence by a past president (1968-70) of the Alpine Club.

E29. EVANS, Joan
The Conways: a history of three generations. Ldn: Museum Press, 1966. 308p, plates, illus. 23cm.
Biography of Sir Martin Conway, starting with his father, ending with his daughter.

E30. EVE, Arthur S. & CREASEY, C. H.
Life and work of John Tyndall. With a chapter on Tyndall as a mountaineer by Lord Schuster. Ldn: Macmillan, 1945. xxxii, 404p, 25 plates, illus. 25cm.
Tyndall was a leading Victorian scientist and mountaineer.

E31. [EVEREST MISCELLANEA]
Assault on Mount Everest. Board game for one or two players. (U.S.A.)

E32. [EVEREST MISCELLANEA]
Everest explorer. Software for computer game. By William Godwin and Don Knowlton. Wayne: Acorn, 1983. For IBM PC/XT (128k) or TRS-80; one disc drive. Requires endless logistical, etc. decisions to get climber to the top.

E33. [EVEREST MISCELLANEA]
Everest the ultimate challenge, 1922-1982. Dolby Stereo, 1983. Sound cassette (90 minutes). Quarry Lane Productions, P.O. Box 1237, Alexandria, Ontario KOC 1AO.

E34. [EVEREST MISCELLANEA]
Mount Everest: a jigsaw puzzle. Heian International Inc. 1,000 pieces. 51 × 73cm. Shows the South Face of Lhotse, from a photograph by Shiro Shirahata.

E35. EVERETT, Boyd N. Jr.
Organization of an Alaskan expedition. Pasadena, CA: Gorak, 1984. 112p, illus, maps. Softback.
Topics include route-planning, glacier flying, regulations, avalanches, equipment, food, climbing, strategy, weather and ethics. Also includes list of mountains with climbed and unclimbed routes.

F

F01. FANTIN, Mario (1920-80)
Cervino 1865-1965 (Matterhorn-Mont Cervin). Fotografie e toti di ...Bologna: Tamari, 1965. 153p, illus, bibl. 29cm. English text included.
Fine photo-history of climbing on this famous peak.

F02. FARQUHAR, Francis Peloubet (1887-1974)
First ascents in the United States, 1642-1900. S.F.: Grabhorn Press, 1948. 12p. 21cm. Presented by the author to members of the A.A.C. at a meeting of the Sierra Nevada section, Berkeley, 1948.

F03. FARQUHAR, F. P.
History of the Sierra Nevada. Berkeley: Univ. California Press in collaboration with the Sierra Club, 1965. xvi, 262p, col. plate, illus, maps, bibl. 28cm. R.P., 1966 twice.
This superb work was prepared by a much loved American climber, mountain historian and book-collector, who was also a past president of the Sierra Club and editor of its Bulletin. His collection of mountain books was given to U.C.L.A.

F04. FARQUHAR, F. P. & PHOUTRIDES, Aristides E.
Mount Olympus. S.F.: Johnck & Seeger, 1929. xiv, 49p, 5 plates, illus, fold. map. 28cm. Boxed. Edition of 950 copies.

F05. FARQUHAR, F. P.
Place names of the High Sierra. S.F.: Sierra Club, 1926. xi, 128p, bibl. 25cm. Edition of 1000 copies of which 200 were printed on all-rag paper. (Sierra Club Publications, 62)
Gives origins of names, bibliographical details of first ascents, biographical notes on persons whose names have been used, etc. A most interesting and carefully compiled work.

F06. FARRER, Reginald (-1920)
Among the hills: a book of joy in high places. Ldn: Headley, [1911]. 326p, plates (some col), illus, fold. map. 22cm.
The author was a well-known botanist and plant-hunter who explored in Burma, China and Tibet.

F07. FARRINGTON, Peter
Cambridge Undergraduate Ladakh Expedition 1977: report. By ...and others. Cambridge, 1977. 137p. Yak. F. 19.

F08. FARIS, John T.
Roaming the eastern mountains. N.Y.: Farrar & Rinehart, 1932. 327p, illus. Appalachians.

F09. FAUX, Ronald
Everest: goddess of the wind. Edinburgh: Chambers, 1978. [xv], 115p, illus. 27cm.
Summary of Everest expeditions including the south-west face, by a British journalist-climber.

F10. FAUX, R.
High ambition: a biography of Reinhold Messner. Ldn: Gollancz, 1982. 180p, plates, illus. 24cm.
Messner is arguably the finest mountaineer of his generation, perhaps of all time.

F11. FAY, Abbott
Ski tracks in the Rockies: a century of Colorado skiing. Evergreen: Cordillera, 1984. 94p, illus. [Large Horiz. format]. Softback.
Stories and photographs.

F12. FAY, Charles Ernest (1846-1931)
The Canadian Rocky Mountains. N.Y.: A.A.C., 1911. 21p, illus, col. map. 35cm. (Alpina Americana series, No. 2 of 3)
Professor Fay was one of the pioneers of Canadian mountaineering.

F13. FEATHERSTONE, B. K.
An unexplored pass: a narrative of a thousand mile journey to the Karakoram Himalayas. Ldn: Hutchinson, [1926]. 295p, plates (1 fold.), illus, map. 25cm.
Exploration of the New (western) Mustagh Pass in 1922: reference to K2.

F14. FEDDEN, Henry Robin Romilly (1908-77)
Alpine ski tour; an account of the High Level Route. With photographs by A. Costa and others. Ldn: Putnam, 1956. 93p, 24 plates, illus, fold. map. 29cm.
Well illustrated account of a crossing of the famous ski-mountaineering route from Chamonix to Zermatt, by a well-known British writer, traveller and climber.

F15. FEDDEN, R.
The Enchanted Mountains: a quest in the Pyrenees. Ldn: Murray, 1962. 124p, 7 plates, illus, maps. 23cm.
A search for the little known Los Encantados peaks, charmingly described. A minor classic.

F16. FEDERATED MOUNTAIN CLUBS OF NEW ZEALAND

Safety in the mountains. Wellington: F.M.C.N.Z., 1938.
—3rd ed. 1949.
—4th ed. n.d.
—5th ed. 1967 [1963?]. 120p, illus. 19cm.
—6th ed. 1978.

F17. FELLOWES, Peregrine Forbes Morant (1883-1955)

First over Everest: the Houston-Mount Everest Expedition 1933. By ...[and others]. Ldn: John Lane Bodley Head, 1933. xx, 279p, 49 plates (some fold.), illus, maps, 3-D viewer (in pkt). 25cm. R.P., 1933 three times, 1934.
—Cheap ed. 1935
—U.S. ed. N.Y.: National Travel Club, 1934. 264p, 31 plates, illus, maps.
—Another ed. N.Y.: Robert McBride, 1934. 264p. 21cm.
This first flight over the summit of Everest, and film record, was a considerable achievement and a most dangerous undertaking.

F18. FELLOWS, Sir Charles (1799-1860)

A narrative of an ascent to the summit of Mont Blanc [made by Charles Fellows and William Hawes]. Ldn: The Author (Printed by Thomas Davison), 1827. [2], viii, 35p, 12 plates, illus. 30-33cm. Fifty copies were printed for private circulation, of which three have coloured plates. Probably all copies were inscribed by the author.
This was the fourteenth ascent of Mont Blanc. Fellows and Hawes adopted a variation of the customary route, i.e. via the Mur de Côte.

F19. FERLET, Réné & POULET, Guy

Aconcagua: South Face. Trans. from the French by E. Noel Bowman. Ldn: Constable, 1956. xii, 209p, 18 plates, illus. 23cm.
First ascent of one of the severest faces in the Andes during which several members of the French team were badly frostbitten.

F20. FERRARI, R. L.

The 1976 Cambridge-Reykjavik Universities Expedition to Vatnajokull, Iceland. By ..., K. J. Miller, G. Owen. Cambridge: The University, 1976. 34 leaves, plates, illus, maps. 29cm. (University of Cambridge, Department of Engineering, special reports, 5)

F21. FIALA, I.

Makalu 1976. Bratislava: Pressfoto, 1977. Portfolio containing 33 large coloured photographs of the 1976 Czech ascent of Makalu. 22cm. Captions in English, French and German.

F22. FIELD, Ernest K.

Mountain search and rescue operations. Edited by ..., prepared by F. D. McLaren. Grand Teton Natural History Association, 1960. Several ptgs.

F23. FIENNES, Sir Ranulph Twistleton-Wykeham (b.1944)

Ice-fall in Norway. Ldn: Hodder, 1972. 160p, 16 plates, illus. 23cm.
Account of an expedition led by the author, a British soldier and explorer.

F24. FILIPPI, Filippo de

The ascent of Mount St. Elias (Alaska) by H.R.H. Prince Luigi Amadeo di Savoia, Duke of the Abruzzi. Narrated by ...Illustrated by Vittorio Sella and trans. [from the Italian] by Signora Linda Villara with the author's supervision. N.Y.: Frederick Stokes. [1899?]/Ldn: Constable, 1900. xvi, 241p, 34 plates (some fold.), illus, 2 fold. col. maps). 28cm. Also large paper (30cm) edition of 100 copies on hand-made paper with mounted photographs. From the original: *La spedizione di S.A.R. il Principe Luigi Amadeo di Savoia, Duca degli Abruzzi, al Monte Sant'Elia (Alaska) 1897.* (Milan: Hoepli, 1900)
The first of three very important and successful expeditions masterminded by the Duke of the Abruzzi. De Filippi was an Italian surgeon, scholar and mountain traveller, and the official recorder of the Duke's expeditions.

F25. FILIPPI, F. de

The Italian expedition to the Himalaya, Karakoram and eastern Turkistan (1913-1914). With chapters by G. Dainelli and J. A. Spranger. Ldn: Arnold, 1932.

xvi, 528p, plates (some fold., some col), illus, maps (2 in pkt). 26cm.
Mainly scientific expedition led by de Filippi. The expedition's reports in Italian cover many volumes.

F26. FILIPPI, F. de

Karakoram and western Himalaya 1909: an account of the expedition of H.R.H. Prince Luigi Amadeo of Savoy, Duke of the Abruzzi. By . . .With a preface by H.R.H., the Duke of the Abruzzi. [Trans. from the Italian by Caroline de Filippi and H. T. Porter.] Illustrations from photographs taken by Vittorio Sella. Ldn: Constable/N.Y.: Dutton, 1912. xvii, 469p, 36 plates, illus. 28cm. Plus portfolio of 18 photographic panoramas, 3 fold. maps, list of illustrations and index. Also de luxe edition plus volume of maps. From the original: *La spedizione nel Karakoram e nell'Himaliaia occidentale 1909* (Bologna: Zanichelli, 1911)
Classic work on the Baltoro region; a most accurate and well illustrated reference source.

F27. FILIPPI, F. de

Ruwenzori: an account of the expedition of H.R.H. Prince Luigi Amadeo of Savoy, Duke of the Abruzzi. [Trans. from the Italian by Caroline de Filippi.] Ldn: Constable/N.Y.: Dutton, 1908. xvi, 403p, 32 plates, illus, 5 maps. 27cm. R.P., 1909. From the original: *Il Ruwenzori* (Milan: Hoepli, 1909)
Classic reference work on this tropical range; the expedition succeeded in climbing all the principal peaks.

F28. FINCH, George Ingle (1888-1969)

The making of a mountaineer. Ldn: Arrowsmith, 1924. 340p, 56 plates, illus. 26cm. R.P., 1924, 1927.
Autobiography; chiefly Alps and Everest, 1922. Finch was a scientist and responsible for the oxygen equipment on Everest. A.C. President, 1959-61.

F29. FINCH, G. I.

Climbing Mount Everest. Ldn: Geo. Philip, 1930. 72p, illus. 19cm. R.P., 1931, 1933, 1935. (Philip's 'New Prospect' readers). N.B.: Finch also wrote pieces with the same title, which appeared in the *Boys' all-round book* (1926) and *Wonder book of the wild* (c.1930).

F30. FIRBANK, Thomas

I bought a mountain. Ldn: Harrap, 1940. 320p. 23cm. (26 ptgs, 1940-57)
—Four Square paperback 1959.
Famous story of a hill farm in Snowdonia; includes a record attempt on the traverse of the 14 peaks over 3000 ft, also a chapter on rock-climbing.

F31. FIRSOFF, Valdemar Axel

Arran with camera and sketchbook. Ldn: Hale, 1951. 230p, illus, fold. map. 22cm.
Includes some scrambling and climbing; attractive book.

F32. FIRSOFF, V. A.

The Cairngorms on foot and ski. Ldn: Hale, 1949. 279p, 35 plates (some fold), illus, fold. map. 23cm.

F33. FIRSOFF, V. A.

The Tatra Mountains. [Ldn]: Lindsay Drummond, [1942]. 128p, illus, map, music. 24cm. R.P., n.d., 1946.
General interest with one chapter on climbing in this small but exciting range.

F34. FIRST AID COMMITTEE OF MOUNTAINEERING CLUBS

First aid: North Wales, Lake District, Scotland. Stockport: F.A.C.M.C., 1938. 19p, plan. 16cm.
This early attempt to organize mountain rescue in Britain led to the formation of the Mountain Rescue Committee, which is still the nationally recognized body, to which most local independent teams are affiliated. For the M.R.C. handbook see under JOURNALS sub-section.

F35. FISHER, Marnie (Editor)

Expedition Yukon. Nelson (Canada), [1972?]. 200p, illus (some col). 26cm.
Canadian centennial celebration expedition to the St. Elias Mountains in 1967, making many first ascents in the Centennial Range and elswhere. Includes history of ascents in the region, prepared by Walter A. Wood.

F36. FITZGERALD, Edward Arthur (1871-1931)

Climbs in the New Zealand Alps: being an account of travel and discovery. By . . .and with contributions by Sir Martin Conway,

Professor T. G. Bonney, C. L. Barrow. Ldn: Fisher Unwin, 1896. xvi, 363p, 46 plates, illus, fold. map (in pkt). 25cm. Edition of 1000 copies. Also de luxe edition of 60 copies numbered and signed, of which only 50 copies were for sale, on Japan paper and bound by Zaehnsdorf.
—2nd ed. 1896. Only 500 copies.
—U.S. ed. N.Y.: Scribner's, 1896. xvi, 363p.
Fitzgerald made a number of good climbs after losing the first ascent of Mount Cook to local climbers. Both he and his book were unpopular with New Zealand mountaineers. His light-hearted style of writing also met with critical disapproval.

F37. FITZGERALD, E. A.
The highest Andes: a record of the first ascent of Aconcagua and Tupungato in Argentina and the exploration of the surrounding valleys. By ...with chapters by Stuart Vignes and contributions by Prof. Bonney [and others]. With 2 maps by A. R. Lightbody. Ldn: Methuen/N.Y.: Scribner's, 1899. xvi, 390p, 45 plates (1 fold), illus. 2 fold. maps. 25cm. Also a numbered edition of 60 copies signed by the author, of which only 50 were for sale.
Fitzgerald was unfit and climbed badly on this expedition, success going to Vignes and the guide Zurbriggen. He also resented the attacks on his previous book and deliberately made this one prosaic. He never climbed again.

F38. FITZGERALD, Kevin
The Chilterns. Ldn: Batsford, 1972. 184p, illus, map, bibl. 23cm.
North-west of London, and easily accessible, these beautiful rolling hills provide fine walking country. Written by a well-known mountaineering personality noted for his elegant and witty prose.

F39. FITZSIMONS, Raymond
The Baron of Piccadilly: the travels and entertainments of Albert Smith, 1816-60. Ldn: Bles, 1967. 192p, 24 plates, illus. 23cm.
Albert Smith made a fortune out of his illustrated lecture on the ascent of Mont Blanc.

F40. FLEMING, Jon W.
Army Mountaineering Association Himachal Pradesh Expedition, 1973: report. [Bythe leader ...and other expedition members.] Aldershot: The Expedition, [1974]. xii, 92p, illus, maps. 30cm. Yak. F. 71.

F41. FLEMING, J. W.
Joint British Army Mountaineering Association/Royal Nepalese Army Nuptse Expedition, 1975. Nuptse 1975: preliminary report. [By ...and others.] Warminster: The Expedition, 1976. 1v. (var. pag), plates, illus, maps. 30cm.

F42. FLEMING, J. W. & FAUX, R.
Soldiers on Everest: the joint Army Mountaineering Association Royal Nepalese Army Mount Everest Expedition, 1976. Ldn: H.M.S.O., 1977. xvi, 239p, 24 plates, illus, maps. 19cm. Softback only.

F43. FORBES, Charles S.
Iceland: its volcanoes, geysers and glaciers. Ldn: Murray, 1860. vii, 335p, plates (1 fold), illus, map. 22cm.
Includes ascent of Snaefells Yokul, etc.

F44. FORBES, James David (1809-68)
Norway and its glaciers visited in 1851: followed by journals of excursions in the high Alps of Dauphiné, Berne and Savoy. Edinburgh: Black, 1853. xxiv, 349p, 10 col. plates, illus, 2 maps (1 fold). 26cm.
Although Forbes visited Norway primarily in the course of his scientific researches into glaciers his book was regarded as a great classic by Cecil Slingsby, the 'Father' of Norwegian mountaineering.

F45. FORBES, J. D.
Travels through the Alps of Savoy and other parts of the Pennine chain with observations on the phenomena of glaciers. Edinburgh: Black, 1843. x, 424p, 9 plates (2 col), illus, 2 maps. 27cm.
—2nd rev. ed. 1845.
—Abridged ed. 1855 entitled *The tour of Mont Blanc and of Monte Rosa.*
—New edition revised and annotated by W. A. B. Coolidge. This edition contains all of Forbes's Alpine writings.

Forbes was a Scottish scientist and traveller who investigated the theory of glaciers and made many observations and mountain expeditions in the Alps. In 1842 he made the first British ascent of a virgin peak, the Stockhorn. He spans the era from De Saussure to Alfred Wills and his books are the first English accounts of systematic Alpine exploration and description of various regions.

F46. FORESTER, Thomas

Norway in 1848 and 1849 containing Rambles among the fjelds and fjords of the central and western districts; ...Ldn: Longmans, 1850. xv, 484p, plates, illus, maps. 23cm.
—Abridged ed. entitled *Rambles in Norway.* Longmans, 1855. xv, 296p. 18cm.

F47. FORSYTH, Sir Thomas Douglas

Report of a mission to Yarkand in 1873. Calcutta: Foreign Department Press, 1875. iii, 3, 573p. [4to].
Forsyth's second mission to Kashgar in 1873-4 was possibly the first expedition to combine exploration with scientific investigation. All members of the party contributed much useful information on the Pamirs, Chinese Turkestan and the Karakoram.

F48. FOTHERGILL, Claud F.

A doctor in many countries. Ldn: Pickering & Inglis, 1945. 168p, plates, illus. 22cm. R.P., 1946.
Includes climbing in the Alps and Corsica in 1920s. Vivid description of descent of the Matterhorn in a storm.

F49. FOUNTAIN, Paul

The great mountains and forests of South America. Ldn: Longmans, 1902. 306p, plates, illus. 24cm. R.P., 1904.

F50. FOX, Joseph Hoyland [Holroyd?] (1833-1915)

Holiday memories. Wellington, Somerset: The Author, 1908. [6], 147p. 28cm.
A lifetime's holiday memories, including mountaineering, by the brother-in-law of F. F. Tuckett, whom he accompanied on many Alpine excursions. Fox was a businessman and leading public figure in Somerset.

F51. FRANCIS, Godfrey Herbert (1927-60)

Mountain climbing. Diagrams drawn by Erik Thorn. Ldn: English Univ. Press, 1958. 192p, 8 plates, illus. 18cm. (Teach Yourself series)
—2nd ed. 1964. 200p.
Instructional. The author was killed climbing on Pillar Rock in the Lake District.

F52. FRANCO, Jean

Makalu: 8470 metres (27,790 ft): the highest peak yet conquered by an entire team. Trans. from the French by Denise Morin. Ldn: Cape, 1957. 256p, 21 plates, illus, maps. 21cm.
Account of 1955 French expedition, written by the leader. The party made the first, second and third ascents.

F53. FRANCO, J. & TERRAY, Lionel

At grips with Jannu. Trans. from the French by Hugh Merrick. Ldn: Gollancz, 1967. 192p, 48 plates, illus. 23cm.
The French ascent of Jannu in 1962 was the most difficult Himalayan climb accomplished up to that time.

F54. FRANCKE, August Hermann

A history of western Tibet: one of the unknown empires. Ldn: Partridge, [1907]. xiv, 191p, plates, illus, maps. 19cm.
Exploration after 1885 in Ladakh, Spiti and Lahoul.

F55. FRASER, Colin

The avalanche enigma. Ldn: Murray/Chicago: Rand McNally, 1966. xvi, 301p, 36 plates, illus, map, bibl. 24cm.
—Rev. ed. entitled *Avalanches and snow safety.* Ldn: Murray/N.Y.: Scribner's, 1978. xiii, 269p, 24 plates, illus, bibl. 23cm.
Deals with the work of the Swiss Federal Institute for Snow and Avalanche Research. Considered to be one of the best English-language works on the subject.

F56. FRASER, Esther

The Canadian Rockies: early travels and explorations. Edmonton: Hurtig, 1969. xvi, 252p, illus, fold. map. 23cm.
Includes all the famous nineteenth century climbers, e.g. Collie, Wilcox, Green, A. O. Wheeler.

F57. FRASER, E.

[A. O. *Wheeler: a biography*. Details not known; mentioned on cover of her other book.]
Wheeler was a founder member of the Alpine Club of Canada and a leading figure at their annual climbing camps.

F58. FRAZIER, Charles

Adventuring in the Andes: the Sierra Club travel guide to Ecuador, Peru, Bolivia, the Amazon Basin, and the Galapagos Islands. By ...with Donald Secreast. S.F.: Sierra Club, 1985. ix, 262p, illus, maps. 22cm. Softback.

F59. FREIDSTON, Jill A. & FESLER, Douglas

Snow sense: a guide to evaluating snow avalanche hazard.
—2nd ed. Anchorage: Alaska D.N.R., 1985. 48p, maps.
Pocket-size field guide.

F60. FREEMAN, Lewis R.

On the roof of the Rockies: the great Columbia icefield of the Canadian Rockies. N.Y.: Dodd Mead, 1925/Ldn: Heinemann, 1926. xv, 270p, 62 plates, illus. 25cm. Binding variations: decorative white cloth; blind-stamped purple cloth.
Photographic surveying expedition.

F61. FRERE, Richard Burchmore

Thoughts of a mountaineer. Ldn: Oliver & Boyd, 1952. vi, 177p, 8 plates, illus. 19cm.
Reminiscences of climbing in Scotland.

F62. FRESHFIELD, Douglas William (1845-1934)

Across country from Thonon to Trent: rambles and scrambles in Switzerland and the Tyrol. Ldn: Spottiswoode, 1865. [8], 135p. 23cm.
The first book by a young man who went on to become A.C. President, 1893-5, editor of the *Alpine Journal,* one of the great mountain explorers, and a leading figure in the Royal Geographical Society. He was also one of the most scholarly and sensitive of mountain writers.

F63. FRESHFIELD, D. W.

Below the snow line. Ldn: Constable/N.Y.: Dutton, 1923. viii, 270p, illus, maps. 23cm.
Climbs in Corsica, the lesser Alps, and elsewhere.

F64. FRESHFIELD, D. W.

The exploration of the Caucasus. With illustrations by Vittorio Sella. [Contributions by J. G. Cockin and others.] Ldn: Arnold, 1896. 2v, plates, illus, maps. 29cm. Also a large paper (33cm) 2v. edition of 100 numbered copies.
—2nd ed. 2v., plates, illus, maps. 29cm. A much less imposing edition than the first.
A magnificent work compiled and illustrated by Freshfield and his friends.

F65. FRESHFIELD, D. W.

Hannibal once more. Ldn: Arnold, 1914. [8], 120p, plates (some fold), illus, maps, bibl. 24cm.
The perennial mystery of Hannibal's crossing of the Alps.

F66. FRESHFIELD, D. W.

Italian Alps: sketches in the mountains of Ticino, Lombardy, the Trentino and Venetia. Ldn: Longmans, 1875. xviii, 385p, 9 plates (some fold., some col), illus, maps. 21cm.
—Another ed. Oxford: Blackwell, 1937. viii, 246p.
—Italian/English ed. Trento, 1956. R.P., 1971.

F67. FRESHFIELD, D. W.

The life of Horace-Bénédict de Saussure. By ...with the collaboration of Henry F. Montagnier. Ldn: Arnold, 1920. xii, 479p, 21 plates, illus, maps, bibl. 25cm.
This book gained Freshfield an Honorary Doctorate of Laws from the University of Geneva. A delightful study of early mountaineering and life in eighteenth century Geneva.

F68. FRESHFIELDS, D. W.

Quips for cranks and other trifles. The Author, 1923. x, 112p. 17cm.
Includes two poems about Coolidge.

F69. FRESHFIELD, D. W.
Round Kanchenjunga: a narrative of mountain travel and exploration. Ldn: Arnold, 1903. xvi, 373p, 41 plates (1 fold), illus, 2 fold. maps, bibl. 26cm.
—Reprint ed. Kathmandu: R. P. Bhandar, 1979. xvi, 367p, illus, maps. 22cm. (Bibliotheca Himalayica, series I, v. 25)
This dangerous and exhausting circuit of Kanchenjunga was a classic of mountain exploration; his second most important book.

F70. [FRESHFIELD, D. W.]
A tramp's wallet of alpine and roadside rhymes. Ldn: Elkin & Matthews, 1890. xii, 87p. 16cm.

F71. FRESHFIELD, D. W.
Travels in the central Caucasus and Bashan: including visits to Ararat and Tabreez and ascents of Kazbek and Elbruz. Ldn: Longmans, 1869. xvi, 509p, 4 plates, illus, 3 fold. maps. 22cm.

F72. FRESHFIELD, D. W.
Unto the hills. Ldn: Arnold, 1914. viii, 119p. 18cm.
Poems.

F73. FRESHFIELD, Jane [Mrs Henry]
Alpine byways: or, Light leaves gathered in 1859 and 1860; by a lady. Ldn: Longmans, 1861. ix, 232p, plates (some col), illus, maps. 21cm.
Classic travel book; tours through the Bernese and Pennine Alps by the Freshfield family.

F74. FRESHFIELD, Mrs Henry
A summer tour in the Grisons and Italian valleys of the Bernina. Ldn: Longmans, 1862. [x], 292p, 4 col. plates, illus, 2 fold. maps. 20cm.
This account of a then little known area sent the first wave of English summer visitors to the Engadine.

F75. FRIEND, Joe
Classic climbs of Australia. Katoomba, Adelaide: Second Back Row, 1983. 111p, plates, illus. 30cm.

F76. FRISON-ROCHE, Roger & TAIRRAZ, Pierre
Mont Blanc and the seven valleys. Trans. [from the French] and adapted by Roland Le Grand with the co-operation of Wilfrid Noyce. Ldn: Kaye/N.Y.: Oxford, 1961. 267p, illus, map. 23cm.
General survey.

F77. FRITH, Henry
Ascents and adventures: a record of hardy mountaineering in every quarter of the globe. Ldn: Routledge, 1884. 320p, illus. 22cm.

F78. FRYXELL, Fritiof N.
The Teton peaks and their ascents. Grand Teton National Park, WY: Crandall Studios, 1932. xiv, 106p, 15 plates, illus, fold. map. 20cm.
—Rev. ed. edited by Phil D. Smith, entitled *Mountaineering in the Tetons: The pioneer period, 1898-1940.* Jackson, WY: Teton Bookshop, [1980]. xiv, 181p, illus. 20cm.
This was the first book on technical climbing in the Tetons and remained the only guide for many years. Fryxell was a geologist and park ranger who pioneered many of the first ascents.

F79. FRYXELL, F. N.
The Tetons: interpretations of a mountain landscape. Berkeley: Univ. California Press, 1938. xiv, 77p, 13 plates, illus, fold. map. 20 cm. R.P., 1946, 1953, 1959, 1966.
An attractive companion volume to the author's climbing history, linked to the geology of the range.

F80. FUKUOKA-KEN HIGH SCHOOL TEACHERS' HINDU KUSH EXPEDITION
The Khwaja Muhammad Range: Central Hindu Kush, 1972. Fukuoka: The Expedition, 1976. 7, 250p, illus, maps. 26cm. In Japanese with English summary. Yak. j. 632.
2nd ascent of Koh-e-Piw and other peaks.

F81. [FURNESS RAILWAY]
Rock-climbing in Cumberland: a note-book for novices: via Furness Railway. Privately printed, [1914]. 44p, illus.

G

G01. GALFY, Ivan & KRISSAK, Milan
Makalu. Ceskoslovenská Horolezecká Expedicia Himaláje 1973. Bratislava: Sport Press, 1978. 218p, illus (many col), map. 27cm. Summary and captions in English, French, German and Russian. Yak. G. 10.
Splendid photo-album of the Czechoslovak 1973 and 1976 expeditions.

G02. GALLAS, F. E.
Land search and rescue.
—2nd ed. [New Zealand]: Federated Mountain Clubs of N.Z., 1981. x, 166p, illus.
The definitive New Zealand rescue manual; concentrates on searches, including the use of helicopters.

G03. GALTON, Sir Francis (1822-1911) (Editor)
Vacation tourists and notes of travel in 1860. [also volumes for 1861: 1862-3]. Cambridge/Ldn: Macmillan, 1861-4. 3v., plates, illus, maps. 24cm.
Three separate annual volumes. Includes various articles on climbing, including his own visit to the Pyrenees in 1860. His Alpine career consisted more or less of this and an ascent of Monte Rosa.

G04. GARDEN, John F.
The Selkirks — Nelson's mountains. Introduction by William Lowell Putnam. Revelstock, B.C: Footprint Pub, 1984. 144p, col. illus, map.
Fine colour photography.

G05. GARDNER, Arthur
The art and sport of alpine photography. Ldn: Witherby, 1927. 224p, 150 plates, illus. 23cm.

G06. GARDNER, A.
Britain's mountain heritage and its preservation as national parks; illustrated by . . .photographs by the author. Ldn: Batsford, 1942. xii, 51p, plates (1 fold), illus, map. 23cm.

G07. GARDNER, A.
The peaks, lochs and coasts of the western Highlands; penned by . . . Ldn: Witherby, 1924. xi, 169p, 100 plates, illus. 23cm.
—2nd rev. ed. enlarged. Edinburgh: R. Grant, 1928.

G08. GARDNER, A.
Sun, cloud & snow in the western Highlands from Glencoe to Ardnamurchan, Mull and Arran. Edinburgh: Grant & Murray, 1933. 122p, plates, illus, map. 24cm.

G09. GARDNER, John Dunn (1811-1903)
Ascent and tour of Mont Blanc: and passage of the Col du Géant, between Sept. 2nd and 7th, 1850. Chiswick, Ldn: C. Whittingham, 1851. 61p. 15cm.
The 38th ascent of Mont Blanc.

G10. GEIGER, Hermann (-1966?)
Alpine pilot. Trans. by Alan Tuppen. Ldn: Cassell, 1956. 104p, 33 plates, illus. 21cm.
Geiger was a Swiss pilot who specialized in mountain rescue by air. Initially he used an aeroplane fitted with skis, later a helicopter.

G11. GEIGER, H.
Geiger and the Alps. Geneva: Atar, [1958?]. 37p, plates (some col), illus, col. map. 29cm.
—Another ed. Trans. by Beatrice Snell. Lucerne: Oscar Bücher, 1966.

G12. GEIST, Roland C.
Hiking, camping and mountaineering. N.Y.: Harper, 1943. ix, 304p, 10 plates, illus, maps.
Includes climbing in north-west U.S.A. and Canadian Rockies.

G13. GEORGE, Hereford Brooke (1838-1910)
The Oberland and its glaciers: explored and illustrated with ice-axe and camera. With 28 photographic illustrations by Ernest Edwards. Ldn: Bennett, 1866. xii, 243p, 11 plates, illus. 28cm.
George was one of the leading climbers of his day. Some of his climbs are described in the book which is also prized for its illustrations. Ernest Edwards was

considered to be the best of the early amateur Alpine photographers, although he was primarily a portrait photographer.

G14. GEORGE, Marian M. (Editor)
A little journey to Switzerland, for home and school. Chicago: A. Flanagan, 1902. 100, 104p, 2 col. plates, illus, map. 20cm.
Children's book; includes Mont Blanc and Matterhorn stories.

G15. GERVASUTTI, GIUSTO (1909-46)
Gervasutti's climbs. Trans. [from the Italian] by Nea Morin and Janet Adam Smith. Ldn: Hart-Davis, 1957. 201p, 15 plates, illus. 22cm. From the original: *Scalate nelle Alpi* (Milan: Garzanti, 1947)
—Softback reprint. Ldn: Diadem, 1978/Seattle: Mountaineers, 1979.
Gervasutti was a leading Italian mountaineer who made many difficult ascents in the Dolomites and Mont Blanc range. He was killed while attempting a new route on Mont Blanc du Tacul.

G16. [GESNER, Conrad (1516-65)]
On the admiration of mountains: the prefactory letter addressed to Jacob Avienus, Physician, in Gesner's pamphlet 'On milk and substances prepared from milk', first printed at Zurich in 1543. A description of the Riven Mountain, commonly called Mount Pilatus, addressed to J. Chrysostome Huber, originally printed with another work of Gesner's at Zurich in 1555.
Trans. [from the Latin] by H. B. D. Soulé. Together with 'On Conrad Gesner' and 'The mountaineering of Theuerdank' by J. Monroe Thorington. Bibliographical notes by W. Dock and J. Monroe Thorington. S.F.: The Grabhorn Press, 1937. [20], 57p, illus. 29cm. Limited edition of 325 copies.
Gesner is usually accorded the distinction of being the first man to climb for sheer pleasure — 'I have resolved to ascend divers mountains each year partly for the worthy exercise of the body and recreation of the mind'.

G17. GIBSON, Jack T. M.
As I saw it. [c. 1976]. (Source *Himalayan Journal,* v. 36, p. 95 & 265.)
Autobiography including climbs in Garhwal Himalaya (Bandarpunch). Not in Yakushi.

G18. GILBERT, Josiah (1814-92) & CHURCHILL, George Cheetham (1822-1906)
The Dolomite Mountains: excursions through Tyrol, Carinthia, Carniola and Friuli in 1861, 1862, and 1863. With a geological chapter and pictorial illustrations from original drawings on the spot. Ldn: Longmans, 1864. xx, 576p, 6 col. plates, illus, 2 fold. maps. 22cm.
An Alpine travel classic by two members of the Alpine Club. Gilbert was a portrait painter; Churchill was a lawyer.

G19. GILBERT, Richard
Memorable Munros: an account of the ascent of the 3000 ft peaks in Scotland. Leicester: Cordee, 1976. [1], 94, [6]p, illus. 23cm. Softback. R.P., 1978.
—2nd ed. revised and expanded. Ldn: Diadem, 1983. [vi], 191p, 16 plates, illus, maps.
Author's climbing diary.

G20. GILBERT, R.
Mountaineering for all. Ldn: Batsford, 1981.

G21. GILBERT, R.
Young explorers. Easingwold, York: G. H. Smith & Son, 1979. [8], 236p, plates (some col), illus, maps. 23cm.
Schoolboy expeditions to Iceland, High Atlas, Lyngen Peninsula and Kolahoi, Kashmir.

G22. GILKISON, W. Scott
Aspiring, New Zealand: the romantic story of the "Matterhorn" of the Southern Alps. Christchurch: Printed by Whitcombe & Tombs, 1951. 80p, 23 plates, illus, maps. 19cm.
Climbing history of Mt. Aspiring (9957 ft), first ascended in 1910; written by a New Zealand climber.

G23. GILKISON, W. S.
Earnslaw, monarch of Wakatipu. Christchurch: Whitcombe & Tombs, 1957. 96p, 9 plates, illus. 18cm.
Description of the area, climbing history and first ascents of adjacent peaks.

G24. GILKISON, W. S.
Peaks, packs and mountain tracks. Auckland: Whitcombe & Tombs, 1940. 120p, 8 plates, illus. 18cm.

G25. GILL, Michael (b.1937)
Mountain midsummer: climbing in four continents. Ldn: Hodder, 1969. 220p, 48 plates, illus, maps. 23cm.
Climbing memoirs of a New Zealand doctor, physiologist and mountaineer. He was a member of some of Hillary's expeditions, climbing Ama Dablam, Taweche and Kangtega. Includes chapters on the Darran Mountains in New Zealand.

G26. GILL, William J.
The river of golden sand: being the narrative of a journey through China and eastern Tibet to Burmah. Edited by Henry Yule. Ldn: Murray, 1880. 2v., illus, maps. 22cm.
—Condensed ed. by Edward Colborne Baber. Ldn: Murray, 1883. 332p, plates (2 fold), illus, map. 21cm.
—Reprinted. Gregg International. 1074p, 9 maps.
Travels in the Minya Konka-Tatsienlu region in 1876-7.

G27. GILLETTE, Ned & REYNOLDS, Jan
Everest grand circle: a climbing and skiing adventure through Nepal and Tibet. Leicester: Cordee/Seattle: Mountaineers, 1985. 264p, col. illus, maps.
First complete circuit of Everest lasting four months; over 300 miles of trekking, climbing and skiing at altitudes between 17,000-23,000 ft. First winter ascent of Pumori.

G28. GILLMAN, Peter & HASTON, Dougal
Eiger direct. Photographed by Christian Bonington. Ldn: Collins, 1966. 183p, 40 plates (some col), illus. 24cm.
—U.S. ed. entitled *Direttissima: the Eiger assault.* N.Y.: Harper, 1966. xiii, 174p, 40 plates, illus. 21cm.
Account of the first direct route during which John Harlin fell to his death. Gillman is a journalist; Haston was a prominent Scottish climber, killed by an avalanche while skiing.

G29. GILLMAN, P.
Fitness on foot (climbing and walking for pleasure). Tadworth: World's Work/Sunday Times, 1978. 128p, plates, illus, bibl. 19cm. Softback.

G30. GIRDLESTONE, Arthur Gilbert (1842-1908)
The high Alps without guides: being a narrative of adventures in Switzerland, together with chapters on the practicability of such mode of mountaineering, and suggestions for its accomplishment. Ldn: Longmans, 1870. x, 182p, plate, illus, 2 maps. 22cm. Probably less than 100 copies.
The Rev. Girdlestone was an enthusiastic but inept climber who had a number of lucky escapes; consequently his book was badly received by his contemporaries. The Alpine Club hold his unpublished letters, some of which tell of his involvement with the Matterhorn tragedy.

G31. GODFREY, Bob & CHELTON, Dudley
Climb! Boulder: Alpine House, 1977. ix, 275p, illus. 28cm.
Illustrations and descriptions of the best in Colorado rock-climbing.

G32. GODLEY, Alfred Denis (1856-1925)
Reliquiae. Edited by C. R. L. Fletcher. O.U.P., 1926. 2v., plates (1 fold), illus. 20cm.
Godley was a scholar, poet and mountaineer, whose mischievous humour showed through his otherwise mournful expression. The second volume of his memoirs includes reprints from his pieces in the *Alpine Journal.* He also contributed to the *Climbers' Club Journal.* He is perhaps best remembered for his poems, 'Snowdonia', 'Switzerland' and 'A wartime lament'.

G33. GOHL, H
Alaska: vast land on the edge of the Arctic. Berne: Kümmerly & Frey, 1970. 140p, illus (some col), maps. [4to]. English text.

G34. GOODMAN, E. J.
New ground in Norway: Ringerike-Telemarken-Saetersdalen. Ldn: Newnes, 1896.

G35. GORDON, Sir Thomas Edward
The roof of the world: being the narrative of a journey over the high plateau of Tibet and the Oxus sources on Pamir.

Edinburgh: Edmonton & Douglas, 1876. xiv, 172p, plates (some fold., some col), illus, map. 27cm.
The author was a member of Forsyth's second mission to Kashgar in 1873-4, one of the first expeditions to combine exploration with scientific investigation. All members contributed much useful information on the areas covered.

G36. GOS, Charles (1885-1949)
Alpine tragedy. Trans. from the French by Malcolm Barnes. Ldn: Allen & Unwin/N.Y.: Scribner's, 1948. x, 282p, 32 plates, illus, maps. 24cm. From the original: *Tragédies alpestres* (Paris Edit. de France, 1940)
Recounts over 20 well-known nineteenth century Alpine accidents. Gos was a Swiss writer and mountaineer whose climbing career was terminated early by illness.

G37. GOS, François Marc Eugene
Rambles in High Savoy. Trans. [from the French] by Frank Kemp. Ldn: Longmans, 1927. 169p, illus, col. map. 25cm.
Well illustrated general interest book.

G38. GOS, F. M. E.
Zermatt and its valley. Trans. [from the French] by F. F. Roget. Ldn: Cassell, 1926. 180p, illus, col. fold. map. 25cm. Binding variations seen: (i) brown shiny cloth; (ii) cloth spine, paperboards, maroon, quarter-bound. The latter has whiter paper, a blank page between front endpaper and half-title, also a blank and back endpaper additional to the other issue.
Well illustated general interest book.

G39. GOSWAMI, S. M.
Everest, is it conquered? Calcutta: [Indian Press for] The Author, [1954]. xvii, 122p, 2 plates, illus, map. 19cm.
The author argues that Hunt's 1953 expedition did not climb Everest.

G40. GRAHAM, Alec & WILSON, Jim
Uncle Alex and the Grahams of Franz Josef. Dunedin: McIndoe, 1983. 224p, illus, maps.
Graham was a leading early guide in the Mount Cook region. The first half of the book is autobiographical; the second half was recently completed by Wilson.

G41. GRAHAM, J. C.
Ruapehu. 1963.

G42. GRAHAM, Peter (1878-1961)
Peter Graham, mountain guide: an autobiography. Edited by [Mrs] H. B. Hewitt. Wellington: Reed/Ldn: Allen & Unwin, 1965. xiv, 245p, 16 plates. 24cm.
—2nd ptg. Wellington: Reed, 1973.
Graham was a New Zealand guide who climbed with Miss Du Faur. He and his brother Alec were the leading New Zealand guides for over thirty years.

G43. [GRAHAM, William Woodman (c.1859-?)]
From the Equator to the Pole: adventures of recent discovery by eminent travellers. Ldn: Isbister, [1886]. 254p, illus, map. 18cm. Part 2. — Climbing the Himalayas, by W. W. Graham.
In 1883 Graham, who was an experienced Alpinist, was the first to visit the Himalaya for pleasure mountaineering. His story first appeared in the magazine *Good Words* (1885). His claim to have climbed Kabru has never been disproved but is no longer taken seriously.

G44. GRANT, Richard Henry (1927-81)
Annapurna II. Ldn: Kimber, 1961. 192p, 8 plates, illus. 23cm.
First ascent.

G45. GRAVES, Robert Ranke (1895-1985)
Goodbye to all that. Ldn: Cape, 1929.
—Rev. ed. Ldn: Cassell, 1957. With new prologue and epilogue.
—Penguin paperback, 1960. R.P., 1961.
Autobiography of the early life of leading British poet and novelist; references to climbing with George Mallory and the Pen-y-Pass crowd.

G46. GRAY, Dennis Dillon (b.1935)
Rope boy. Ldn: Gollancz, 1970. 320p, 27 plates, illus. 23cm. R.P., 1979, 1980.
Climbing autobiography of English mountaineer, now administrator of the British Mountaineering Council.

G47. GRAY, William R.
Pacific Crest Trail. Washington, DC: National Geographic, 1975. 200p, illus, maps.

G48. GREEN, John Richard (1837-83)
Stray studies from England and Italy. Ldn: Macmillan, 1876. viii, 421p. 19cm.
English historian; his book includes some scathing comments about alpinists and alpine travel books of his day (see Milne, *Modern mountaineering*).

G49. GREEN, Roger Lancelyn
A. E. W. Mason. Ldn: Max Parrish, 1952. 272p, plate, illus. 23cm.
Biography of Alfred Edward Woodley Mason (1865-1948), English novelist and climber. His best known climbing novel is *Running water,* a thriller which climaxes on the Brenva ice-ridge on Mont Blanc.

G50. GREEN, William Spotswood (1847-1919)
Among the Selkirk glaciers: being the account of a rough survey in the Rocky Mountain regions of British Columbia. Ldn & N.Y.: Macmillan, 1890. xvi, 251p, 9 plates, illus, fold. map. 20cm.
The Rev. Green was an Irish civil servant. He was one of the first to climb in Canada where he made the first ascent of Mount Bonney in the Selkirks in 1888.

G51. GREEN, W. S.
The high alps of New Zealand: or, A trip to the glaciers of the antipodes with an ascent of Mount Cook. Ldn: Macmillan, 1883. xvi, 350p, frontis, 2 maps. 20cm.
—Facsimile reprint. Christchurch: Capper Press, 1976.
Green's uncompleted ascent of Mount Cook, by a route which was not finished until many years later, marks the start of high alpine climbing in New Zealand.

G52. GREENBANK, Anthony
A book of survival. Wolfe, 1967.

G53. GREENBANK, A.
Climbing, canoeing, skiing and caving. Kingswood, Surrey: Elliott Right Way Books, 1964. 156p, plates, illus, bibl. 19cm.

G54. GREENBANK, A.
Climbing for young people. Ldn: Harrap, 1977. 128p, illus. 23cm.
—Piccolo paperback, 1977.

G55. GREENBANK, A.
Climbing mountains. Bridlington: Peter Haddock Ltd, 1973. 63p, illus. 16cm. (Project Book series, 128)

G56. GREENBANK, A.
Climbing rocks. Bridlington: Peter Haddock Ltd, 1973. 63p, illus. 16cm. (Project Books series, 127)

G57. GREENBANK, A.
Enjoy your rock-climbing. Ldn: Pelham, 1976. 150p, 8 plates, illus. 23cm.

G58. GREENBANK, A.
Instructions in rock-climbing. Ldn: Museum Press, 1967. 125p, 8 plates, illus. 23cm.

G59. GREENBANK, A.
Instructions in rock-climbing. Ldn: Museum Press, 1963. 159p, 8 plates, illus. 23cm.

G60. GREENBANK, A.
Walking, hiking and backpacking. Ldn: Constable, 1977.

G61. GREENE, Raymond (1901-82)
Moments of being: random recollections. Ldn: Heinemann, 1974. ix, 180p, plates, illus. 25cm.
The author was doctor-climber on pre-war expeditions to Everest and Kamet, reaching the summit of the latter.

G62. GREGORY, Alfred (b.1913)
The picture of Everest: a book of full-colour reproductions of photographs of the Everest scene. Chosen and explained by . . .Ldn: Hodder/N.Y.: Dutton, 1954. [96p], 43 col. illus. 28cm. Also de luxe binding of gilt-stamped vellum with dark blue linen-paper dust wrapper and logistical chart of ascent on rear end-paper.

G63. GREGORY, John Walter
The great Rift valley; being the narrative of a journey to Mount Kenya and Lake Baringo, with some account of the geology, natural history . . .etc. Ldn: Murray, 1896. xxi, 422p, plates (some fold. col), illus, maps. 25cm.
Dr. Gregory, who also travelled through

the Aberdare Range to the west of Mount Kenya in the 1870s, reached the Lewis Glacier on Mount Kenya in 1893.

G64. GREGORY, J. W. & GREGORY, C. W.

To the alps of Chinese Tibet: an account of a journey of exploration up to and among the snow-clad mountains of the Tibetan frontier. Ldn: Seeley Service, 1923. 321p, plates (1 fold), illus, maps. 23cm.
—U.S. ed. Philadelphia, 1924.
Account of four months' travel by Dr. Gregory and his son in 1922 in the Minya Konka-Tatsienlu region.

G65. GREIG, Andrew

Men on ice. Edinburgh: Cannongate Publishing, 1977. 51p.
Poems; dedicated to Dougal Haston.

G66. GREINER, James

Wager with the wind: the Don Sheldon story. N.Y.: Rand McNally, 1974. 256p, illus. 24cm.
Biography of legendary Mt. McKinley glacier pilot who died in 1975.

G67. GRIBBLE, Francis Henry

The early mountaineers. Ldn: Fisher Unwin, 1899. xiv, 338p, 48 plates, illus. 23cm.
Authoritative and detailed record of pre-nineteenth century mountaineering in the Alps and Pyrenees.

G68. GRIBBLE, F. H.

The story of alpine climbing. Ldn: Newnes, 1904. 180p, 20 plates, illus, bibl. 16cm. (The Story of ...series)
—Rev. & enlarged ed. Ldn: Hodder, [c.1912]. 184p.
Children's series; good little summary.

G69. GRIBBON, P. W. F.

Scottish East Greenland Expedition 1963: general report. By ...[and others]. 1964.
Members made 21 first ascents in the Angmagssalik district and the second ascent of Rytterknagten via the north ridge.

G70. GRIBBON, P. W. F.

University of St. Andrew's West Greenland Expedition, 1965: general report. By ...[and others]. 1966.
Sixteen first ascents in the Sukkertoppen district to the south of the Evighedsfjord.

G71. GRIFFIN, Arthur Harold

Adventuring in Lakeland. Ldn: Hale, 1980. 189p, illus. 23cm.
Covers all types of Lake District mountaineering except hard rock-climbing. The author has written numerous books about Lake District life and customs.

G72. GRIFFIN, A. H.

Long days in the hills. Ldn: Hale, 1974. 188p, 32 plates, illus. 23cm.
British Isles.

G73. GRIFFIN, Margaret

Tiquimani. Stellenbosch, South Africa: Kosmo Pub., 1965. 164p, 13 plates, illus. 22cm.
Account of the 1983 South African expedition to the Cordillera Real, Bolivia.

G74. GROOM, Arthur

One mountain after another. Sydney: Angus & Robertson, 1949. R.P., 1951.
Australia — MacPherson Range, etc; general description.

G75. GROVE, Florence Crauford (1838-1902)

'The frosty Caucasus': an account of a walk through part of the range and of an ascent of Elbruz in the summer of 1874. With illustrations engraved by Ed. Whymper from photographs taken during the journey by H. Walker. Ldn: Longmans, 1875. x, 341p, 6 plates, illus, fold. map. 20cm. The first issue was bound in blue cloth. The second issue, with errata slip, was bound in decorative (reindeer & sled) grey cloth or plain green cloth.
Grove was one of the ablest British climbers of his day. A.C. President, 1884-6. He led the condemnation of guideless climbing in the 1870s, against the Rev. Girdlestone.

G76. GUMMA-KEN HIGH SCHOOL TEACHERS' INDIAN HIMALAYA EXPEDITION 1980
First ascent of Sharmili-CB53 (6096m) in Himachal Pradesh; and trekking in Ladakh-Zanskar-Central Lahoul. Maebashi: The Expedition, 1981. [x], 290p, illus (some col), maps. 26cm. In Japanese with English summary. Yak. j. 266.

G77. GUNMA-KEN HIMALAYAN EXPEDITION COMMITTEE
Ascent of Dhaulagiri I via the SE-ridge, 1978. Maebashi: Gunma Mountaineering Union, 1980. [36], 306p, col. illus, maps. 26cm. In Japanese with English summary. Yak. j. 265.

G78. GUNMA-KEN HIMALAYAN EXPEDITION COMMITTEE
Dhaulagiri IV, 1972. Maebashi: Gunma-ken Mountaineering Union, 1974. [26], 197p, illus (some col), maps. 26cm. In Japanese with English summary. Yak. j. 263.

G79. GUNMA-KEN LADIES' GANGOTRI EXPEDITION
Mountain of the Heart-dancing Holy Place. Gunma: The Expedition, 1981. [12], 107p, illus, maps. In Japanese with English summary. Yak. j. 267.
Expedition to Bhagirathi II (6512m) in 1980.

G80. GURUNG, Harka Bahadur
Annapurna to Dhaulagiri: a decade of mountaineering in Nepal Himalaya, 1950-1960. Kathmandu: Department of Information, Ministry of Information & Broadcasting, 1968. ix, 122p, col. plates, illus, map. 23cm.
Summarizes about 100 expeditions.

G81. GURUNG, H. B.
Vignettes of Nepal. Kathmandu: Sajha Prakashan, 1980. xv, 435p, illus (some col), maps. 22cm.
Includes chapter on his experiences with the 1971 international Everest expedition to climb the south-west face.

H

H01. HABELER, Peter
Everest, impossible victory: conquering Everest without oxygen. Trans. [from the German] by David Heald. Ldn: Arlington Books, 1979. 223, col. plates, illus, map. 25cm. From the original: *Der Einsame Sieg* (Munich: Goldmann, 1978)
—U.S. ed. entitled *The lonely victory: Mount Everest '78.* N.Y.: Simon & Schuster, 1979. 224p.
First ascent without oxygen by Reinhold Messner and the author.

H02. HACKETT, Peter H.
Mountain sickness: prevention, recognition and treatment. N.Y.: A.A.C., 1980. 29p. (An A.A.C. Climber's Guide)
—Rev. ed. A.A.C., [1983]. 77p. 17cm.

H03. HAGEN, Toni
Mount Everest: formation, population and exploration of the Everest region. By ...[and others]. Trans. [from the German] by E. Noel Bowman. Ldn: O.U.P., 1963. xvi, 195p, 31 plates, illus, maps. 23cm. From the original: *Mount Everest-Aufbau, Erforschung und Bevölkerung des Everest Gebietes* (Zurich: Orell Füssli, 1959)
Includes a 1:25,000 scale map of Everest.

H04. HAGEN, T.
Nepal: the kingdom in the Himalayas. Trans. [from the German] by B. M. Charleston. Berne: Kümmerly & Frey, 1960/N.Y.: Rand McNally, 1960/Ldn: Geographia, 1961/New Delhi: Oxford Book & Stationery, 1961. 117p, plates (some col), illus, map. 30cm.
—3rd ed. Chicago: Rand McNally, 1971. 180p, plates, map. 30cm.
The author, a Swiss geologist, travelled extensively in Nepal, and his book is the best general account of the country.

H05. HAGEN, Victor von
South America called them. Ldn: Hale, 1949. [xii, 401p?]
—T.B.C. ed.
—Scientific Book Club ed.
Includes the Ecuador expeditions of La Condamine and Alexander von

Humboldt; and Charles Darwin's expeditions to Tierra del Fuego and Chile. Written by a well-known explorer.

H06. HAGERMAN, Percy (1869-1950)
Notes on mountaineering in the Elk Mountains of Colorado, 1908-1910. Denver: Colorado Mountain Club, 1956. 28p. Prepared from typescript dated 1912. Hagerman was one of the first Americans to climb solely for pleasure. Together with Harold Clark he explored and climbed most of the major peaks in the Elk Range.

H07. HAINES, Aubrey
Mountain fever: historic conquests of Rainier. Portland: Oregon Historical Society, 1962. xiii, 257p, 9 plates, illus, 3 maps. 23cm.

H08. HALAS, Alojz & KELE, Frantisek
Hindukus '74 Bratislava: Nakladatelstvo CSTK-Pressfoto, 1978. [9p], 33 plates (mostly col), illus, map. 22 × 19cm. Summary and captions in English, French and German.
Czech ascent of Noshaq (7492m).

H09. HALAS, A. & KELE, F.
Hoggar-Kibo. Bratislava, 1980. Portfolio of 4 maps and 33 large colour photographs. Captions in English, Russian, Slovakian, German and French.

H10. HALASA, J. & SLACHTA, F.
Velka Fatra (The great Fatra). [Bratislava], 1981. 26p text, 154 col. illus. [8vo]. English summary.
Photo-album of mountain range in Slovakia.

H11. HALES, Jane
Memories of a modest mountaineer. Holt: The Author, [1984]. 30p. 21cm.
Climbing in the Alps in 1920s.

H12. HALL, Arthur Vine
"Table Mountain": pictures with pen and camera. Cape Town/Ldn: Juta, [1897?]. 23p, plates (some col), illus. 23cm.
—3rd ed. Cape Town: Miller/Ldn: Sampson Low Marston, [1900].

H13. HALL, Donald Alan
On top of Oregon. Corvallis, OR: Golden West Press, [1975]. [4], 180p, illus. 23cm.
Studies of four major Cascade peaks — Three Sisters, Mt. Washington, Three fingered Jack, Mt. Jefferson.

H14. HALL, Lincoln
White limbo: the first Australian climb of Mount Everest. McMahons Point: Weldon, 1985. 262p, col. illus, map.
Complete ascent of the Great Couloir.

H15. HALL, Richard Watson
The art of mountain tramping: practical hints for both walker and scrambler among the British peaks. Ldn: Witherby, 1932. 191p, 4 plates, illus. 23cm. (Sports & Pastimes Library series)

H16. [HALL, R. W.]
On Cumbrian Fells: papers on rock-climbing with other pieces in prose and verse. By 'Hobcarton'. Whitehaven, Cumberland: Whitehaven News, 1926. 76p.

H17. HALL, R. W.
Some Cumbrian climbs and equipment. Cockermouth, Cumberland: The Author, [1923]. 35p. 19cm.

H18. HALL, Vernon
A scrapbook of Snowdonia. Stockwell, 1982. 132p, illus.
Virtually a history of the Pen y Gwryd Hotel, a famous hostelry for climbers and fishermen. It has an 'Everest Room' with expedition members' signatures on the ceiling.

H19. HALLWORTH, Rodney
The last flowers on earth. Maidstone: Angley Books, 1966. 167p, 9 plates, illus. 21cm.
Account of the ill-fated Royal Navy East Greenland mountaineering expedition to Schweizerland, written by a journalist.

H20. HAMER, Samuel H.
The Dolomites: with . . .illustrations in colour by Harry Rountree. Ldn: Methuen, 1910. xi, 305p, col. plates, illus, map. 23cm.

—2nd ed. entitled *A wayfarer in the Dolomites.* Methuen, 1926. xv, 207p, plates, map. 20cm.
Includes some climbing history; mainly descriptive.

H21. HAMILTON, Helen
Mountain madness. Ldn: Collins, 1922. x, 274p, 11 plates, illus. 19cm.
Reminiscences of climbing as a young woman around Chamonix in the early twentieth century.

H22. HANKINSON, Alan (b.1926)
Camera on the crags: a portfolio of early rock climbing photographs by the Abraham Brothers. Selected and written by . . .Ldn: Heinemann, 1975. [vi], 42p, 96 plates, illus. 29cm. R.P., 1979.
The author is a climber-writer resident in the Lake District.

H23. HANKINSON, A.
The first tigers: the early history of rock climbing in the Lake District. Ldn: Dent, 1972. xviii, 196p, 16 plates, illus. 23cm.
—Rev. ed. Keswick: Melbecks Books, 1984.
Covers the period from the earliest eighteenth century records to 1914.

H24. HANKINSON, A.
The mountain men: an early history of rock climbing in North Wales. Ldn: Heinemann Educational Books, 1977. x, 202p, illus. 23cm.
Covers the period from about 1800 to 1914.

H25. HANOTEAU, Guillaume
The Alps I love. By . . ., M. Aldebert & Michael Serraillier. N.Y.: Tudor Pub. Co., 1963. ?p, illus (some col). 26cm.
Photo-album.

H26. HARA, Makota & ASAMI, Masao
Makalu 1970: the first ascent by the south-east ridge. Nagoya: Privately printed for the Tokai Section, Japanese Alpine Club, 1971. var. pag, illus, 2 maps.
In Japanese with English summary. Yak. J. 585.

H27. HARDIE, Norman D.
In highest Nepal: our life among the Sherpas. Ldn: Allen & Unwin, 1957. 191p, plates, illus, maps. 22cm.
Account of life with the Sherpas by a New Zealand mountaineer, a member of the 1954 Baruntse and 1955 Kanchenjunga expeditions. Includes climbing.

H28. HARDING, David E.
Alpine New Zealand. Wellington: Millwood, 1980. 112p, plates, illus, 2 maps.

H29. HARDING, John
Avalanche: proceedings of a symposium for skiers, ski-mountaineers and mountaineers, with accounts of experiences of avalanches in Scotland, Europe and the Himalaya. By . . ., Michael Baker & Edward Williams. Ldn: Alpine Club, 1980. 62p, illus.

H30. HARDING, Warren
Downward bound: a mad! guide to rockclimbing. By Warren 'Batso' Harding. With illustrations by Beryl 'Beasto' Knauth. Englewood Cliffs, NJ: Prentice-Hall, 1975. 204p, illus. 21cm.
Part instructional, part a caricature of contemporary climbing and personalities. Written by a leading American rock-climber.

H31. HARE, James R. (Editor)
Hiking the Appalachian Trail.
—3rd ptg. 1977. 2v., 2009p, col. illus. 23cm.
Accounts of 46 men and women who did the trail from end to end.

H32. HARKER, George
Easter climbs: (the British Alpine Club). Ldn: Sherratt & Hughes, 1913. 141p, group port. 19cm.
Walking in the Lake District, Snowdonia, etc., 1883-1912, by a group of Manchester businessmen.

H33. HARMON, Byron
128 views of the Canadian Rockies: . . .specially selected, the results of five years' wandering in the Rockies . . .,

photographed by Byron Harmon. Banff: The Author, 1911. 1v. of illus. 18 × 26cm.
The author's photographs helped to make the Canadian Rockies world famous.

H34. HARMON, B.
Canadian Rockies: a series of eighteen hand-coloured Van Dyck photogravures. Banff: Byron Harmon, [1929]. 38p, 18 plates. Spiral bound.
Photo-album; general views.

H35. HARPER, Arthur Paul (1865-1955)
Memories of mountains and men. Christchurch: Simpson & Williams, 1946. 208p, plates, illus. 22cm.
Autobiographical memoirs, with plenty of fascinating mountaineering material. A worthy sequel to his first book.

H36. HARPER, A. P.
Pioneer work in the Alps of New Zealand: a record of the first exploration of the chief glaciers and ranges of the Southern Alps. Ldn: Fisher Unwin, 1896. xvi, 336p, 39 plates, illus, map. 23cm. Plus 20 copies on Japan paper in the British Museum.
Harper was a New Zealander who made several first ascents and did much exploration and survey work in the 1890s with Charles Douglas and G. E. Mannering. He was one of the pillars of the climbing world in New Zealand, and greatly revered by men of the younger generation. such as Scott Russell, just as he had looked up to the members of the Alpine Club.

H37. HARPER, Stephen
Ladykiller Peak: a lone man's story of twelve women on a killer mountain. Ldn: World Distributors, 1965. 124p, 18cm. Consul paperback.
Written by a journalist who followed this international women's expedition to Cho Oyu (8156m), which resulted in the death of Claude Kogan and three others.

H38. HARRER, Heinrich (b.1912)
I come from the Stone Age. Trans. from the German by Edward Fitzgerald. Ldn: Hart-Davis, 1964. 256p, 32 plates (some col), illus. 24cm. From the original: *Ich komme aus der Steinzeit* (Berlin: Ullstein, 1963)
—U.S. ed. N.Y.: Dutton, 1965.
—Book club ed.
Includes climbing all the Equatorial Carstenz Range in New Guinea.

H39. HARRER, H.
Return to Tibet. Ldn: Weidenfeld & Nicolson, 1984. vii, 184p, col. plates, illus. 23cm.
Sequel to *Seven years in Tibet.* The author retraces his journeys, describing present-day Tibet under Chinese rule.

H40. HARRER, H.
Seven years in Tibet. Ldn: Hart-Davis, 1953. xiii, 288p, plates, illus. 23cm.
—U.S. ed. N.Y.: Dutton, 1953. 314p, illus, maps.
—Reprint society ed.
Harrer escaped from internment in India during World war II and made his way to Lhasa, where he found favour in high circles.

H41. HARRER, H.
The White Spider: the history of the Eiger's North Face. Trans. from the German by Hugh Merrick. Ldn: Hart-Davis, 1959. v, 240p, 41 plates (1 col, 1 fold), illus. 24cm. Several ptgs. From the original: *Die weisse Spinne: Die Geschichte der Eiger-Nordwand* (Berlin: Ullstein, 1958)
—U.S. ed. N.Y.: Dutton, 1960.
—2nd rev. ed. with 10 additional chapters by Harrer & Kurt Maix. Hart-Davis, 1965.
—3rd rev. ed. 1976.
—Another ed. Granada, 1979.
—Rev. ed. Granada, 1983. 315p.
The author, an Austrian mountaineer, took part in the first ascent of the Eiger North Face in 1938 after there had been several attempts and fatalities.

H42. HARRIS, George W. & HASLER, Graeme
The Mount Cook alpine region. Wellington: Reed, 1971. 224p, illus (some col). 29cm. Cover title *A land apart.*
Chiefly photographs, with historical details, route guides, etc.

H43. HARRIS, Walter B.
Tafilet: the narrative of a journey of exploration in the Atlas mountains and the oases of the north-west Sahara. Illustrated by Maurice Romberg. Edinburgh: Blackwood, 1895. xii, 386p, plates, illus, maps. 22cm.

H44. Harrison, Frederic (1831-1923)
My alpine jubilee, (1851-1907). Ldn: Smith Elder, 1908. x, 141p, plate, port. 20cm.
Nostalgic letters and essays; his Alpine career was slight.

H45. HART, J.
The climbers. Univ. Pittsburgh Press, 1978. 72p.
Poems.

H46. HART, John Lathrop Jerome
Fourteen thousand feet: a history of the naming and early ascents of the high Colorado peaks. Denver: Colorado Mountain Club, 1925. 51p, map. 23cm.
—Rev. ed. with *A climber's guide to the high Colorado peaks* by Elinor Eppich Kingery. 71p, plates, illus, map. 23cm. R.P., 1972, 1977.
A little classic on Colorado mountaineering.

H47. HARVARD, Andrew & THOMPSON, Todd
Mountain of storms: the American expeditions to Dhaulagiri, 1969 & 1973. N.Y.: Chelsea House/New York Univ. Press, 1974. xii, 210p, illus. 26cm.
The 1969 expedition ended in the loss of seven members through a fall of ice. Members of the 1973 expedition made the fourth ascent.

H48. HARVARD MOUNTAINEERING CLUB
Wickersham Wall Expedition, 1963: Report.

H49. HASHIMOTO, S. (Editor)
Annapurna South, 7150m: via the untrodden East ridge. Tokyo: Dôryu Mountaineering Club, 1973. 16, 79p, illus, maps. 26cm. In Japanese with English summary. Yak. j. 31.
Ascent to central peak of Annapurna South.

H50. HASSE, Dietrich
Cordillera Real: Berliner Jubilaüms-Expedition, 1969. [Berlin]: The Expedition, 1969. 64p, illus, maps. 22cm. Summaries in English and Spanish.
Climbs in Bolivia.

H51. HASTON, Dougal (1940-77)
The Eiger. Ldn: Cassell, 1974. [10], 170p, 16 plates, illus. 23cm.
History of modern routes on the North Face. Haston took part in the first direct ascent route.

H52. HASTON, D.
In high places. Ldn: Cassell, 1972/N.Y.: Macmillan, 1973. [8], 168p, 16 plates, illus. 23cm. R.P., 1973 twice.
—Arrow paperback. Ldn: Hutchinson, 1974.
Climbing autobiography of leading Scottish climber, whose very severe climbs included the south-west face of Everest. He was killed in an avalanche while skiing.

H53. HAUSER, Günter
White mountain and tawny plain. Trans. from the German by Richard Rickett. Ldn: Allen & Unwin, 1961. 224p, 15 plates, illus, maps. 23cm. Abridged from the original: *Ihr Herren Berge* (Stuttgart: Engelhorns Verlag, 1959)
Climbing in the Peruvian Cordilleras Blanca and Vilcanota.

H54. HAVERGAL, Frances Ridley
Swiss letters and alpine poems: by the late Frances Ridley Havergal; edited by her sister, J. Miriam Crane. Ldn: Nisbet, 1882. vii, 356p, plates, illus. 21cm.
The author's mountaineering experiences were slight but her book contains some delightful descriptions of her excursions.

H55. HAWES, Sir Benjamin (1797-1862)
A narrative of an ascent to the summit of Mont Blanc, made during the summer of 1827 by Mr William Hawes and Mr Charles Fellows. By ...[from material supplied by his brother William]. Ldn: printed for Benjamin Hawes by Arthur Taylor, 1828. 35p, plate. 25cm. Variations: some copies have a plate depicting heights; others a plate of de

Saussure's ascent. Some copies have more variations overall, i.e. slightly larger, title finishing at '1827', insertion of 'junior' (i.e. printed for Benjamin Hawes junior). These copies appear to have the plate of heights.

H56. HAWTHORNE, Hildegarde & MILLS, Esther Burrell
Enos Mills of the Rockies.
Biography of famous Longs Peak guide, naturalist and conservationist.

H57. HAYDEN, Ferdinand Vandeveer (1829-87)
Sun pictures of Rocky Mountain scenery: with a description of the geographical and geological features, ... [with] photographic views along the line of the Pacific rail road, from Omaha to Sacramento. N.Y.: J. Bien, 1870. viii, 150p, 30 plates, illus. 32cm.
In 1867 Hayden was appointed geologist-in-charge of the U.S. geological and geographical survey of the territories, which occupied him for twelve years. In 1877 he issued his *Geological and geographical atlas of Colorado.* His surveyors made many ascents in Colorado, details of which are contained in the official reports (for which see under UNITED STATES GEOLOGICAL AND GEOGRAPHICAL SURVEYS). Extracts from these reports are quoted in Bueler, *Roof of the Rockies.*

H58. HAZARD, Joseph T.
Glacier playfields of Mount Rainier National Park. Seattle: Western Printing, 1920. 96p, illus.
Contains account of the first ascent of Fuhrer Finger Route; and a chapter on the Cascade peaks.

H59. HAZARD, J. T.
Pacific crest trails: from Alaska to Cape Horn. Seattle: Superior Pub, 1946. 317p, illus. [8vo].
—Rev. ed. Superior Pub, 1948. 352p.
Includes first-hand accounts of ascents of numerous peaks.

H60. HAZARD, J. T.
Snow sentinels of the Pacific north-west. Seattle: Lowman & Hanford, 1932. 249p, illus. 24cm.

History of exploration and climbing on the principal peaks of the Cascades and Olympic Mountains.

H61. HEALD, Weldon F.
Sky Island. Princeton, 1967. 166p, illus. 25cm.
The spectacular Chiricahua Mountains in Arizona.

H62. HEATH, Donald & WILLIAMS, David Reid
Man at high altitude.
—2nd ed. N.Y./Ldn: Churchill Livingstone, 1981. 347p, illus.
Probably the most authoritative book on high altitude.

H63. HECKEL, Vilem (1918-70)
Climbing in the Caucasus. Text by Josef Styrsa. Ldn: Spring Books, [1958]. 208p, plates (some col), illus. 28cm.
Photo-album by well-known Czechoslovak mountain photographer.

H64. [HECKEL, V.]
Profily. Z prací mistru ceskoslovenskí fotografie. Prague: Olympia, 1981. 25p, 18 plates, illus. 30cm. Text in Czech, Russian, English, German and French.
Biographical photo-album of the celebrated Czech photographer who was killed by the Huascarán landslide in Peru.

H65. HECKMAIR, Anderl (b.1906)
My life as a mountaineer. Trans. [from the German] by Geoffrey Sutton. Ldn: Gollancz, 1975. 224p, 16 plates, illus. 23 cm. R.P., 1978. From the original: *Mein Leben als Bergsteiger* (Munich: Nymphenburger, 1972)
Climbing memoirs of a leading pre-war German climber and guide, who took part in the first ascent of the Eiger North Face in 1938.

H66. 'HEDERATUS'
Cambridge nightclimbing. Ldn: Chatto & Windus, 1970. 95p, 32 plates, illus. 23cm.
Wall and roof climbing is a traditional Cambridge sport.

H67. HEDIN, Sven Anders (1865-1952)
My life as an explorer. Trans. [from the Swedish] by Alfhild Hueback. N.Y.:

Garden City Pub, 1925. xi, 544p, illus, maps. 25cm.
—U.K. ed. Ldn: Cassell, 1926. xii, 498p, col. plate, illus. 25cm.
Hedin travelled extensively in his youth in the Caucasus, western Persia and Mesopotamia, and climbed Demavend, c.1891. He mapped large areas of the Pamirs and Tibet. His only major ascent was an attempt on Mustagh Ata in 1894, reaching 6150 metres, a considerable achievement. His best known work on mountain exploration is *Trans-Himalaya.*

H68. HEDIN, S. A.

Trans-Himalaya: discoveries and adventures in Tibet. Ldn: Macmillan, 1909-13. 3v. plates (some fold. col), illus, maps. 24cm.
—Cheap 3v. ed. 1919? [Colonial Library ed.?]
—Another ed. Greenwood, 1968.
—Another ed. 1978.
The Trans-Himalaya is a recognized section of the Himalaya, lying to the north of the Kumaun Himalaya, in Tibet. Although of interest it does not contain any peaks of great height.

H69. HEIM, Arnold & GANSSER, August

The throne of the gods: an account of the first Swiss expedition to the Himalayas. Trans. [from the German] by Eden and Cedar Paul. Ldn: Macmillan, 1939. xxvi, 236p, 120 plates, illus, fold. map (in pkt). 24cm. From the original: *Thron der Götter* (Zurich: Morgarten, 1938)
Superbly illustrated account of chiefly geological expedition, which explored the area around Kailas in Tibet.

H70. HEINE, Arnold J.

Mountaincraft manual. Wellington: National Mountains Safety Council of New Zealand, 1971. 170p, illus. Cover title: *Mountaincraft: your basic manual.*
Includes specific sections on New Zealand conditions.

H71. HELLIWELL, R.

The rambler's and climber's North Wales. Roscoe Publications, 1949.

H72. HENDERSON, Kenneth Atwood (Editor)

Manual of American mountaineering. N.Y.: A.A.C., 1941. 179p, illus.
Privately printed for purposes of copyright and not available for distribution.
—Public edition entitled *The American Alpine Club's handbook of American mountaineering.* Boston: Houghton Mifflin, 1942. 239p, illus, bibl. 19cm.
—Another ed. entitled *The handbook of American mountaineering.* Cambridge, MA: Riverside Press, ?
Comprehensive instruction manual which was used as the basis for the U.S. Army's *Manual on mountain warfare.* Henderson was a pioneer climber with Underhill and Fryxell in the 1930s.

H73. HERLIGKOFFER, Karl Maria

Nanga Parbat: incorportating the official report of the expedition of 1953. Trans. [from the German] and additional material supplied by Eleanor Brockett and Anton Ehrenzweig. Ldn: Elek, 1954. 254p, 54 plates (some col), illus. 23cm. From the original: *Nanga Parbat 1953* (Munich: Lehmanns, 1954)
—U.S. ed. N.Y.: Knopf, 1954. xviii, 263, viiip, illus. 22cm. No colour plates. Title sometimes quoted as *The killer mountain.*
—Panther paperback, 1956.
Summarizes the earlier attempts on the mountain. German mountaineer Herligkoffer led the successful 1953 expedition, which was distinguished by Hermann Buhl's outstanding solo summit climb.

H74. HERZOG, Maurice (b.1919)

Annapurna: conquest of the first 8000-metre peak (26,493 feet). Trans. from the French by Nea Morin and Janet Adam Smith. Ldn: Cape, 1952. 288p, 28 plates, illus, maps (1 col. fold.). 21cm. Several ptgs.
—U.S. ed. N.Y.: Dutton, 1953. 316p, illus, fold. map. 22cm.
—Fontana paperback, 1956.
—Another ed. Bath: Cedric Chivers, 1974.
—Various book club editions.
One of the great landmarks in mountaineering, breaking a psychological barrier, not unlike the first 4-minute mile.

H75. HEWITT, Rodney & DAVIDSON, Mavis
The mountains of New Zealand. Wellington: Reed, 1954. 128p, illus, map. 26cm.
—Another ed. Ldn: Phoenix House, 1954.
Chiefly illustrations with supporting text.

H76. HIEBELER, Toni (1930-84)
North Face in winter: the first winter climb of the Eiger's North Face, March 1961. Introduced and trans. [from the German] by Hugh Merrick. Ldn: Barrie & Rockcliff, 1962. 121p, 15 plates, illus. 23cm.
—U.S. ed. Philadelphia: Lippincott, 1963.
The author, who participated in the climb, was a well-known German journalist, publisher and climber.

H77. HILLARY, Sir Edmund Percival (b.1919)
Boys' book of exploration. Edited by . . .Ldn: Cassell, 1957. x, 196p, illus. 23cm.
Includes extracts from five Himalayan books.

H78. HILLARY, E. P.
Challenge of the unknown. N.Y.: Dutton, 1958. 221p, illus. 21cm.
Various adventures including three climbs.

H79. HILLARY, E. P. & LOWE, George
East of Everest: an account of the New Zealand Alpine Club Himalayan Expedition to the Barun Valley in 1954. Ldn: Hodder/N.Y.: Dutton, 1956. 71p, 48 plates, illus, maps. 25cm. R.P., 1956.

H80. HILLARY, E. P.
From the ocean to the sky. Ldn: Hodder/N.Y.: Viking, 1979. 273p, 8 col. plates, illus, maps. 24cm.
—Large print ed. Leicester: Ulverscroft, 1980.
1500 mile adventure up the Ganges to climb Akash Parbat and Nar Parbat.

H81. HILLARY, E. P.
High adventure. Ldn: Hodder/N.Y.: Dutton, 1955. 256p, illus. 21cm.
—Companion Book Club ed. Ldn. 1956.
—Paperback ed. Hodder, 1958.
Chiefly about his climbs on Everest.

H82. HILLARY, E. P. & DOIG, Desmond
High in the thin cold air. N.Y.: Doubleday, 1962. xii, 254p, 41 plates (mostly col), illus, maps. 24cm.
—U.K. ed. Ldn: Hodder, 1963. 287p, 31 plates, illus. 22cm.
Search for the Yeti, physiological research and climbing including an almost disastrous attempt on Makalu. Ascent of Ama Dablam.

H83. HILLARY, E. P.
No latitude for error. Ldn: Hodder, 1961. 255p, illus, maps. 24cm.
Crossing of Antarctica.

H84. HILLARY, E. P.
Nothing venture, nothing win. Ldn: Hodder/N.Y.: Coward McCann & Geoghegan, 1975. 319p, 32 plates (some col), illus. 25cm.
—Coronet paperback, 1977.
Autobiography.

H85. HILLARY, E. P.
Schoolhouse in the clouds. Ldn: Hodder/N.Y.: Doubleday, 1964. xii, 180p, 32 col. plates, illus. 22cm.
—Penguin paperback. 1968.
Includes ascents of Kangtega and Taweche.

H86. HILLARY, E. P. & HILLARY, Peter
Two generations. Ldn: Hodder, 1984. 223p, 24 plates, illus, maps.
Father and son write their own separate stories. Peter Hillary includes a lengthy account of his attempt on Lhotse from Everest's Western Cwm.

H87. HILLARY, Louise Mary (- ?)
High time. Ldn: Hodder, 1973. 192, illus (some col), maps. 23cm.
A family trek in the land of the Sherpas, written by the wife of Edmund Hillary.

H88. HILLARY, L. M.
Keep calm if you can: round the world with the Hillary family. Ldn: Hodder, ? [viii], 159p, illus, maps. 22cm.
Chapter on the Himalaya.

H89. HILLARY, L. M.
A yak for Christmas: the story of a Himalayan holiday. Ldn: Hodder, 1968. 208p, illus, maps. 22cm.
—U.S. ed. Garden City, NY: Doubleday, 1969. 255p.
—T.B.C. ed. 1969.

H90. HILLARY, Peter
A sunny day in the Himalayas. Ldn: Hodder, 1980. 166p, col. plates, illus. 24cm.
Ama Dablam.

H91. HILLS, Denis Cecil
My travels in Turkey. Ldn: Allen & Unwin, 1964. 252p, 25 plates, illus, maps. 22cm.
Includes climbing in various parts of Turkey.

H92. HIMALAYAN ASSOCIATION OF JAPAN
Badakshan to Nuristan: trekking and climbing in northern Afghanistan. Tokyo: The Association, 1977. 168p, illus, maps. 26cm. In Japanese with English summary. Yak. j. 552.
Expedition to Koh-i-Bura, Koh-i-Munjan and other peaks.

H93. HIMALAYAN ASSOCIATION OF JAPAN
First ascent of Kanjeralwa: account of expedition to Kanjiroba Himal, 1973. Tokyo: The Association, 1976. 173p, illus, maps. 26cm. In Japanese with English summary. Yak. j. 549.

H94. HIMALAYAN ASSOCIATION OF JAPAN
Nun expedition 1975. Fukushima: The Association, 1978. 112p, illus (some col), maps. 26cm. In Japanese with English summary. Yak. j. 555.
Ascent of Nun by members of the Japan-India Joint Kashmir Expedition.

H95. HIMALAYAN ASSOCIATION OF JAPAN
Trisul 7120m. H. A. J. Garhwal Himalaya Expedition 1978. Fukushima: The Association, 1979. 143p, illus, maps. 26cm. In Japanese with English summary. Yak. j. 556.
Ascents of Trisul I & II, and other peaks.

H96. HINCHLIFF, Thomas Woodbine (1825-82)
Summer months among the Alps: with the ascent of Monte Rosa. Ldn: Longmans, 1857. xviii, 312p, 4 plates, illus, 3 maps (fold. col). 21cm.
A classic of the 'Golden Age'. Hinchliff was a lawyer, botanist and traveller, whose climbing career was curtailed by a shotgun accident to his hand. He was President of the Alpine Club, 1875-7 and his book and his personality were decisive influences on contemporary mountaineering.

H97. HIND, C. Lewis (1862-1927)
The diary of a looker-on. 1908.
Hind was a writer, art critic and magazine editor. His book includes a humorous account of an ascent of the Ortler (see Lee, *Lure of the hills*).

H98. HINDLEY, Geoffrey
The roof of the world. Ldn: Aldus, 1971. 191p, illus (some col), maps (some col). 27cm. (Aldus Encyclopaedia of Discovery and Invention series) R.P., 1973, 1974.
—Another ed. Ldn: Readers' Digest Assoc., 1981.

H99. HIRST, John
Songs of the mountaineers. Collected and edited by ...for the Rucksack Club. Manchester: Rucksack Club, [1922]. [8], 124p. 18cm. Words only issued in various guises — linen-backed paper; limp leather cover; for binding with Rucksack Club Journal. Music published in 3v, or as separate songs.
—New ed. entitled *Climbing songs.* [c.1960]. 83p.
Climbing songs; contains many lyrics by Geoffrey Winthrop Young.

H100. HOARE, Robert John
The high peaks. Ldn: Ginn, [1966]. 80p, illus, maps. 20cm.

H101. HOEHNEL, Ludwig von
Discovery of Lakes Rudolf and Stephanie: a narrative of Count Samuel Teleki's exploring and hunting expedition in eastern Equatorial Africa in 1887 and 1888. Ldn: Longmans, 1894. 2v., 2 fold. col. plates, illus, maps. 26cm.
Count Teleki and Ludwig von Höhnel

were the first to begin the thorough exploration of Mount Kenya in 1887. Approaching from the south-west they reached a height of c.4270 metres.

H102. HOHLE, Per

The mountain world of Norway. Oslo: Dreyers Forlag, [1956?]. 167p, illus (some col). 26cm.
Photo-album; general illustrations.

H103. HOKKAIDÔ UNIVERSITY ALPINE CLUB & ACADEMIC ALPINE CLUB OF HOKKAIDÔ

Account of the Karakorum Expedition: Shumari Kunyang Chhish. Sapporo: The Club, 1981. 125p, illus (some col), maps. 26cm. In Japanese with English summary. Yak. j. 667.
First ascent of Kunyang Chhish North (7108m) in 1979.

H104. HOLDEN, Peter (Editor)

Trent Polytechnic Hindu Kush Expedition 1975: report. [Nottingham]: The Expedition, [1977]. 32, xxxvip, plates, illus, map. 30cm. Yak. H. 227.
Climbing in the Mandaras Valley.

H105. HOLDGATE, Martin

Mountains in the sea: the story of the Gough Island expedition. Ldn: Macmillan/N.Y.: St. Martin's, 1958. xvi, 222p, 36 plates, illus, maps.

H106. HOLMES, Peter

Mountains and a monastery. Ldn: Bles, 1958. 191p, 8 plates, illus, 2 fold. maps. 22cm.
First ascents in 1956 in Spiti, at the head of the Ratang Nulla.

H107. HOLMES, W. Kersley

Tramping Scottish hills. 1946.
—2nd ed. (?) entitled *on Scottish hills.* 1962.

H108. HOOKER, Sir Joseph Dalton (1817-1911)

Himalayan journals: or, Notes of a naturalist in Bengal, the Sikkim and Nepal Himalaya, the Khasia Mountains, etc. Ldn: Murray, 1854. 2v., plates, illus, 2 maps. 23cm.
—2nd rev. ed. 2v.
—Minerva Library edition. Ldn: Ward Lock, 1891. xxxii, 574p, plates, illus, 2 maps. 18cm. R.P., 1892, 1893, 1905.
—Another ed. Reprint of 1855 ed. New Delhi: Today and Tomorrow's Printers & Publishers, 1969. 2v. in one. No maps.
Hooker was the first to make an almost complete circuit of Kanchenjunga in the years 1848-50: a classic of early Himalayan travel and exploration.

H109. HOOKER, J. D. & BALL, John

Journal of a tour in Marocco and the Great Atlas. With an appendix by George Maw, Ldn: Macmillan, 1878. xvi, 499p, 8 plates (1 fold), illus, fold. maps. 23cm.
Comprehensive account of the vegetation and geology, and of climbs in the Atlas Mountains.

H110. HOPE, G. S.

The Equatorial glaciers of New Guinea. By ...[and others]. Rotterdam, 1976. xii, 244p, illus, map. [8vo].

H111. HORNADAY, William T.

Camp-fires in the Canadian Rockies. N.Y.: Scribner's/Ldn: Werner Laurie, 1906. xix, 353p, 53 plates, illus, maps. 25cm.

H112. HORNBEIN, Thomas Frederick (b.1930)

Everest: the West Ridge. Intro. by W. E. Siri and edited by D. Brower. S. F.: Sierra Club, 1965/Ldn: Allen & Unwin, 1966. 200p, 84 col. plates, illus, maps. 35 × 27cm. (Exhibit Format series)
—Abridged ed. S.F.: Sierra Club/Ballantine Books, 1966. 160p, col. illus, maps. 24cm. R.P., 1968.
—Rev. ed. Ldn: Allen & Unwin, 1971. 181p, illus. 22cm.
—Another ed. Seattle: Mountaineers, 1980. 240p, col. illus. 24cm.
First ascent of the West Ridge and traverse down normal route.

H113. HORNBY, Emily

Mountaineering records. [By] E. H. [Compiled by M. L. Hornby]. Liverpool: Thompson, 1907. viii, 352p. 23cm.
Record of ascents, 1873-95, by a leading woman climber of her generation.

H114. HORROBIN, D. F.
Oxford University Expedition to Nepal, 1963: general report. Oxford: D. Parchment, 1964. iv, 46p, illus, map. [8vo]. Yak. H. 242.

H115. HORT, Arthur Fenton (Editor)
Life and letters of Fenton John Anthony Hort. Ldn: Macmillan, 1896. 2v., plate, port. 22cm.
Hort was an original Alpine Club Member. His Alpine career was curtailed by ill-health, although he continued to visit the Alps until a few years before his death.

H116. HOTCHKISS, Bill
Climb to the high country. N.Y.: Morrow, 1978.
Poems.

H117. HOUSTON, Charles S. (b.1913)
Going high: the story of man and altitude. Burlington, VT: The Author, 1980. xii, 211p, illus. [8vo].
—Rev. enlarged ed. entitled *Going higher.* Burlington: The Author, 1983. xii, 273p, col. plates, illus, bibl. 22cm.
Comprehensive study of effects of altitude, particularly on climbers.

H118. HOUSTON, C. S. & BATES, Robert
K2: the savage mountain. N.Y.: McGraw-Hill, 1954. 334p, illus (some col), map. 22cm.
—U.K. ed. Ldn: Collins, 1955. 192p, 24 plates, illus. 22cm.
—Softback ed. with additional material and more illustrations. Seattle: Mountaineers/Ldn: Diadem, 1979. 395p, illus. 21cm.
Despite failure to reach the summit, this expedition is considered to be one of the pinnacles of American Himalayan mountaineering — a dramatic story which almost resulted in the destruction of the whole party during the descent.

H119. HOWARD, William (1793-1834)
A narrative of a journey to the summit of Mont Blanc, [*made on 12th July*] *1819.* Baltimore: Fielding Lucas, 1821. [6], 49p, plate, illus. 17cm.
—Republished. Lucas Brothers, 1856.
Ninth ascent of Mont Blanc and the first by Americans. Howard's companion, Dr. Jeremiah Van Rensselaer (1793-1871) also wrote a short account of their climb, published in magazine form only. Both accounts were reprinted in the *Alpine Journal.*

H120. HOWARD-BURY, Charles Kenneth (1883-1963)
Mount Everest: the reconnaissance, 1921. By . . .and other members of the Mount Everest Expedition. Ldn: Arnold/N.Y.: Longmans, 1922. xii, 356p, 33 plates, illus, 3 fold. maps. 26cm. Also large paper edition, numbered and limited to 200 copies, with 14 extra plates.
The author led the expedition. This book and the two others recounting the stories of the 1922 and 1924 expeditions form a very handsome record of the courage and daring of the early Everesters.

H121. HOWARTH, David
The sledge patrol. Ldn: Collins, 1957. 255p, 8 plates, illus, maps. 21cm.
Exciting account of mountain warfare in 1943 in north-east Greenland.

H122. HOWARTH, D.
We die alone. Ldn: Collins, 1955. 255p, plates, illus. 22cm.
—Reprint Soc. ed. 1957.
—Fontana paperback entitled *Escape alone.*
Remarkable escape across the arctic mountains of Nazi-occupied Norway.

H123. HOYTE, John
Trunk road for Hannibal: with an elephant over the Alps. Ldn: Bles, 1960. 190p, plates, illus, maps, bibl. 21cm.
An empirical test to determine over which pass Hannibal crossed the Alps.

H124. HUBBARD, Bernard R.
Cradle of the storms.
—2nd ed. N.Y.: Dodd Mead, 1935. xv, 285p, illus, maps. 22cm.
—4th ed. 1937.
Account of the author's 1934 expedition to investigate the volcanoes of the Alaskan peninsula and Aleutian Islands chain; climbing on Unimak volcanoes, Aghileen Pinnacles, etc.

H125. HUDOWALSKI, Grace L.

The Adirondack Forty-sixers. By . . .[and others]. Albany, NY: Peters Print for the Adirondack Forty-sixers, 1958. 147p, illus. Limited edition of 400 copies.
History of group of people who have climbed all the peaks in the Adirondacks over 4000 ft.

H126. HUDSON, Charles (1828-65) & KENNEDY, Edward Shirley (1817-98)

Where there's a will there's a way: an ascent of Mont Blanc by a new route and without guides. Ldn: Longmans, 1856. xvi, 95p, plate, illus, col. map, 21cm.
—2nd ed. with accounts of two ascents of Monte Rosa. xvi, 114p.
The Rev. Hudson was the leading amateur mountaineer of his day. He made the first ascent of the highest point of Monte Rosa and the first guideless ascent of Mont Blanc. He was killed in the Matterhorn accident. Kennedy accompanied him in numerous guideless ascents, edited the second series of *Peaks, passes and glaciers* and was A.C. President, 1861-3.

H127. HUF, Hans

English mountaineers: A. Wills, J. Tyndall, E. Whymper, C. Dent, A. F. Mummery. Herausgegeben von [Edited by] . . .Bamberg: C. C. Buchners Verlag, 1925. 88p, illus. 19cm.
English reader for German schools; contains extracts from the works of those named.

H128. HUMBLE, Benjamin Hutchinson (-1977)

The Cuillin of Skye. Ldn: Hale, 1952. xvi, 144p, 49 plates, illus. 26cm.
—Facsimile edition. Ernest Press, 1986. With an appreciation of Ben Humble by W. H. Murray. Limited edition of 2000 copies, including 250 subscribers' copies, numbered and specially bound.
The principal book on the history of climbing in Skye. Humble was a Scottish climber, latterly active in the field of mountain rescue. He wrote and edited various publications relating to holidaying in Scotland.

H129. HUMBLE, B. H.

On Scottish hills. Ldn: Chapman & Hall, 1946. 128p, illus, maps. 26cm. R.P., 1948.
Illustrations with supporting text.

H130. HUMBLE, B. H.

Songs for climbers. Edited by . . .and W. M. McClellan. Glasgow: Wm. McClellan, [1938]. 30p. 22cm.

H131. HUMBLE B. H.

The songs of Skye: an anthology. Stirling: Eneas Mackay, 1934.
—Reissued, 1955.

H132. HUMBLE B. H.

Tramping in Skye. Edinburgh: Grant & Murray, 1933, xii, 144p, 15 plates, illus. 19cm.
—2nd enlarged ed. Glasgow: Wm. McClellan, 1947.
Walking tours around the island.

H133. HUMBOLDT, Alexander, Freiherr von

Humboldt's travels and discoveries in South America.
—2nd ed. Ldn: J. W. Parker, 1846. viii, 278p, illus. 15cm.
Humboldt made the first recorded ascent in Venezuela, that of the coastal peak Silla de Avila, in 1799. More important were his expeditions in Ecuador (1802-3), with his attempts on Cotopaxi and Chimborazo.

H134. HUMBOLDT, A. & BONPLAND, Aimé

Personal narrative of travels to the equinoctial regions of America during the years 1799-1804. Trans. & edited by Thomasina Ross. Ldn: Henry G. Bohn, 1852-3. 3v. 20cm. (Bohn's Scientific Library series).
—Reissued, 1870-1. 3v.

H135. HUNT, Henry John Cecil, Baron Hunt of Llanvair Waterdine (b.1910)

The ascent of Everest. Ldn: Hodder, 1953. xx, 300p, 56 plates (some col), illus. 23cm. Several ptgs.
—U.S. ed. entitled *Conquest of Everest.* N.Y.: Dutton, 1954.
—Abridged ed. for schoolchildren. Ldn:

Univ. Ldn Press, 1954. Senior version, 160p; junior version, 96p.
—Companion Book Club ed. 1954.
—R.U. ed. 1955
—Paperback ed. Hodder, 1953. also 1957.
—Great Venture series ed. Ldn: Tandem, 1973.
John Hunt led the successful British expedition in 1953, and subsequently became the 'father figure' of post-war British mountaineering. He was President of the A.C. in 1956-8, which included the Centenary celebrations.

H136. HUNT, J.
Life is meeting. Ldn: Hodder, 1978. 286p, 16 plates, illus. 24cm.
—R.U. ed. 1979.
Autobiography of this professional soldier, mountaineer, administrator and public figure.

H137. HUNT, J.
My favourite mountaineering stories. Edited by ...With line decorations by Douglas Phillips. Ldn: Lutterworth Press, 1978. 127p. 23cm.
Anthology of 12 extracts from books by Noyce, Shipton, Smythe, and others.

H138. HUNT, J.
Our Everest adventure: the pictorial history from Kathmandu to the summit. Leicester: Brockhampton Press/N.Y.: Dutton, 1954. 128p, illus. 25cm.
Chiefly previously unpublished photographs; companion volume to *Ascent of Everest.*

H139. HUNT, J. & BRASHER, Christopher
The Red Snows: an account of the British Caucasus expedition 1958. Ldn: Hutchinson, 1960. 176p, 17 plates, illus, map. 22cm. R.P., 1960.
—T.B.C. ed. 1960.
Includes useful summary history of climbing in the Caucasus.

H140. HUNTER, Robert
Chris Bonington. Ldn: Hamilton, 1983. 64p.
Biography for young readers.

H141. HUNTER, R.
Winter skills. Ldn: Constable, 1982.
Instructional.

H142. HUTCHINGS, James Mason
In the heart of the Sierras: the Yosemite Valley, both historical and descriptive. Published at the Old Cabin, Yosemite Valley; and at Pacific Press Pub. House, Oakland, 1886. 496p, illus. 22cm.
Includes attempts on Half Dome.

H143. HUTT VALLEY TRAMPING CLUB
In search of New Zealand. Edited by G. E. Mabin. 1934.
Interesting material.

H144. HUTT VALLEY TRAMPING CLUB
Hills and valleys. Edited by G. E. Mabin. 1936.
Interesting material.

H145. HUXLEY, Anthony Julian (Editor)
Standard encyclopaedia of the world's mountains. Ldn: Weidenfeld & Nicolson/N.Y.: Putnam's, 1962. 383p, 16 col. plates, illus, maps. 24cm. R.P., 1964, 1969.
Pleasant reference work.

H146. HUXLEY, Leonard
Life and letters of Sir Joseph Dalton Hooker, O.M., G.C.S.I.; based on materials collected and arranged by Lady Hooker. Ldn: Murray, 1918. 2v. plates (1 fold.), illus, map, ports. 23cm.
Joseph Hooker (1817-1911) was a famous British botanist and explorer. He accompanied James Ross to the Antarctic (1839-43) as assistant surgeon. In 1848-9 he made two journeys which comprised an almost complete circuit of Kanchenjunga, described in his book *Himalayan journals.* In the 1870s he made a tour in Morocco and the Atlas Mountains with John Ball, another famous botanist-alpinist.

I

I01. IMPERIAL COLLEGE EAST GREENLAND EXPEDITION, 1963

Preliminary report. 1964.
Scientific and climbing expedition. Seventeen first ascents and other climbs in the Bersaerkbrae area and adjoining glaciers of the East Staunings Alps.

I02. [INDIAN MOUNTAINEERING FOUNDATION]

Second Indian Expedition to Mount Everest February-June 1962 . . .: souvenir brochure. New Delhi: Published on behalf of the Indian Mountaineering Foundation by the Armed Forces Information Office, [1962]. 24p, illus. 24cm.

I03. [INDIAN MOUNTAINEERING FOUNDATION]

Indian Mount Everest Expedition, 1965. New Delhi: Published on behalf of the Indian Mountaineering Foundation by the Armed Forces Information Office, Ministry of Defence, [1965]. 44p, illus. 27cm. Yak. I. 23.

I04. INDIAN MOUNTAINEERING FOUNDATION

Indian Mountaineering Foundation: Silver Jubilee '58-'83. [New Delhi: I.M.F., 1983]. [4], 128p, illus (some col), ports. 21cm. Softback.
Record of the first 25 years' work of Indian climbers with useful information about the I.M.F. and mountaineering in India.

I05. INDIAN NANDA DEVI EXPEDITION, 1981

Nanda Devi Expedition, 1981: the first ascent by men and women: report. illus (some col).

I06. INDO-JAPANESE NANDA DEVI EXPEDITION, 1976

Nanda Devi traverse 1976: preliminary report of the . . .[Tokyo]: The expedition, 1976. 18p, plates, illus. 26cm. In Japanese with photo captions in English.

I07. INGRAM, John Anthony

Fellcraft: some advice for fellwalkers. Ldn: Stanley Paul, 1964. 140p, 12 plates, illus. 19cm. R.P., 1968.

I08. INNERLEITHEN ALPINE CLUB

Principal excursions of the Innerleithen Alpine Club during the years 1889-94; with a memoir of . . .Robert Mathison, first president of the Club. Galashiels: John McQueen for the Club, 1895. 311p, plates, illus. 20cm.
—2nd ed. 1897.

I09. IRAN-JAPAN MOUNT MANASLU JOINT EXPEDITION, 1976

Friendship going beyond Manaslu. Nagano: Shinano-Mainichi-Newspaper, 1977. 290p, illus (some col), maps. 26cm. In Japanese with English summary. Yak. j. 517.
Account of ascent of Manaslu, 1976.

I10. IRISH ANDEAN EXPEDITION, 1980

Report. [The Expedition]. 20p, illus, map.
Cordillera Blanca, Peru (Nevado Caraz, Alpamayo, Artesonraju).

I11. IRISH GREENLAND EXPEDITION, 1968

Report.

I12. IRISH KISHTWAR HIMALAYAN EXPEDITION

Report. The Expedition, [1977]. 29p, illus.

I13. IRVING, Robert Lock Graham (1877-1969)

The Alps. Ldn: Batsford, 1938. viii, 120p, 81 plates, illus. 22cm.
—U.S. ed. N.Y.: Scribner's, 1940. R.P., 1942.
—Rev. ed. Batsford, 1942.
—Rev. ed. Batsford, 1947.
General description.

I14. IRVING, R. L. G.

A history of British mountaineering. Ldn: Batsford, 1955. xvi, 240p, 31 plates, illus. 23cm.
Pleasant reading but not a profound work.

I15. IRVING, R. L. G.
The mountain way: an anthology in prose and verse. Collected by ...Ldn: Dent/N.Y.: Dutton, 1938. xxii, 656p. 20cm.
Still one of the best mountaineering anthologies. Selected from general literature, mountaineering 'classics', *Alpine Journal,* etc. The quoted dates of some of the extracts do not agree with publication dates.

I16. IRVING, R. L. G.
The mountains shall bring peace. Oxford: Blackwell, 1947. iv, 47p. 18cm.
In this pamphlet Irving explains the benefits he has received from climbing and suggests greater participation in mountaineering as a means to achieving international peace, brotherhood and co-operation.

I17. IRVING, R. L. G.
The romance of mountaineering. Ldn: Dent/N.Y.: Dutton, 1935. xiv, 320p, plates, illus. 24cm. R.P., 1935, 1946.
Basically a history of mountaineering, written with great enthusiasm and feeling, no doubt with a view to encouraging young climbers. Includes many interesting passages and excerpts from original accounts. Well worth reading but now somewhat neglected.

I18. IRVING, R. L. G.
Ten great mountains. Ldn: Dent, 1940. xii, 213p, 15 plates, illus. 23cm. R.P., 1942, 1947.
—T.B.C. ed.
Climbing history of Snowdon, Ben Nevis, Ushba, Mt. Logan, Everest, Nanga Parbat, Kanchenjunga, Mont Blanc, Matterhorn and Mt. Cook.

I19. IRWIN, William Robert
Challenge: an anthology of the literature of mountaineering. Edited by ...N.Y.: Columbia Univ. Press, 1950. xx, 444p. 23cm.
Consists of the editor's introduction, short biographies of authors of extracts quoted, and lists of books on mountaineering.

I20. ISHERWOOD, Dick
Hong Kong Mountaineering Club Expedition to Lamjung Himal, Spring 1974. [Report], narrative section by ...and others. 39p, 9 plates, illus, map.

I21. IZZARD, Ralph William Burdick
The Abominable Snowman adventure. Ldn: Hodder, 1955. 302p, illus. 21cm.
—U.S. ed. N.Y.: Doubleday, 1955. 250p, illus.
Account of the four-month *Daily Mail* Himalayan Yeti expedition of 1954, organized by the author.

I22. IZZARD, R. W. B.
An/The innocent on Everest. Ldn: Hodder, 1954. 256p, 31 plates, illus. 21cm. R.P., 1955.
—U.S. ed. N.Y.: Dutton, 1954. 319p.
Izzard was the *Daily Mail* correspondent covering the 1953 Everest expedition.

J

J01. JACKSON, Eileen Montague (b.1910?)
Switzerland calling: a true tale of a boy and girl's wonderful summer holidays climbing in the Alps; announcer: "Miss Tarzan", Eileen Montague Jackson. Ldn: Black, 1927. vii, 237p, plates, illus. 22cm.
A teenager's enthusiastic account of climbing around Zermatt. A very fast climber, her prospects of a brilliant mountaineering career were curtailed by serious illness a few years later.

J02. JACKSON, Herbert & Mary
Lakeland pioneer rock-climbers: based on the visitors' books of the Tysons of Wasdale Head. Clapham, Yorks: Dalesman Books, 1980. 168p, illus. 22cm. Softback.
Comprises lists of names from the visitors' books of Row Farm, Wasdale Head, 1876-86; includes a few accounts of climbs.

J03. JACKSON, John Angelo
More than mountains. Ldn: Harrap, 1955. 213p, 29 plates, illus, maps. 22cm.
Himalayan reminiscences by an outdoor

pursuits instructor. Includes Somamarg, Nilkanta, Yeti hunting, Kanchenjunga reconnaissance.

J04. JACKSON, Monica & STARK, Elizabeth

Tents in the clouds: the first women's Himalayan expedition. Ldn: Collins, 1956. 255p, 24 plates, illus, maps. 22cm.
Expedition to the Jugal Himal, Nepal in 1955, and ascent of Gyalgen Peak (6706m).

J05. JACKSON, M.

The Turkish time machine. Ldn: Hodder, 1966. 159p, 8 plates, illus, map. 21cm.
Climbs on the Cilo-Sat mountains of south-east Turkey.

J06. JACOBSON, Frederick L.

The meek mountaineer: a climber's armchair companion. N.Y.: Liveright, 1974. xv, 192p, illus, map. 21cm.
Mostly guided climbing in the Alps.

J07. JAMES, Mervyn

Mountains. With 27 illustrations by Rigby Graham. Brewhouse Press [for the Author], 1972. 46p, 16 col. plates (1 fold), illus. 26cm. Edition limited to 200 copies.
Mainly around Wastwater & Wasdale Head, Lake District: mountain poems.

J08. JAMES, Ronald (b.1933)

Rock face: techniques of rock climbing. Ldn: B.B.C., 1974. 118p, illus. 20cm.
Text accompanying television series.

J09. JAPAN EVEREST SKIING EXPEDITION

Mount Everest: Yûichirô Miura and the Japanese Everest Skiing Expedition. Photos by Akira Kotani and Kazunari Yasuhisa. Tokyo: Bungei-shunju, 1970. var. pag., 90 col. plates, illus, maps. 30 × 25cm. In Japanese with English summary. Yak. j. 521.
Photo-album of 1970 expedition.

J10. JAPAN MANASLU WEST WALL EXPEDITION

Manaslu West Wall, 1971. Tokyo: The Expedition/Yama-to-Keikokusha, 1974. var. pag., illus (some col), maps. 26cm. In Japanese with English summary. Yak. j. 567.
Successful ascent.

J11. JAPAN MOUNTAINEERING ASSOCIATION

At the end of the White Glacier. K2 (8611m). By the . . .Japan K2 Expedition. Tokyo: Kôdan-sha, 1978. 162p, col. illus, map. 30cm. In Japanese with English summary. Yak. j. 537.
Japan 1977 K2 expedition.

J12. [JAPAN TIMES]

Mount Fuji. Tokyo: Japan Times, 1970. 118p, illus (some col), map. 26cm.

J13. JAPAN WOMEN'S MANASLU EXPEDITION

Manaslu 1974: account of the . . .. Tokyo: Meikei-dô, 1977. var. pag., plates (some col), illus, maps. 26cm. In Japanese with English summary. Yak. j. 538.

J14. JAPANESE ALPINE CLUB

Official report of the Japanese Mount Everest Expedition, 1969-1970. Tokyo: ?, 1972. 2v. [Vol. I–Mountaineering account], illus, map. In Japanese with English summary.

J15. JAPANESE ALPINE CLUB

Chomolangma-Tibet: official account of the Japanese Alpine Club Chomolangma expedition. Tokyo: Kôdan-sha, 1981. 151p, illus (some col), maps, 31cm. In Japanese with English summary. Yak. j. 532.

J16. JAPANESE ALPINE CLUB

Manaslu, 1952-53. Tokyo: Mainichi-Newspaper, 1954. var. pag., plates, illus, maps. 26cm. In Japanese with English summary. Yak. j. 525.
Official account of 1952 & 1953 expeditions. Many illustrations.

J17. JAPANESE ALPINE CLUB

Manaslu, 1954-56. Tokyo: Mainichi-Newspaper. var. pag., plates, illus, map. 26cm. In Japanese with English summary. Yak. j. 526.
Official accounts of 1954 Manaslu attempt and ascent in 1956; numerous illustrations.

J18. JAPANESE ALPINE CLUB
Mount Everest 1975. Tokyo, [1975?]. 100p col. illus. [4to]. Picture captions also in English.

J19. [JAPANESE ALPINE CLUB]
Indo-Japanese Women's 2nd Joint Himalayan Expedition, 1976: Expedition Committee report. Tokyo: Japanese Alpine Club, 1976. 72p, illus, maps. 26cm. In Japanese with English summary. Yak. j. 519.
Account of ascent of Abi Gamin (7355m) in 1975.

J20. JAROS, J. & KALVODA, J.
Geological structure of the Himalayas: Mt. Everest-Makalu section. Prague, 1978. 69p, illus, maps. [8vo]. In English. Not in Yakushi.

J21. JAVELLE, Jean Marie Ferdinand Émile (1847-83)
Alpine memories. With a biographical and literary notice by Eugène Rambert. Trans. [from the French] and with an introduction by W. H. Chesson. Ldn: Fisher Unwin, 1899. viii, 444p, 4 plates, illus. 21 cm. From the original: *Souvenirs d'un alpiniste* (Lausanne: Payot, 1886).
Climbing memoirs of a French-born Swiss schoolmaster. His finest climb was probably the first ascent of the Tour Noire by the eastern face. His writing attempted to describe his ecstatic emotions but his style was not good and, unfortunately, was imitated by others. He died of tuberculosis, contracted while climbing in Corsica.

J22. JAYAL, Narendra Dhar (1926-58)
Nandu Jayal and Indian mountaineering: a tribute to Major Narendra Dhar Jayal. Printed and published at the College of Military Engineering, Dapodi-Poona 12, [c.1961]. [viii], 134p, 5 plates, illus. 25cm.
Articles by Jayal and his friends. Not in Yakushi. Jayal visited the Alps and participated in a number of Himalayan climbs from 1946 onwards. In 1954 he became the first principal of the Himalayan Mountaineering Institute. He died of pulmonary oedema on Cho Oyu.

J23. JEFFERS, Leroy (1878-1926)
Atop Katahdin (Maine's highest peak). By . . .et al. Bangor & Aroostook Railroad, [c.1920]. 32p, illus.

J24. JEFFERS, L.
The call of the mountains: rambles among the mountains and canyons of the United States and Canada. N.Y.: Dodd Mead, 1922/Ldn: Fisher Unwin, 1923. xvi, 282p, 65 plates, illus. 24cm. R.P., 1923.
In 1919 New York librarian Jeffers made a solo first ascent of the north (lower) peak of Mount Moran, in the then little known Teton range, about which he wrote widely later. As a member of several leading mountaineering clubs he was well-known and had formed in 1916 the Bureau of Associated Mountaineering Clubs of North America. He died in an aeroplane crash.

J25. JENKINSON, Bruce
Mountain recreation. Christchurch, N.Z.: Privately published, 1976. 89p, plates, illus.
Unfinished memoirs published posthumously as a tribute to a talented New Zealand mountaineer, who also climbed in North and South America. Jenkinson was a leading figure in the lives of the group of friends described in Aat Verwoorn's book.

J26. JEROME, John
On mountains — thinking about terrain. N.Y.: Harcourt Brace Jovanovich, 1978. —U.K. ed. Ldn: Gollancz, 1979. xx, 262p, illus.
General interest — mountain structure, playground, environment.

J27. JIRAK, Ivan L. (Editor)
A.K. [Angeda Kimonhon] handbook. 322p, illus, maps.
Chapters on climbing techniques, equipment and locations; (U.S.A.).

J28. JIRAK, I. L.
El Sangay expedition. The Author, [1963]. Sangay is an extremely active volcano in Ecuador, Also includes Cordillera Blanca, Peru.

J29. JOHNSTON, Sir Harry Hamilton (1858-1927)

The Kilima-Njaro expedition: a record of scientific exploration in eastern Equatorial Africa . . .Ldn: Kegan Paul Trench, 1886. xvi, 572p, plates (2 fold. col), illus, maps. 24cm.

Johnston was a well-known British adminstrator and explorer, and author of several books on Africa. He produced an excellent map of the Kilimanjaro region and pushed exploration higher than before, reaching c.16,300 ft.

J30. JOINT SERVICES EXPEDITION TO CHILEAN PATAGONIA, 1972-73

Preliminary report. The Expedition, [1973]. [30p], plates, illus, maps. 30cm.

Traverse of the northern ice-cap.

J31. JONES, Anthony S. G.

Some thoughts on the organisation of mountain search and rescue operations. With *Notes on mountain rescue first aid* (by Dr. Ieuan W. Jones). [Bangor]: Ogwen Valley Mountain Rescue Organisation, 1973. 90p, illus. 21cm. R.P., 1973. Softback.

Manual prepared by North Wales rescue team.

J32. JONES, Christopher

Climbing in North America. Berkeley: Published for the A.A.C. by Univ. California Press, 1976. xii, 392p, illus. 23cm.

—Softback ed. Diadem, 1979.

Authoritative and well-illustrated history of climbing in North America.

J33. JONES, David

Rock climbing in Britain. Ldn: Willow Books, Collins, 1984. 192p, illus (chiefly col). 31cm.

Details of equipment and training required, with 100 full page colour illustrations of extremely hard climbs.

J34. JONES, Harry

The regular Swiss round in three trips. Ldn: Strahan, 1865. vii, 393p, plates, illus, map. 17cm.

—2nd ed. 1868.

Refers to Whymper and the Matterhorn disaster.

J35. JONES, Owen Glynne H. (1867-99)

Rock-climbing in the English Lake District. Ldn: Longmans, 1897. xxvi, 284p, 39 plates, illus. 24cm.

—2nd ed. Keswick: Abraham, 1900. lxiv, 322p. With a memoir [of O. G. Jones by W. M. Cook] and portrait of the author . . .and appendix [of new climbs] by G. & A. Abraham.

—3rd ed. Keswick: Abraham, 1911. lxiv, 384p. Appendix II (pp. 317-79) added by G. & A. Abraham.

—Facsimile reprint of 2nd ed. Manchester: E. J. Morten, 1973.

The first part of a classic trilogy completed by the Abraham Brothers. Jones was an English schoolmaster and leading rock-climber, killed on the Dent Blanche.

J36. JULYAN, Robert Hixson

Mountain names. Seattle: Mountaineers, 1984. 276p, illus.

Stories behind the names of more than 300 peaks.

K

K01. KAIN, Conrad (1883-1934)

Where the clouds can go. Edited, with additional chapters by J. Monroe Thorington. N.Y.: A.A.C., 1935. [xiv], 456p, 19 plates, illus. 23cm.

—Another ed. Boston: Charles T. Branford/Ldn: Bailey & Swinfen, 1954.

—Another ed. N.Y.: A.A.C., 1979. xxviii, 456p, plates, illus. 23cm.

Austrian Kain was the most famous guide employed by the Alpine Club of Canada. He guided the first ascent of Mt. Robson in 1913; two other great climbs of his were Mt. Louis and Bugaboo Spire, which he considered to be his hardest.

K02. KANAI, Hiroo

Index gazetteer of the Himalaya. Japan Nepal Society, 1984. 70p.

Alphabetical listing of place-names in the Himalaya, including mountains, rivers and other features, giving grid references.

K03. KARR, Heywood W. Seton

Shores and alps of Alaska. Ldn: Sampson Low, 1887. xvi, 248p, illus, 3 maps (2 col). 23cm.

This British naval officer made the first reconnaissance, in 1886, of the Mount St. Elias region.

K04. KAWASAKI TEACHERS' HINDU KUSH EXPEDITION, 1977

Snow of the Oxus: the ascent of Koh-i-Daraz in 1977. Kawasaki: The Expedition, 1978. 116p, illus, maps. In Japanese with English summary. Yak. j. 360.

K05. KAWASAKI TEACHERS' HINDU KUSH EXPEDITION, 1979

To the unknown peak. Kawasaki: The Expedition, 1980. 216p, illus, maps. 26cm. In Japanese with English summary. Yak. j. 361.
First ascent of Bindu Gol Zom II (6214m).

K06. KAZAMI, Takehide

The Andes. Tokyo: Kodansha International/Ldn: Ward Lock, [c.1970]. 118p, col. illus. 18cm. (This Beautiful World series)
General interest.

K07. KAZAMI, T.

The Himalayas: a journey to Nepal. Tokyo: Kodansha International/LDN: Ward Lock/Delhi: Allied Publishers, 1968. 154p, col. illus. 18cm. (This Beautiful World series)

K08. KAZAMI, T.

Jungal Himal: photo-album of the Himalayas. Tokyo: Shinchô-sha, 1959. var. pag., illus, maps. 31cm. In Japanese with English summary. Yak. j. 180.
Photo-album of 1958 expedition led by Kyûya Fukata.

K09. KEAY, John

The Gilgit game: the explorers of the western Himalayas, 1886-95. Ldn: Murray, 1979. xiii, 277p, illus, 3 maps. 22cm.
—Similar edition by Readers' Union Book Club, 1979.

K10. KEAY, J.

When men and mountains meet: the explorers of the western Himalayas, 1820-75. Ldn: Murray, 1977. x, 277p, 16 plates, illus, maps, bibl. 23cm.
—U.S. ed. Hamden, CT: Archon Books, 1982. 277p, illus, maps, bibl.
—Softback ed. Murray, 1983.

K11. KEENLYSIDE, Francis

Peaks and pioneers: the story of mountaineering. Ldn: Elek, 1975. 248p, illus (some col), maps. 31cm.
Fine picture-history book.

K12. KELLY, Dennis

Mountain search for the lost victim. Edited by Hugh Marsh. Montrose: The Author, 1973. 283p. [8vo].

K13. KELSO, T. McMillan

A trip to Mt. Rainier in 1899. Carlton: Minikin, 1985. 20p. 59 × 74 millimetres. Limited edition of 150 numbered copies. Also special full leather edition of 26 lettered copies.

K14. KENNETT, John

The story of Annapurna. Retold and adapted by . . .from Maurice Herzog's *Annapurna.* Bombay: Blackie, 1955. 72p, illus. [8vo].
Story of the first ascent.

K15. KERASOTE, Edward

Navigations: one man explores the Americas and discovers himself. Harrisburg: Stackpole, 1986. 192p, illus.
Includes climbs in Ecuador, Bolivia, Argentina, Chile.

K16. KEY, Charles E.

A book of recent exploration. Ldn: Harrap, 1946.
—T.B.C. ed. 1948. 233p, 12 plates, illus, maps. 21cm.
Chapters on Tibet, Arctic, Everest, Kanchenjunga, Karakoram.

K17. KHANNA, Y. C.

Saser Kangri, yellow goddess of the Karakoram; the first ascent. Delhi: R. K. Puram (Indo-Tibet Border Police), 1980. xii, 144p, 29 plates, illus (some col), map. 23cm.
Saser Kangri (7672m) was one of the highest unclimbed peaks prior to this Indian ascent in 1973. It had been attempted several times.

K18. KILBOURNE, Frederick W.
Chronicles of the White Mountains. Boston: Houghton Mifflin, 1916. xxxii, 433p, illus, maps. 21cm. Several ptgs.
Early history of the White Mountains.

K19. KILGOUR, William T.
Twenty years on Ben Nevis: being a brief account of the life, work and experiences of the observers at the highest meteorological station in the British Isles. Paisley: A. Gardner, [1905]. iv, 154p, 18 plates, illus. 20cm.
—2nd ed. 1906 with chapter on meteorology. 171p.
—Facsimile of 2nd ed. with added tailpiece drawings. Anglesey Books, 1985. Softback.
The observatory was formally opened on 17 October, 1883.

K20. KING, Alfred Castner
Mountain idylls and other poems. Chicago: F. H. Revell, 1901. 120p, illus. 19cm.

K21. KING, Clarence (1842-1901)
Mountaineering in the Sierra Nevada. Boston: J. R. Osgood, 1872. [v], 292p. 21cm. Green or maroon cloth; t.e.g.; gilt lettering; title page with or without monogram. Also large paper (23cm) copies for presentation by the author.
—U.K. ed. Ldn: Sampson Low, 1872. v, 292p. 22cm. Brown cloth, gilt blocked (saddlebags & guns).
—Another ed. Ldn: Sampson Low, 1872. viii, 292p. 20cm. Reset and slightly smaller format. Frontispiece in some copies. Green cloth, gilt blocked (peaks & eagle on spine).
—'4th ed'. Boston: Osgood, 1874. viii, 308p, 2 col. fold. maps. 20cm. With new preface and additional chapter on Mt. Whitney. Also large paper edition.
—Another ed. Ldn: Sampson Low, 1874. No preface. Frontispiece. Brown cloth (saddlebags & guns).
—Reprint ('5th ed'). Boston: Osgood, 1875.
—Reprint ('6th ed'). Boston: Ticknor, 1886.
—Reprint ('7th ed').
—Reprint ('8th ed').
—Reprint ('9th ed'). [c.1888].
—Another ed. N.Y.: Scribner's, 1902. xiv, 378p. 20cm. Entirely reset. R.P., 1909, 1911, 1915, 1923.
—Another ed. Ldn: Fisher Unwin, 1903. xiv, 378p. 20cm. R.P., 1907?
—Another ed. N.Y.: W. Norton, 1935. Edited by Francis P. Farquhar. 320p, illus. 23cm.
—Another ed. N.Y.: Norton, 1946. Reset on lighter weight paper. Bound in blue cloth.
—Another ed. Ldn: A. & C. Black, 1947. 320p, 8 plates, illus. 22cm. Edited and with a preface by Francis P. Farquhar. First [sic] English edition. 1000 copies.
—Reprint of 1872 edition. Univ. Nebraska Press, 1970.
This book is the greatest mountain classic of the U.S.A. King was a geologist, and was a member of the 1864 California survey when he made his famous ascent of Mt. Tyndall in the Sierra Nevada.

K22. [KING, C.]
Clarence King memoirs [and] The Helmet of Mambrino. N.Y.: Putnam for the King Memorial Committee of the Century Association, 1904. vii, 429p, plates, ports. 22cm.
Memories of King by various people who knew him; and his short story, 'The Helmet of Mambrino', the best thing he ever wrote.

K23. KING, Samuel William (1821-68)
The Italian valleys of the Pennine Alps: a tour through all the romantic and less-frequented 'vals' of northern Piedmont, from the Tarentaise to the Gries. Ldn: Murray, 1858. x, 558p, 10 plates, illus, 3 fold. maps. 22cm.
The Rev. King was a member of the Alpine Club but his climbing career was very short and his reputation rests on this lengthy cross-country tour with his wife in 1855, described in delightful detail in his book. He died and is buried at Pontresina.

K24. KING, Benjamin E. ['Tom'] (1929-85)
In the shadow of the giants: mountain ascents past and present. San Diego: Barnes/Ldn: Tantivy, 1981. 287p, illus, maps. 24cm.
Historical details plus accounts of his own

ascents of various peaks, e.g. Mont Blanc, Matterhorn. Includes a good chapter on Fujiyama.

K25. KING, Thomas Starr
The White Hills: their legends, landscape and poetry. Boston: Crosby Nichols, 1860. 403p?
—Another ed. Boston, 1862. 403p, illus, map. 20cm.
—Another ed. Boston: Crosby & Ainsworth, 1866. 403p.
—Another ed. Boston: Woolworth, Ainsworth, 1869. xv, 403p, illus. 20cm.
—Another ed. Boston: Chick & Andrews, 1871. 403p.
History and description of the White Mountains, including an ascent of Mt. Washington.

K26. KINGSLEY, Mary Henrietta (1862-1900)
Travels in West Africa. 1897
The author, sister of novelist Charles Kingsley, made an ascent of Mount Cameroon by a new route in 1895, during the course of an enterprising expedition, vividly described in her book. She died of enteric fever while nursing Boer War prisoners.

K27. KINGSLEY, Norman
Icecraft. Glendale, CA: La Siesta Press, 1975. 120p, illus.

K28. KINZL, Hans (-1979) & SCHNEIDER, Erwin
Cordillera Blanca (Perú). Innsbruck: Universitäts-Verlag Wagner, [1950]. [4], 167p, illus, fold. map (in pkt). 27cm. Introductory text in German, English and Spanish.
This fine photo-album, prepared by members of the three outstanding D.Oe.A.V. expeditions (1932-39), was used as a guidebook in the 1950s.

K29. KIRK, Ruth
Exploring Mount Rainier. Seattle: Univ. Washington Press, 1968.

K30. KIRKPATRICK, William Trench (1858-1941)
Alpine days and nights. By . . .with a paper by the late R. Philip Hope. Ldn: Allen & Unwin, 1932. 198p, 12 plates, illus. 21cm.
Collection of articles first published in the *Alpine Journal* during the years 1900-31, relating to his climbs with R. P. Hope.

K31. KIRKUS, Colin F. (1910-42)
"Let's go climbing". Ldn: Nelson, 1941. 208p, 15 plates, illus, map. 21cm. R.P., 1946.
—Another ed. 1960. Nelson Juniors series. 3-200p. 19cm. Softback.
Instructional book for youngsters, written by a climber who dominated Welsh rock-climbing with Menlove Edwards in the 1930s. A cousin of Wilfrid Noyce, Kirkus was killed in World War II.

K32. KITTO, H. D. F.
In the mountains of Greece. Ldn: Methuen, [1933]. ix, 150p, plates, illus, map. 19cm.

K33. KLUCKER, Christian (1853-1928)
Adventures of an Alpine guide. Trans. from the third German edition by Erwin and Pleasaunce von Gaisberg. Edited and with additional chapters by H. E. G. Tyndale. Ldn: Murray, 1932. xiv, 329p, 16 plates, illus. 23cm. From the original: *Erinnerungen eines Bergführers* (Zurich: Rentsch, 1930).
Memoirs of a great guide. In 1890 he made several difficult new climbs with Norman-Neruda, and in 1893 he participated in the first traverse of the Peuterey Arête on Mont Blanc. Overall he made dozens of new ascents and continued climbing until he died.

K34. KNIGHT, Edward Frederick
Where three empires meet: a narrative of recent travel in Kashmir, western Tibet, Gilgit and the adjoining countries. Ldn: Longmans, 1893. xvi, 495p, illus, map. 22cm.
—New cheap ed. 1893. R.P., 1894, 1897. xv, 528p, illus, map. 19cm.
—Colonial Library ed. 1894. R.P., 1895. xv, 528p.
—Silver Library ed. 1903. R.P., 1905. xv, 528p.
—Reprinted 1971. 528p.
Reference Nanga Parbat. The author saw active service in the gorges of the Karakoram during the Hunza-Nagar expedition.

K35. Knoop, Faith Yingling
A world explorer: Sir Edmund Hillary. Champaign, IL: Garrard, 1970.
—U.K. ed. entitled *Sir Edmund Hillary.* Ldn: F. Watts, [1974]. 96, [4]p, col. illus, maps. 22cm.

K36. KNOWLTON, Elizabeth
The naked mountain. N.Y./Ldn: Putnam's, 1933. [xii], 335p, 24 plates, illus. 24cm.
—Another ed. N.Y.: Junior Literary Guild, 1934. 335p.
—Another ed. Seattle: Mountaineers, 1980.
Account of the 1932 German-American expedition to Nanga Parbat, the first since Mummery's attempt in 1895. Written by an American climber who accompanied the party as press reporter.

K37. KNOX, C. F.
Cambridge East Greenland Expedition 1963: general report. By ...[and others].
Members made 25 first ascents in the Gully-Sefstrom-glacier area of the Stauning Alps, and opened up five new passes.

K38. KNOX, Raymond (Editor)
A thousand mountains shining: stories from New Zealand's mountain world. Wellington: Reed, 1985. [vii], 237p, maps (endpapers).
Collection drawn from explorers, mountaineers, writers and poets.

K39. KOBE UNIVERSITY KARAKORUM EXPEDITION 1976.
Sherpa Kangri 1976: [report of the ...]. [Kobe]: The Expedition, 1976. 8p, plates (some col), illus, maps. 26cm. In Japanese with English summary as insert. Yak. j. 597.

K40. KOGAN, Georges & LEININGER, Nicole
The ascent of Alpamayo: an account of the Franco-Belgian expedition to the Cordillera Blanca in the high Andes. Trans. [from the French] by Peter E. Thompson. Ldn: Harrap, 1954. 134p, 32 plates, illus, maps. 21cm. From the original: *Cordillère Blanche* (Paris: Arthaud, 1952)
Misled by darkness the party reached in fact only the northern end of the summit ridge. The first ascent was made in 1957 by Günter Hauser's party.

K41. KOHLI, M. S. (b.1931)
Indians on Everest. [Source: Indian Mountaineering Federation Silver Jubilee booklet, p.71.]

K42. KOHLI, M. S.
Last of the Annapurnas. Delhi: Ministry of Information & Broadcasting, 1962. 143p, plates (some col), illus, map. 23cm.
First ascent of Annapurna III (7555m), second highest of the four principal Annapurna peaks; it was climbed at the first attempt.

K43. KOHLI, M. S.
Nine atop Everest: story of the Indian ascent. Bombay: Orient Longmans, 1969. xxviii, 384p, 56 plates (some col), illus. 25cm.
Kohli led this successful 1965 expedition. Now a businessman, his career has included service with the Indian Navy and the Indo-Tibet Border Police

K44. KOLB, Fritz
Himalaya venture. Trans. [from the German] by Laurence Wilson. Ldn: Lutterworth Press, 1959. 148p, 15 plates, illus, 3 maps. 22cm. From the original: *Einzelgänger im Himalaya.* (Munich: Bruckmann, 1957)
Lightweight climbing and exploration, in 1939 and 1946, in Lahoul and Padar, by two Austrians who were interned in India during World War II.

K45. KOPP, Hans (b.1910)
Himalaya shuttlecock. Trans. from the German by H. C. Stevens. Ldn: Hutchinson, 1957. 191p, illus, map. 21cm.
—Adventurers Club ed., n.d. 191p, 15 plates. 23cm.
Kopp escaped from internment in India and crossed the Himalaya by various means six times while on the run. He was accompanied by Heinrich Harrer part of the time.

K46. KOR, Layton
Beyond the vertical. Edited by Bob Godfrey. Boulder: Alpine House, 1983. 215p, col. illus. 31cm.

Well illustrated portrait of leading American climber, with contributions by numerous well-known climbers. At his peak Kor's drive and energy earned him the reputation as American mountaineering's most legendary figure.

K47. KRAPF, John Lewis

Travels, researches and missionary labours . . .in eastern Africa . . ., with an appendix respectiong the snowcapped mountains of eastern Africa. Ldn: Trüber, 1860. liii, 566p, plates (2 fold., some col), illus, maps. 24cm.

Krapf was the first to sight Mount Kenya, in 1849, his companion Rebmann having sighted Kilimanjaro the previous year. They were the earliest European explorers of the Kilimanjaro and Kamaba regions.

K48. KUGY, Julius (1858-1944)

Alpine pilgrimage. Trans. [from the German] by H. E. G. Tyndale. Ldn: Murray, 1934. xxii, 374p, 21 plates, illus, fold. map. 23cm. From the original: *Aus dem Leben eines Bergsteigers* (Munich: Rother, 1925.)

One of the most fascinating of Alpine books written by an Austrian climber who became a legend in his own lifetime. He was particularly knowledgeable about the Julian Alps.

K49. KUGY, J.

Son of the mountains: the life of an Alpine guide. Trans. [from the German] by H. E. G. Tyndale. Ldn: Nelson, 1938. xii, 200p, 9 plates, illus. 21cm. From the original: *Anton Oitzinger: ein Bergführerleben* (Graz: Verlag Leykam, 1925)

Biography of Anton Oitzinger, Kugy's friend and guide.

K50. KUKACKA, Miroslav

Nizke Tatry. Bratislava: Vydavatel'stvo Osveta, 1962. Volume of mostly illustrations. Summaries in English, German and Russian.

Tatra Mountains.

K51. KUMAR, Kiran Inder [Narinder?]

Expedition Kinner Kailash [6473m]. Delhi: Vision Books, 1981. 116p, illus (some col), map. 24cm.

K52. KUMAR, Narinder [Narendra?] (b.1933)

Kanchenjunga: first ascent from the north-east spur. Delhi: Vision Books/Ldn & The Hague: East-West Publications, 1978. 156p, illus, 2 maps. 27cm.

K53. KUMAR, N.

Nilakantha: story of the Indian expedition of 1961. Delhi: Ministry of Information & Broadcasting, 1965. xiv, 140p, illus, map. 22cm.

—2nd ed. entitled *Nilakantha: the first ascent.* Delhi: Vision Books, 1979. xii, 119p, 16 plates, illus. 25cm.

K54. KUMAR, N. & AHLUWALIA, H. P. S.

Trisul ski expedition. Delhi: Vikas Pub, 1978. xi, 148p, illus, map. 22cm.

Account of 1976 expedition.

K55. KYOTO MOUNTAINEERING CLUB

Bogda (I) in the Tien-Shan of China: Kyoto Mountaineering Club 1981 expedition. Edited by Kyôko Endô. Kyoto: The Club. 110p, illus (some col), maps. 26cm. In Japanese with English summary. Yak j. 240.

First ascent of main Bogda peak (5445m).

L

L01. LACHAPELLE, Edward R.

The ABC of avalanche safety.

—2nd ed. Seattle: Mountaineers/Leicester: Cordee/Vancouver: Douglas & McIntyre, *1978.* [64p], illus, bibl. 18cm. Softback.

—Another ed. Seattle: Mountaineers, 1985. 96p.

L02. LAMB, Elkanah J.

Memories of the past and thoughts of the future. United Brethren Pub. House, 1906.

Autobiography of the Rev. Lamb who made the first descent of the East Face of Longs Peak, Colorado, in 1871. Subsequently he settled nearby and became the first professional mountain guide in the United States.

L03. LAMB, G. F. (Editor)
Living dangerously. Ldn: Allen & Unwin, 1958. 139p. 19cm. Softback.
Young adult book; includes 'A blizzard on Mount Everest' by J. L. Longland (pp. 63-74), taken from Cobham's *Tight corners.*

L04. LAMB, G. F.
Thrilling exploits of modern adventure. Ldn: Harrap, 1957. 217p, plates, illus, maps. 19cm. R.P., 1958, 1961.
Includes Tazieff's descent into the crater of an active volcano; Greenland ice-cap; Benuzzi on Mt. Kenya; Nanga Parbat.

L05. LAMBERT, Raymond (b.1914) & KOGAN, Claude
White fury: Gaurisankar and Cho Oyu. Trans. [from the French] by Showell Styles. Ldn: Hurst & Blackett, 1956. 176p, 15 plates, illus. 22cm. From the original: *Record à l'Himalaya* (Paris: Editions France-Empire, 1955).
Account of the Franco-Swiss expedition of 1954, reconnoitring the difficult Gaurisankar (7145m) and Menlungtse. The party then attempted Cho Oyu (8156m) being beaten by winter gales. Lambert, a Swiss guide, made an heroic attempt to gain Everest's south summit in 1952. Claude Kogan, a leading French climber, died on Cho Oyu in 1959.

L06. LANE, Rose Wilder
Peaks of Shala. N.Y./Ldn, 1923. 349p, illus. 23cm.
The mountains of Albania.

L07. LANGE, Harald
Kilimanjaro: the white roof of Africa. Seattle: Mountaineers, 1985. 176p, plates, illus (mostly colour), 5 maps. From the original: *Kilimandscharo; das Weisse Dach Afrikas.*
Text includes history, planning a climb of the main peak, routes, regulations, facilities and general description.

L08. LANGMUIR, Eric
Mountain leadership: the official handbook of the Mountain Leadership Training Boards of Great Britain. Edinburgh: Scottish Council of Physical Recreation, [1969]. 89p, illus. 24cm.
—Rev. ed. 1973. 119p.
—New ed. entitled *Mountaincraft and leadership.* Scottish Sports Council/ Leicester: Cordee-B.M.C./Edinburgh: Scottish Sports Council, 1984. 361p, illus, bibl. 23cm. By Langmuir and others.

L09. LANGUEPIN, Jean-Jacques
To kiss high heaven. Trans. from the French by Mervyn Savill. Ldn: Kimber, 1956. 199p, 7 plates, illus. 22cm. From the original: *Himalaya, passion cruelle* (Paris: Flammarion, 1955).
Expedition to Nanda Devi in 1951 when the summit pair disappeared.

L10. LARDEN, Walter (1855-1919)
Argentine plains and Andine glaciers: life on an estancia, and an expedition into the Andes. Ldn: Fisher Unwin, 1911. 320p, plates, illus, map. 23cm.
Includes an attempt on Aconcagua.

L11. LARDEN, W.
Guide to the walks and climbs around Arolla. Ldn: S. Chick, 1908. x, 138p, plates, illus. 15cm.

L12. LARDEN, W.
Recollections of an old mountaineer. Ldn: Arnold, 1910. xv, 320p, 17 plates, illus. 24cm.
Climbing memoirs of a British alpinist, schoolmaster and naval instructor who did much to popularize Arolla as a climbing centre.

L13. LATROBE, Charles Joseph (1801-75)
The alpenstock: or, Sketches of Swiss scenery and manners, MDCCCXXV-MDCCCXXVI. Ldn: R. B. Seeley, 1829. x, 388p, 3 plates, illus. 23cm.
—2nd ed. W. Burnside, [1939]. x, 366p, plates, illus. 17cm. Variations seen or noted: (i) 3 plates, grey binding, uncut; (ii) 4 plates & vignette, crimson cloth, a.e.g.; (iii) 7 steel engravings & 3 woodcuts, no roman dates on title page, mauve binding, blind stamped, gilt decoration on front & spine, a.e.g. The last probably a late issue.

L14. LATROBE, C. J.
The pedestrian: a summer's ramble in the Tyrol and some of the adjoining provinces,

MDCCCXXX. Ldn: R. B. Seeley & W. Burnside, 1832. iv, 349p, map. 21cm. Binding variations noted: crimson cloth, gilt lettering; green cloth, paper label.

L15. LATHROP, Theodore G.
Hypothermia: killer of the unprepared. —Rev. ed. Portland: Mazamas, 1970. 23p.

L16. LATTA, William S.
The ascent of the Lions: 5th September and subsequent days, 1903. By ..., John F. and Robert P. Latta. Vancouver City Archives, 1953. 22p, illus.
First-hand account of a first ascent by three young brothers.

L17. LAW, Donald
Starting mountaineering and rock-climbing. Newton Abbot: David & Charles, 1977. 143p, illus. 23cm.

L18. LEAMER, Laurence
Ascent: the spiritual and physical quest of Willi Unsoeld. N.Y.: Simon & Schuster, 1982. 392p, illus, map. 22cm.
Unofficial biography of leading American mountaineer Willi Unsoeld (1926-78), killed in an avalanche on Mount Rainier. His climbs included first ascents of Masherbrum and the West Ridge of Everest. He also had a distinguished academic career.

L19. LE BLOND. Elizabeth Alice Frances (née Hawkins-Whitshead) (1861-1934)
Adventures on the roof of the world. Ldn: Fisher Unwin/N.Y.: Dutton, 1904. xvi, 333p, 32 plates, illus. 22cm. R.P., 1907.
—Pocket ed. Shilling Library series. Ldn: Nelson, [c.1916].
Excerpts from accounts of Alpine climbs by well-known figures.

L20. LE BLOND, E. A. F.
Day in, day out. Ldn: Bodley Head, 1928. 264p, 16 plates, illus. 23cm.
Autobiography; includes some references to climbing. Mrs Le Blond (who also wrote under her other married names, i.e. Mrs Fred Burnaby, Mrs Main) was a wealthy society woman who originally went to Switzerland for health reasons. She climbed extensively in the Alps and later in Norway. She was the founder and first president of the Ladies Alpine Club, 1907.

L21. LE BLOND, E. A. F.
The high Alps in winter: or, Mountaineering in search of health. By Mrs Fred Burnaby. Ldn: Sampson Low, 1883. xx, 204p, 5 plates illus, 2 maps (1 fold). 18cm.

L22. LE BLOND, E. A. F.
High life and towers of silence. By the author of 'The high Alps in winter'. Ldn: Sampson Low, 1886. xii, 195p, 7 plates, illus. 19cm.
Alpine climbs.

L23. LE BLOND, E. A. F.
Hints on snow photography. By Mrs Main. Ldn: Sampson Low, Marston, 1894. 15p, 14 plates, illus. 22cm.

L24. LE BLOND, E. A. F.
Mountaineering in the land of the midnight sun. Ldn: Fisher Unwin, 1908. xii, 304p, 64 plates, illus, map. 23cm.
First ascents in the Lyngen Peninsula.

L25. LE BLOND E. A. F.
My home in the Alps. By Mrs Main. Ldn: Sampson Low, 1892. viii, 131p. 20cm.
Miscellaneous pieces about guides and alpine life; much of the material first appeared in the *St. Moritz Post.*

L26. LE BLOND, E. A. F.
True tales of mountain adventure for non-climbers young and old. Ldn: Fisher Unwin, 1902. xviii, 299p, 36 plates, illus. 22cm. R.P., 1903, 1906.
—U.S. ed. N.Y.: Dutton, 1903.
—Pocket ed. Shilling Library series. Ldn: Nelson, [c.1915].

L27. LE CONTE, Joseph Nisbet (1823-1901)
Autobiography of Joseph Le Conte [Senior]. Edited by William Dallam Armes. N. Y.: Appleton, 1903.
—Another ed. Berkeley: Univ. California Press, ?. Edition of 500 numbered copies.
Le Conte was an explorer of the Sierra Nevada and friend of John Muir.

L28. LE CONTE, J. N.
A journal of ramblings through the High Sierras of California by the "University Excursion Party". S.F.: Francis &

Valentine, 1875. 103p, 9 plates, illus. 22cm. Bound in blue cloth. The exact number of copies issued is unknown but is unlikely to exceed 120.
—Reprinted in *Sierra Club Bulletin,* v. III, No. 1, January, 1900, pp. 1-107.
—Publication No. 21 of the Sierra Club. S.F., 1900. Reprint from *Sierra Club Bulletin.*
—Abridged version published by Le Conte in *Overland Monthly,* New Series, v. VI, S.F., Oct/Nov/Dec, 1885.
—Another ed. S.F.: Sierra Club, 1930. xvi, 154p, 5 plates, illus. 22cm. Edited by Francis P. Farquhar. Edition of 1500 copies.
—Edition of 500 copies issued as part of the reprint of Volumes I-VI of the *Sierra Club Bulletin.* Sierra Club, 1950.
—Another ed. S.F.: Sierra Club, 1960. xvi, 150p, 8 plates. 22 cm. Minor changes in pagination, and restoration of all the original illustrations. Edition of 2500 copies.
A record of a trip in 1870 during which John Muir joined the party for a few days. The book is regarded as one the greatest classics of early Californian mountain travel.

L29. LE CONTE, Joseph Nisbet Jr. (1870-1950)
The High Sierra of California. N.Y.: A.A.C., 1907. 16p, illus, fold. map. 35cm. (Alpina Americana series, 1)

L30. LEE, Chip
On edge: the life and climbs of Henry Barber. By . . .with David Roberts and Kenneth Andrasko. Boston: Appalachian Mountain Club, 1982. xxvii, 291p, illus. 24cm.
Biography of a leading American rock-climber, written by a fellow-student.

L31. LEE, Frank Harold
The lure of the hills: an anthology. Ldn: Harrap, 1928. 253p. 18cm.

L32. LEICESTER POLYTECHNIC STUDENTS ØKSFORD EXPEDITION, 1970.
Official Report.
Loppa Peninsula, Finnmark, arctic Norway.

L33. LEIFER, Walter
Himalaya, mountains of destiny: meeting place of Russian, Chinese, Indian spheres of influence. A study of geopolitics. Trans. from the German by Ursula Prideaux. Ldn: Gallery Press, 1962. x, 176p, illus. 22cm.

L34. LE MESURIER, W. H.
An impromptu ascent of Mont Blanc in 1881. Ldn: Elliot Stock, 1882. 76p, 7 plates, illus, map. 22cm.

L35. LEONARD, Richard
Belaying the leader: an omnibus on climbing safety. S.F.: Sierra Club, 1956. vii, 85p, illus. Several ptgs.

L36. LEONARD, R.
Mountain records of the Sierra Nevada. Compiled by . . .& the Committee on Mountain Records. S.F.: Sierra Club, 1 May 1937. 115p. 27cm. Numbered copies.

L37. LÉPINEY, Jacques de & Tom de
Climbs on Mont Blanc. Trans. [from the French] by Sydney Spencer. Ldn: Arnold, 1930. xii, 179p, 16 plates, illus. 22cm. From the original: *Sur les crêtes du Mont Blanc.* (Chambéry: Dardel, 1929).
French brothers who made many fine climbs in the 1920s, including the North face of the Aiguille du Plan and Pointe de Lépiney.

L38. LEWIN, Walter Henry
Climbs. Ldn: The Author, 1932. xviii, 226p, 16 plates, illus. 23cm. Limited edition of 250 numbered and signed copies.
Climbing reminiscences (Britain, Alps, Canadian Rockies, South Africa).

L39. LEWIS, H. Warren
You're STANDING on my FINGERS!. Berkeley, CA: Howell-North Books, 1969. 268p, illus, maps. 24cm.
Lighthearted account of climbing with a growing family on the ranges of North America.

L40. LEYLAND, Peter
The naked mountain. Ldn: Heinemann, 1951. xix, 83p. 19cm. (New Heinemann Poetry)

L41. LIEBENBERG, Doyle P.

The Drakensberg of Natal. Cape Town: Bulpin, 1972. x, 178p, 24 plates (some col), illus, maps. 25cm.
Includes climbing and list of recorded climbs. Written by a South African climber who made a number of pioneer ascents in the Drakensberg in 1930s & 1940s.

L42. LINDSAY, M.

Three got through. 1946.
British Trans-Greenland Expedition, 1934. The author and his two companions discovered and surveyed the Kronprins-Frederiks-Berge on the east coast.

L43. LITTLE, Archibald John

Mount Omi and beyond: a record of travel on the Tibetan border. Ldn: Heinemann, 1901. xv, 272p, plates (1 fold. col), illus, map. 24cm.
Account of journeys in 1892-97. The author passed close by vast snow-covered ranges which remained practically unexplored by Europeans. Omi-shan is a sacred mountain in north-west Szechuan.

L44. LIVESEY, Peter

Rockclimbing. Wakefield: E.P. Publishing, 1978/Seattle: Mountaineers, 1979. 116p, illus. 21cm. (E.P. Sport series)
Authoritative presentation of modern rock-climbing techniques by a leading British climber; profusely illustrated.

L45. LODGE, Sir Oliver

Why I believe in personal immortality. Ldn: The Author, 1928. viii, 151p. Less than 10 copies are thought to exist.
—1st public edition. Ldn: Cassell, 1928.
The eight pages referring to the deaths of Mallory and Irvine were omitted from the public edition.

L46. LONGMAN, William & TROWER, Henry

Journal of six weeks' adventures in Switzerland, Piedmont, and on the Italian lakes: by W.L. and H.T., June, July, August, 1856. Printed by Spottiswoode [for the Authors], 1856. 123p, 1 fold. col. plate, map. 21cm.
Longman's first Alpine tour. Although his climbing career was undistinguished he rose to become president of the Alpine Club (1872-4), his great contribution being the fostering and publication of many early Alpine classics, including the publications sponsored by the Alpine Club.

L47. LONGSTAFF, Thomas George (1875-1964)

Mountain sickness and its probable cause. Ldn: Spottiswoode, 1906. 56p. 22cm.
Written as a graduation thesis. He qualified as a doctor but never practised, having private means.

L48. LONGSTAFF, T. G.

This my voyage. Ldn: Murray/N.Y.: Scribner's, 1950. [xii], 324p, 23 plates, illus, maps. 23cm. R.P., 1951.
Longstaff climbed on most ranges in the northern hemisphere and was one of the great early Himalayan climber-explorers. His greatest success was the ascent in 1907 of Trisul (7120m), which remained for 21 years the highest peak climbed. His authoritative climbing memoirs have scarcely received their due.

L49. LOUGHMAN, Michael

Learning to rock climb. S.F.: Sierra Club, 1981. 141p, illus.

L50. LOVELOCK, James

Climbing. With a chapter on artificial climbing by Trevor Jones. Ldn: Batsford, 1971. 185p, 16 plates, illus. 23cm.

L51. LOWE, Jeff

The ice experience. Chicago: Contemporary Books/Leicester: Cordee, 1979. xiii, 211p, illus. 23cm.
Instructional book written by leading American climber.

L52. LOWE, W. George

Because it is there. Ldn: Cassell, 1959. viii, 216p, plates, illus, maps. 22cm.
—U.S. ed. entitled *From Everest to the South Pole.* N.Y.: St. Martin's Press, 1961.
Memoirs of New Zealand climber and explorer who took part in the 1953 Everest expedition. Chiefly about his antarctic experiences.

L53. LOWERY, L. G.

Mountains are for climbing. San Antonio: Naylor, 1973.

L54. LUCKHOFF, C. A.
Table Mountain: our national heritage after three hundred years. Cape Town: A. A. Balkema, 1951. 152p, 125 plates, illus. 28cm.
Lavish monograph with sections on geology, flora and climbing.

L55. LUKAN, KARL (b.1923) & NOYCE, Wilfrid
The Alps. Trans. from the German by Margaret Shenfield. Ldn: Thames & Hudson, 1961. 312p, 230 plates, illus, maps. 28cm. From the original: *Die Alpen von Mont Ventoux zum Kahlenberg.*
—Rev. ed. 1963
—U.S. ed. N.Y.: Putnam's, 1963. 312p.
Illustrated climbing history. Wilfrid Noyce's contribution is chiefly introductory.

L56. LUKAN, K.
The Alps and alpinism. Edited by . . .Trans. [from the German] by Hugh Merrick. Ldn: Thames & Hudson, 1968. 200p, plates (some col), illus. 29cm.
—U.S. ed. N.Y.: Coward McCann, 1968

L57. LUKAN, K.
Mountain adventures. Ldn: Collins/N.Y.: Franklin Watts, 1972. 128p, illus (chiefly col), col. maps. 26cm. Softback R.P., 1978.
Illustrated summary of the mountaineering world; suitable for young adults.

L58. LUNN, Sir Arnold Henry Moore (1883-1974)
Alpine ski-ing at all heights and seasons.
—2nd rev. ed. Ldn: Methuen, 1926. xiv, 106p, plates, illus. 18cm.
—U.S. ed. N.Y.: Dutton, n.d. xii, 116p, plates, illus. 17cm.

L59. LUNN, A. H. M.
The Alps. Ldn: Williams & Norgate, 1914. 256p, bibl. 18cm. (Home University library of modern knowledge, 91)
History of climbing in the Alps and a long chapter on the Alps in literature.

L60. LUNN, A. H. M.
And the floods came: a chapter of war-time autobiography. Ldn: Eyre & Spottiswoode, 1942. 237p. 23cm.

L61. LUNN, A. H. M.
And yet so new. Ldn, 1958. 244p.

L62. LUNN, A. H. M.
The Bernese Oberland. Ldn: Eyre & Spottiswoode, 1958. 215p, 16 plates (1 fold. col), illus. 21cm.
—Rev. & enlarged ed. Ldn: Allen & Unwin, 1973.
General interest.

L63. LUNN, A. H. M.
A century of mountaineering, 1857-1957; [Centenary tribute to the Alpine Club from the Swiss Foundation for Alpine Research]. Ldn: Allen & Unwin, 1957. [4], 263p, 24 plates (some col), illus. 25cm.
Lunn, who knew many of the great figures of mountaineering well, rose to the occasion with this fascinating insight into world mountaineering. His best and most sought-after book.

L64. LUNN, A. H. M.
Chapters from my life.

L65. LUNN, A. H. M.
Come what may: an autobiography. Ldn: Eyre & Spottiswoode, 1940. 482p. 22cm.
—U.S. ed. Boston: Little Brown, 1941. [viii], 348p.

L66. LUNN, A. H. M.
The complete ski-runner. Ldn: Methuen, 1930. 213p, plates, illus. 23cm. (The complete series)

L67. LUNN, A. H. M.
The cradle of Switzerland. Ldn: Hollis & Carter, 1952. xiii, 226p, plates, illus. 19cm.

L68. LUNN, A. H. M.
Cross-country ski-ing. Ldn: Methuen, 1920. viii, 118p, plates, illus. 16cm.

L69. LUNN, A. H. M.
The Englishman in the Alps, being a collection of English prose and poetry relating to the Alps. Edited by . . .O.U.P., 1913. xx, 294p. 18cm.
An elegant little anthology.

L70. [LUNN, A. H. M.]
Guide to Montana and district. Ldn: H. Marshall, 1907. 79p, 1 fold. plate (in pkt), illus. 19cm. Preface signed A.H.M.L.

L71. LUNN, A. H. M.
A history of skiing. O.U.P., 1927. xv, 492p, 24 plates, illus. 23cm.
Approximately 80 pages are devoted to the history of winter mountaineering, both on foot and on ski.

L72. LUNN, A. H. M.
Matterhorn centenary. Ldn: Allen & Unwin/N.Y.: Rand McNally, 1965. 144p, 25 plates, illus. 22cm.
Celebrates the first 100 years' climbing on the Matterhorn.

L73. LUNN, A. H. M.
Memory to memory. Ldn: Hollis & Carter, 1956. 268p, plates, illus, port. 23cm.

L74. LUNN, A. H. M.
Mountain jubilee. Ldn: Eyre & Spottiswoode, 1943. xii, 287p, plates, illus. 23cm.
Chapters on various Alpine themes.

L75. LUNN, A. H. M.
Mountains of memory. Ldn: Hollis & Carter, 1948. xii, 248p, plates, illus. 23cm.

L76. LUNN, A. H. M.
The mountains of youth. O.U.P., 1925. [8], 192p, 20 plates, illus. 22cm. R.P., 1930.
—Reissued 1943. Ldn: Eyre & Spottiswoode. R.P., 1949.

L77. LUNN, A. H. M.
Oxford mountaineering essays. Ldn: Arnold, 1912. xi, 237p. 20cm.
One of the best volumes of mountain essays.

L78. [LUNN, A. H. M.]
Portrait of a pioneer: Sir Arnold Lunn, 1883-1974. Zurich: De Clivo Press, [1979]. 20p, ports. Text of Arnold Lunn Memorial Lecture given by Walter Amstutz on 10 May 1979, under the auspices of the Ski Club of Great Britain and the Alpine Ski Club.

L79. LUNN, A. H. M.
Ski-ing. Ldn: E. Nash, 1913. 256p, plates, illus. 20cm.

L80. LUNN, A. H. M.
Ski-ing for beginners. Ldn: Methuen, 1924. xi, 127p, plates, illus. 18cm.
—2nd rev. ed. 1926.

L81. LUNN, A. H. M.
The story of ski-ing. Ldn: Eyre & Spottiswoode, 1952. 224p. 24cm.

L82. LUNN, A. H. M.
The Swiss and their mountains: a study of the influence of mountains on man. Ldn: Allen & Unwin, 1963. 167p, 24 plates (some col), illus. 23cm.

L83. LUNN, A. H. M.
Switzerland and the English. Ldn: Eyre & Spottiswoode, 1944. x, 258p, plates, illus. 22cm. R.P., 1945.

L84. LUNN, A. H. M.
Switzerland: her topographical, historical and literary landmarks. Ldn: Harrap, 1928. 320p, illus. 18cm. (Kitbag series).

L85. LUNN, A. H. M.
Switzerland in English prose and poetry. Edited by . . .Ldn: Eyre & Spottiswoode, 1947. xxvii, 262p, 17 plates, illus. 22cm. (New Alpine library).
Anthology.

L86. LUNN, A. H. M.
'Unkilled for so long'. Ldn: Allen & Unwin, 1968. 175p, plate, port. 23cm.
A volume of general autobiography.

L87. LUNN, A. H. M.
Zermatt and the Valais. Ldn: Hollis & Carter, 1955. x, 211p, plates, illus. 20cm.

L88. LYMAN, Tom (b.1943?)
Bouldering and outcrop climbing. Brattleboro: Stephen Greene, 1978. 144p, illus.

L89. LYMAN, T. & RIVIERE, Bill
The field book of mountaineering and rock climbing. N.Y.: Winchester Press, 1975. [8], 213p, illus. 24cm.

L90. LYNAM, Joss
Irish peaks. Ldn: Constable, 1982. 250p, illus, maps.

M

M01. MCCALLUM, John D.
Everest diary: based on the personal diary of Lute Jerstad, one of the first five Americans to conquer Mount Everest. Chicago: Follett Pub, [1966]. x, 213p, 28 plates, illus. 22cm.

M02. MCCLYMONT, W. G.
The exploration of New Zealand. Wellington: Department of Internal Affairs, 1940. xv, 202p, plates (2 fold.), illus, maps, bibl. 22cm. (New Zealand centennial surveys, 3)
—2nd ed. O.U.P., 1959.
Standard work on New Zealand exploration as a whole.

M03. MCCORMICK, Arthur David (1860-1943)
An artist in the Himalayas. Ldn: Fisher Unwin, 1895. xii, 306p, plate, illus, map. 23cm.
His own account of Conway's 1892 Karakoram Expedition. McCormick was a landscape artist and watercolourist who illustrated Conway's Alpine books and other mountaineering books.

M04. M'CORMICK, Joseph
A sad holiday.
—2nd ed. Ldn: James Nisbet & Co./Cassel Petter & Galpin, 1866.
A lecture delivered before the Liverpool College on the Matterhorn accident.

M05. MCCOWAN, Dan
Hill-top tales. Toronto: Macmillan, 1948. [xi], 266p, illus.
24 tales of climbing, exploring, etc. in the Canadian Rockies.

M06. MACDONALD, Hugh
On foot: an anthology selected by . . .O.U.P., 1942. 320p. 16cm.
Includes extracts from mountaineers, mountain poets and others about the British Isles and the Alps.

M07. MACGREGOR, John
The ascent of Mont Blanc: a series of four views; printed in oil colours by George Baxter; the original sketches and the description by J. Macgregor. [G. Baxter], [1855]. 4p, 4 col. plates, illus. 19 × 27cm.

M08. MACGREGOR, John
Tibet: a chronicle of exploration. Ldn: Kegan Paul, 1970. x, 373p, illus, maps. 22cm.
—U.S. ed. N.Y./Washington: Praeger, 1970.
—2nd ed. 1972.
European exploration from the 16th century to the 1904 Younghusband expedition; also the exploits of the Indian Pundits.

M09. MACHETTO, G. & BINI, Gianfranco
Annapurna: spedizione italiana nel Nepal, 1973. Pero/Milan: Virginia, [1974?]. 183p (mostly col. plates). 30 × 23cm.
—2nd ed. Pero, 1980.
Photo-album in Italian and English of the 1973 Italian Annapurna expedition.

M10. MACINNES, Hamish
Beyond the ranges: five years in the life of Hamish MacInnes. Ldn: Gollancz, 1984. xi, 202p, plates, illus. 24cm.
Includes the remote Llanganati range in Ecuador, ballooning, film-making, etc.

M11. MACINNES, H.
Call-out. Ldn: Hodder, 1973. 190p, 16 plates, illus. 23cm. 3rd ptg, 1974.
—Penguin paperback.
The work of the Glencoe Mountain Rescue Team.

M12. MACINNES, H.
Climb to the lost world. Ldn: Hodder, 1974. 224p, 32 plates (some col), illus. 23cm.
—Penguin paperback.
Climbing the Great Prow of Roraima, Guyana; a severe climb in appalling conditions.

M13. MACINNES, H.
Climbing. Scottish Y.H.A., 1963. 86p, illus. 18cm.
—2nd ed. Stirling: Scottish Y.H.A., 1964. 84p, illus. 19cm.

M14. MACINNES, H.
High drama: mountain rescue stories from four continents. Ldn: Hodder/Seattle: Mountaineers. 1980. 208p, plates, illus. 23cm.

M15. MACINNES, H.
International mountain rescue handbook. Ldn: Constable/N.Y.: Scribner's 1972. 218p, illus. 23cm. R.P., 1976.
—Scribner's paperback.
—New ed. Constable, 1984. 268p.

M16. MACINNES, H.
Look behind the ranges: a mountaineer's selection of adventures and expeditions. Ldn: Hodder, 1979. 271p, plates (some col), illus. 24cm.
Reminiscences of a famous Scottish climber.

M17. MACINNES, H.
Sweep search. Ldn: Kaye & Ward, 1985. 192p, 8 plates, illus, map.
Memories of eighteen years' mountain rescue.

M18. MACINTYRE, Neil
Attack on Everest. Ldn: Methuen, 1936. viii, 172p. 20cm.
Summary of various attempts taken from articles originally published in the *News Chronicle.*

M19. MCLANE, Alvin R.
Silent cordilleras: the mountain ranges of Nevada. [Reno, 1978]. 118p, illus, 2 maps. 28cm.

M20. MACLEAN, F. W.
Three weeks amongst the upper regions of the Alps, with a comment on 'mountaineering' and the 'Matterhorn catastrophe'. Hampstead: [The Author?], 1865. 44p. 21cm.

M21. MCMORRIS, William Bruce
The real book of mountaineering. Garden City, NY: Doubleday, 1958. 217p.
—Rev. ed. Ldn: Dobson 1961. 192p, illus. 21cm.

M22. MCNEIL, Fred H.
Wy'East 'The Mountain': a chronicle of Mount Hood, known to the Indians, who worshipped it as Wy'east. Portland: Metropolitan Press, 1937. 244p, illus. 22cm.
Cascade Range, western U.S.

M23. MACROW, Brenda G.
Unto the hills [photographs by Robert M. Adams]. Edinburgh: Oliver & Boyd, [1946]. 111p, illus. R.P., 1947.

M24. MCSPADDEN, J. Walker.
The Alps as seen by the poets. Ldn/N.Y.: Crowell, 1912. [xii], 222p, 16 plates, illus. 21cm.
Attractive anthology of general alpine poetry.

M25. MADDEN, Cecil
Living dangerously: 37 stories of adventure on land, at sea, in the air and investigating the unknown. Collected by ...Ldn: Allen & Unwin, 1936. 286p, plates, illus. 21cm.
Chapters on Everest, Nanda Devi, Mt. Waddington. Not in Yakushi.

M26. MAEDA, Shinzo
The Nippon Alps Kamikochi. 108p. Text in Japanese and English.
Fine photo-album on the Japanese alps by one of Japan's best photographers.

M27. MAEDER, Herbert (b.1930)
The mountains of Switzerland: the adventure of the high Alps. Edited, with photographs and commentary, by ...Trans. [from the German] by Hendrik P. B. Betlem. Ldn: Allen & Unwin, 1968. 288p, illus (some col), 30cm. From the original: *Die Berge der Schweiz* (Olten: Walter Verlag, 1967)
—U.S. ed. Walker, 1969.
Includes sections on geology, flora and fauna. Heavily illustrated, with supporting text.

M28. MAEDER, H.
The lure of the mountains. Edited and selection of photos by ...Ldn: Elsevier-Phaidon/N.Y.: Crowell, 1975. [6], 138p, col. illus. 30cm. From the original: *Lockende Berge* (Zurich: Silva-Verlag, 1971)
Elaborate anthology comprising nine extracts from well-known authors, e.g. Whymper.

M29. MAGNONE, Guido
West face. Trans. from the French by J. F. Burke. Ldn: Museum Press, 1955. 166p, 13 plates, illus. 23cm. From the original: *La Face Ouest des Drus* (Paris: Amiot-Dumont, 1953)
Account of the first ascent of the very imposing rock face of the Dru in which Magnone participated. His many notable ascents included Fitzroy and Makalu.

M30. MAHONEY, Michael
Harry Ayres: mountain guide. Christchurch: Whitcoulls, 1982. 160p, 16 plates, illus. 21cm.
Legendary New Zealand guide invited to Everest 1953 by Shipton and rejected by Hunt. Hillary considered Ayres would have been the strongest member of the party.

M31. [MAINICHI-NEWSPAPER (Editor)]
Everest. Tokyo: Mainichi-Newspaper, 1970. 202p, col. illus, panorama, map. 30 × 21cm. In Japanese with English summary. Yak. j. 687.
Photo-album of Japanese Alpine Club 1970 expedition.

M32. MAIN, Lindsay
Mountaincraft. Wellington: New Zealand Mountain Safety Council
—2nd ed. 1980. ix, 181p, illus. (Mountain Safety Manual, 3)

M33. MAITLAND, Frederic William
The life and letters of Leslie Stephen. Ldn: Duckworth, 1906. ix, 510p, 5 plates, illus. ports, bibl. 24cm.
—U.S. facsimile ed. Detroit: Gale Research, 1968.
Biography of one the most famous Victorian mountaineers.

M34. MAJORS, Harry M.
Mount Baker, a chronicle of its historic eruptions and first ascent. Edited by . . .Seattle: Northwest Press, 1978. 226p, illus. 22cm. Limited edition of 1000 numbered copies. Spiral-bound.

M35. MALARTIC, Yves
Tenzing of Everest. Trans. [from the French] by Judith B. Heller. Ldn: Kimber/N.Y.: Crown, 1954. 285p, illus. 22cm. From the original: *La conquête de l'Everest par le Sherpa Tenzing* (Paris: Scorpion, 1953)

M36. MANCHESTER UNIVERSITY
Hindu Kush Expedition, 1977: [final report]. Enfield: The Expedition, [1978]. 14p, illus, map. 30cm.

M37. MANDOLF, Henry Ikarus (1897-1972)
Basic mountaineering. Edited by . . .San Diego: Sierra Club, 1961. 112p, illus.
—2nd ed. 1967.
—3rd ed.

M38. MANNERING, George Edward (1862-1947)
Eighty years in New Zealand: embracing fifty years of New Zealand fishing. Christchurch: Simpson & Williams, 1943. 255p, plates, illus. 23cm.
Miscellaneous reminiscences of a varied life written in old age. Includes some climbing.

M39. MANNERING, G. E.
Mount Cook and its surrounding glaciers. Auckland: Whitcombe & Tombs, [192?]. 1v (chiefly illus, map). 22 × 29cm.

M40. MANNERING, G. E.
With axe and rope in the New Zealand alps. Ldn: Longmans, 1891. xii, 139p, 17 plates, illus, map. 24cm.
Memoirs of a New Zealand mountaineer who was responsible for much exploration and survey work in the Mount Cook area. Co-founder of the New Zealand Alpine Club with A. P. Harper.

M41. MANNIN, Ethel
Confessions and impressions.
First volume of autobiography; some of her novels include climbing.

M42. MANNIN, E.
Privileged spectator. Ldn: Hutchinson, [1938].
Second volume of autobiography; discusses the writing of her mountain novel, *Men are unwise.*

M43. MANNIN, E.
Brief voices. Ldn: Hutchinson, 1959.
Third volume of autobiography; war-time holidays in the Lakes, and her novel, *Late have I loved thee,* which includes climbing.

M44. MANNING, Harvey & MILLER, Tom
The North Cascades. [Text by Harvey Manning. Photographs by Tom Miller.] Seattle: Mountaineers, 1964. 95p, illus, maps, bibl. 31cm.
Photo-album; spectacular photography. Includes Ptarmigan Traverse.

M45. MANNING, H.
The wild Cascades: forgotten parkland. S.F.: Sierra Club, 1965? 128p, illus, fold. map. 35cm.
—Softbound ed. 160p.

M46. MANNING, Robert E. (Editor)
Mountain passages: an Appalachian anthology. Boston: Appalachian Mountain Club, 1982. [xv], 229p, 22 plates, illus.
Selections from the first 100 years of America's oldest mountaineering journal.

M47. MARAINI, Fosco (b.1912)
Karakoram: the ascent of Gasherbrum IV. Trans. from the Italian by James Cadell.. N.Y.: Viking Press/Ldn: Hutchinson, 1961. 320p, 80 plates (some col), illus, maps, bibl. 24cm. From the original: *Gasherbrum 4°.* (Bari: Leonardo da Vinci, 1959)
This finely illustrated book by an Italian mountaineer-scholar is a worthy successor to de Filippi's great work on the same region.

M48. MARAINI, F.
Secret Tibet. Trans. from the Italian by Eric Mosbacher. Ldn: Hutchinson, 1952. 306p, plates, illus, map, bibl. 25cm.
—U.S. ed. N.Y: Viking Press, 1953.
—R.U. ed. 1954. 251p.
Personal account of Giuseppe Tucci's second trip to Lhasa in 1948; finely illustrated.

M49. MARAINI, F.
Where four worlds meet: Hindu Kush 1959. Trans. from the Italian by Peter Green. Ldn: Hamish Hamilton/N.Y.: Wolf & Harcourt Brace, 1964. xii, 290p, 100 plates (some col), illus, maps. 25cm. From the original: *Parapàmiso* (Bari: Leonardo da Vinci, 1963)
—Another ed. R.U./Hamish Hamilton, 1965.
Ascent of Saraghrar. Another of Maraini's finely illustrated works.

M50. MARCH, William
Improvised rescue techniques. Edinburgh: Jacobean Press, 1974. [ix], 94p, illus. 21cm. Spiral-bound. Cover title: *Improvised techniques in mountain rescue.*

M51. MARCH, W.
Modern rope techniques in mountaineering: incorporating 'Improvised techniques in mountain rescue'. Manchester/Milnthorpe: Cicerone Press, 1976. 127p, illus. 17cm. R.P., 1977.
—2nd rev. ed. 1978.
—3rd rev. ed. 1985.

M52. MARCH, W.
Modern snow and ice techniques. Manchester/Milnthorpe: Cicerone Press, 1973. 66p, 7 plates, illus. 16cm. R.P., 1974-77.
—2nd ed. 1980. 72p.
—Completely rev. ed. 1984. 96p.

M53. MARINER, Wastl
Mountain rescue techniques. Drawings by Fritz and Gert Ebster. First aid instructions by Hans Heinz Seidel. Revised by and trans. from the German by O. T. Trott & K. G. Beam. Innsbruck: Austrian Alpine Club/Seattle: Mountaineers, 1963. 200p, illus. 21cm.

M54. MARKHAM, Sir Clements R. (1830-1916)
A memoir on the Indian Surveys. Ldn: W. H. Allen, 1871. xxv, 303p, fold. col. plates, maps. 29cm.
—2nd ed. Ldn: Allen/Stanford: King Trübner, 1878. xxix, 481p, 5 maps. 28cm.
—Reprint of 2nd ed. Amsterdam, 1968.
Markham was widely travelled and gives a history of Himalayan survey work during his service with the Survey of India.

M55. MARRIOTT, Michael
Mountains and hills of Britain: a guide to the uplands of England, Scotland and Wales. Ldn: Willow Books Collins, 1982. 176p, illus (some col), maps. 27cm.

M56. MARSH, Terry
Summits of Snowdonia: a guide to the 600-metre mountains of Snowdonia. Ldn: Hale, 1984. 192p, illus. 18 maps.

M57. MARSHALL, Howard Percival
Men against Everest. Ldn: Country Life, 1954. 64p, 17 plates, illus. 23cm.
History up to first ascent.

M58. MARSHALL, Robert
Arctic wilderness: exploring the central Brooks Range. Berkeley: Univ. California Press, 1956. xxvi, 171p, illus, maps (1 fold.). 24cm.
—2nd ed. entitled *Alaska wilderness.* Univ. California Press, 1970. 173p, plates, illus. 23cm. Softbound. R.P., 1973.
Account of Marshall's four trips to the northern Koyukuk drainage basin and Brooks Range, 1929, 1930-1, 1938-9. Includes mountaineering experiences (about 28 peaks, mostly first ascents).

M59. MARTY, Sid
Men for the mountains. Seattle: Mountaineers, 1978. 270p. 23cm.
A Park Warden's anecdotes including climbing, rescues, etc.

M60. M[ARTYN] T[homas] (1735-1825)
Sketch of a tour through Swisserland: with an accurate map. Ldn: G. Kearsley, 1787. 98p, map. 18cm. Bound with *an appendix containing catalogues of paintings ...in different parts of Italy.* This has its own title-page and is separately paginated.
—New ed. 1788. With *An appendix to the Sketch of a tour through Swisserland, containing a short account of an expedition to the summit of Mont Blanc, by M. De Saussure of Geneva, in August last;* paginated 99-127.
—[2nd ed.] 131p. 18cm. The main title-page is altered to read: *Sketch of a tour through Swisserland: with an accurate map. A new edition, to which is added a short account of an expedition to the summit of Mont Blanc, by M. De Saussure, of Geneva.* The title-page of the supplement reads: *A short account of an expedition to the summit of Mont Blanc, by M. De Saussure of Geneva, in August last; in order to ascertain the height of that celebrated mountain, the loftiest point of the three ancient continents, and to make a variety of observations and experiments of the form and structure of the mountain, the state of the air, with many other curious particulars.*

M61. MASON, Gene W.
Minus three. Englewood Cliffs, NJ: Prentice-Hall, 1970. 190p, col. illus. 23cm.
Account of his ascents of McKinley, Aconcagua and Kilimanjaro.

M62. MASON, Kenneth (1887-1976)
Abode of snow: a history of Himalayan exploration and mountaineering. Ldn: Hart-Davis/N.Y.: Dutton, 1955. xii, 372p, 20 plates, illus. 23cm. R.P., 1955.
Mason was Superintendent of the Survey of India. His book is the most authoritative one volume reference source on the historical and geographical background to the entire Himalayan range, with a remarkably concise and comprehensive history of Himalayan exploration.

M63. MASON, K.
Completion of the link connecting the triangulations of India and Russia, 1913. Dehra Dun: Survey of India, 1914. (Records of the Survey of India, v.6)
Mason went to the 17,000 ft survey stations on the Sino-Russian frontier and worked southwards over the Taghdumbash Pamir. Not in Yakushi.

M64. MASON, K.
Exploration of the Shaksgam Valley and Aghil Ranges, 1926. Dehra Dun: Geodetic Branch Office, Survey of India, 1928. xii, 182p, plates (1 fold. col), illus, map (in pkt). 26cm. (Records of Survey of India, v.22)
Important survey expedition with reference to K2.

M65. MASON, K.
Routes in the western Himalaya, Kashmir etc.: with which are included

Montgomerie's routes, revised and re-arranged. Vol. 1. Punch, Kashmir and Ladakh. Dehra Dun: Trigonometrical Survey of India, 1922. xvii, 273p, fold. col. plates, maps (in pkt). 26cm.
—Additions and corrections, [1925].
—2nd ed. Calcutta: Government of India Press, 1929. 223p, map.

M66. MATHEWS, Charles Edward (1834-1905)
The annals of Mont Blanc: a monograph. Ldn: Fisher Unwin, 1898. xxiv, 368p, 28 plates, illus, fold. map, bibl. 23cm. Two different bindings seen: brown-orange cloth with green leather labels: grey cloth with gilt illustration on front cover.
—U.S. ed. Boston: Page, 1900. xxiv, 367p, fold. col. map. 23cm.
A history of climbing on Mont Blanc by an original member of the Alpine Club and President, 1878-80.

M67. MATSUURA, Teruo
K2 West face: the first ascent, by the Waseda University K2 Expedition, 1981. Tokyo: Waseda Univ. A.C., 1982. 24p (9 in English), 4 col. plates, illus, map. Paper-bound. Yak. j. 855.

M68. MATSUURA, T.
West ridge of K2: first ascent by the Waseda University Alpine Club K2 Expedition, 1981. Tokyo: Waseda Univ. A.C., 1983. 144p, col. illus, 2 maps. Summary and photo captions in English. Horiz. format. Yak. j. 855.
Dramatic, finely reproduced colour illustrations.

M69. MATTHEWS, Donald Stafford
Medicine my passport. Ldn: Harrap, 1957. 256p, illus.
Autobiography; references to 1954 Kanchenjunga reconnaissance expedition.

M70. MAY, Julian
Hillary and Tenzing: conquerors of Mt. Everest. Creative Ed., 1972. 40p.

M71. MAY, William G.
Mountain search and rescue techniques. Boulder: Rocky Mountain Rescue Group, 1972.

M72. MAZAMAS
Oregon, out of doors: Mount Hood. Portland: Mazamas, 1920. 121p, illus.

M73. MAZEAUD, Pierre (b.1929)
Naked before the mountain. Trans. [from the French] by Geoffrey Sutton. Ldn: Gollancz, 1974. 256p, 24 plates, illus. 23cm. From the original: *Montagne pour un homme nu* (Paris: Arthaud, 1971). First published in Germany as *Schritte himmelwärts* (Hering-Verlag, 1968)
Memoirs of a French lawyer, politician and mountaineer who survived the disaster on the Pillar of Frêney with Walter Bonatti.

→ **M74. [MAZUCHELLI, Elizabeth Sarah ('Nina') (1832-1914)]**
The Indian Alps and how we crossed them: being a narrative of two years' residence in the eastern Himalaya and two months' tour into the interior, by a lady pioneer [i.e. Nina Mazuchelli], illustrated by herself. Ldn: Longmans, 1876. xvii, 612p, 10 col. plates, illus, fold. map. 27cm.
—U.S. ed. N.Y.: Dodd Mead, [1876?].
A handsome volume, described by Freshfield as a 'trivial and topographically obscure narrative'. The author and her Army chaplain husband followed the Nepal-Sikkim frontier along the Singalila Ridge.

M75. MEADE, Charles Francis (1881-1975)
Approach to the hills. Ldn: Murray/N.Y.: Dutton, 1940. [x], 265p, 16 plates, illus. 23cm. R.P., 1941.
—Albemarle Library ed. Murray, 1948.
Some Alpine stories plus the author's Himalayan experiences; he attempted Kamet three times, 1910-3.

M76. MEADE, C. F.
High mountains. Ldn: Harvill Press, 1954. 136p, 11 plates, illus. 22cm.
Examines the question of mountains and nature mysticism.

M77. MEANY, Edmond Stephen (1862-1935)
Mount Rainier: a record of exploration. Edited by . . .Portland: Binford & Morts/N.Y.: Macmillan, 1916. xii, 325p, 17 plates, illus. 23cm.

Extracts from the accounts of explorers, 1792-1914. The author was a president of The Mountaineers.

M78. MEANY, E. S.

Mountain camp fires. Seattle: Lowman & Hanford, 1911. viii, 90p, plates, illus. 19cm.
Volume of songs and poems.

M79. MELBOURNE UNIVERSITY MOUNTAINEERING CLUB

Equipment for mountaineering: a guide to the choice of equipment for the bush walker, rock climber, caver and mountaineer.
—2nd ed. Melbourne Univ. Press, 1965. 120p.

M80. MELDRUM, Kim & ROYLE, Brian

Artificial climbing walls. Ldn: Pelham, 1970. 69p, 12 plates, illus. 23cm.
Their design and use.

M81. MENDENHALL, Ruth Dyar & John Dale (1911-83)

Introduction to rock and mountain climbing. Illustrated by Vivian Mendenhall. Harrisburg, PA: Stackpole Books, 1969. 192p, illus. 19cm.
—2nd ed. entitled *Beginner's guide to rock and mountain climbing.* Stackpole, 1975. xv, 202p, col. plates, fold. map. 21cm.
—3rd rev. ed. entitled *Challenge of rock and mountain climbing.*

M82. MERRICK, Hugh (pseud. Harold A. Meyer) (1898-1980)

The Alps in colour. Text by ..., photographs by Robert Löbl. Ldn: Constable, 1970. 237p, col. illus. 29cm.

M83. MERRICK, H.

The perpetual hills: a personal anthology of mountains. Ldn: Newnes, 1964. 247p, plates, illus. 26cm.

M84. MERRICK, H.

Rambles in the Alps. Written and illustrated by . . .Ldn: Country Life, 1951. 128p, illus, maps. 29cm.

M85. MERZBACHER, Gottfried (1846-1926)

The central Tian-Shan Mountains, 1902-1903. Published under the authority of the Royal Geographical Society. Ldn: Murray/N.Y.: Dutton, 1905. x, 294p, 18 plates, illus, fold. map. 23cm.
Mountain exploration on the Sino-Russian frontier. The author was a German climber and explorer, active in the Dolomites, Caucasus and ranges of central Asia.

M86. MESSNER, Reinhold (b.1944)

The big walls: history, routes, experiences. Trans. from the German by Audrey Salkeld. Ldn: Kaye & Ward/N.Y.: Oxford, 1978. 144p, illus (some col). 27cm.
Includes Alpine climbs, Nanga Parbat south face, Dhaulagiri south face, Aconcagua south face. Messner, a German-speaking Italian from the South Tyrol, is the leading figure in modern mountaineering. He has climbed all of the fourteen 8000-metre peaks.

M87. MESSNER, R.

The challenge: two men alone at 8000m. Trans. from the German by Noel Bowman and Audrey Salkeld. Ldn: Kaye & Ward/N.Y.: Oxford, 1977. 205p, 16 col. plates, illus. 24cm.
Unsuccessful attempt on Lhotse south face in 1975 with Cassin's expedition; followed by his Alpine-style ascent of Hidden Peak (8068m) with Peter Habeler.

M88. MESSNER, R.

Everest: expedition to the ultimate. Trans. from the German by Audrey Salkeld. Ldn: Kaye & Ward/N.Y.: Oxford/Delhi: Vision Books, 1979. 254p, 32 col. plates, illus. 24cm.
First ascent without oxygen with Peter Habeler.

M89. MESSNER, R. & GOGNA, Alessandro

K2 mountain of mountains. Trans. [from the German] by Audrey Salkeld. Ldn: Kaye & Ward/N.Y.: Oxford, 1981. 176p, illus, (chiefly col). 27cm.
History and 1979 expedition.

M90. MESSNER, R.
The seventh grade: most extreme climbing. Ldn: Kaye & Ward/N.Y.: Oxford, 1974. 160p, 4 col. plates, illus. 21cm.
Accounts of Messner's early Alpine climbs and training.

M91. MESSNER, R.
Solo Naga Parbat. Trans. from the German by Audrey Salkeld. Ldn: Kaye & Ward/N.Y.: Oxford/Delhi: Vision Books, 1980. 268p, illus (some col). 24cm.
Solo ascent of the Diamir Flank by a new route in 1978.

M92. MEYER, Hans (1858-1929)
Across East African glaciers: an account of the first ascent of Kilimanjaro. Trans. from the German by E. H. S. Calder. Ldn: George Philip, 1891. xx, 404p, 21 plates, illus, 3 col. fold. maps. 26cm. Also a limited numbered edition of 50 copies on Japanese vellum, signed by the author. From the original: *Ostafrikanische Gletscherfahrten: Forschungsreisen im Kilimandscharo-Gebiet* (Leipzig, 1890)
First undisputed ascent of Kibo Peak; handsome volume.

M93. MEYER, H.
In the high Andes of Ecuador: Chimborazo, Cotopaxi, etc. Ldn: Williams & Norgate, 1908. Plates, illus. In portfolio. 24 large quarto chromolithographic plates, from paintings by Rudolf Reschreiter and 20 plates with 40 phototypes from the originals of various artists and explorers. Preface and 24 pages of explanatory text by Meyer, abstracted from his lengthy book, *In den Hoch-Anden von Ecuador* (Berlin: Reimer, 1907).

M94. MEYERS, George
Yosemite climber: action photographs from the world's leading rock-climbing area. Ldn: Diadem/Modesto, CA: Robbins Mountain Letters, 1979. 96p, illus (chiefly col). 29cm. R.P., 1983.
Fine photo-album.

M95. MEYERSTEIN, E. H. W.
The climbers: an ode on the Eton masters who lost their lives descending the Piz Roseg on August 17th, 1933. Ldn: Metcalfe & Cooper, 1934. 5p. 28cm.

M96. MICHELET, Jules
The mountain. From the French of Michelet by the translator of 'The Bird' [W. H. D. Adams]; with . . .illustrations from designs by Percival Skelton. Ldn: Nelson, 1872. xvi, 323p, illus. 26cm.
—Another ed. 1886. 260p, illus. 21cm.

M97. MIDDLETON, Dorothy
Victorian lady travellers. Ldn: Routledge & Kegan Paul, 1965. xiii, 182p, 12 plates, illus, map, bibl. 23cm. Also 2nd ptg.
Includes Fanny Bullock Workman.

M98. MILBURN, Geoff
Helyg, Diamond Jubilee, 1925-1985. Climbers' Club, 1985. 255p, illus (some col). Also limited edition of 500 numbered copies signed by the author.
This cottage in North Wales was the first successful climbers' hut in Britain, and was a centre for leading rock-climbers for over 20 years.

M99. MILBURN, Kenneth
Beyond the Swale. Glossop: The Author, 1981. 41p, illus. [8vo?]. Limited edition of 100 numbered copies signed by the author.
Essays, poems, photographs and sketches by a climber; mountains and natural history.

M100. MILES, John C.
Koma Kulshan: the story of Mt. Baker. Seattle: Mountaineers, 1984. 232p, illus. maps, bibl.
Blend of facts and legends about the mountain, including climbing, accidents and rescues.

M101. MILL, Hugh Robert
The record of the Royal Geographical Society, 1830-1930. Ldn: R.G.S., 1930. xvi, 288p, illus. 24cm.

M102. MILLER, Keith J. (Editor)
The Cambridge Staunings Expedition, 1970. Vol. 1. General report and the glaciological projects. Cambridge: Univ. Cambridge, Dept. of Engineering, 1971. 66 leaves, illus, fold. map. 30cm.
East Greenland.

M103. MILLER, K. J.
A photographic album of the 1972 East Greenland Expedition from Cambridge

University. Cambridge: Univ. Cambridge, Dept. of Engineering, 1974. 1v. (chiefly illus). 30cm. (C.U.E.D. Special project report, 3)

M104. MILLER, K. J.
Continents in collision: the International Karakoram Project. Ldn: Geo. Philip, [1982]. [xi], 212p, 32 plates, illus (some col), 11 maps, bibl. 29cm.
150th anniversary expedition of the Royal Geographical Society. Includes climbing narratives.

M105. MILLER, Luree
On top of the world: five women explorers in Tibet. U.S./U.K.: Paddington Press/Canada: Random House, 1976. 222p, illus, maps. 24cm.
—Another ed. Seattle: Mountaineers, 1984. 222p.
Includes Nina Mazuchelli, Isabella Bird, Fanny Bullock Workman.

M106. MILLS, Enos A.
The Rocky Mountain wonderland. Boston: Houghton Mifflin, [1915]. xiv, 363p, plates, illus. 21cm.

M107. MILLS, E. A.
Spell of the Rockies. Boston: Houghton Mifflin, 1911. [xii], 356p, 24 plates, illus. 20cm. R.P., 1929.
—U.K. ed. Ldn: Constable, 1912. xii, 356p.
Mills was the best known of the Longs Peak guides. As a naturalist the establishment of the Rocky Mountain National Park was largely due to his efforts. One of the greatest of John Muir's disciples. The book includes climbing, e.g. Blanca Peak solo in winter.

M108. MILLS, E. A.
Wild life on the Rockies. Boston: Houghton Mifflin, 1909. xii, 263p, plates, illus. 21cm.
Mountain exploration and natural history.

M109. MILLS, Ernest James Edward (1926-62)
Airborne to the mountains. Ldn: Jenkins/N.Y.: Barnes, 1961. 202p, 32 plates, illus, maps. 23cm.
Army expedition to McKinley region. Describes the mixture of excitement, boredom, dangers, discomforts, fatigue and frayed nerves.

M110. MILNE, Malcolm
The book of modern mountaineering. Ldn: Barker/N.Y.: Putnam's, 1968. 304p, illus (some col). 30cm.
Chiefly pictorial with supporting text by well-known climbing personalities.

M111. MILNER, Cyril Douglas
All about taking pictures in the hills with your camera. Ldn: Focal Press, 1955. 56p, 16 plates, illus. 16cm.

M112. MILNER, C. D.
The Dolomites. Ldn: Hale, 1951. xiv, 105p, 97 plates, illus, maps. 26cm. R.P., 1952.
Well illustrated survey of climbing in this important region.

M113. MILNER, C. D.
Mont Blanc and the Aiguilles. Ldn: Hale, 1955. xvi, 176p, 65 plates, illus, maps. 24cm.
Well illustrated survey of climbing in this important region.

M114. MILNER, C. D.
Mountain photography: its art and technique in Britain and abroad. Ldn: Focal Press, 1945. 238p, illus. 25cm. R.P., 1946.
—Rev. ed. in smaller format entitled *The photoguide to mountains for the backpacker and climber.* Focal Press, 1977. 184p, illus. 18cm.

M115. MILNER, C. D.
Rock for climbing. Ldn: Chapman & Hall, 1950. viii, 128p, illus. 26cm.
Photographs of many classic rock-climbs, mostly British Isles, with supporting text.

M116. MILTON, John P.
Nameless valleys, shining mountains: the record of an expedition into the vanishing wilderness of Alaska's Brooks Range. N.Y., 1970. xxiii, 195p, illus. 24cm.

M117. MILTON, William Fitzwilliam, Viscount Milton & CHEADLE, Walter Butler

The North-west passage by land: being the narrative of an expedition from the Atlantic to the Pacific, undertaken with a view of exploring a route across the continent. 1865.
—2nd ed. 1865.
—3rd ed. Ldn: Cassell Petter & Galpin, 1865. xxiv, 400p, plates (2 fold. col), illus, maps. 23cm.
—5th ed. 1866.
—7th ed. 1867.
Story of a very adventurous journey, across Canada, starting from Quebec. The young men were the first tourists to cross the Rockies by the Yellowhead Pass.

M118. [MISCELLANEOUS]

Oh, what a mountain! [U.S.A.]: Milton Bradley Co., 1980. Board game for four players.
'Sky-high fun with hazards that push, shove and sweep you from the mountain path.'

M119. MITCHELL, Elyne

Australia's alps. Sydney: Angus & Robertson, 1946. xii, 185p, 52 plates, illus. 25cm. R.P., 1946.
—2nd ed. smaller format. Sydney, 1962.
The Snowy Mountains: the main attraction is high mountain skiing.

M120. MITCHELL, Richard G. Jr.

Mountaineering first aid: a guide to accident response and first aid care. Seattle: Mountaineers, [1972]. 96p, illus. 22cm. R.P., 1975.
—2nd ed. 1977. 101p. 22cm.
—3rd ed. 1985. by M. Lentz, S. C. MacDonald & J. Carline. 110p,

M121. MITCHELL, R. G.

Mountain experience: the psychology and sociology of adventure. Chicago: Univ. Chicago Press, 1983. 288p.
Study of ordinary people in search of extraordinary adventure, for the discovery of self in work, play and other vital fields of self-expression.

M122. M.I.T. OUTING CLUB

Fundamentals of rock-climbing. M.I.T. Outing Club, Massachusetts Institute of Technology, 1956.
—Softback ed. 1973.

M123. MIURA, Yuichiro

The man who skied down Everest. [Trans. from the Japanese by Eric Perlman.] S.F.: Harper Row, 1978. xii, 170p, illus. [8vo].

M124. MOFFAT, Gwen

On my home ground. Ldn: Hodder, 1968. 256p, 15 plates, illus. 23cm.
Second volume of autobiography.

M125. MOFFAT, G.

Space below my feet. Ldn: Hodder, 1961. 286p, 7 plates, illus. 21cm.
—Penguin paperback. 1976.
First volume of autobiography. The author was a professional mountain guide and has latterly become a prolific writer of mountain thrillers and other books.

M126. MOFFAT, G.

Survival count: a personal journey towards conservation. Ldn: Gollancz, 1972. 175p, 8 plates, illus. 23cm.
Third volume of autobiography.

M127. MOFFAT, G.

Two Star Red: a book about R.A.F. mountain rescue. Ldn: Hodder, 1964. xviii, 206p, 16 plates, illus, maps. 21cm.
A history of the various teams in Britain and elsewhere; and the author's involvement with some of their rescues.

M128. MOLEMAAR, Dee (b.1918)

The challenge of Rainier: a record of the explorations and ascents, triumphs and tragedies on the Northwest's greatest mountain. Seattle: Mountaineers, 1971. xx, 332p, illus. 26cm.
—Rev. ed. 1973.
—Updated ed. 1979. 368p. 23cm.

M129. MOLONY, Eileen (Editor)

Portraits of mountains. Ldn: Dobson, 1950. 117p, 12 plates, illus. 23cm.
Essays on British mountains by well-known climbers.

M130. MONCRIEFF, Ascot Robert Hope

Romance of the mountains. By . . .[i.e. A. R. Hope Moncrieff] Ldn: J. Hogg, [1888]. viii, 376p, plates, illus. 20cm.

M131. MONKHOUSE, Frank & WILLIAMS, Joe

Climber and fellwalker in Lakeland. Newton Abbot: David & Charles, [1972]. 214p, 17 plates, illus, maps. 23cm.
Good general survey.

M132. MONKHOUSE, Patrick

On foot in North Wales. Glasgow: Maclehose, 1934. 247p, illus.
—Another ed. [1986?] in one volume with M133.

M133. MONKHOUSE, P.

On foot in the Peak. Glasgow: Maclehose, 1932. 196p, illus.
—Another ed. [1986?] in one volume with M132.

M134. MONZINO, Guido

The 1973 Italian Everest expedition/La spedizione italiana all'Everest 1973. Milan/Verona, 1976. 256p, 23 col. plates, illus, 2 maps, bibl. 38cm.
In Italian and English.

M135. MOON, Kenneth

Man of Everest: the story of Sir Edmund Hillary. Ldn: Lutterworth Press, 1962. 96p, col. plate, port. 19cm.

M136. MOORCROFT, William (-1825) & TREBECK, George

Travels in the Himalayan provinces of Hindustan and the Panjab; in Ladakh and Kashmir; in Peshawar, Kabul, Kunduz and Bokhara, from 1819 to 1825. Prepared for the press from original journals . . .by Horace Hayman Wilson. Ldn: Murray, 1841. 2v., plates (1 fold.), illus, map. 24cm.
—Facsimile ed. introduced by G. J. Alder. Karachi/Oxford: O.U.P., 1979. 2v. 23cm.
Moorcroft was one of the first to describe routes into the Karakoram. He explored much of Ladakh, placed correctly the Karakoram and Saltoro passes, and his accurate records were a great addition to the knowledge of the western Himalaya.

M137. MOORE, Adolphus Warburton (1841-87)

The Alps in 1864: a private journal. [The Author], 1867. x, 360p, 10 maps. 24cm. Edition of 100 copies for private circulation.
—1st public edition. Edinburgh: Douglas, 1902. xxxvi, 444p, 22 plates, illus, 10 maps. 26cm. Edited by A. B. W. Kennedy.
—Another ed. Oxford: Blackwell, 1939. 2v. Edited by E. H. Stevens.
Moore made extensive Alpine tours in the years 1860-81 including this one with Whymper and Horace Walker in 1864. The Alpine Club hold his later unpublished diaries, parts of which were incorporated into the 1902 edition, including his account of the first ascent of the famous Brenva ice-ridge on Mont Blanc.

M138. MOORE, J. E. S.

To the Mountains of the Moon: being an account of the modern aspect of Central Africa, and of some little known regions traversed by the Tanganyika Expedition in 1899 and 1900. Ldn: Hurst & Blackett, 1901. xvi, 350p, 1 fold. col. plate, illus, maps. 24cm.
The party ascended the Mubuku Valley to Bujongolo and climbed to the main ridge of Mt. Baker by the East Baker Glacier in March, 1900.

M139. MOORE, J. H.

Tears of the Sun-god. Ldn: Faber, 1965. 194p, illus. 23cm.
—T.B.C. ed.
Includes chapters on Roraima and some ascents in the Sierra Nevada de Cocuy, Colombia.

M140. MOORE, Terris (b.1908.)

Mount McKinley: the pioneer climbs. College: Univ. Alaska Press, 1967. xvi, 202p, col. plate, illus, maps. 24cm.
—Paperback ed. 1981.
Written by an American climber who made the first ascent of Minya Konka in 1932. He also climbed several Alaskan peaks and pioneered glacier landing tecniques.

M141. MORAN, Martin

The Munros in winter: 277 summits in 83 days. Newton Abbot: David & Charles, 1986. 240p, col. illus, maps. 24cm.
Scotland.

M142. MORAVETZ, Bruno (Editor)
The big book of mountaineering. Woodbury, NY/Ldn: Barron's, 1980. 284p, col. illus. 34cm.
Contributions by many leading climbers.

M143. MORDECAI, D.
The Himalaya: an illustrated summary of the world's highest mountain ranges. Calcutta: Daw Sen, 1966. 28p, 30 plates, illus. 18 × 31cm.
Annotated list of 569 peaks over 20,000 ft in the Himalaya, Karakoram and Hindu Kush.

M144. MORIN, Micheline (1899-1972)
Everest — from the first attempt to the final victory. Ldn: Harrap/N.Y.: John Day, 1955. 205p, illus (some col), maps. 21cm. From the original: *Everest, du premier assault à la victoire* (Paris: Arthaud, 1953).

M145. MORIN, Nea E. (née Barnard) (b.1905)
A woman's reach: mountaineering memoirs. Ldn: Eyre & Spottiswoode/N.Y.: Dodd Mead, 1968. 188p, 25 plates, illus. 23cm.
Memoirs of one of the leaders in the development of women's climbing; includes a list of first feminine ascents.

M146. MORLEY, M.
Carolina mountains. Boston: Houghton Mifflin, 1913.

M147. MORRIS, James Humphry/Jan (b.1927)
Coronation Everest. Ldn: Faber/N.Y.: Dutton, 1958. 146p, 8 plates, illus. 23cm.
—Schools ed. 1963.
—Another ed. Faber, 1970. 146p. 21cm.
Fascinating account of the first ascent told by the *Times* correspondent who relayed the news to England on the eve of Coronation Day.

M148. MORRIS, J.
Conundrum. Ldn: Faber, 1974. 160p. 23cm.
Autobiography with retrospective chapter on Everest.

M149. MORRIS, John (1896-1981)
Hired to kill: some chapters of autobiography. Ldn: Hart-Davis, 1960. 272p, illus, map. 22cm.
Interesting chapters on his part in the 1922 Everest expedition; also a journey in 1927 in the Hunza area, north of Distaghil Sar.

M150. MORRIS, J.
Traveller from Tokyo. Ldn: Cresset Press, 1943. 163p. 21cm.
Chapter on mountaineering in Japan.

M151. MORRIS, Maurice O.
Rambles in the Rocky Mountains. Ldn, 1864.

M152. MORRISEY, Thomas
20 American peaks and crags. Chicago: Contemporary, 1978. 210p, illus.
Panorama of American climbing — from the low cliffs of the Appalachians to the heights of the western Rockies.

M153. MORRISON, Tony
The Andes. Amsterdam: Time Life Books, 1976. 184p, col. illus, map. 27cm. (World's Wild Places series)
Beautiful pictures; emphasis on natural history.

M154. MORRISON, T.
Land above the clouds. Ldn: Deutsch, 1974.
Deals with the whole Andean chain; emphasis on wildlife.

M155. MORSE, Randy
The mountains of Canada. Edmonton: Hurtig/Seattle: Mountaineers, 1978. 150p, col. illus, bibl. 31cm.

M156. MORSE, R.
The Naked Mountain: an adventure to the deadliest peak in the Himalaya. Toronto: Fleet, 1982. 200p, 7 col. plates, illus. 24cm.
1980 Canadian attempt on the Rupal Flank of Nanga Parbat.

M157. MOSER, Brian & TAYLOR, Donald
The cocaine eaters. Ldn: Longmans, 1965.
Includes ascent of Pico La Reina in the Sierra Nevada de Santa Marta, Colombia.

M158. MOSSO, Angelo
Life of man on the high Alps. Trans. from the 2nd ed. of the Italian by E. Lough Kiesow. Ldn: Fisher Unwin, 1899. xv, 342p, illus. 26cm. From the original: *Fisologia dell'uomo sulle Alpi.* (Milan: Treves, 1897)

M159. MOULD, Daphne Desirée Charlotte Pochin
The mountains of Ireland. Ldn: Batsford, 1955. 160p, 32 plates, illus. 23cm.
Good general survey.

M160. MOUNTAIN RESCUE ASSOCIATION
Mountain rescue equipment and techniques. Co-ordinated by the ...[N.Y.]: A.A.C., 1967. 15p, illus. 28cm. (Mountain rescue and safety education program, article 6)

M161. MOUNTAINEERING ASSOCIATION
A short manual of mountaineering training. By W. C. Burns, F. Shuttleworth & J. E. B. Wright. Ldn: M.A., 1948.
—2nd ed. 1952.
—3rd ed. 1955. 64p, illus. 19cm.
—4th ed. rev. by J. E. B. Wright. 1960.
—5th ed. 1962.
—6th ed. rev. by Peter Gentil. Kaye & Ward, 1964. 78p.

M162. MOUNTAINEERS
The mountain climber's notebook. Seattle: Mountaineers, 1946. 135p, illus.

M163. MOUNTAINEERS
Mountaineer's handbook: the techniques of mountain climbing. Seattle: Superior Pub, 1948. 160p, illus.

M164. MOUNTAINEERS
Mountaineering: the freedom of the hills. Seattle: Mountaineers, 1960. Edited by Harvey Manning. [xiii], 430p, plates, illus. 23cm. R.P., 1967.
—3rd ed. 1974. Edited by Peggy Ferber. [xv], 478p.
—4th ed. 1982. Edited by E. Peters. 550p, illus. 24cm. R.P., 1983.
Internationally recognised instruction manual.

M165. MUDDOCK, J. E. (Editor)
The "J.E.M." guide to Switzerland: the Alps and how to see them.
—2nd ed. Ldn: N. pub., 1882. 274p, plates, illus, maps. 18cm.
—6th ed. rev. & corrected. 1886. xxxii, 412, xxxvp, illus, maps. [12mo].
—8th ed. rev. & corrected.
Includes articles on glaciers, avalanches and mountaineering.

M166. MUIR, John (1838-1914)
The mountains of California. Illustrated from preliminary sketches and photographs furnished by the author. N.Y.: Century/Ldn: Fisher Unwin, 1894. xv, 381p, illus, 2 maps. 20cm. R.P., 1903, 1904, 1907.
—9th ed. enlarged. 1911. 389p. R.P., 1913, 1917, 1921 (i.e.. 12th ptg)
—New ed. Boston: Houghton Mifflin, [1926?]. 2v. 20cm.
—Another ed. N.Y.: Doubleday, 1961.
—Facsimile of original edition. Berkeley: Ten Speed, 1977. 389p, 14 plates, illus, maps.

M167. MUIR, J.
My first summer in the Sierra. [With illustrations from drawings made by the author in 1869 and from photographs by Herbert W. Gleason.] Boston: Houghton Mifflin/Ldn: Constable, 1911. viii, 354p, 12 plates, illus. 21cm. R.P., 1911.
—Another ed. 1916. 272p, illus, fold. map. 19cm.
—Facsimile reprint. 1979. Softback.

M168. MUIR, J.
Steep trails: [California, Utah, Nevada, Washington, Oregon, Grand Canyon]. Edited by William Frederic Badè. Boston: Houghton Mifflin, [1918?]. xi, 391p, 12 plates, illus. 22cm. Also large paper edition of 350 copies.

M169. MUIR, J.
Travels in Alaska. [Prepared for publication by Marion Randall Parsons.] Boston: Houghton Mifflin, 1915. [xii], 329p, 12 plates, illus. 21cm. Also large paper (23cm) edition of 450 copies, with 5 extra illustrations. R.P., 1916 (5th ptg)
—New ed. 1918. 390p.
—Facsimile ed. 1979. With introduction by Edwin Way Teale. Softback.

M170. MUIR, J.
The writings: manuscript edition. Boston: Houghton Mifflin, 1916-24. 10v. 23cm. 750 numbered sets. (Kimes 341).
—Sierra edition. 1917-24. 10v. 19cm.
Muir was a Scottish-born naturalist who emigrated to the United States in early boyhood. He visited Alaska and the Arctic and was very active in California. Founder and President of the Sierra Club; also a founder member of the A.A.C. He exercised considerable influence over American concepts of mountains. As an ardent lover of all natural scenes, animals and open-air life, he was largely responsible for the establishment of Yosemite and other areas as national parks.

M171. MUIR, J.
The Yosemite. N.Y.: Appleton-Century, 1912. 284p, illus, maps. 21cm. R.P., 1935.
—Another ed. With notes and intro. By Frederic R. Gunsky. N.Y.: Doubleday, 1962. 225p, illus, bibl. (Natural History Library series).

M172. MUIR, J.
Yosemite and the Sierra Nevada. Selected writings of John Muir and 64 photographs by Ansel Adams. Boston: Houghton Mifflin, 1948. xix, 132p, illus. 26cm.
Ansel Easton Adams (1902-84) was one of the most famous of all American mountain photographers.

M173. MULGREW, Peter D.
No place for men. Wellington: Reed, 1964. 199p, 24 plates, illus. 23cm.
—U.K. ed. Ldn: Nicholas Vane, 1965. 1st ed. reprinted.
—U.S. ed. entitled *I hold the heights.*
—Another ed. Auckland: Collins, 1975.
Account of Hillary's 1960 expedition to Makalu, experimenting with the effects of high altitude climbing without oxygen. The author was severely crippled by frostbite.

M174. MULLER, Edwin Jr. (1892-1963)
They climbed the Alps. N.Y./Ldn: Cape, 1930. [x] 217p, 16 plates, illus. 22cm.
Résumé of various classic nineteenth century ascents.

M175. MULLER, J. W.
First aid to naturers. N.Y.: Platt & Peck, [1913]. 240p, illus. 19cm.
Skit on the lure of the wild. In the passage on mountaineering it is suggested that people who climb mountains for sport are known as mountaineers; while those who descend are known as survivors. There are also professional survivors, who are called guides.

M176. MULLICK, B. N.
The sky was his limit: the life and climbs of Sonam Gyatso [1923-68]. Dehra Dun: Palit & Dutt, 1970. 200p, illus. 22cm.
Biography of well-known Indian mountaineer whose expeditions included Everest, Cho Oyu, Annapurna III.

M177. MULLIKAN, Mary Augusta & HOTCHKISS, Anna M.
The nine sacred mountains of China: an illustrated record of pilgrimages made in the years 1935-1936. Hong Kong: Vetch & Lee, 1973. xx, 156p, col. plates, illus.

M178. MUMM, Arnold Louis (1859-1927)
The Alpine Club Register. Ldn: Arnold, 1923-8. 3v. 23cm.
Details of all members elected to the Alpine Club from 1857 to 1890, including bibliographical details of their published writings. The volumes cover the periods 1857-63; 1864-76; 1877-90. The dates refer to date of election to the club. The A.C. have typescripts of projected volumes covering the years 1891-1895 & 1896-1901. Invaluable reference source.

M179. MUMM, A. L.
Five months in the Himalaya: a record of mountain travel in Garhwal and Kashmir. Ldn: Arnold/N.Y.: Longmans, 1909. xvi, 263p, 28 plates (4 fold.), illus, 2 fold. maps. 26cm.
Account of the 1907 expedition to Trisul with Longstaff.

M180. MUMEY, Nolie
The Teton Mountains: their history and tradition. With an account of the early fur trade, trappers, missionaries, mountain men and explorers who blazed the trails around the inspiring peaks. Denver:

Artcraft, 1947. xxiii, 462p, illus, fold. map, bibl. 24cm. Limited edition of 700/750? copies signed by the author. Lists the earliest attempts on the peaks.

M181. MUMMERY, Albert Frederick (1855-95)

My climbs in the Alps and Caucasus. [Illustrated by Joseph Pennell and others.] Ldn: Fisher Unwin, 1895. xii, 360p, 11 plates (some col). 28cm. Also edition on Japan paper of 24 numbered and signed copies of which only 20 were for sale. R.P., 1895.
—U.S. ed. N.Y.: Scribner's, 1895.
—2nd ed. [4th ptg]. Ldn: Fisher Unwin, 1908. With intro. by Mrs Mummery and an appreciation by J. A. Hobson. Portrait of author substituted for picture of Aiguille Verte.
—Another ed. Ldn: Nelson, [1913]. With intro and appreciation as 1908 ed.
—Another ed. Oxford: Blackwell, 1936. Edited by H. E. G. Tyndale, with intro. by M. Mummery. R.P., 1946.
—Another ed. N.Y.: Barrows Mussey, [1937]. xxiii, 256p, illus. 21cm.
—Facsimile reprint of 1895 ed. Lawrence, MA: Quarterman Pub, 1974.
Mummery was an expert rock-climber and alpinist who made many important climbs in the Mont Blanc region. He led an expedition to Nanga Parbat in 1895, with Collie and Bruce, and disappeared whilst reconnoitring.

M182. MUNDAY, Walter Alfred Donald (1890-1950)

The unknown mountain. Ldn: Hodder, 1948. xx, 268p, 31 plates, illus, fold. map. 23cm.
—Reprinted. Seattle: Mountaineers.
The Canadian author and his wife discovered Mt. Waddington, in the Coast Mountains of British Columbia, in 1925 and spent nearly ten years trying to climb it.

M183. MUNDELL, Frank

Stories of alpine adventure. Ldn: Sunday School Union, [1898]. 158, [2]p, illus. 19cm.
—Another ed. (two books in one) entitled *Stories of alpine adventure and balloon adventure.* Ldn: Sunday School Union, n.d. 158p, 158p, illus. 19cm. Preface to balloon section dated 1897.
Includes Mont Blanc, Matterhorn and other famous early stories.

M184. MURPHY, Dervla

Eight feet in the Andes. Ldn: Murray, 1983.
—Another ed. Ldn: Century, 1985. 274p, map. 22cm.
—Large print ed. Isis, 1985.
Account of a high-level trek by a well-known travel writer, her daughter and a four-footed friend.

M185. MURRAY, William Hutchinson (b.1913) & WRIGHT, J. E. B.

The craft of climbing. Ldn: Kaye, 1964. 77p, 16 plates, illus. 23cm. Boards.

M186. MURRAY, W. H.

Mountaineering in Scotland. Ldn: Dent, 1947. xii, 252p, 32 plates, illus. 22cm. R.P., 1962.
—Aldine paperback. 1966.
—Reissued in one volume with *Undiscovered Scotland.* Diadem, 1979.
Murray was prominent in Scottish rock and winter climbing in the 1930s, accomplishing many severe new routes. He has also written climbing novels and general books on the Scottish Highlands.

M187. MURRAY, W. H.

The Scottish Himalayan Expedition. [Maps and diagrams by Robert Anderson.] Ldn: Dent, 1951. xiv, 282p, 36 plates (some col), illus, maps. 22cm.
Account of small private expedition to Garhwal Himalaya (Bethatli, Punchi Chuli, etc.).

M188. MURRAY, W. H.

The story of Everest. [Maps and diagrams by Robert Anderson.] Ldn: Dent/N.Y.: Dutton, 1953. ix, 193p, 23 plates, illus. 23cm. R.P., May 1953.
—Rev. ed. 1953. x, 198p. R.P., Aug. 1953.
—Rev. ed. Nov. 1953. x, 218p.
—New ed. 1953. x, 230p.
—Book club ed.
History up to first ascent.

M189. MURRAY, W. H.
Undiscovered Scotland: climbs on rock, snow and ice. [Maps and diagrams by Robert Anderson.] Ldn: Dent, 1951. viii, 232p, 24 plates, illus. 22cm.
—Reissued in one volume with *Mountaineering in Scotland.* Diadem, 1979.

M190. MUSTON, A. J.
[Report of the] British Army Axel Heiberg Expedition, 1972. By ...and others. [Donnington]: The Expedition, [1972?]. 1v. (var. pag.), fold. plate, illus, maps. 30cm.
Arctic.

M191. MUSTON, A. J.
Report of the British Army West Greenland Expedition, 1971. By ...and others. [Donnington]: The Expedition, [1971?]. 1v. (var. pag.), illus, maps. 30cm.

N

N01. [NAESS, Arne]
Tirich Mir. By members of the Norwegian Himalayan Expedition. Trans. [from the Norwegian] by Sölvi and Richard Bateson. Ldn: Hodder, 1952. 192p, 39 plates, illus. 23cm. From the original: *Tirich Mir Til Topps. Den Norske Himalaia-Ekspedisjonen.* (Oslo: Gyldendale, 1950)
First major ascent in the Hindu Kush; Tirich Mir is the highest peak.

N02. NAGASAKI UNIVERSITY ACADEMIC ALPINE CLUB
Account of the Hindu-Kush Expedition of the ...: Koh-e-Bandaka. Nagasaki: The Club, 1971. 72p, illus (some col), maps. 26cm. In Japanese with English summary. Yak. j. 488.
Expedition to Koh-e-Bandaka.

N03. NAGAYAMA, Mokuo
Snowbridge. Tokyo: Hokuseido, 1976.
Poems.

N04. NAGOYA YMCA ALPINE CLUB
Putha Hiunchuli, 7246m. Account of the expedition of autumn, 1972. Nagoya: The Club, 1974. [12], 85p, illus, maps. 26cm. In Japanese with English summary. Yak. j. 504.
Ascent in 1972.

N05. NARAZAKI, Muneshige
Hokusai–the thirty-six views of Mt. Fuji. Tokyo/N.Y./S.F.: Kodansha International, 1968.

N06. NATIONAL GEOGRAPHIC SOCIETY
America's magnificent mountains. Prepared by the special publications Division. Washington, DC: National Geographic Society, 1980. 207p, col. illus. 26cm.
Includes Sierra Nevada, Cascades, Coast Mountains, McKinley, Aspen's Rockies, Mexico's volcanoes, Great Smokies, North Appalachians.

N07. NATIONAL RAILWAY CLIMBERS' CLUB
Karakorum: Prupoo Burhaka. Tokyo: The Club, 1978. 374p, illus (some col), maps. 26cm. In Japanese with English summary. Yak. j. 435.
Expedition to Prupoo Burhaka, an unnamed peak, c.7000m, in 1977.

N08. NAVARRA, Fernand
The forbidden mountain. Trans. from the French by Michel Legat. Ldn: Macdonald, 1956. x, 174p, 15 plates, illus, maps. 23cm. From the original: *L'expédition au Mont Ararat.* (Bordeaux: Biere, 1953)
Ascent of Ararat in search of Noah's Ark.

N09. NAVARRA, F.
The Noah's Ark expedition. Coverdale House, 1974.
Mt. Ararat.

N10. NEGRI, N. C.
The valley of shadows: the story of an arctic expedition. Ldn: Muller, [1956?]. vii, 196p, plates, illus, maps. 20cm.
General account of Lyngen Winter Survey Expedition, 1954-55 to arctic Norway; ascent of Medagstind, Tromma Citadel, description of winter conditions.

N11. NEVE, Arthur (-1919)
Picturesque Kashmir. Ldn: Sands, 1900. xvi, 163p, illus. 25cm.
Well illustrated account of the mountains and glaciers of the district, with description of some of his climbs, e.g. Panamik Peak. The author and his brother Ernest were medical missionaries.

N12. NEVE, A.
Thirty years in Kashmir. Ldn: Arnold, 1913. viii, 316p, 17 plates, illus, fold. map. 23cm.
Holiday expeditions to Nun Kun, Nanga Parbat, etc.

N13. NEVE, Ernest
Beyond the Pir Panjal: life among the mountains and valleys of Kashmir. Ldn: Fisher Unwin, 1912. 320p, plates (1 fold. col), illus, map. 23cm.
—Popular ed. entitled *Beyond the Pir Panjal: life and missionary enterprise in Kashmir.* Ldn: Church Missionary Society, 1914. viii, 178p, illus, map. 22cm. R.P., 1915.
The brothers Arthur and Ernest Neve climbed and travelled extensively in Kashmir, Baltistan and Ladakh in the course of their medical duties. This book includes an account of the ascent of the highest of the Kolahoi peaks in 1911 with Kenneth Mason.

N14. NEW, Charles
Life, wanderings and labours in Eastern Africa: with an account of the first successful ascent [sic] of the Equatorial snow mountain, Kilima Njaro. Ldn: Hodder, 1873. xiii, 528p, plates (1 fold. col), illus, map. 22cm.
—2nd ed. 1874.
New made the second serious attempt on Kilimanjaro in 1871, reaching c.15,000 ft at the then snowline; he described the snow as 'lying on ledges of rock in masses, like large sleeping sheep'.

N15. NEWBY, George Eric (b.1919)
Great ascents: a narrative history of mountaineering. Newton Abbot: David & Charles/N.Y.: Viking Press/Vancouver: Douglas, David & Charles, 1977. 208p, illus (some col). 26cm.
Attractively produced selection of mountaineering highlights.

N16. NEWBY, G. E.
A short walk in the Hindu Kush. Ldn: Secker & Warburg, 1958. 247p, 25 plates, illus, fold. map. 22cm.
—Arrow Books ed., 1961.
—Reprinted from 1st ed. Hodder, 1972.
—Pan Books, 1974.
—Another ed. Ldn: Harvill Press, 1983. 276p.
Two non-mountaineers attempt 19,880 ft Mir Samir in north-east Afghanistan and explore the remote region of Nuristan. Classic work by well-known writer and traveller.

N17. NICHOLS, Starr Hoyt
Monte Rosa: the epic of an alp. Boston: Houghton Mifflin, 1883, 148p. 19cm.
Poetic rendering of an ascent, in flowery language.

N18. NICOLSON, Marjorie
Mountain gloom and mountain glory: the development of the aesthetics of the infinite. Ithaca: Cornell, 1959.
—Another ed. N.Y.: Norton, 1963.
Scholarly study of the development of appreciation of mountains in western literature, leading up to the start of mountaineering.

N19. NICOLSON, Nigel
The Himalayas. Amsterdam: Time Life Books, 1975. 184p, col. illus. 27cm. (World's Wild Places series.)

N20. NIHON UNIVERSITY NEPAL HIMALAYA EXPEDITION
First ascent of Sita Chuchura, 1970. Tokyo: The Expedition, 1974. 15, 67p, illus, maps. 25cm. In Japanese with English summary. Yak j. 540.
Sita Chuchura, an unnamed 6611m peak in Dhaulagiri Himal.

N21. NOCK, Peter
Rock climbing. Ldn: Foyle, 1963. 96p, 4 plates, illus. 19cm.
—Edited and rev. by Donald Law. Foyle, 1975. 80p.

N22. NOEL, John Baptist Lucius
Through Tibet to Everest. Ldn: Arnold, 1927. 302p, 20 plates, illus. 22cm.
—U.S. ed. entitled *Story of Everest.*

Boston: Little Brown, 1927. xiv, 258p, illus. 23cm.
—Kingfisher Library ed. Ldn: Arnold, 1931. 302p, plates, illus. 18cm.
—U.S. ed. Blue Ribbon Books, 1931. 258p.
Account of the first three attempts on Everest by the photographer to the 1922 & 1924 expeditions.

N23. NOORBERGEN, Rene
The Ark file. Mountain View, CA: Pacific Press, 1974.
—Another ed. Ldn: New English Library, 1980. 3-216p, illus, maps. 23cm.
Expeditions to discover Noah's Ark.

N24. NORMAN-NERUDA, Ludwig (1864-98)
The climbs of Norman-Neruda. Edited, and with an account of his last climb, by May Norman-Neruda. Ldn: Fisher Unwin, 1899. xii, 335p, 30 plates, illus. 23cm.
Norman-Neruda was a leading climber of his day, some of his ascents still being highly regarded. He was taken ill and died during a climb.

N25. NORRIS, Dermot
Kashmir, the Switzerland of India: a descriptive guide with chapters on skiing and mountaineering, etc. Calcutta: Newman/Ldn: Forster Groom Field Press, [1932]. 294, xiip, illus, maps. 19cm.

N26. NORTHEY, William Brook
The land of the Gurkhas: or, The Himalayan Kingdom of Nepal. With a chapter by C. G. Bruce. Cambridge: Heffer & Sons, [1937]. x, 248p, illus, map. 23cm.
—Reprinted. N.Y.: Ams Press, 1975.
Northey served twenty years with the Gurkhas and gives an account of the geography, history, ethnology, etc. of Nepal.

N27. NORTH LONDON HINDU KUSH EXPEDITION, 1978
Report. The Expedition, [1979?]. 32p, illus, maps.
Ascent of Thui II.

N28. NORTH OF ENGLAND KISHTWAR EXPEDITION, 1978
[*Report*]. [*Bakewell*]: The Expedition, [1979]. 40p, maps. 22cm.

N29. NORTHERN IRELAND YOUTH EXPEDITION, 1980
Polish peaks: an account of the . . .to the Polish Tatras. Belfast: Published for the . . .by the Standing Conference of Youth Organizations in Northern Ireland, 1981. 43p. 30cm.
Climbing expedition.

N30. NORTON, Boyd
The Grand Tetons. 128p, col. plates. [4to].
Describes history and personal adventures — climbing, snow-shoeing, backpacking, etc.

N31. NORTON. Edward Felix (1884-1954)
The fight for Everest: 1924. By . . . and other members of the expedition. Ldn: Arnold/N.Y: Longmans, 1925. xii, 372p, 32 plates (some col), illus, fold. map. 26cm.
Norton took over the leadership of the 1924 expedition during which he climbed to a height of c.28,100 ft without oxygen.

N32. NOTT, David
Angels four: the first ascent of the face of Angel Falls, the highest waterfall in the world. Englewood Cliffs, NJ: Prentice-Hall, 1972. 191p, illus, maps. [8vo]. Also 2nd, 3rd ptgs.
This 3,000 ft Venezuelan waterfall is named after the stunt flyer Jimmy Angel who discovered it.

N33. NOTT, D.
Into the Lost World. Englewood Cliffs, NJ: Prentice-Hall, 1975. 186p, illus. 22cm.
Descent into the summit caverns of Roraima, Guyana, inspiration for Conan Doyle's novel about prehistoric monsters.

N34. NOYCE, Cuthbert Wilfrid Frank (1917-62)
The climber's fireside book. Compiled by . . .Ldn: Heinemann, 1964. xvi, 268p, 16 plates, illus. 22cm.
Anthology which follows the development of climbing.

N35. NOYCE, C. W. F.
Climbing the Fish's Tail. Ldn: Heinemann, 1958. xiv, 150p, 25 plates, illus. 21cm.
Uncompleted ascent of Machapuchare, Nepal Himalaya.

N36. NOYCE, C. W. F.
Everest is climbed. By . . .and R. Taylor. Harmondsworth, Middx: Penguin Books, 1954. 31p, illus. 19 × 23cm. (Puffin Picture book)

N37. NOYCE, C. W. F.
Mountains and men. Ldn: Bles, 1947. 160p, 17 plates, illus, maps. 25cm.
—2nd ed. with rev. preface. 1954.
Autobiography, including wartime climbing at Sonamarg in the Himalaya. Ends with his accident on Great Gable and rescue by Rusty Westmorland, leading to the formation of the Keswick Mountain Rescue Team. Noyce was one of the best climber-writers of his generation. He died in a climbing accident in the Pamirs.

N38. NOYCE, C. W. F.
Poems. Ldn: Heinemann, 1960. 98p. 23cm.

N39. NOYCE, C. W. F.
Scholar mountaineers: pioneers of Parnassus. With wood-engravings by R. Taylor. Ldn: Dennis Dobson, 1950. 164p, 12 plates, illus. 22cm.
Essays on the effect of mountains on various historical figures, e.g. Dante, Keats, Nietzsche, Wordsworth and others.

N40. NOYCE, C. W. F.
South Col: one man's adventure on the ascent of Everest, 1953. Ldn: Heinemann, 1954/N.Y.: Sloane, 1955. xx, 303p, 52 plates (some col), illus, maps. 22cm. Also 2nd ptg.
—Abridged ed. New Windmill series. Heinemann, 1956.
Noyce's work on the Lhotse face opened the way to the South Col. One of the best personal accounts of an Everest expedition.

N41. NOYCE, C. W. F.
The springs of adventure. Ldn: Murray, 1958. xii, 240p, 16 plates, illus. 22cm.
—U.S. ed. Cleveland: World Pub., 1958. 255p.
An examination of man's reasons for seeking adventure; includes mountaineering examples.

N42. NOYCE, C. W. F.
They survived: a study of the will to live. Ldn: Heinemann, 1962. xiv, 202p, 12 plates, illus. 22cm.
—U.S. ed. N.Y: Dutton, 1963.
Includes mountaineering examples.

N43. NOYCE, C. W. F.
To the unknown mountain: ascent of an unexplored twenty-five thousander in the Karakoram. Ldn: Heinemann, 1962. xii, 183p, 13 plates, illus. 22cm.
Ascent of Trivor.

N44. NOYCE, C. W. F. & MCMORRIN, Ian (Editors)
World atlas of mountaineering. Ldn: Nelson, 1969. 224p, 48 plates, illus (some col), 32 maps. 28cm.
—U.S. ed. N.Y: Macmillan, 1970.
Informative and well illustrated; the maps are the weakest part.

N45. NÜNLIST, Hugo
Spitsbergen: the story of the 1962 Swiss Spitsbergen expedition. Ldn: Kaye/N.Y.: Barnes, 1966. 191p, 24 plates, illus, maps. 24cm. From the original: *Spitsbergen* (Zurich: Orell Fussli, 1963)
Describes the pleasures and drawbacks of climbing in Spitsbergen.

N46. NYKA, J.
In the Polish Tatra Mountains. Warsaw: Interpress, 1971. 127p, illus (some col).
General interest.

N47. NYQUIST, F. P. (Editor)
Jotun Heimen: challenge of a mountain wilderness. Oslo, 1977. English text.

O

O01. [OESTERREICHISCHER ALPENVEREIN]
Cordillera Huayhuash Perú: ein Bildwerk über ein tropisches Hochgebirge. [Edited by the 1954 Andes Expedition of the Oe.A.V.] Innsbruck: Tiroler Graphik, [1955]. 42p text in German, Spanish and English, 63 plates, illus. 27cm.
Fine photo-album with introductory text.

O02. OGAKI HIMALAYAN COMMITTEE
Ascent of Sha-i-Anjuman. Edited by the Committee. Ôgaki: The Committee, 1969. var. pag., illus (some col), 35 sheets of maps. 21cm. In Japanese with English summary. Yak. j. 112.
Hindu Kush expedition in 1968.

O03. OKADA, Koyo
Mount Fuji. Tokyo: Hobundo Co., 1959.

O04. O'KANE, Walter Collins
Trails and summits of the White Mountains. Boston: Houghton Mifflin, 1925. [xi], 308p, 24 plates, illus. 17cm.
Eastern U.S.A.

O05. OKAYAMA UNIVERSITY ALPINE CLUB
Dhaulagiri V, 1975. Okayama: The Club, 1976. 255-432p, illus (some col), maps. In Japanese with English summary. Yak. j. 141.
Offprint of mountaineering section of official report (Yak. j. 140).

O06. OKAYAMA UNIVERSITY SCIENTIFIC & MOUNTAINEERING EXPEDITION
Okayama University Nepal Himalaya Expedition, 1975. Scientific research in Nepal and first ascent of Dhaulagiri V. Okayama: The Executive Committee, 1976. 433p, illus (some col), maps. In Japanese with English summary. Yak. j. 104.

O07. OKI, Masato
Dhaula Himal: journey in northwest Nepal. Nagoya: The Author, 1968. 77p, illus, maps. 18cm. In Japanese with English summary. Yak. j. 143.
Personal account of Aichi-ken Mountaineering Union expedition to Dhaulagiri II in 1965.

O08. OKI, M. & TOKUNAGA, Susumu
From Kashmir to Swat in 1971: account of the Meijô University 2nd Himalayan expedition. Nagoya: The Expedition, 1971. 63p, illus, maps. 26cm. In Japanese with English summary. Yak. j. 148.
Ascents of Kolahoi etc.

O09. OKI, M. & SAWADA, Munechika
From Mir Samir to Falaksar: account of the Meijô University first Himalayan expedition. Nagoya: Meijô Univ. Alpine Club, 1970. 41p, illus, maps. 26cm. In Japanese with English summary. Yak. j. 147.
Ascent of Mir Samir in the Hindu Kush.

O10. OLIVER, William Dudley
Crags and craters: rambles in the island of Réunion. Ldn: Longmans, 1896. xiv, 213p, illus, fold. map. 20cm.
Includes climbs on Piton des Neiges, Salazes, etc.

O11. OLSEN, John Edward
The climb up to hell. Ldn: Gollancz, 1962. 191p, 16 plates, illus. 22cm. R.P., 1963. —U.S. ed. N.Y.: Harper Row, 1963. 212p.
Rescue of Corti from the Eigerwand in 1957.

O12. OPPENHEIM, Edwin Camillo (1868-1941)
New climbs in Norway: an account of some ascents in the Sondmore district. Ldn: Fisher Unwin, 1898. x, 257p, plate, illus. 21cm.

O13. OPPENHEIM, E. C.
The reverberate hills. Ldn: Constable, 1914. viii, 56p. 20cm. R.P., 1921.
Poems.

O14. OPPENHEIMER, Lehmann J. (1868-1916)
The heart of Lakeland. Ldn: Sherratt & Hughes, 1908. [xiv], 196p, 38 plates, illus. 24cm.
Lehmann was an artist-climber who was killed in World War I. He encouraged his fellow-climbers in many new climbs and is best remembered for his pioneer work on the Buttermere crags.

O15. ORLOB, Helen
Mountain rescues. N.Y.: Nelson, 1963. 176p, illus. [8vo].
Accounts of rescues in the western U.S., Canada and McKinley.

O16. ORMES, Robert M.
Farewell to Ormes: a Colorado mountain life in retrospect. Colorado Springs:

Hardlea Press, 1984. 189p, illus. 22cm. Boards.
Autobiography of Colorado climber active in the 1930s and author of a well-known guidebook to the region.

O17. OSAKA CITY UNIVERSITY ALPINE CLUB
Expedition to Langtang Lirung, 1978. Osaka: The Club, 1980. [44], 195p, illus (some col), maps. 26cm. In Japanese with English summary. Yak. j. 117.
First ascent.

O18. OSAKA CITY UNIVERSITY ALPINE CLUB
The first ascent of Kanjiroba Himal in 1970. Osaka: The Club, 1972. [26], 184p, illus, maps. 26cm. In Japanese with English summary. Yak. j. 116.
The club's third Himalayan expedition.

O19. OUNDLE SCHOOL
Expedition to Ecuador, 1975: report. [Peterborough]: Oundle School, 1975. 94 leaves. 32cm.

O20. OUTRAM, Sir James, Bart (1864-1925)
In the heart of the Canadian Rockies. N.Y.: Macmillan, 1905. xiv, 466p, illus, 3 maps (1 fold). 23cm. R.P., 1906, 1923.
Complete account of the exploration of the range. Outram made first ascents of Assiniboine, Columbia, Forbes and other peaks. Originally a clergyman, he succeeded to the title in 1912 and spent most of his life in Canada after 1900.

O21. OXFORD EXPEDITION TO THE HINDU KUSH, 1977
[*Report*]. The Expedition, 1978. 31 leaves, maps. 30cm.

O22. OXFORD HIMALAYAN EXPEDITION, 1973
[*Report*[. East Hanney: The Expedition, [1974]. 36p, illus, maps. 30cm.

O23. OXFORD UNIVERSITY
Baffin Island Expedition, 1976: [report]. Oxford: The Expedition, [1977]. 40p, illus. 30cm.

O24. OXFORD UNIVERSITY MOUNTAINEERING CLUB
Expedition to Kishtwar Agyasol '81: report. The Expedition, [1982?]. 28p, map.

O25. OXLEY, T. Louis
Jacques Balmat: or, The first ascent of Mont Blanc, a true story. [Trans. from the French from a narrative by Venance Payot.] Ldn: Kerby & Endean, 1881. 38p. 19cm.
Only in recent times has Dr. Paccard's part in the first ascent of Mont Blanc been recognized as superior to Balmat's.

P

P01. PACKARD, Winthrop
White Mountain trails: . . . to the summit of Mount Washington and other summits of the White Hills. Boston, 1917. xiv, 311p, plates, illus. 22cm.

P02. PACKE, Charles Jr. (1826-96)
A guide to the Pyrenees: especially intended for the use of mountaineers. Ldn: Longmans, 1862. xvi, 130p, plates (2 fold., some col), illus, maps. 18cm.
—2nd ed. rewritten and much enlarged. 1867.
Packe was largely responsible for opening up the Pyrenees as a climbing district and his guide remained the standard work until the turn of the century.

P03. PALLIS, Marco
Peaks and lamas. Ldn: Cassell, 1939. iii-xx, 428p, 72 plates, illus, maps. 25cm. With a chapter by Colin Kirkus.
—U.S. ed. 1940.
—Rev. U.S. ed. 1942.
—3rd rev. U.S. ed. N.Y.: Knopf, 1949. xiii, 397p.
—3rd rev. & enlarged U.K. ed. Ldn: Woburn Books, 1974. xvii, 435p.
Expeditions to Garhwal and Sikkim but largely about Tibetan Buddhism.

P04. PALLIS, M.
The way and the mountain. Ldn: Peter Owen, 1960. 216p, illus. 22cm. R.P., 1961.

Mountain mysticism. Chapter illustrating the concept that all true paths lead to enlightment, i.e. the top of the mountain.

P05. PALLISER, John

The journals, detailed reports and observations relative to the explorations by Captain Palliser. Ldn: Eyre & Spottiswoode, 1863.

Palliser led an expedition, 1857-60, into the unknown wilds of western Canada to prospect for possible railway routes. One of his companions was Dr. James Hector who accomplished much of the very rough exploration.

P06. PALMER, Howard (1883-1944)

Edward W. D. Holway: a pioneer of the Canadian alps. Minneapolis: Univ. Minnesota Press, 1931. xiv, 81p, plates, illus, map, bibl. 22cm.

Holway and Palmer made many first ascents in the Selkirks.

P07. PALMER, H.

Mountaineering and exploration in the Selkirks: a record of pioneer work among the Canadian alps. 1908-1912. N.Y.: Putnam, 1914. xxviii, 439p, 139 plates, illus, maps (1 col, 3 fold.). 24cm.

The principal work on the Selkirk Range.

P08. PALMER, William Thomas

The complete hillwalker, rock-climber and cave explorer. Ldn: Pitman, 1934. xii, 219p, illus. 22cm.

Palmer wrote numerous topographical books touching on climbing.

P09. PALMER, W. T.

Odd corners in Derbyshire: rambles, scrambles, climbs and sport. Ldn: Skeffington, [1940].

P10. PARES, Bip

Himalayan honeymoon. Ldn: Hodder, 1940. 301p, plates (some col), illus, maps. 23cm.

References to 1938 Everest expedition.

P11. PARKER, E. W. (Editor)

Adventure today. Ldn: Longmans, 1955. x, 182p, illus. 17cm. (Heritage of Literature series)

Includes two mountaineering extracts.

P12. PARKER, E. W.

Real adventure. Selected by . . .Edited by W. T. Hutchins. Ldn: Longmans, ?.

—New ptg. 1954. 175p, illus. 17cm. (Heritage of Literature series)

Includes three mountaineering extracts.

P13. PARROT, Friedrich

Journey to Ararat. Trans. [from the German] by W. D. Cooley. Ldn: Longmans, 1845. xii, 375p, fold. plate, illus, map. 24cm. From the original: *Reise zum Ararat* (Berlin: Haude & Spenerschen, 1834)

—U.S. ed. N.Y., 1846. 389p.

First ascent of Ararat. One of Monte Rosa's summits bears his name.

P14. PASCOE, John Dobrée (b.1908)

Great days in New Zealand exploration. Wellington: Reed, 1959.

P15. PASCOE, J. D.

Great days in New Zealand mountaineering: the rock and the snow. Wellington: Reed/Ldn: Bailey & Swinfen, 1958. 199p, 16 plates, illus, maps, bibl. 23cm.

Climbing history of selected peaks throughout New Zealand.

P16. PASCOE, J. D.

Land uplifted high. Christchurch: Whitcombe & Tombs, 1952. xii, 235p, plates, illus, maps. 23cm. R.P., 1961.

Sequel to *Unclimbed New Zealand,* continuing the author's climbing adventures; with interesting reviews of the literature of climbing and exploration in New Zealand.

P17. PASCOE, J. D.

The mountains the bush and the sea: a photographic report. Christchurch: Whitcombe & Tombs, 1950. [x], 100p, map. 28cm.

Photo-album.

P18. PASCOE, J. D.

Mr. Explorer Douglas. Wellington: Reed, 1957. xx, 331p, plates, illus, 4 maps, bibl. 25cm.

Douglas was a Westland explorer who worked with Harper and Mannering.

P19. PASCOE, J. D.
Over the Whitcombe Pass. Christchurch: Whitcombe & Tombs, 1960.
Exciting account taken from Jakob Lauper's 1863 narrative, originally translated by R. L. Holmes and published in the *Canterbury Provincial Gazette,* 6 July 1863. Lauper was the only survivor of the first west-east crossing of the Whitcombe Pass, discovered in 1861 by Samuel Butler.

P20. PASCOE, J. D.
Unclimbed New Zealand: alpine travel in the Canterbury and Westland ranges, Southern Alps. Ldn: Allen & Unwin, 1939. 238p, 50 plates (some fold., some col), illus, maps, bibl. 25cm.
—2nd ed. 1950. 244p.
—3rd ed. 1954.
The author's pioneering climbs and explorations between the wars, with historical sections on Samuel Butler, etc.

P21. PATERSON, M.
Mountaineering below the snow-line; or, The solitary pedestrian in Snowdonia and elsewhere. With etchings by Mackaness. Ldn: Redway, 1886. viii, 307p, 4 plates, illus. 19cm.
Hillwalking in the British Isles and Norway.

P22. PATEY, Thomas Walton (1932-70)
One man's mountains: essays and verses. Ldn: Gollancz, 1971. 287p, 23 plates, illus. 23cm. R.P., 1972, 1973, 1975, 1978.
The climbs and writings of a well-known Scottish humorist and mountaineer, who climbed the Muztagh Tower and Rakaposhi. Includes televised rock-climbs and 'The Ballad of Joe Brown'. Patey died in an abseiling accident.

P23. PAULKE, Wilhelm (-1949) & DUMLER, Helmut
Hazards in mountaineering. Trans. from the German by E. Noel Bowman. Ldn: Kaye & Ward/N.Y.: Oxford, 1973. 161p, illus (2 col). 21cm.

P24. PAUSE, Walter
Extreme Alpine rock: the 100 greatest Alpine rock climbs. Ldn: Granada, 1979. [10], 202p, illus, maps. 29cm. From the original: *Im Extremen Fels* (Munich: BLV Verlag, 1977).

P25. PAUSE, W.
Salute the mountains: the hundred best walks in the Alps. Trans. [from the German] by Ruth Michaelis-Jena and Arthur Ratcliffe. Ldn: Harrap, 1962. 211p, illus, maps. 26cm. From the original: *Bergheil: die 100 schönsten Bergwanderungen in den Alpen* (Munich: BLV Verlag, 1958)

P26. PAYNTER, Thomas
The ski and the mountain. Ldn: Hurst & Blackett, 1954. 212p, 11 plates, illus. 22cm.
Ski-mountaineering instruction and reminiscence.

P27. PEACOCKE, Thomas Arthur Hardy
Mountaineering. Ldn: Black, 1941. viii, 211p, 8 plates, illus. 19cm. R.P., 1943, 1953, 1954.

P28. PEARSE, Reginald O.
Barrier of spears: drama of the Drakensberg. [Cape Town]: Howard Timmins, 1973. xii, 304p, 20 col. plates, illus. 29cm.
Lavish monograph including some climbing history and list of first ascents. The best overall work on the range.

P29. PEARSON, Grant H.
My life of high adventure. By . . .and Philip Newill. Englewood Cliffs, NJ: Prentice-Hall, 1962. xviii, 237p, 16 plates, illus. 22cm.
—Another ed. N.Y.: Ballantine, 1972. [xix], 234p.
Includes 1932 McKinley expedition, the first to climb both north and south peaks.

P30. PEASCOD, William (1920-1985)
Journey after dawn. Milnthorpe: Cicerone Press, 1985. [xiii], 173p, plates, illus. 24cm.
Autobiography of pre-war pioneer Lakeland climber and artist.

P31. PEATTIE, Roderick
Friendly mountains, Green, White and Adirondacks. Edited by ...N.Y.: Vanguard Press, 1942. 341p, plates, illus. 24cm.

P32. PEATTIE, R.
The Great Smokies and the Blue Ridge: the story of the southern Appalachians. Edited by ... N.Y.: Vanguard Press, 1943. 372p, illus. 23cm.

P33. PEATTIE, R.
The incurable romantic. 1941.
Autobiography of American academic, geographer and mountaineer.

P34. PEATTIE, R.
Pacific Coast ranges. Edited by ...N.Y.: Vanguard Press, 1946. 402p, illus, 4 maps. 23cm.
Chapters by different contributors on various aspects including climbing.

P35. PEATTIE, R.
Sierra Nevada: the range of light; with an introduction by Donald Culross Peattie. By ...[and others]. N.Y.: Vanguard Press, 1947. 398p, plates, illus, fold. map. 24cm. (American Mountain series, 5)
General account; includes story of Yosemite climbing.

P36. PECK, Annie Smith (1853-1935)
A search for the apex of America: high mountain climbing in Peru and Bolivia including the conquest of Huascarán with some observations on the country and people below. N.Y.: Dodd Mead, 1911. xx, 370p, 64 plates, illus, map. 24cm.
—U.K. ed. entitled *High mountain climbing in Peru and Bolivia: a search for the apex of America, including the conquest of Huascarán.* Ldn: Fisher Unwin, 1912. Same details as U.S. ed.
Miss Peck was the driving force on all her Andean expeditions, many of her failures being due to the indifferent performance of her companions. She also climbed the Matterhorn and was a founder member of the A.A.C.

P37. PEDGLEY, David
Mountain weather: a practical guide for hillwalkers and climbers in the British Isles. Milnthorpe: Cicerone Press, 1979. 112p, illus, maps. 18cm.

P38. PELLY, Richard C. (Editor)
Report of the Cambridge Hindu Kush Expedition, 1972, 20th June-10th September. Haslemere: The Expedition, [1973]. 83p, plates, illus, maps. 30cm.

P39. PENBERTHY, Larry
Acute mountain sickness — Type R: including suggestions on climbing Mt. Rainier. Seattle: Altitude Medical Publishing, 1977. 48p, illus. 21cm.

P40. PERCIVAL, Walter
Mountain memories. Ldn: Jacey, 1962. [4], 120p. 22cm.
Alpine climbing reminiscences.

P41. PERRIN, Jim
Menlove: the life of John Menlove Edwards; with an appendix of his writings. Ldn: Gollancz, 1985. 347p, plates, illus. 24cm.
Biography of leading between-wars British climber, who was also a talented writer.

P42. PERRIN, J.
Mirrors in the cliffs. Edited by ...With cartoons by Sheridan Anderson. Ldn: Diadem, 1983. 688p, 33 plates, illus. 23cm.
Anthology of 100 mountaineering articles.

P43. PERRIN, J.
On and off the rocks. Ldn: Gollancz, 1986. 192p, illus. 25cm.
Collected essays

P44. PERRY, Alexander W.
Welsh mountaineering: a practical guide to the ascent of all the principal mountains in Wales. Ldn: Upcott Gill, 1896. 172p, maps. 15cm.

P45. PETIT, Louis Carl & Joseph
Mountains in the desert: exploration and adventure in the Tefedest Range of the central Sahara. N.Y.: Doubleday, 1954. 218p.

P46. PETNUCH, M.
Rock fever: origins of a mid-western climber. Jackness, 1979. 59p, illus.

P47. PETZOLDT, Patricia
On top of the world: my adventures with my mountain-climbing husband. N.Y.: Crowell, 1953. viii, 248p, illus. 21cm.
—U.K. ed. Ldn: Collins, 1954. 254p. 8 plates, illus. 21cm.
—Panther paperback. 1956.
Biography of Paul Petzoldt, Grand Teton guide amd member of the 1938 American K2 expedition.

P48. PETZOLDT, Paul
The wilderness handbook. N.Y.: W. W. Norton, 1974. 286p, illus. 19cm.
Instructional book, including climbing, written for the National Outdoor Leadership School, Lander, Wyoming.

P49. PHILIPS, Francis (1830-98)
A reading party in Switzerland: with an account of the ascent of Mont Blanc on the 12th and 13th of August 1851. Manchester: The Author, 1851. 49p. 19cm.
Philips made the ascent with Albert Smith; it was his only major climb.

P50. PHILLIMORE, R. H.
Historical records of the Survey of India. Collected and compiled by . . .Dehra Dun: Survey of India, 1945-62. 5v., plates (some fold.), illus, maps. 30cm.
Covers the period from the eighteenth century to 1861.

P51. PICKERING, William H.
Guide to the Mt. Washington Range. 1882.

P52. PICKMAN, Dudley Leavitt
Some mountain views. Boston: Manthorne, 1933. 94p, 38 plates, illus. [8vo] Edition of 500 copies.
Reminiscences of mountaineering in the 1870s including the Matterhorn, Jungfrau, Monte Rosa, Fuji, etc.

P53. PIERRE, Bernard
A mountain called Nun Kun. Trans. from the French by Nea Morin and Janet Adam Smith. Ldn: Hodder, 1955. 189p, 16 plates, illus, maps. 21cm. From the original: *Une montagne nommée Nun Kun* (Paris: Amiot-Dumont, 1954)
An early French success in the Himalaya, and a new women's height record for Claude Kogan.

P54. PIGEON, Anna & ABBOT, Ellen
Peaks and passes: [particulars of six mountaineering tours . . .between the years 1869 and 1876]. Ldn: The Authors, 1885. 31p. 18cm. Prepared for private circulation.
Summary of dates and times of ascents by two sisters who made numerous Alpine expeditions.

P55. PILKINGTON, Lawrence (1855-1941)
An Alpine valley and other poems. Wood-engravings by Margaret Pilkington. Ldn: Longmans, 1924. 70p, illus. 23cm.
Pilkington and his brother Charles (1850-1918) were among the leading guideless Alpine climbers of the 1870s and pioneers of British rock-climbing.

P56. PILKINGTON, L.
The hills of peace and other poems. Ldn: Longmans, 1930. 48p. 20cm.

P57. PILLEY, Dorothy
Climbing days. Ldn: Bell/N.Y.: Harcourt Brace, 1935. xiv, 352p, 64 plates, illus. 23cm.
—2nd ed. with additional material, 'Retrospection'. Ldn: Secker & Warburg, 1965.
—Facsimile ed. 1986.
The author of this classic book was a leading British climber between the wars. Her book covers climbs over twenty years around the world, chiefly in the 1920s. Her husband Ivor Richards was also a fine climber and writer, who occasionally wrote for the *Alpine Journal, etc.*

P58. PLATT, William
The joy of mountains. Ldn: Bell, 1921. 80p, 16 plates. 18cm. Hardback or limp cloth.
School primer; includes the Mont Blanc and Matterhorn stories etc.

P59. PLUNKETT, The Hon. Frederica Louisa Edith
Here and there among the Alps. Ldn: Longmans, 1875. viii, 195p. 20cm.
Account of her Alpine rambles, written to encourage other young ladies.

P60. POKORNA, Lida
High Tatras Expedition, Himalaya 69: (Tatranská Expedicia Himaláje 1969). [Issued in English by the participants ...English version: Lida Pokorna.] Stary Smokovec: The Expedition, 1968. [33p], illus (some col). 25cm.

P61. POKORNY, George
International directory of mountaineering clubs and organizations. By ...[and others]. [Montana]: Mountain Press, 1979. xii, 162p. Large format paperback. Sponsored by the Chicago Mountaineering Club.
An attempt to compile a list of names and addresses.

P62. POLLINGTON, S. W. (Editor)
Loughborough University Mountaineering Club Kishtwar Himalayan Expedition, 1976. Loughborough: The Expedition, [1978]. 36 plates, illus. 30cm.

P63. POOLE, Michael Crawford
The love of mountains. N.Y.: Crescent/Ldn: Octopus, 1980. 96p, col. illus, map. 33cm.

P64. PORTWAY, Christopher (b.1923)
Journey along the spine of the Andes. Yeovil: Oxford Illustrated Press, 1984. viii, 216p, col. plates, illus. 23cm.
Chiefly a trek through the northern highlands of Peru east of the main ranges, along the Inca royal road. Includes an ascent of Chimborazo.

P65. POST, Austin & LACHAPELLE, E. R.
Glacier ice. Seattle: Mountaineers/Univ. of Washington, 1971. 110p, illus. [4to].
Study written by two experts; dramatic aerial pictures.

P66. POUCHER, William Arthur (b.1891)
The Alps. Ldn: Constable, 1983. 204p, col. illus.
This book and all his others are photo-albums, unless otherwise stated.

P67. POUCHER, W. A.
Backbone of England. Ldn: Country Life, 1946. 208p, illus. 29cm.
Pennines.

P68. POUCHER, W. A.
Camera in the Cairngorms. Ldn: Chapman & Hall, 1947. 144p, illus, maps (endpapers). 26cm.

P69. POUCHER, W. A.
Climbing with a camera: the Lake District. Ldn: Country Life, 1963. 108p, illus.

P70. POUCHER, W. A.
Escape to the hills. Ldn: Country Life, [1943]. viii, 216p, illus. 30cm.
—Rev. ed. 1952.
British Isles generally.

P71. POUCHER, W. A.
Highland holiday: Arran to Ben Cruachan. Ldn: Chapman & Hall, 1945. 104p, illus, maps (endpapers). 26cm.

P72. POUCHER, W. A.
The Highlands of Scotland. Ldn: Constable, 1983. 206p, col. illus. 27cm. R.P., 1985.

P73. POUCHER, W. A.
Journey into Ireland. 1953.

P74. POUCHER, W. A.
The Lake District. 1982.

P75. POUCHER, W. A.
Lakeland holiday. Ldn: Chapman & Hall, 1942. 112p, illus. 28cm.

P76. POUCHER, W. A.
Lakeland journey. Ldn: Chapman & Hall, 1945. 128p, illus. 29cm.

P77. POUCHER, W. A.
The Lakeland peaks: a pictorial guide. Ldn: Constable, 1960. 367p, illus. 18cm.
—9th ed. 1983.
Pictorial route guide.

P78. POUCHER, W. A.
Lakeland scrapbook. Ldn: Chapman & Hall, 1950. 136p, illus. 29cm.

P79. POUCHER, W. A.
Lakeland through the lens: a ramble over fell and dale. Ldn: Chapman & Hall, 1940. 152p, illus. 26cm.

P80. POUCHER, W. A.
The magic of Skye. Ldn: Chapman & Hall, 1949. 223p, illus. 29cm.
—Small format ed. Ldn: Constable, 1980.
The most highly prized of his books.

P81. POUCHER, W. A.
Magic of the Dolomites. Ldn: Country Life, 1951. 144p, illus. 29cm.

P82. POUCHER, W. A.
North-west Highlands. Ldn: Country Life, 1954. 128p, illus. 29cm.

P83. POUCHER, W. A.
Over Lakeland fells. Ldn: Chapman & Hall, 1948. 152p, illus, maps. 29cm.

P84. POUCHER, W. A.
The Peak and Pennines from Dovedale to Hadrian's Wall: a pictorial guide to walking in this region. Ldn: Constable,
—2nd ed. 1973. 420p, illus.
—4th ed. 1983. 456p.
Pictorial route guide.

P85. POUCHER, W. A.
Peak panorama: Kinder Scout to Dovedale. Ldn: Chapman & Hall, 1946. 120p, illus. 29cm.

P86. POUCHER, W. A.
Scotland. 1980.

P87. POUCHER, W. A.
Scotland through the lens: Loch Tulla to Lochaber. Ldn: Chapman & Hall, 1943. 119p, illus, maps (endpapers). 26cm.

P88. POUCHER, W. A.
The Scottish peaks: a pictorial guide to walking in this region. Ldn: Constable, 1965. 18cm.
—2nd rev. ed. 1968.
—3rd rev. ed. 1971.
—4th rev. ed. 1974. 454p.
—5th ed. 1979.
—6th ed. 1982.
Pictorial route guide.

P89. POUCHER, W. A.
Skye.

P90. POUCHER, W. A.
Snowdon holiday. Ldn: Chapman & Hall, 1943. 127p, illus. 29cm.

P91. POUCHER, W. A.
Snowdonia through the lens: mountain wanderings in wildest Wales. Ldn: Chapman & Hall, 1941. 124p, illus. 29cm.

P92. POUCHER, W. A.
Wales. 1981.

P93. POUCHER, W. A.
Wanderings in Wales. Ldn: Country Life, 1949. 208p, illus.

P94. POUCHER, W. A.
The Welsh peaks: a pictorial guide to walking in this region and to the safe ascent of its principal mountain groups. Ldn: Constable, 1962. 405p, illus. 18cm.
—2nd ed. 1965.
—3rd ed. 1967.
—4th ed. 1970.
—5th ed. 1973.
—8th ed. 1983.
Pictorial route guide.

P95. POUCHER, W. A.
The Yorkshire Dales and the Peak District. Ldn: Constable, 1984. 200p, col. illus.

P96. POWELL, Paul Sidney
Just where do you think you've been? Wellington: Reed, 1970. 211p, 16 plates, illus, maps. 24cm.
New Zealand climbing reminiscences.

P97. POWELL, P. S.
Men aspiring. Wellington: Reed, 1967. 183p, plates, illus, maps. 25cm.
New Zealand climbing on the Southern Alps and on Mt. Aspiring.

P98. PRABODHANAND, Swami & ANAND, Swami
Across Gangotri glaciers. Bombay: Popular Book Depot, [1961]. 62p, illus.
Six Hindu monks travel to Badrinath from Gangotri across glaciers in Garhwal Himalaya. Not in Yakushi.

P99. PRAEGER, Robert Lloyd
The way that I went: an Irishman in Ireland. Dublin: Hodges Figgis, 1947. 416p, illus.

P100. PRAG, Per
Mountain holidays in Norway. Compiled by ...Oslo: Norway Travel Assoc., [1963]. 200p, illus. 21cm.
Includes details of first ascents, general description, etc; a narrative guidebook.

P101. PRICE, Larry W.
Mountains and men: a study of process and environment. Berkeley: Univ. California, 1981. xxi, 506p, illus, maps, bibl. 26cm.

P102. PUSKAS, Arno & KORSALA, J.
Fanske Vrchy. Svet Pattisicoviek (Fan's Mountains, Tadzikistan, U.S.S.R.). Bratislava, 1981. Portfolio with 3 maps and 33 large colour photographs. Captions in Slovakian, Russian, German and English.

P103. PUSKAS, A. & URBANOVIC, Ivan
Nanga Parbat 8125m. Bratislava: Sport, 1974. 140, xxxxip, illus (some col), 4 maps. 27cm. Summary and captions in English and German.
Report of the Czechoslovak expeditions in 1969 and 1971.

P104. PUTNAM, William Lowell
The Great Glacier and its House: the story of the first center of alpinism in North America, 1885-1925. N.Y.: A.A.C., 1982. 223p, illus, maps, bibl. 30cm.
Glacier House was an hotel on the railway, situated near the summit of Rogers Pass in the Selkirk Range.

P105. PYATT, Edward Charles (1916-85) & Marguerite E.
The boys' book of mountains and mountaineering. Ldn: Burke, 1963. 144p, illus, maps. 26cm.
Interesting illustrations.

P106. PYATT, E. C.
British crags and climbers. An anthology chosen by Edward C. Pyatt and Wilfrid Noyce. Ldn: Dobson, 1952. 235p, 16 plates, illus. 22cm.
Extracts, mainly from club journals, illustrating the development of climbing in Britain.

P107. PYATT, E. C.
A climber in the west country. Newton Abbot: David & Charles, 1968. 204p, 16 plates, illus, maps. 23cm.
Narrative guide.

P108. PYATT, E. C.
Climbing and walking in south-east England. Newton Abbot: David & Charles, 1970. 173p, illus, plans, bibl. 23cm.
Narrative guide.

P109. PYATT, E. C.
The Guiness book of mountains and mountaineering facts and feats. Enfield, Middx: Guinness Superlatives, 1980. 256p, illus (some col), maps. 25cm.
Attractive and interesting reference book.

P110. PYATT, E. C.
Mountains of Britain. Ldn: Batsford, 1966. 216p, 30 plates, illus, maps. 23cm.
General description of the mountains and the development of climbing on them.

P111. PYATT, E. C.
Where to climb in the British Isles. Ldn: Faber & Faber, 1960. 287p, 17 plates, illus. 19cm.
Narrative guide to the crags and outcrops of Britain, in each county.

P112. PYE, Sir David Randall (1886-1960)
George Leigh Mallory: a memoir. Ldn: O.U.P., 1927. [12], 183p, 6 plates, illus. 21cm.
Pye climbed with Mallory in Skye. While this book has been superseded by Robertson's biography, it remains the most touching portrayal of one of the most enigmatic figures in mountaineering history.

R

R01. [R, L.N.R.]
A short account of our trip to the Sierra Nevada Mountains. Ldn: J. Martin, [1884?]. 49p. 18cm.

R02. RADAU, Hans
Illampu: adventure in the Andes. Ldn/N.Y.: Aberlard Schumann 1961. From the original: *Illampu-Abenteuer in den Anden* (Düsseldorf: Hoch Verlag, 1958)

R03. RADCLIFFE, Peter
Land of mountains: tramping/hiking and climbing in New Zealand. Wellington: Methuen/Seattle: Mountaineers, 1979. 164p, illus (some col). 28cm.
Covers ten regions from North Island volcanoes to the Darran Mountains, with notes on historical and geographical features; chiefly pictorial.

R04. R.A.E. MOUNTAINEERING CLUB
Kishtwar Himalayan Expedition, 1980.: report. The Expedition, [1981?]. 35p, illus.
Ascent of Flat Top.

R05. RAEBURN, Harold (1865-1926)
Mountaineering art. Ldn: Fisher Unwin, 1920. xii, 274p, 29 plates, illus. 20cm.
Raeburn was typical of the new spirit of Scottish mountaineering at the turn of the century. He was an outstanding Alpinist and also visited Norway, the Caucasus and Himalaya.

R06. RAMOND DE CARBONNIÈRES, Baron Louis-François Élizabeth (1762-1827)
Travels in the Pyrenees: containing a description of the principal summits, passes and vallies. Trans from the French of M. Ramond by F. Gold. Ldn: Longmans, 1813. viii, 324p. 24cm. Being a trans. of part I of *Observations faites dans les Pyrénées* (Paris: Belin, 1789)
Ramond was an important mountaineering pioneer, who explored the Pyrenees and made the first ascent of Mont Perdu in 1802.

R07. RANDALL, Glenn
Breaking point: challenge on Alaska's Mt. Hunter. Denver: Chockstone, 1984. 160p, 8 plates, illus, map.
Three men repeat John Waterman's 146 day solo ascent of the south spur.

R08. RANDALL, G.
Vertigo games. Sioux City, IA: W. R. Publications, 1983. 125p, col. illus. Softback.
Contemporary climbing in Colorado; spectacular pictures.

R09. ROYAL ARMY ORDNANCE CORPS
R.A.O.C. Greenland Expedition, 1979: report. 59p, illus, maps.
East Greenland — Staunings Alps and Lyell Land.

R10. RATTI, Achille, Pope Pius XI (1857-1939)
Climbs on Alpine peaks. Trans. from the Italian by J. E. C. Eaton. Ldn: Fisher Unwin, 1923. 136p, 16 plates, illus. 23cm. R.P., 1925.
—U.S. ed. Boston: Houghton Mifflin, 1923. 139p, illus. 21cm.
—Essex Library ed. Ldn: Benn, 1929. xxx, 128p. 17cm.

R11. RAWLING, Cecil Godfrey
The great plateau: being an account of exploration in central Tibet 1903, and of the Gartok Expedition, 1904-1905. Ldn: Arnold, 1905. xii, 324p, illus, 2 fold. maps. 23cm.

Rawling did some fine exploration in western Tibet in 1903, and was one of the first to plan an expedition to Everest.

R12. RAWLING, C. G.
The land of the New Guinea Pygmies. Ldn: Seeley Service, 1913.
Account of very rough exploration in 1910-11 with A. F. R. Wollaston, trying to reach the Carstenz peaks.

R13. RAWSON, David H.
"Search": (the story of the development of search and rescue in Taranaki). New Plymouth, N.Z.: The Author, 1979. [14], 198p, 64 plates, illus. 22cm.
Mt. Egmont and eastern Taranaki, New Zealand.

R14. READER, John
Kilimanjaro. Ldn: Elm Tree Books, Hamish Hamilton/N.Y.: Universe, 1982. xii, 84p, plates, illus (mostly col), maps. 31cm.
Spectacular pictures of climbing on Africa's highest peak.

R15. RÉBUFFAT, Gaston (1921-85)
Between heaven and earth. By . . .and Pierre Tairraz. Trans. from the French by Eleanor Brockett. Ldn: Vane/N.Y.: Oxford, 1965. 183p, illus (some col). 23cm. From the original: *Entre terre et ciel* (Paris: Arthaud, 1962)
—Rev. ed. Ldn: Kaye & Ward/N.Y.: Oxford, 1970.
Rébuffat was a famous French mountain guide and film-maker. He was a member of the party who made the first ascent of Annapurna in 1950, the first ascent of a 8000-metre peak.

R16. RÉBUFFAT, G.
Men and the Matterhorn. Trans. from the French by Eleanor Brockett. Ldn: Vane/N.Y.: Oxford, 1967. 222p, illus (some col). 25cm. From the original: *Cervin, cime exemplaire* (Paris: Hachette, 1965)
—Rev. ed. Ldn: Kaye & Ward/N.Y.: Oxford, 1973. 27cm.

R17. RÉBUFFAT, G.
The Mont Blanc massif: the 100 finest routes. Trans. from the French by Jane and Colin Taylor. Ldn: Kaye & Ward/N.Y.: Oxford, 1975. 239p, illus (some col). 27cm. From the original: *Le massif du Mont Blanc* (Editions Denoël, 1973)
Lavishly illustrated, with route diagrams and descriptions.

R18. RÉBUFFAT, G.
Mont Blanc to Everest. Trans. [from the French] by Geoffrey Sutton: captions by Wilfrid Noyce. Ldn: Thames & Hudson/N.Y.: Studio-Crowell, 1956. 158p, 77 plates (some col), illus (2 fold.). 26cm. From the original: *Du Mont Blanc à l'Himalaya.* (Grenoble: Arthaud, 1955)
Chiefly pictorial, tracing Rébuffat's climbing career.

R19. RÉBUFFAT, G.
On snow and rock. Trans. from the French by Eleanor Brockett with technical assistance from J. E. B. Wright. Ldn: Nicholas Kaye, 1963. 191p, col. plates, illus. 24cm.
—2nd ed. Ldn: Vane/N.Y.: Oxford, 1965. 208p, illus. 24cm.
—Revised and reissued as *On ice and snow and rock.* Trans. by Patrick Evans. Ldn: Kaye & Ward/N.Y.: Oxford, 1971. 191p, illus (some col). 29 cm.
From the originals : *Neige et roc* (Paris: Hachette, 1959) and *Glace, neige et roc* (Paris: Hachette, 1970)
Lavishly illustrated work of instruction by a master of the art.

R20. RÉBUFFAT, G.
Starlight and storm: the ascent of six great north faces of the Alps. Trans. [from the French] by Wilfrid Noyce and Sir John Hunt. Ldn: Dent, 1956. xxii, 122p, 37 plates, illus, maps. 23cm. From the original: *Étoiles et tempêtes* (Paris: Arthaud, 1954)
—U.S. ed. N.Y.: Dutton, 1957. 189p.
—New ed. with different illustrations. Ldn: Kaye & Ward/N.Y.: Oxford, 1968. 224p.
Accounts of his own ascents; expressive and lyrical.

R21. REID, J. M.
Mount Everest. The Newdigate Prize poem, 1922. Ldn: Basil Blackwell, 1922.

R22. RENDU, Louis, Bishop of Savoy
Theory of the glaciers of Savoy. Trans. [from the French] by Alfred Wills, to which are added the original memoir and supplementary articles by P. G. Tait and John Ruskin. Edited . . .by George Forbes. Ldn: Macmillan, 1874. viii, 216p, map. 22cm. Text in English and French. From the original: *Théorie des glacières de la Savoie* (Chambéry, 1840)

R23. RENWICK, George
Romantic Corsica: wandering in Napoleon's isle; with a chapter on climbing by T. G. Ouston. Ldn: Fisher Unwin, 1909. 333p, plates (1 fold. col), illus, map. 23cm.

R24. REUTHER, David & THORN, John (Editors)
The armchair mountaineer. N.Y.: Scribner's, 1984. [x], 342p, illus.
Collection of 50 short pieces: interesting historical survey from wide variety of sources, including well-known climbers.

R25. REY, Guido (1861-1935)
The Matterhorn. With an introduction by Edmondo de Amicis. Trans. from the Italian by J. E. C. Eaton. With . . .plates and . . .drawings by Edoardo Rubino. Ldn: Fisher Unwin, 1907. 336p, 35 col. plates, illus. 27cm. Also 15 copies on Japan paper, numbered and signed by the publisher. R.P., 1908, 1913. From the original: *Il Monte Cervino* (Milan: Hoepli, 1904)
—Rev. ed. with two additional chapters by R. L. G. Irving. Oxford: Blackwell, 1946. R.P., 1949
One of the principal books on the early history of the Matterhorn, written by a wealthy Italian climber with a great passion for the mountain.

R26. REY, G.
Peaks and precipices: scrambles in the Dolomites and Savoy. Trans. from the Italian by J. E. C. Eaton. Ldn: Fisher Unwin/N.Y.: Dodd Mead, 1914. 238p, 48 plates, illus. 27cm. From the original: *Alpinismo acrobatico* (Turin: Lattes, 1914)

R27. REYNOLDS, Kev
Mountains of the Pyrenees. Milnthorpe: Cicerone Press, 1982. 151p, illus, maps, bibl.
Includes historical survey of climbing, descriptions of the mountains, and appendices.

R28. RHODES, Daniel P.
A pleasure-book of Grindlewald. N.Y.: Macmillan, 1903. xv, 235p, illus, fold. map. 21cm.
Approximately one-quarter of the book concerns mountaineering.

R29. RICHARD, Colette
Climbing blind. Trans. [from the French] by Norman Dale. Ldn: Hodder, 1966/N.Y.: Dutton, 1967. 159p, 4 plates, illus. 21cm. From the original: *Des cimes aux cavernes* (Mulhouse: Editions Salvator, 1965)
The climbing and caving experiences of a young blind girl.

R30. RICHMOND, William Kenneth
Climber's testament. Ldn: Redman, 1950. 8, 246p, 36 plates, illus. 23cm.
Reflections on climbing.

R31. RICKMERS, Willi Rickmer (1873-1965)
Ski-ing for beginners and mountaineers. Ldn: Fisher Unwin, 1910. 176p, plates, illus, bibl. 20cm.
The author climbed in Britain, the Alps, Caucasus and Pamirs, and was also an accomplished skier.

R32. RIDGEWAY, Rick
The boldest dream: the story of twelve who climbed Mount Everest. N.Y.: Harcourt Brace Jovanovich, 1979. xii, 244p, 8 plates, illus. 22cm.
This party of American men and women got two climbers to the top.

R33. RIDGEWAY, R.
The last step: the American ascent of K2. By . . .With introduction by Senator Edward M. Kennedy and prelude by James W. Whittaker. Seattle: Mountaineers, 1980. viii, 301p, 32 col. plates, illus. 27cm.
Ridgeway was one of three to reach the summit without oxygen in 1978.

R34. RIDGWAY, John
Cockleshell journey: the adventures of three men and a girl. Ldn: Hodder, 1974. 213p, plates, illus, map (endpapers). 23cm.
Rubber-boat voyage in southern Patagonia, including the first attempted crossing of the Gran Campo Nevado ice-cap.

R35. RIDLEY, Norman M.
Royal Air Force Expedition to the Sierra Nevada de Santa Marta in Colombia, 1974. Report by ...[and others]. The Expedition, [1975?]. 1v. (var. pag), illus, maps. 30cm.

R36. RIEGER, Edward
Up is the mountain: and other views. Portland: Binfords & Mort, 1973. 184p, illus.
Includes climbing on Mt. Hood.

R37. RITTERBUSH, Philip C.
Report of the 1970 expedition to the Nevado del Huila, Central Andean Cordillera, Colombia, July 1970. By ...and other members of the expedition; with an account of the original ascent by Erwin Kraus. Cali: Museo Departmental de Historia Natural, [1970?]. 43p, plates, illus, maps, bibl. 27cm. (Occasional publication of the Museo Departmental de Historia Natural)

R38. ROBBINS, Leonard Harman
Mountains and men. N.Y.: Dodd Mead, 1931. [xiii], 324p, plates, illus, maps. 21cm.
Tales of great mountain ascents around the world.

R39. ROBBINS, Royal
Advanced rockcraft. Illustrated by Sheridan Anderson. Glendale, CA: La Siesta Press, 1973. 95p, illus. 21cm.
The author is a leading American climber.

R40. ROBBINS, R.
Basic rockcraft. Illustrated by Sheridan Anderson. Glendale, CA: La Siesta Press, 1971. 70p, illus. 21cm.

R41. ROBERTS, Athol R.
Himalayan Holiday: an account of the New Zealand Himalayan Expedition, 1953. By ...[and others]. Christchurch, N.Z.: Whitcombe & Tombs, 1954. 44p, plates, illus, map. 22cm.

R42. ROBERTS, David S. (b.1943)
Deborah: a wilderness narrative. N.Y.: Vanguard Press, 1970. 188p, 8 plates, illus, maps. 24cm.
Attempt on the east ridge of Deborah, Alaska.

R43. ROBERTS, D. S.
Great exploration hoaxes. S.F.: Sierra Club, 1982. x, 182p, plates, illus. 24cm.
Chapters on Dr. Cook and Mt. McKinley; Maestri and Cerro Torre.

R44. ROBERTS, D. S.
Moments of doubt: and other mountaineering writings of ... Seattle: Mountaineers, 1986. [xvi], 238p.
Chapters on famous mountains and climbers.

R45. ROBERTS, D. S.
The mountain of my fear. N.Y.: Vanguard Press, 1968. 157p, illus, fold. map. 24cm.
—U.K. ed. Ldn: Souvenir Press, 1969. 157p, 16 plates, illus. 23cm. Without fold. map.
—Quality Book Club ed. 1969.
West face of Mt. Huntingdon, Alaska.

R46. ROBERTS, Dennis
I'll climb Mount Everest alone: the story of Maurice Wilson. Ldn: Hale, 1957. 158p, 17 plates, illus. 23cm.
Fatal solo attempt by non-mountaineer in 1934.

R47. ROBERTS, Eric Bernard (1945-79)
Welzenbach's climbs: a biographical study and the collected writings of Willo Welzenbach. Reading: West Col/Seattle: Mountaineers, 1981. 271p, illus. 22cm.
Welzenbach was Germany's leading between-wars climber. He perished in an terrible storm on Nanga Parbat in 1934. Roberts was a noted British alpinist.

R48. ROBERTS, Michael (1902-48)
Collected poems: edited with introductory memoir by Janet Roberts. Ldn: Faber, 1958. 3-226p. 21cm.

Includes mountaineering poems; Roberts was not only one of the best poets of his generation but also an able and enthusiastic mountaineer. He married Janet Adam Smith.

R49. ROBERTS, M.
Michael Roberts: Selected poems and prose. Edited and with an introduction by Frederic Grubb. Manchester: Carcanet Press, 1980. [ix], 205p, port, bibl. 23cm.
Includes mountaineering items; the bibliography lists his reviews of climbing books, etc.

R50. ROBERTS, M.
A portrait of Michael Roberts. Edited by T. W. Eason and R. Hamilton. Chelsea: College of S. Mark & S. John, 1949. xii, 72p, plates, ports, bibl. 23cm.

R51. ROBERTSON, David
George Mallory. Ldn: Faber, 1969. 279p, 17 plates, illus. 23cm.
—U.S. ed. entitled *Mallory of Everest.*
Definitive biography written by Mallory's son-in-law.

R52. ROBERTSON, D.
West of Eden: a history of the art and literature of Yosemite. Yosemite Natural History Association and Wilderness Press, [1984]. 174p, illus (some col).
Fine book dealing with the literature, painting and photography of a spectacular region.

R53. ROBERTSON, Max (Editor)
Mountain panorama: a book of winter sports and climbing. Ldn: Parrish, 1955. 128p, illus. 24cm.
Includes contributions by Hunt, Longland, Lunn, Noyce et al.

R54. ROBINSON, Anthony Melland (1907-50)
Alpine roundabout. Ldn: Chapman & Hall, 1947. x, 214p, 8 plates, illus. 23cm.

R55. ROBINSON, Bart & HARMON, Don
Columbia Icefield: a solitude of ice. Banff: Altitude, 1981. 112p, plates, illus. 28cm.
Fine photo-album of the most impressive ice-field in the Canadian Rockies.

R56. ROBINSON, John W.
The San Gabriels: southern California mountain country. San Marino, [1977]. 124p, illus. 29cm.

R57. ROCH, André
Climbs of my youth. Ldn: Lindsay Drummond, 1949. 160p, 17 plates, illus. 22cm. From the original: *Les conquêtes de ma jeunesse* (Neuchâtel: Attinger, 1943)
Roch was one of the great inter-war Swiss climbers. He climbed in the Himalaya in 1939 and 1947, and was a member of the 1952 Everest expedition.

R58. ROCH, A.
Everest 1952. Edited by Marcel Kurz. Ldn: Allen & Unwin, 1953.

R59. ROCH, A.
On rock and ice: mountaineering in photographs. Ldn: Black, 1947. xvip, 87 plates, illus. 25cm. From the original: *In Fels und Eis: ein Photo-Tourenbuch.* (Zurich: Amstatz Erdeg, 1946)
Fine portfolio of Alpine routes.

R60. ROCK, J. F.
The Amnye Ma-chhen Range and adjacent regions: a monographic study. Rome: Instituto Italiano per il Medio ed Estremo Oriente, 1956. xi, 194p, plates (some fold. some col), illus, maps. 26cm. (Serie Orientale Roma, 12)
Rock explored the region in 1926, including the gorges of the Yellow River and Gynd-par Range. He estimated the height of Amne Machin at 6400 metres (actually 6282m).

R61. ROCK CLIMBING CLUB OF JAPAN
Everest 8848m: Japanese expedition to Mt. Everest, 1973. Tokyo: Rock Climbing Club, Japan, 1974. 43p, illus. 26cm. Preliminary report. Diary and captions in English. Yak. j. 792.
Attempt on south-west face and ascent via south-east ridge.

R62. ROCKHILL, William Woodville
The land of the lamas: notes of a journey through China, Mongolia and Tibet. Ldn: Longmans/N.Y.: Century, 1891. viii, 399p, illus, maps. 23cm.

—Reprint. Taiwan: Ch'eng Wen, 1972. 399;.
—Reprint. Delhi: Asian Publ. Services, 1975. 399p.
Narrative of a journey in 1888 in the Minya Konka-Tatsienlu region.

R63. ROGET, François Frédéric
Altitude and health. Ldn: Constable, 1919. xii, 186p. 23cm. (Chadwick Library)
Three lectures delivered in London for the Chadwick Trust.

R64. ROGET, F. F.
Hints on alpine sports; with a supplement on mountaineering and winter sports clothing. Ldn: Burberrys, [1912]. 55p, illus. 23cm.
Clothing manufacturer's publication.

R65. ROGET, F. F.
Ski runs in the high Alps. Illustrations by L. M. Crisp. Ldn: Fisher Unwin, 1913. 312p, 25 plates, illus, 6 fold. maps. 23cm.
The principal book in English by a Swiss academic who was outstanding among the pioneers of ski-mountaineering.

R66. ROMM, Michael D.
The ascent of Mount Stalin. Trans. [from the Russian] by Alec Brown. Ldn: Lawrence & Wishart, 1936. xii, 270p, 32 plates, illus. 23cm.
Mt. Stalin (now Pik Communism, 7495m) was discovered in 1913. One of the official tasks of the 1933 Russian scientific expedition to the western Pamirs was the ascent of the peak.

R67. RONGZU, Zhang
Mount Qomolangma: the highest in the world. 1981. 64p, illus (some col), maps. Text in English, Spanish and Japanese.
Discusses formation of the peak, geological structure, flora and fauna, and adaptation of life to altitude. Not in Yakushi.

R68. ROPER, Steve & STECK, Allen
Fifty classic climbs of North America. S.F.: Sierra Club/Ldn: Diadem, 1979. 324p, illus, maps. 28cm.
Illustrations, route diagrams and descriptions.

R69. ROSCOE, Donald Thomas
Mountaineering: a manual for teachers & instructors. Ldn: Faber, 1976. [x], 181p, 8 plates, illus. 23cm.
Comprehensive manual written by a British mountaineering instructor.

R70. ROSE, Eugene A.
High odyssey: the first solo winter assault of Mt. Whitney and the Muir Trail area, from the diary of Orland Bartholomew, and photographs taken by him. Berkeley: Howell-North Books, 1974. 160p, illus, maps. 23cm.
Remarkable six-month solo ski-mountaineering expedition in 1928 through the Sierra Nevada.

R71. ROSENBERG, John D.
The darkening glass: a portrait of Ruskin's genius. Ldn: Routledge Kegan Paul, 1963.
The best one-volume biography of John Ruskin (1819-1900). Although Ruskin's general health and upbringing prevented him from indulging in serious mountaineering, he exercised considerable influence over his contemporaries by the magnificence of his descriptive mountain writing. He was elected to the Alpine Club on the strength of his book *Modern painters* (v.4), which includes the famous chapter, 'Of Mountain Glory'.

R72. ROSS, Malcolm (1864-1930)
Aorangi: or, The heart of the Southern Alps. New Zealand. Wellington: New Zealand Survey, 1892.

R73. ROSS, M.
A climber in New Zealand. Ldn: Arnold/N.Y.: Longmans, 1914. xx, 316p, 24 plates, illus. 23cm.
Chiefly concerning the Mount Cook area. Ross was a founder member of the New Zealand Alpine Club.

R74. ROSS, M.
First traverse of Mount Cook. Wellington: Evening Post, 1906. 32p. 23cm.

R75. ROSSIT, Edward A.
Northwest mountaineering. Caldwell, ID: Caxton, 1965. 206p, illus. [8vo].

R76. ROSSIT, E. A.
Snow camping and mountaineering. N.Y.: Funk & Wagnalls, 1970. 276p, illus. 21cm.

R77. ROTH, Abraham
The Doldenhorn and Weisse Frau: ascended for the first time by Abraham Roth, and Edmund von Fellenberg. Coblenz: Baedeker/Ldn: Williams & Norgate, 1863. 82p, 13 col. plates, illus, fold. map. 26cm. English translation and eleven sketches by P. C. Gosset.
This finely illustrated book includes accounts of earlier attempts. Von Fellenberg (1838-1902) was the most successful pioneer of the Bernese Alps. Philip Charles Gosset (1838-1911) made the earliest attempts on the Weisse Frau with von Fellenberg, with whom he also attempted the Doldenhorn in 1862. Gosset is better known for his account of the fatal accident involving the guide J. J. Bennen on the Haut de Cry in 1864 (see Tyndall, *Hours of exercise*).

R78. ROTH, Arthur
Eiger: wall of death. N.Y.: Norton/Ldn: Gollancz, 1982. 350p, illus, maps. 24cm.
History of climbing on the Eigerwand.

R79. ROTH, Hal
Pathway in the sky: the story of the John Muir Trail. Berkeley: Howell-North, 1965. 231p, illus, maps (endpapers).

R80. ROWELL, Galen
Alaska: images of the country. By . . .and John McPhee. S.F.: Sierra Club, 1981. 144p, illus. [4to]. Boxed. Edition of 500 copies signed by the author and photographer.
—Another ed. 160p, map.
Rowell is a leading American climber and fine mountain photographer.

R81. ROWELL, G.
High and wild: a mountaineer's world. S.F.: Sierra Club, 1979. 160p, col. illus. 31cm.
—2nd ed. entitled *High and wild: essays on wilderness adventure.* S.F.: Lexikos, 1983. [xiv], 207p.
Climbs and ski-touring — High Sierra, Cirque of the Unclimbables, McKinley in a day, etc.

R82. ROWELL, G.
In the throne room of the mountain gods. S.F.: Sierra Club/Ldn: Allen & Unwin, 1977. x, 326p, illus (some col). 29cm.
Unsuccessful attempt on K2.

R83. ROWELL, G.
Many people come, looking, looking. Seattle: Mountaineers, 1980. ix, 164p, col. illus, maps. 31cm.
Account of Rowell's experiences with three Himalayan expeditions — Nun Kun, Thorungtse, Trango Tower.

R84. ROWELL, G.
Mountains of the Middle Kingdom: exploring the high peaks of China and Tibet. S.F.: Sierra Club in assoc. with A.A.C./Ldn: Century, 1985. [xvi], 192p, illus (many col), maps. 31 × 26cm.
Rowell was one of the first western climbers to explore the newly opened areas in China — Mustagh Ata, Tian Shan, Minya Konka, Amne Machin, etc.

R85. ROWELL, G.
Vertical world of Yosemite: a collection of photographs and writings on rock climbing in Yosemite. Edited by . . .Berkeley: Wilderness Press, [1974]. xiv, 208p, illus. 29cm. Softback ed., 1981.
Illustrated and with articles on climbs by leading climbers.

R86. ROWLAND, E. G.
The ascent of Snowdon. Illustrated by Jonah Jones. Criccieth: Cidron Press, 1956. 21, iiip, illus, map. 20cm. Many reprints by (1) Vector and (2) Cicerone Press.

R87. ROWLAND, E. G.
Hillwalking in Snowdonia: camera studies by W. A. Poucher. Ldn: Camping & Open Air Press, 1951. 83p, plates, illus, map. 22cm. R.P., 1952.
—New & fully rev. ed. Criccieth: Cidron Press, 1958. Many reprints by (1) Vector and (2) Cicerone Press.

R88. [ROYAL AIR FORCE]
Mountain rescue handbook. Ldn: H.M.S.O., 1952.
—2nd ed. 1968. 178p, illus. 22cm. Softback.
—3rd ed. 1972. 152p. Softback.

R89. ROYAL MILITARY COLLEGE OF SCIENCE SHRIVENHAM

[Report of] the R.M.C.S. Andean Expedition to the Sierra Nevada de Santa Marta, Colombia, South America. Shrivenham: The Expedition, [1973?]. 1v. (var. pag), plates, illus, maps. 30cm.

R90. ROYAL NAVY AND ROYAL MARINES MOUNTAINEERING CLUB

Norland Expedition, 1978: report. The Expedition, [1979]. [32p]. plates, illus. 31cm.

R91. ROYAL REGIMENT OF FUSILIERS

Expedition to the Ahaggar Mountains, Southern Algeria, 1979: report of the 2nd Battalion. 89p, illus, maps.
Expedition to cross the Ahaggar from south to north on foot.

R92. RUDGE, E. C. W.

Mountain days near home. Illustrated with photographs by the author, and drawings by his wife. Wellingborough: W. D. Wharton, 1941. viii, 75p, plates, illus. 23cm.
Climbing in Britain.

R93. RUNDLE, John

The Tararua book. Wellington: Millwood, 1981. 104p, plates, illus, map. [4to].
Interesting New Zealand range.

R94. RUSK, Claude Ewing (1871-1931)

Tales of a western mountaineer: a record of mountain experiences. Boston: Houghton Mifflin, 1924. xiv, 309p, 31 plates, illus. 20cm.
—Facsimile reprint plus 28 pages of biography and new illustrations. Seattle: Mountaineers, [1978]. Softback.
Rusk taught himself climbing on the peaks of the Cascade Range, becoming especially expert on Mt. Adams. He led the 1910 Mazamas expedition to McKinley to investigate Dr. Cook's alleged ascent of 1906.

R95. RUSSEL, A.

The Rockies. Edmonton: Hurtig, 1975. ?p, col. illus.
Canadian Rockies photo-album.

R96. RUSSELL, Franklin

The mountains of America: from Alaska to the Great Smokies. N.Y.: Abrams, 1975. 224p, illus (mostly col), maps. 33cm.
Photo-album.

R97. RUSSELL, Jean (b.1939)

Climb if you will: a commentary on Geoff Hayes and his club, the Oread Mountaineering Club. Compiled and edited by ...in association with Jack Ashcroft. Ashbourne: M. J. Russell, [1974]. xiv, 222p, illus. 23cm.
Geoff Hayes was killed in 1971 in a rock-climbing accident in the Lake District.

R98. RUSSELL, R. Scott

Mountain prospect. Ldn: Chatto & Windus, 1946. xvi, 248p, 47 plates, illus, maps. 22cm.
These climbing memoirs deserve more recognition than hitherto accorded them. Russell gives a fascinating account of summer camps with the great New Zealand pioneer A. P. Harper, as well as relating his experiences in the Arctic and Karakoram.

R99. RUTTLEDGE, Hugh L. (1884-1961)

Everest 1933. Ldn: Hodder, 1934. xvi, 390p, 59 plates, illus, 3 fold. maps. 27cm. 4 ptgs.
—U.S. ed. entitled *Attack on Everest.* N.Y.: McBride, 1935. xx, 339p. 3-D viewer (in pkt).
—National Travel Club ed. N.Y., 1935.
1936. xx, 299p, illus. 23cm. This 'popular' edition consists only of the narratives forming the major part of the original work.
—B.J. ed. 1938. R.P., 1943, 1947.
Ruttledge led this major British attempt which got very near the top.

R100. RUTTLEDGE, H. L.

Everest: the unfinished adventure. Ldn: Hodder, 1937. [xvi], 295p, 63 plates, illus, 2 fold. maps. 27cm.
Ruttledge led this major British expedition which achieved little because of an early monsoon.

R101. RYMILL, John
Southern lights.
Antarctica. Account of the British Graham Land Expedition, 1934-37, led by the author.

S

S01. SABIN, Edwin L.
The Peaks of the Rockies. Denver: Denver & Rio Grande Railroad, [1916]. 36p, illus. 18cm.

S02. SACK, John
The Butcher: the ascent of Yerupaja. N.Y.: Rinehart, 1952. ix, 213p, illus. 22cm.
—U.K. ed. entitled *The ascent of Yerupaja.* Ldn: Jenkins, 1954. 191p, 9 plates, illus. 20cm.
Account of the first ascent of the highest peak in the Cordillera Huayhuash, Peru.

S03. ST. HELENS MOUNTAINEERING CLUB
Andean Expedition, 1977: [report]. St. Helens: St. Helens Mountaineering Club, [1978]. 18 leaves, 30 cm.
Cordillera Urubamba, Peru.

S04. SALT, Henry Stephen
On Cambrian and Cumbrian hills: pilgrimages to Snowdon and Scawfell. Ldn: Fifield, 1908. 128p, 2 plates, illus. 18cm.
—Paperback ed. 1911.
—Rev. ed. Ldn: Daniel, 1922. 124p.

S05. SANDEMAN, R. G.
A mountaineer's journal. [Carmarthen: Druid Press], 1948. 168p, 14 plates, illus. 23cm.
Climbing in Scotland.

S06. SANREI ASCENT CLUB
Hachindar Chish Expedition. Tokyo: The Club, 1981. [20], 142p, illus (some col), maps. 26cm. In Japanese with English summary. Yak. j. 317.
Attempt on Hachindar Chish (7163m) in 1978.

S07. SANSOM, George S.
Climbing at Wasdale before the first World War. Somerset, Castle Cary Press, 1982. 100, [xx]p, 12 plates, illus, map. 28cm. Edition of 1000 copies.

S08. SANUKI, Matao & YAMADA, Keiichi
The Alps. Ldn: Ward Lock, 1970. 146p, illus (some col), maps. 19cm. (This beautiful World series)

S09. SARKAR, B.
Gangotri. Calcutta, 1971. Vol. 1
References to Indian expeditions 1967/68 in Garhwal (Kedarnath Dome, Radhanath Parbat, Satopanth). Not in Yakushi. Source: Sircar, p. 166.

S10. SAUNDERS, Charles Francis
The southern sierras of California. Boston: Houghton Mifflin, 1923. xii, 367p, plates, illus. 21cm.
—U.K. ed. 1924.

S11. SAYRE, Woodrow Wilson (b.1919)
Four against Everest. Englewood Cliffs, NJ; Prentice-Hall, 1964. 259p, illus (some col), maps. 24cm. R.P., 1964.
—U.K. ed. Ldn: Arthur Barker, [1964]. 251p.
—Paperback ed. Prentice-Hall, 1968.
—Paperback ed. N.Y.: Tower, 1968.
Unauthorized attempt by the North Col Route, without porters.

S12. SCANLAN, A. B.
Egmont: the story of a mountain. Wellington: Reed, 1961. 200p, 16 plates, illus, maps. 23cm.
This 8260 ft mountain is a popular peak on the North Island, New Zealand. Includes legends, Maori tribal history, exploration and ascent. The author made 130 ascents of the peak.

S13. SCANLAN, A. B.
Mountains of Maoriland. New Plymouth, N.Z.: Thomas Avery, 1949. 115p, illus. [4to].
Well illustrated.

S14. SCARR, Josephine
Four miles high. Ldn: Gollancz, 1966. 188p, 33 plates, illus, maps. 22cm.
Account of two women's expedition to the Himalaya (Kulu and Jagdula Himal).

S15. SCAYLEA, Josef
Moods of the mountain. Seattle: Superior Pub., 1968.
Attractive photo-album of Mt. Rainier.

S16. SCEVA, Paul H.
Recollections of the 'Old Man of the Mountains'. Tacoma, WA: The Author, [1973]. 248p, illus.
The author was manager of Rainier National Park Company.

S17. SCHALLER, George B.
Stones of silence: journeys in the Himalaya. Ldn: Deutsch, 1980. ix, 292p, 12 col. plates, illus, maps. 24cm.
—U.S. ed. N.Y.: Viking Press, 1980. 292p, 14 col. plates, illus, maps. 24cm.
The author travelled in search of rare and elusive animals; a book for all who are concerned with man's effect on the mountain environment.

S18. SCHLAGINTWEIT, Hermann
Results of a scientific mission to India and High Asia. Undertaken between the years 1854 and 1858 by order of the directors of the Honourable East India Company. By . . ., Adolphe Schlagintweit and Robert Schlagintweit. Leipzig: Brockhaus/Ldn: Trübner, 1861-66. 4v. 33 × 27cm. Plus atlas. 95 × 63cm.
The Schlagintweits made interesting explorations in the Kumaun Himalaya and claimed to have reached a height of over 22,000 ft, probably on Abi Gamin in the Kamet Group.

S19. SCHMOE, Floyd W.
Our greatest mountain: a handbook for Mount Rainier National Park. N.Y.: Putnam's, 1925. 366p, 45 plates, illus, map. 21cm.
Includes chapter with advice on climbing Mt. Rainier.

S20. SCHMOE, F. W.
A year in paradise. N.Y.: Harper, [1959]. 235p, 20 plates, illus. [8vo].
—Another ed. Seattle: Mountaineers, ?. 235p.
Includes some climbs, e.g. Rainier.

S21. SCHNEIDER, Anne & Steven
Climber's sourcebook. Garden City, NY: Anchor Press/Doubleday, 1976. xii, 340p, illus. 21cm. Paper-bound.
Sections on U.S. tuition centres, equipment suppliers, climbing areas, clubs and addresses, etc.

S22. SCHNEIDER, Steven
High technology: guide to modern mountaineering equipment. Chicago: 1980. 211p.

S23. SCHOMBERG, Reginald Charles Francis
Kafirs and glaciers: travels in Chitral. Ldn: Hopkinson, 1938. 287p, 25 plates, illus, fold. map. 23cm.
Includes excellent description of the mountains and glaciers in Chitral.

S24. SCHOMBERG, R. C. F.
Peaks and plains of central Asia. Ldn: Hopkinson, 1933. 288p, 8 col. plates, illus. 23cm.
During this expedition Schomberg visited the Tian-Shan and Bogdo Ola.

S25. SCHOMBERG, R. C. F.
Unknown Karakoram. Ldn: Hopkinson, 1936. 244p, 23 plates, illus, map (in pkt). 23cm.
Exploring north of the main range, in the Raskam, Shaksgam, Oprang and Braldu valleys.

S26. SCHUSTER, Claud, Baron Schuster (1869-1956)
Men, women and mountains: days in the Alps and Pyrenees. Ldn: Nicholson & Watson, 1931. xvi, 143p, 13 plates, illus. 25cm. R.P., 1931.
Miscellaneous essays by a past president of the Alpine Club.

S27. SCHUSTER, C.
Mountaineering: the Romanes lecture delivered in the Sheldonian Theatre, 21 May 1948. Oxford: Clarendon Press, 1948. 32p. 23cm.

S28. SCHUSTER, C.
Peaks and pleasant pastures. Oxford: Clarendon Press, 1911. 227p, 9 plates, illus, maps. 24cm.
His best book; a minor classic.

S29. SCHUSTER, C.
Postscript to adventure. Ldn: Eyre & Spottiswoode, 1950. 214p, 9 plates, illus. 23cm.
Miscellaneous papers read before the Alpine Club and others, including 'Tyndall as a mountaineer'.

S30. SCHWATKA, Frederick
A summer in Alaska. Philadelphia: John Huber, 1891. 418p, illus. 23cm.
The author's party in 1886 was the first to make an attempt on Mount St. Elias.

S31. SCOTT, Douglas Keith (b.1941)
Big wall climbing. Ldn: Kaye & Ward/N.Y.: Oxford, 1974. xii, 348p, illus. 21cm. R.P., 1981.
History of severe big-wall climbing and climbers, written by a leading British mountaineer. Very well illustrated.

S32. SCOTT, D. K.
The Cilo Dag Mountains of south-east Turkey: [report of an expedition organised by the Nottingham Climbers' Club]. [Nottingham]: [The Club], [1966]. 72p, plates, illus, maps. 26cm.

S33. SCOTT, D. K.
Midlands Hindu Kush Expedition in 1967. Report, written by ...& W. Cheverst. Nottingham: The Expedition, [1968]. 62p, plates (some fold.), illus, maps. 25cm.

S34. SCOTT, D. K. & MACINTYRE, Alex
The Shishapangma expedition. Ldn: Granada/Seattle: Mountaineers, 1984. 322p, illus, maps. 24cm.
Spring 1982 expedition to climb the south-west face, with historical detail about climbers and travellers in the region. The book ends with tributes to MacIntyre who died on Annapurna shortly afterwards.

S35. SCOTT, D. K.
Tibesti. [Nottingham]: The Author, [1965]. 78p, plates, illus, map. 25cm.
Account of the Nottingham Tibesti Expedition, 1965.

S36. SCOTT, John D.
We climb high: a thumbnail chronology of the Mazamas, 1894-1969. Published by the Mazamas on the day of their Seventy-Fifth Anniversary, July 19, 1969. Portland: Mazamas, 1969. [6], 94p, illus. 26cm. Softback.
The Mazamas grew out of the Oregon Alpine Club. The author was an active member, a past president and journal editor.

S37. SCOTT, J. M.
Gino Watkins. Ldn: Hodder, 1935. xviii, 317p, plates, illus, maps. 23cm.
—B.J. ed.
Watkins (1907-1932) was a good climber who became a driving force in arctic exploration. He discovered the highest mountains in Greenland (now named after him) but drowned while out hunting in a kayak.

S38. SCOTTISH HINDU KUSH EXPEDITION, 1968
Report. [Edinburgh]: The Expedition, [1968?]. [26p], illus, maps. 35cm.

S39. SCOTTISH HINDU KUSH EXPEDITION, 1970
Scottish expedition to the roof of the world. Aberdeen: The Expedition, [1971?]. 20p, illus, maps. 30cm.

S40. SCOTTISH PERUVIAN ANDES EXPEDITION, 1976
Report. The Expedition, [1977?]. [41p], illus, map. 30cm.
Huayanay massif, Cordillera Vilcabamba, Peru.

S41. SEAVER, George
Francis Younghusband: explorer and mystic. Ldn: Murray, 1952. 391p, 12 plates, illus, 4 maps. 22cm.
Biography of well-known British soldier and Tibetan traveller who was a leading figure in organizing the early Everest expeditions.

S42. SEGHERS, Carroll Jr.
The peak experience: hiking and climbing for women. Indianapolis: Bobbs-Merrill, 1979. 302p, illus. [8vo].

S43. SELIGMAN, Gerald Abraham
Snow structures and ski-fields: being an account of snow and ice forms met with in nature and a study on avalanches and snowcraft. With an appendix on Alpine weather by C. K. M. Douglas. Ldn: Macmillan, 1936. xii, 555p, fold. plates, illus, bibl. 23cm.
—Another ed. Brussels: Adam, 1962. 555p.
Long regarded as a leading work on the subject.

S44. SERRAILLIER, Ian
Everest climbed. Illustrated by Leonard Roseman. Oxford: Geoffrey Cumberlege, O.U.P., 1955. viii, 60p, illus. 19cm.
Narrative poem of the first ascent of Everest.

S45. SETNICKA, Tim J.
Wilderness search and rescue. Boston: Appalachian Mountain Club, 1980. [xi], 640p, plates, illus.
Very comprehensive manual by former Yosemite rescue leader.

S46. SHAIRP, John Campbell
Life and letters of James David Forbes. By . . ., Peter Guthrie Tait and A. Adams-Reilly. Ldn: Macmillan, 1873. xvi, 598p, illus, map. 23cm.
Biography of the Scottish scientist who was one of the first to carry out systematic Alpine exploration, and also visited Norway in the course of his glaciological studies. He spans the era from de Saussure to Alfred Wills.

S47. SHARMA, Man Mohan
Of gods and glaciers: on and around Mt. Rataban. Delhi: Vision Books, 1979. vii, 152p. 25cm.
First Indian ascent of Mt. Rataban in the Zanskar range of Ladakh by all-women team.

S48. SHARMA, M. M.
Through the valley of gods: travels in the central Himalayas. Delhi: Vision Books, 1977. xiv, 278p, illus, 4 maps. 24cm.
—2nd ed. 1978.

S49. SHAW, C. A.
Tales of a pioneer surveyor. Edited by Raymond Hull. Toronto: Longman Canada, 1970.
References to Collie.

S50. SHEBL, James M.
King, of the mountains. Drawings by Bjorklund. Stockton, CA: Pacific Center for Western Historical Studies/Univ. Pacific Press, 1974. 76p.
Clarence King.

S51. SHERMAN, Paddy (b.1928)
Cloud walkers: six climbs on major Canadian Peaks. Maps by John A. Hall. Toronto: Macmillan of Canada, 1965. [9], 161p, 16 plates, illus, maps. 21cm.
—U.S. ed. N.Y.: St. Martins, 1965. Also 2nd ptg.
—Another ed. Ldn: Macmillan, 1966. [12], 161p, 16 plates, illus, maps. 23cm. Also 2nd ptg.
—Paper-bound ed. Seattle: Mountaineers, 1979.
Mounts Fairweather, Logan, Waddington, Slesse, Robson & Howson.

S52. SHERMAN, P.
Expeditions to nowhere. Seattle: Mountaineers, 1981. [9], 226p, illus. 24cm.
Holiday climbs around the world — Huascarán, Kilimanjaro, McKinley, Aconcagua, Illimani.

S53. SHERRING, Charles Atmore
Western Tibet and the British borderland: the sacred country of Hindus and Buddhists; with an account of the government, religions and customs of its peoples. Ldn: Arnold, 1906. xv, 376p, illus, 2 fold. maps. 25cm.
—Reprinted. Delhi: Cosmo Pub, 1974.
Exploration in Garhwal and Ladakh in 1905 with T. G. Longstaff in the

neighbourhood of Mt. Kailas; with a chapter by Longstaff on his attempt on Gurla Mandhata.

S54. SHERWILL, Walter S.

Notes upon a tour in the Sikkim Himalayah Mountains undertaken for the purpose of ascertaining the geological formation of Kunchinjinga and the perpetually snow-covered peaks in its vicinity. Calcutta: The Author, [1852?]. 59p, plate, illus. 22cm.

S55. SHIH CHAN-CHUN

The conquest of Minya Konka. Trans. [from the Chinese] by Huang Kai-Ping. Peking: Foreign Languages Press, 1959. [13], 54p, illus. 19cm.
Chinese ascent in 1957.

S56. SHINSHÛ UNIVERSITY ALPINE CLUB & ACADEMIC ALPINE CLUB

Annapurna II — 1971. Nagano: Shinshû Univ. A.C. & Academic A.C., 1972. 239, [3]p, illus, map. 26cm. In Japanese with English summary. Yak. j. 354.
Unsuccessful attempt in 1971.

S57. SHIPTON, Diana

The antique land. Decorations by Jill Davis. Ldn: Hodder, 1950. 219p, plates, illus, map. 23cm.
Eric Shipton's wife's account of life in and around Kashgar, 1946-8, when he was British Consul.

S58. SHIPTON, Eric Earle (1907-77)

Blank on the map. Text drawings by Bip Pares. Ldn: Hodder, 1938. xviii, 299p, 36 plates, illus, 3 maps (1 fold. col). 23cm.
Exploration of the Shaksgam area north of the main Karakoram range in 1937.

S59. SHIPTON, E. E.

Land of tempest: travels in Patagonia, 1958-62. Ldn: Hodder/N.Y.: Dutton, 1963. 224p, 17 plates, illus, maps. 23cm. R.P., 1963.
Traverses of the southern ice-cap.

S60. SHIPTON, E. E.

The Mount Everest Reconnaissance Expedition, 1951. Ldn: Hodder/N.Y.: Dutton, 1952. 128p, illus, maps. 27cm. R.P., 1953.
Confirmation of the southern route via the Khumbu ice-fall and Western Cwm. This has become the normal route up Everest via the South Col.

S61. SHIPTON, E. E.

Mountain conquest. By the editors of 'Horizon' Magazine. Author: Eric Shipton in consultaion with Bradford Washburn. N.Y.: American Heritage Pub, 1966/Ldn: Cassell, 1967. 153p, illus (some col), maps. 27cm. (Cassell Caravel series)
Survey of world mountaineering.

S62. SHIPTON, E. E.

Mountains of Tartary. Ldn: Hodder, [1951]. 224p, 23 plates, illus, map (endpapers). 23cm.
While British Consul at Kashgar, Shipton attempted Muztagh Ata, Chakragil and Bogdo Ola.

S63. SHIPTON, E. E.

Nanda Devi. Drawings in the text by Bip Pares. Ldn: Hodder, 1936. xvi, 310p, 27 plates, illus, map (endpaper). 23cm. R.P., 1936.
—B.J. ed. 1939.
Shipton and Tilman carried out one of the great pieces of mountain exploration, penetrating the Rishi Gorge to the Nanda Devi Sanctuary.

S64. SHIPTON, E. E.

The six mountain-travel books. Ldn: Diadem/Seattle: Mountaineers, 1985. 800p, map. 23cm.
Includes *Nanda Devi, Blank on the map, Upon that mountain, Mountains of Tartary, Everest reconnaissance expedition, Land of tempest.*

S65. SHIPTON, E. E.

That untravelled world: an autobiography. Ldn: Hodder/N.Y.: Scribner's, 1969. 286p, 16 plates, illus. 23cm. R.P., 1970, 1977.
Shipton was arguably the greatest mountain explorer of all time. He took part in five Everest expeditions but is best known for his private lightweight expeditions, often with Tilman. In later years he spent much of his time exploring and climbing in Patagonia and Tierra del Fuego.

S66. SHIPTON, E. E.
Tierra del Fuego — the fatal lodestone. Ldn: Charles Knight, 1973. 1745p, illus, maps. 23cm.
—R.U. ed. 1974. viii, 175p, 8 plates, illus. 22cm.
History of discovery and colonization. Chapter on his first approach to the remote Mount Burney (actually on the mainland).

S67. SHIPTON, E. E.
The true book about Everest. Illustrated by F. Stocks. Ldn: Muller, 1955. 142p, illus. 19cm.
—U.S. ed. entitled *Men against Everest.* Englewood Cliffs, NJ: Prentice-Hall, [1956]. 161p, illus, map. 21cm.

S68. SHIPTON, E. E.
Upon that mountain. Ldn: Hodder, 1943. 222p, 31 plates, illus. 21cm. R.P., 1943, 1944, 1947.
—R.U./Hodder ed. 1945.
—Pan paperback. 1956.
Early climbing autobiography.

S69. SHIRAHATA, Shiro
The Alps. N.Y.: Rizzoli, 1980. vii, [104], xliip, col. illus. 37cm. slipcase.
Magnificent photo-album.

S70. SHIRAHATA, S.
Nepal Himalaya. Tokyo: Yama-Kei Pub/S.F.: Heian International, 1983. 232p, 115 col. plates, illus. 37 × 27cm. Slipcase.
Companion volume to his work on the Alps; very high quality photography and printing.

S71. SHIRAKAWA, Yoshikazu
The Alps. Text by Max Wyss. Ldn: Thames & Hudson, 1973. 136p, 56 col. plates, illus, maps.

S72. SHIRAKAWA, Y.
The Himalayas. Tokyo: Kôdan-sha/N.Y.: Abrams, 1972. 300p, illus (some col), maps. 43cm. Slipcase.
—2nd ed. 1975.
—Concise ed. N.Y.: Abrams. 1977.

S73. SHIZUOKA UNIVERSITY ALPINE CLUB
Churen Himal 1970. Shizuoka: The Club, 1973. var. pag., illus, maps. 26cm. In Japanese with English summary. Yak. j. 322.
First ascent of Churen Himal, central peak, autumn 1970.

S74. SHIZUOKA UNIVERSITY ALPINE CLUB
Teram Kangri. Shizuoka: The Club, 1978. var. pag., illus (some col), maps. 26cm. In Japanese with English summary. Yak. j. 323.
First ascent of Teram Kangri I & II in 1975.

S75. SIMONOV, Yevgeny
Conquering the Celestial Mountains. Trans. from the Russian by G. Ivanov-Mumjiev. Moscow: Foreign Languages Pub. House, 1958. 130p, 31 plates, illus. 20cm.
Climbs in the Tian-Shan.

S76. SINGER, Armand E.
Essays on the literature of mountaineering with a section of exemplary pieces and a bibliography. [Morgantown]: West Virginia Univ. Press, 1982. xv, 158p. 23cm. Softback.
Includes pieces on several well-known climbing books, and other interesting discourses.

S77. SINGH, Gyan (b.1918)
Lure of Everest: story of the first Indian expedition. Delhi: Publications Division, Ministry of Information & Broadcasting, 1961. xiii, 212p, 41 plates, illus. 22cm.
The author led this first all-Indian attempt on Everest in 1960. He was at the time Principal of the Himalayan Mountaineering Institute in Darjeeling.

S78. SINIGAGLIA, Leone (1868-1944)
Climbing reminiscences of the Dolomites. With an introduction by Edmund J. Garwood. Trans. [from the Italian] by Mary Alice Vialls. Ldn: Fisher Unwin, 1896. xxiv, 224p, 39 plates, illus, fold. map. 26cm. Also 30 numbered & signed copies on Japan paper, bound by Zaehnsdorf. Cover title: *Climbing in the*

Dolomites. From the original *Ricordi alpini delle Dolomiti*.
This Italian mountaineer was by profession a musician and composer. He died of a heart attack on the eve of being sent as slave labour to Nazi Germany.

S79. SIRCAR, S. Joydeep
Himalayan handbook. Calcutta: The Author, 1979. 168p. 22cm. Softback. (Vol. 1, A-K (36p) originally appeared in 1974.)
Lists every Himalayan peak over 20,000 ft and summarizes every attempt and ascent with bibliographical references.

S80. SKOCZLAS, Adam
Stefano, we shall come tomorrow. Ldn: Poets' and Painters' Press, 1962. 33p, 10 plates, illus. 24cm.
Death of Stefano Longhi on the Eigerwand in 1957. This was one of the largest rescue operations ever mounted in the Alps. His companion Corti was saved.

S81. SLESSER, C. G. Malcolm (b.1926)
The Andes are prickly. Ldn: Gollancz, 1966. 254p, 29 plates, illus, maps. 23cm.
Scottish expedition climbing in the Peruvian cordilleras Huayhuash and Urubamba.

S82. SLESSER, C. G. M.
Red Peak: a personal account of the British-Soviet Pamir expedition 1962. Ldn: Hodder/N.Y.: Coward-McCann, 1964. 256p, 20 plates (some col), illus. 23cm.
Wilfrid Noyce and Robin Smith, two leading British climbers, were killed on this unhappy expedition.

S83. SLINGSBY, William Cecil (1849-1929)
Norway: the northern playground. Sketches of climbing and mountain exploration in Norway between 1872 and 1903. Edinburgh: Douglas, 1904. xx, 425p, plates, illus. maps. 23cm.
—Reissued with a biographical note by G. W. Young. Oxford: Blackwell, 1941. xxviii, 227p, illus, map. 21cm.
Slingsby was one of the leading climbers of his generation, climbing in Britain and the Alps; but he is still revered in Norway as the 'Father' of Norwegian mountaineering. His book remains the classic, indispensable work on the region.

S84. SMEETON, Miles
A taste of the hills. Ldn: Hart-Davis, 1961. 207p, illus, map. 22cm.
Includes a light-hearted attempt on Tirich Mir, Hindu Kush, with Tenzing.

S85. SMITH, Albert Richard (1816-60)
Mont Blanc. Ldn: The Author, 1852. 88p. 18cm. Only a few copies printed for private circulation.
Smith was an English writer with a passion for Mont Blanc. After his ascent in 1851 he produced an illustrated lecture based on his experiences. This ran for six years and made him a rich man. The popularity of this public entertainment coincided with the start of the 'Golden Age' of Alpine mountaineering.

S86. SMITH, A. R.
The story of Mont Blanc. Ldn: David Bogue, 1853. xii, 219p, plate, illus. 21cm. The plate is coloured or plain.
—U.S. ed. N.Y.: Putnam, 1853. x, 208p, plate. 20cm.
—2nd [ed.] ptg. Bogue, 1854.
—2nd ed. enlarged. Bogue, 1854. xvi, 299p, illus. 18cm.
—Reprint. Ldn: Kent, 1857. Kent was Bogue's successor.
—Reprinted with new title-page. Kent, 1860.
—Facsimile reprint of 1853 ed. Reading: Gastons-West Col, 1974.

S87. SMITH, A. R.
The story of Mont Blanc, and a Diary to China and back. Privately printed, 1860. xvi, 299p, 60p. 17cm. Reprint of 1854 enlarged edition bound with another story. This version has a new title-page and reprinted dedication. On the title-page (recto) there are two photographs of handbills of the two lectures and (verso) two photographs of Albert Smith and of the exterior of the Egyptian Hall. On the dedication page are two photo portraits. Memorial edition. [Details from copy in Alpine Club Library.]

S88. SMITH, A. R.
A boy's ascent of Mont Blanc; written by himself. Ldn: Houlston & Wright, [1859]. Fictional variation. In the *Boy's Birthday Book* . . .by Mrs S. C. Hall et al. Pp. 9-145.
—Reissued with slightly altered title-page. Ldn: Maxwell, [1870].

S89. SMITH, A. R.
The story of Mont Blanc. Ldn: Beeton, [1860]. In the *Boy's Own Magazine,* v.VI, parts 8-12. Illus. 18cm. Reprint of the 1854 edition.

S90. SMITH, A. R.
Mont Blanc. By . . .with a memoir of the author by Edmund Yates. Ldn: Ward Lock, [1860]. xxxvi, 299p, plate. 17cm. Pictorial boards.
—Another ed. Ldn: Ward Lock & Tyler, [1860]. xxxvi, 299p, plate. 17cm. Bound in cloth, blind and gilt stamped.
—Reprint entitled *A boy's ascent of Mont Blanc.* Ldn: Ward Lock & Tyler, [c.1871]. Altered title-page. Cloth, blind and gilt stamped.
N.B.: There are two plates used in these editions: a glacier scene, and a woodland hill cottage.

S91. [SMITHIANA]
A handbook of Mr. Albert Smith's ascent of Mont Blanc. Illustrated by Mr. William Beverley. With twenty-five outline engravings of the views. First represented at the Egyptian Hall, Piccadilly, Monday Evening, March 15, 1852. Ldn: ?, 1852. 28p, illus.
—Another ed. Ldn: Savill & Edwards, 1852. [2], 31p, illus. 11 × 19cm.
—4th ed. [1853]. Savill & Edwards.
—Another ed. [1854]. Ldn: Chappell, [1854]. 29p.
—Another ed. Ldn: The Author, 1856.
Probably six editions in all: the illustrations differ in number and subjects. The pictures were published by Madame de Chatelain as colouring books. See also the following references in the *Alpine Journal: Miniature Mont Blanc* (v. 19, p. 273); *Exercises in colouring: Mont Blanc* (v. 19, p. 272); *Notice of entertainment, Mt. Blanc to China* (v. 18, p. 564). The A.A.C. Library also has an item entitled *Handbook of the miniature Mont Blanc* (1855).

S92. [SMITHIANA]
Mr. Albert Smith's ascent of Mont Blanc, Holland and up the Rhine. Egyptian Hall, Piccadilly. Every evening (except Saturday) at eight o'clock. 8p, illus. 22cm.
Lecture programme. Programmes were also issued in the form of a lady's fan; see illustration in Hindley's *Roof of the world.*

S93. [SMITHIANA]
The Mont Blanc room at the Egyptian Hall. Presented, by Mr. Albert Smith, to the ladies in the gallery, on the occasion of the 1856th representation of 'Mont Blanc', March 1, 1858.
Lithograph.

S94. [SMITHIANA]
The new game of the ascent of Mont Blanc. Large coloured lithograph (16″ × 20″) comprising 54 wiews in compartments of England, France, Switzerland. and incidents of Alpine adventure. Mounted on linen, folding to octavo size, Ldn: Charles Warren (from C. Adler's Printing Establishment, Hamburg, [c.1852]).
Rare children's game; the first to reach the summit took the pool built up by fines during the game. Colour illustration in Keenlyside, *Peaks and pioneers.*

S95. [SMITHIANA]
L'Echo du Mont Blanc. Polka dedicated to his friend Albert Smith by Jullien. Ldn: Jullien, [c.1858]. 8p. 34cm.
Referred to in the advertisements in the handbook as 'Les Echos de Mont Blanc Polka, composed by M. Jullien'. Also known as the 'Chamonix Polka'?

S96. [SMITHIANA]
The 'Mont Blanc' Quadrilles. Composed by J. H. Tully. Ldn: Charles Jeffreys, Soho Square.
Described in the advertisement in the handbook as follows: 'The title-page by Brandard is illustrative of the most interesting portions of the ascent, copied, by favour, from Mr. Beverley's renowned dioramic views of Mont Blanc . . .the quadrilles have produced a perfect furore of delight at all the fashionable soirées dansantes of the season . . .'. John Brandard, born Birmingham 1812, was a younger brother of Robert Brandard,

etcher and engraver after J. W. M. Turner. John Brandard also commenced as an engraver but was working for M. & N. Hanhart, Lithographers by the 1840s. He had a soft, gentle touch, his speciality being opera and ballet subjects.

S97. SMITH, B. Webster
Pioneers of mountaineering. Ldn: Blackie, [1930]. 224p, 8 plates, illus. 20cm.

S98. SMITH, B. W.
True stories of modern adventure. Ldn: ?, [1930]. 221p, illus. R.P., 1931, 1934.
—Rev. ed. 1936.
Chapter on Everest. Not in Yakushi.

S99. SMITH, George Alan
The armchair mountaineer: a gathering of wit, wisdom and idolatry. Edited by ...and Carol D. Smith. N.Y.: Pitman, 1968. xvi, 361p, illus (some col). 26cm.
Anthology.

S100. SMITH, G. A.
Introduction to mountaineering. N.Y.: A. S. Barnes, 1957.
—U.K. ed. Ldn: Yoseloff, 1960. xiv, 128p, plate, illus. 26cm.
—Rev. ed. Yoseloff, 1967. xiv, 134p.

S101. SMITH, Howard E. Jr.
The complete beginner's guide to mountain climbing. N.Y.: Doubleday, 1977. xi, 241p, illus. 24cm.

S102. SMITH, Janet Adam (b.1906?)
Mountain holidays. Ldn: Dent, 1946. xii, 194p, 32 plates, illus. 22cm. R.P., 1946.
Pre-war Alpine reminiscences of the well-known Scottish climber who married the poet Michael Roberts (1902-48). A minor classic.

S103. SMITH, Phil D.
Knots for mountaineering, camping, climbing utility, rescue, etc. Twenty-nine Palms, CA: The Desert Trail, 1953. 24p, illus. Softback.

S104. SMITH, Roger S. D.
Malvern College Iceland Expedition, 1978: preliminary report. [Compiled by ...(expedition leader)]. Malvern: The Expedition, 1978. 8p, illus, maps. 30cm.

S105. SMITH, R. S. D.
Synopsis of mountaineering in south Greenland. Belper: The Author, [1972]. 16 leaves, maps. 31cm.

S106. SMITH, R. S. D.
The winding trail. With cartoons by Sheridan Anderson. Ldn: Diadem, 1981. 477p, 32 col. plates, illus. 23cm.
Anthology; a selection of articles and essays for walkers and backpackers.

S107. SMITH, Walter Parry Haskett (1859-1946)
Climbing in the British Isles. [Vol] 1: England, by ...With twenty-three illustrations by Ellis Carr. Ldn: Longmans, 1894. xii, 162p, illus. 16cm. [Vol] 2: Wales and Ireland. Wales by ...Ireland by H. C. Hart. With thirty-one illustrations by Ellis Carr. Ldn: Longmans, 1895. viii, 197p, illus. 16cm.
—Facsimile reprint of Irish section entitled *Climbing in the British Isles: Ireland.* Dublin: privately printed, [1974].
—Facsimile reprint of both volumes in one. [Glasgow]: Ernest Press, 1986.
The first guidebook to British rock-climbing; Part 3 (Scotland) was planned but never executed.

S108. SMYTHE, Frank Sydney (1900-49)
The adventures of a mountaineer. Ldn: Dent, 1940. viii, 228p, 17 plates, illus. 22cm. R.P., 1941, 1945, 1949.
Frank Smythe was a British mountaineer who climbed extensively in the Alps. His Himalayan expeditions included the 1930 attempt on Kanchenjunga, first ascent of Kamet, and Everest twice. He was a fine photographer and one of the most prolific and widely-read pre-war climbers.

S109. SMYTHE, F. S.
Again Switzerland. Ldn: Hodder, 1947. viii, 248p, 33 plates, illus, map (endpaper). 23cm.
First visit to the Alps after the war.

S110. SMYTHE, F. S.
An Alpine journey. Ldn: Gollancz, 1934. 351p, 48 plates, illus, fold. map. 24cm.
—B.J. ed. 1940.
Traversing the Alps of eastern Switzerland.

S111. SMYTHE, F. S.
Alpine ways. Ldn: Black, 1942. 106p, illus, map. 28cm.
Photo-album

S112. SMYTHE, F. S.
British mountaineers. Ldn: Collins, 1942. 48p, 8 col. plates, illus. 23cm. Some illustrations/captions wrongly printed. (Britain in Pictures series)
—Another ed. Bahamas: Britain in Pictures Publishers, [n.d]. Repeats errors in illustrations. Also seen bound in cloth as well as usual boards.
—Reprinted with corrections and variations in illustrations. Boards. Ldn: Collins, 1946.

S113. SMYTHE, F. S.
A camera in the hills. Ldn: Black, 1939. 147p, illus. 28cm. R.P., 1942, 1946, 1948.
Photo-album.

S114. SMYTHE, F. S.
Camp Six; an account of the 1933 Mount Everest expedition. Ldn: Hodder, 1937. xii, 307p, 36 plates, illus. 23cm.
—B.J. ed. 1938. R.P., 1941.
—New ed. Ldn: Black, 1956. xii, 219p, 8 plates, illus. 23cm.
One of his best books, with its revelations of his experiences at the highest camp and his solo attempt on the summit, one of the great efforts in Everest history.

S115. SMYTHE, F. S.
Climbs and ski-runs: mountaineering and ski-ing in the Alps, Great Britain and Corsica. Edinburgh: Blackwood, 1929. xx, 307p, 61 plates, illus. 23cm. R.P., 1930, 1931.
—Cheap ed. 1933.
—Another ed. Toronto, 1934.
—New ed. Ldn: Black, 1957. xii, 197p.
His first and perhaps his best book.

S116. SMYTHE, F. S.
Climbs in the Canadian Rockies. Ldn: Hodder/N.Y.: Norton, 1950. x, 260p, 34 plates (2 col), illus, maps. 23cm.
His last book; includes climbing in the northern Lloyd George Range.

S117. SMYTHE, F. S.
Edward Whymper. Ldn: Hodder, 1940. xiv, 330p, 24 plates, illus. 2 fold. maps. 22cm.
This remains the only biography of the most famous mountaineer of all time.

S118. SMYTHE, F. S.
Kamet conquered. Ldn: Gollancz, 1932. xvi, 420p, 50 plates, illus, fold. map. 24cm. Reprinted several times. Some first editions lack the two photogravures following the title-page?
—Cheap ed. 1933.
—B.J. ed. 1938.
—Uniform ed. Hodder, 1947.
This first ascent of Kamet (7756m) was a fine achievement, following a series of attempts dating back to 1855.

S119. SMYTHE, F. S.
The Kanchenjunga adventure. Ldn: Gollancz, 1930. 464p, 48 plates, illus. 24cm. R.P. 1931.
—First cheap ed., October 1931. R.P., 1932-37.
—B.J. ed. 1946.
Unsuccessful 1930 international expedition led by G. L. Dyrenfurth, resulting in the deaths of two climbers. Smythe was one of three British climbers.

S120. SMYTHE, F. S.
The mountain scene. Ldn: Black, 1937. ix, 153p, illus. 28cm. R.P., 1938.
Photo-album.

S121. SMYTHE, F. S.
The mountain top: an illustrated anthology from the prose and pictures of Frank S. Smythe. Ldn: St. Hugh's Press, 1947. 45p, illus. 16cm. Misprinted copy seen.
A diminutive curiosity.

S122. SMYTHE, F. S.
The mountain vision. Ldn: Hodder, 1941. xii, 308p, 16 plates, illus. 23cm. R.P., 1942.
—Uniform ed. Hodder, 1946. R.P., 1950.
Essays on aspects of the mountains and mountaineering, illustrating Smythe's rather romantic and mystical attitude to climbing.

S123. SMYTHE, F. S.
Mountaineering holiday. Ldn: Hodder, 1940. xiv, 229p, 24 plates, illus, map. 23cm.
—B.J. ed. 1941. R.P., 1943.
—Uniform ed. Hodder, 1950. xiv, 229p.
Climbing on the Dauphiné Alps and the Brenva face of Mont Blanc.

S124. SMYTHE, F. S.
Mountains in colour. Ldn: Parrish, 1949. 155p, col. illus. 29cm.
—U.S. ed. entitled *Behold the mountains: climbing with a color camera.* N.Y.: Chanticleer Press, 1949. 155p, col. illus. 29cm.
Photo-album.

S125. SMYTHE, F. S.
My Alpine album. Ldn: Black, 1940. 147p, illus, map. 28cm. R.P., 1947.
Photo-album.

S126. SMYTHE, F. S.
Over Tyrolese hills. Ldn: Hodder, 1936. xvi, 292p, 36 plates, illus, map. 23cm. R.P., 1936, 1937.
—B.J. ed. 1938.
The title is misleading — the book covers many areas of the Austrian Alps.

S127. SMYTHE, F. S.
Over Welsh hills. Ldn: Black, 1941. 101p, illus. 28cm. R.P., 1942, 1945.
Photo-album.

S128. SMYTHE, F. S.
Peaks and valleys. Ldn: Black, 1938. xi, 129p, illus. 28cm.
Photo-album, partly illustrating his Himalayan travels described in his book *Valley of flowers.*

S129. SMYTHE, F. S.
Rocky Mountains. Ldn: Black, 1948. 149p, illus (some col), map. 29cm.
Photo-album; Canadian Rockies.

S130. SMYTHE, F. S.
Snow on the hills. Ldn: Black, 1946. 119p, plates, illus. 33cm.
Photo-album.

S131. SMYTHE, F. S.
The spirit of the hills. Ldn: Hodder, 1935. xiv, 308p, 36 plates, illus. 23cm.
—B.J. ed. 1937. R.P., 1938, 1941.
—Uniform ed. Hodder, 1946. R.P., 1950.
Reminiscences of the mountains and climbing in all their aspects, drawn from his own experiences, and illustrating his romantic, mystical approach to climbing.

S132. SMYTHE, F. S.
Swiss winter. Ldn: Black, 1948. 125p, illus (some col). 29cm.
Photo-album.

S133. SMYTHE, F. S.
The valley of flowers. Ldn: Hodder, 1938. xiv, 322p, 16 col. plates, illus, fold. map. 23cm. Also a limited edition of 250 numbered copies signed by the author.
—Uniform ed. Hodder, 1947.
—U.S. ed. N.Y.: Norton, 1949. 322p.
—Another ed. 1986. (Plant Hunters series)
After ascending Kamet Smythe continued his travels in the Garhwal Himalaya and Bhyundar Valley.

S134. SMYTHE, Anthony G.
Rock climbers in action in Snowdonia. Written by . . . Illustrated by John Cleare. Captions(descriptions and layout by Robin G. Collomb. Ldn: Secker & Warburg, 1966. 127p, 32 plates, illus. 25cm. R.P., 1967.
Superbly illustrated account of contemporary personalities and hard climbs.

S135. SNAILHAM, Richard
Sangay survived: the story of the Ecuador volcano disaster. Ldn: Hutchinson, 1978. 192p, illus, maps. 23cm.
Snailham and his companions were overwhelmed by an eruption near the summit of this extremely active volcano.

S136. SNAITH, Stanley
Alpine adventure. Ldn: Percy Press, 1944. vi, 153p, 8 plates, illus. 20cm. R.P., 1946.

S137. SNAITH, S.
At grips with Everest. Ldn: Percy Press, 1937. xvi, 240p, 8 plates, illus. 20cm.
—U.S. ed. N.Y.: Oxford, 1938. 258p, illus. 20cm.
—2nd ed. Percy Press, 1945. xii, 164p.

S138. SNAITH, S.

The mountain challenge. Ldn: Percy Press, 1952. x, 158p, 8 plates, illus. 19cm.
Includes McKinley, Pamirs, New Zealand, etc.

S139. SNELLING, John

The sacred mountain: travellers and pilgrims at Mount Kailas in western Tibet, and the great universal symbol of the sacred mountain. Ldn: East West Pub., 1983. xii, 241p, plates, illus, maps. 24cm.
Mt. Kailas (22,000 ft) lies inside Tibet and is regarded as the most sacred mountain in Asia. The book gives a record of visits by western travellers and a discussion of the mountain's religious significance.

S140. SNOW, Sebastian (b.1929)

Half a dozen of the other. Ldn: Hodder, 1972. 222p, plates, illus. 23cm.
Includes climbing Chimborazo, Cotopaxi and Sangay in Ecuador. The engagingly eccentric author is well-known for his South American travels.

S141. SNYDER, Howard (b.1945)

Hall of the mountain king. N.Y.: Scribner's, 1973. xii, 207p, illus. 24cm.
Snyder took part in an expedition to Mt. McKinley in 1967 when seven men died. For an opposing view see Wilcox, *White winds.*

S142. SOMERVELL, Theodore Howard (1890-1975)

After Everest: the experiences of a mountaineer and medical missionary. Ldn: Hodder, 1936. xiv, 339p, 22 plates, illus, fold. map. 23cm.
—B.J. ed. 1938. R.P., 1939, 1947, 1950.
Apart from climbing and medicine, Somervell was a skilled amateur painter and musician. He took part in the 1922 & 1924 Everest expeditions, and was president of the A.C., 1962-4.

S143. SOPER, N. Jack (1934)

The Black Cliff: the history of rock climbing on Clogwyn du'r Arddu. By . . ., Ken Wilson and Peter Crew. Based on the original research of Rodney Wilson. Ldn: Kaye & Ward, 1971. 158p, illus. 22cm.
The definitive record of climbing on one of Britain's biggest and most famous cliffs. The authors are all well-known climbers.

S144. SOUND HERITAGE

In the Western Mountains: early mountaineering in British Columbia. Compiled and edited by Susan Leslie. Victoria, B.C.; Aural History Program, 1980. iv, 76p, illus. 27cm. Softback. (Sound Heritage, Vol VIII, no. 4)
Original accounts and photographs, from the Provincial Archives of British Columbia. A sound cassette with the climbers telling their stories was also issued.

S145. SOUND HERITAGE

Mountaineering at the Coast. Produced by Susan Leslie. Aural History, Provincial Archives of British Columbia. Cassette accompanying the Sound Heritage book.

S146. SOUTH AFRICAN RAILWAYS

Mountaineering in South Africa. [Compiled by W. C. West] Issued by the General Manager, South African Railways, in co-operation with members of the Mountain Club of South Africa. Johannesburg: South African Railways, 1914. 62p, plates, illus, maps. 22cm.
Covers the Cape Mountains and the Drakensberg.

S147. SOUTH OF ENGLAND EAST KULU EXPEDITION, 1978

[Report]. The Expedition, [1979]. 16p, illus, maps. 32cm.

S148. SPECTORSKY, Auguste C.

The book of the mountains: being a collection of writings about the mountains in all of their aspects. Edited by . . .N.Y.: Appleton-Century-Crofts, 1955. 492p, illus. 25cm.
Anthology of the literature of mountaineering in its widest sense.

S149. SPEER, Stanhope Templeman

On the physiological phenomena of the mountain sickness, as experienced in the ascent of the higher Alps. Ldn [Lincoln-cum-Fields]: T. Richards, 1853. 51p. 20cm. Offprint from medical journal.
In this paper Speer alludes to two climbs he made from Chamonix in 1844 when still a medical student. However, his greatest climb was in 1845, being the first ascent of the highest point of the Wetterhorn. His

account, which appeared in the November 1, 1845 issue of the *Athenæum* was widely read in public libraries and is thought to have played a greater part in the beginnings of mountaineering as a sport than the ascent and book by Alfred Wills. Speer's narrative was 'discovered' by the Alpine Club in the 1890s and republished in the *Alpine Journal.*

S150. SPENCER, Sydney (1862-1950) (Editor)

Mountaineering. By ...and others. Ldn: & Philadelphia, n.d. 383p, plates (some fold., some col), illus, maps, bibl. 23cm. (Lonsdale Library series, 18) (N.B.: The date of publication is usually given as 1934 but Arnold Lunn, in his *Century of mountaineering* (p. 39) suggests that the date was 1927.)
An omnibus work, with a great deal of useful information, which was still in print in the 1950s, but now something of a period piece.

S151. SPENDER, E. Harold (-1925?)

In praise of Switzerland: being the Alps in prose and verse. Ldn: Constable, 1912. xvi, 291p. 23cm.
Attractive anthology.

S152. SPENDER, E. H.

Through the high Pyrenees. With illustrations and supplementary sections by H. Llewellyn Smith. Ldn: Innes, 1898. xii, 370p, 31 plates, illus. 5 maps (1 fold.), bibl. 24cm.
One of the few books on climbing in the Pyrenees.

S153. SPRING, Bob & Ira

High adventure: mountain photography by ...Text by Norma and Patricia Spring. Seattle: Superior Pub., [1951]. 115p, illus. 31cm. Also 100 copies signed by Bob and Ira Spring.
Outstanding photographs of the mountains of the Pacific North-west.

S154. SPRING, B. & I.

High worlds of the mountain climber. Photographs by ...Text by Harvey Manning. Seattle: Superior Pub., 1959. 142p, illus. 27cm. Also an edition of 2000 numbered copies signed by Manning and the Springs.
Photo-album; mountains of the western U.S.

S155. SPRING, B. & I.

North Cascades National Park. By ...& Harvey Manning. Seattle: Superior Pub., 1969. 143p, illus (some col), maps. [4to].
Contains some of the best of Harvey Manning's climbing tales, with illustrations by the Springs.

S156. STARK, Freya

Traveller's prelude. Ldn: Murray, 1950. xiii, 346p, plates, illus, map. 23cm.
—Penguin paperback. 1962.
A promising Alpine career as a young woman was curtailed by illness and frailty, but she went on to become a noted explorer of the Middle East. Her biggest climb was Monte Rosa from the Marinelli Hut. Interesting references to contemporary climbers, particularly W. P. Ker.

S157. STARR, Frederick

Fujiyama — the sacred mountain of Japan. Chicago: Covici-McGee, 1924.

S158. STEAD, Richard

Adventures on the high mountains: romantic incidents and perils of travel, sport and exploration throughout the world. Ldn: Seeley Service/Philadelphia: Lippincott, 1908. [xi], 328p, 16 plates, illus. [8vo].

S159. STEAD, R.

Daring deeds of great mountaineers: true stories of adventure, pluck and resource in many parts of the world. Ldn: Seeley Service, 1921. 3-259p, 9 plates, illus. 22cm.
Contents similar to his book *Adventures.*

S160. STEEL, William Gladstone

The mountains of Oregon. Portland: David Steel, successor to Hines the Printer, 1890. 112p, illus, maps, bibl. 23cm.
Chronicles of the Oregon Alpine Club, predecessor of the Mazamas. Includes Oregon bibliography.

S161. STEELE, Peter R. C. (b.1935)
Doctor on Everest. Line drawing by Phoebe Bullock. Ldn: Hodder, 1972. 222p, 24 plates, illus. 23cm.
—Book club ed.
A personal and professional eye-view of the controversial and unhappy 1971 international expedition.

S162. STEELE, P. R. C.
Medical care for mountain climbers. Line drawings by Phoebe Bullock. Ldn: Heinemann, 1976. xii, 220p, illus. 19cm. Limp-bound.
Concise and authoritative expedition handbook.

S163. STEELE, P. R. C.
Two and two halves to Bhutan; a family journey in the Himalayas. Line drawings by Phoebe Bullock. Ldn: Hodder, 1970. 191p, 16 plates, illus. 23cm.
—Book club editions, 1970.
Dr. Steele and his family travelled through the remote Himalayan Kingdom of Bhutan; with a little climbing on the side, in the Monlarkarchhung region.

S164. STEPHEN, Sir Leslie (1832-1904)
Men, books and mountains. Collected by S. O. A. Ullman, Ldn: Hogarth Press, 1956. 247p.
Includes climbing on Mont Blanc, etc.

S165. STEPHEN, L.
The playground of Europe. Ldn: Longmans, 1871. xii, 321p, 3 plates, illus. 20cm.
—Enlarged & rev. ed. 1894. xii, 339p. R.P., 1895.
—Silver Library ed. 1899. xiv, 339p, 3 plates, illus. 19cm. R.P., 1901, 1904, 1907, 1910, 1924.
—U.S. ed. N.Y.: Putnam, 1909. 384p.
—Another ed. Oxford: Blackwell, 1936. 243p. with intro. by Winthrop Young. R.P., 1946.
—Another ed. N.Y.; New Mountaineering Library, 1940.
(N.B.: Stephen varied the contents in different editions; none contains all his mountain writings.)
Stephen is one of the most famous personalities in mountaineering, and his book ranks among the best in climbing literature. The piece on Switzerland in winter is perhaps his finest.

S166. STEVEN, Campbell
The Island hills. Ldn: Hurst & Blackett, 1855. 190p, 23 plates, illus, maps. 23cm.
Walks and scrambles on most of Scotland's island hills.

S167. STEVEN, C.
The story of Scotland's hills. Ldn: Hale, 1975. 192p, plates, illus, map. 23cm.

S168. STEVENS, W. Bertrand
Victorious mountaineer: memoir of Henry Pierce Nichols, 1850-1940. Stockport: Cloister Press, 1943. 78p. [12mo].
The Rev. Nichols climbed in the Canadian Rockies; mentioned in Outram's book.

S169. STOBART, Tom
Adventurer's eye: the autobiography of Everest film-man Tom Stobbart. Ldn: Odhams Press, 1958. 256p, plates, illus. 23cm.
—Popular Book Club ed.
—U.S. ed. entitled *I take pictures for adventure.* N.Y.: Doubleday, 1958. 288p, 32 plates.
Includes attempt on Nun Kun, Antarctica and Everest.

S170. STOCK, E. Elliot
Scrambles in storm and sunshine among the Swiss and English alps. Ldn: John Ouseley, [1910]. 210p, plates, illus. 24cm.

S171. STODDARD, S. R.
The Adirondacks. Albany, 1874. 204p, illus.

S172. STODDART, Anna
Life of Isabella Bird Bishop. N.Y.: Dutton, 1908.

S173. STONOR, Charles
The Sherpa and the Snowman. Ldn: Hollis & Carter, 1955. xii, 209p, plates, illus. 23cm.
Account of the 1953-4 *Daily Mail* Himalayan Yeti expedition, organized by Ralph Izzard.

S174. STROUDE, Ben C.
Merseyside Himalayan Expedition, 1977: report. Wirral: The Expedition, [1978?]. 34p, illus. 21cm.

S175. STUART-WATT, Eva
Afirca's dome of mystery: comprising ...and a girl's pioneer climb to the crater of [Kilimanjaro]. Ldn: Marshall, 1930. 215p, plates (1 fold.), illus. map. 26cm.

S176. STUCK, Hudson (1863-?)
The ascent of Denali (Mount McKinley): a narrative of the first complete ascent of the highest peak in North America. N.Y.: Scribner's/Ldn: Bickers, 1914. xx, 188p, 34 plates, illus, fold. map. 22cm. The U.K. ed. is identical apart from the cover, which is red, gilt lettered; whereas the U.S. one is blue, with different lettering and a picture.
—2nd ed. 1918. R.P., 1921, 1925.
—Facsimile reprint. Seattle: Mountain Craft/Vancouver: Cordee, 1977. With intro. notes by Bradford Washburn and the diary of Walter Harper.
Archdeacon Stuck also climbed in Britain, Colorado, Canadian Rockies and Mt. Rainier.

S177. STUTFIELD, Hugh Edward Millington (1858-1929) & COLLIE, John Norman (1859-1942)
Climbs & exploration in the Canadian Rockies. Ldn: Longmans, 1903. xii, 343p, 52 plates, illus. fold. map. 23cm.
One of the classics of the Canadian Rockies.

S178. STYLES, Frank Showell (b.1908)
Backpacking in the Alps and Pyrenees. Ldn: Gollancz, 1976. 191p, plates, illus, maps. 23cm.

S179. STYLES, S.
Blue remembered hills. Ldn: Faber, 1965. 189p, plates, illus, map. 21cm.
Climbing reminiscences of a British climber and prolific writer, including fiction. His climbing has taken him to the Alps, Pyrenees, Norway and Himalaya.

S180. STYLES, S.
Climber in Wales. By ...(S.S. of the *Birmingham Post*). Birmingham: Cornish Brothers, [1948]. 85p, 21 plates, illus. 22cm.

S181. STYLES, S.
The climber's bedside book. Ldn: Faber, 1968. 256p. 21cm.
A miscellany of mountain stories, and notes on 50 names famous in mountaineering history and on 100 notable mountains.

S182. STYLES, S.
First on the summits. With diagrams by R. B. Evans. Ldn: Gollancz, 1970. 157p, 12 plates, illus, maps. 23cm.
—Quality Book Club ed. 1971.
Covers the Matterhorn, Cook, Grépon, Nanga Parbat, McKinley, Nanda Devi, Everest, Mont Blanc, K2, Mt. Kenya, Kanchenjunga, Muztagh Tower.

S183. STYLES, S.
The forbidden frontiers: the Survey of India from 1765 to 1949. Ldn: Hamilton, 1970. 160p, 12 plates, illus. 23cm.
Surveying the frontiers with Nepal, Tibet and Afghanistan.

S184. STYLES, S.
The foundations of climbing. Ldn: Paul, 1966. 142p, 12 plates, illus. 22cm.
—Reissued as an Arrow paperback entitled *Arrow book of climbing.*

S185. STYLES, S.
Getting to know mountains. Edited by Jack Cox. Ldn: Newnes, 1958. 160p, 8 plates, illus. 19cm.

S186. STYLES, S.
How mountains are climbed. Ldn: Routledge, 1958. xii, 158p, 8 plates, illus. 19cm.

S187. STYLES, S.
Introduction to mountaineering. Ldn: Seeley Service, [1954?]. 159p, 8 plates, illus. 22cm. (Beaufort Library series).

S188. STYLES, S.
Look at mountains. Ldn: Hamilton, 1962. 95p, illus. 19cm.

S189. STYLES, S.
Mallory of Everest. Ldn: Hamilton, 1967. 157p, 10 plates, illus, maps. 23cm.
—U.S. ed. N.Y.: Macmillan, 1967. 174p.

S190. STYLES, S.
Men and mountaineering: an anthology of writings by climbers. Edited by . . .Ldn: Hamilton, 1968. 207p. 23cm.

S191. STYLES, S.
The moated mountain. Ldn: Hurst & Blackett, 1955. 255p, 21 plates, illus. 22cm.
Attempt on Baudha, Manaslu district, Nepal.

S192. STYLES, S.
Modern mountaineering. Ldn: Faber, 1964. 189p, 8 plates, illus. 23cm.

S193. STYLES, S.
The mountaineer's weekend book. Ldn: Seeley Service, [1950]. 408p, illus. 19cm.
—Rev. ed. 1962.
Fascinating compendium of songs, stories, information and verses.

S194. STYLES, S.
Mountains of North Wales. Ldn: Gollancz, 1973. 175p, 20 plates, illus, map. 23cm.

S195. STYLES, S.
Mountains of the midnight sun. Ldn: Hurst & Blackett, 1954. 208p, 14 plates, illus. 22cm.
Climbing on the Lyngen Peninsula, northern Norway.

S196. STYLES, S.
On top of the world: an illustrated history of mountaineering and mountaineers. Ldn; Hamilton/N.Y.: Macmillan, 1967. xx, 278p, 32 col. plates, illus, maps. 26cm.

S197. STYLES, S.
Rock and rope. Ldn: Faber, 1967. 174p, 8 plates, illus. 21cm.

S198. SUFRIN, Mark
To the top of the world: Sir Edmund Hillary and the conquest of Everest. N.Y.: Platt & Munk, 1966. 94p, illus. [4to].

S199. SUTTON, Geoffrey J. S. (b.1930)
Artificial aids in mountaineering. Ldn: Mountaineering Assoc., 1962. 60p, illus. 19cm. (Teaching Manual No. 2–Modern Methods, complementary to *A short manual of mountaineering training.*)
—2nd ed. Ldn: Nicholas Kaye, 1962. 64p, illus. 19cm.

S200. SUTTON, G. J. S. & NOYCE, Wilfrid
Samson: the life and writings of Menlove Edwards. Edited, with a biographical memoir, by . . .[Stockport: Cloister Press, 1961.] vi, 122p, 8 plates, illus. 23cm.
Essays, short stories and poems by John Menlove Edwards (1910-58), leading British inter-wars climber, whose life ended in tragedy.

S201. SUTTON, George
Glacier Island: the official account of the British South Georgia Expedition, 1954-55. Ldn: Chatto & Windus, 1957. 224p, 15 plates, illus, maps. 23cm.
—Book club ed.
Expedition to these antarctic islands with climbing as the prime objective, making first ascents in the Allardyce Range.

S202. SUTTON, John
Hypoxia: man at high altitude. Edited by . . ., Norman Jones & Charles Houston. N.Y.: Thieme-Stratton, 1982. 210p, illus.
Papers given at the Second Hypoxia Symposium, Banff, 1981; many directly related to high-altitude mountaineering.

S203. SWIFT, Hildegarde Hoyt
From the eagle's wing: a biography of John Muir. N.Y., 1962. 287p, illus. 21cm.

S204. SWINSON, A.
Beyond the frontiers: the biography of Colonel F. M. Bailey, explorer and special agent. Ldn: Hutchinson, 1971. xiii, 246p, plates, illus. 23cm.

S205. [SWISS ALPINE CLUB]
Vocabulary for alpinists/Vocabulaire pour alpinistes/Vocabolario per alpinisti. Swiss Alpine Club, 1966. 4 sections × 16p.
Comparative mountaineering vocabulary in English, French, German and Italian.

S206. SWISS FOUNDATION FOR ALPINE RESEARCH
Everest: the Swiss Everest expeditions. Ldn & N.Y.: Hodder, 1954. xvi, [28p] 144 plates (some col), illus. 28cm.
Photo-album of the two 1952 expeditions, introduced by Othmar Gurtner.

S207. SWISS FOUNDATION FOR ALPINE RESEARCH
The first 10 years of the S.F.A.R. Zurich: S.F.A.R., 1951. 48p, col. plate, illus, fold. map. 28cm. Limited edition of 750 copies.
Includes references to Dhaulagiri, etc.

S208. SYMONDS, John
The great beast: the life of Aleister Crowley. Ldn: Rider, 1951. 316p, plates, illus. 24cm.
—Rev. ed. expanded & entitled *The great beast: life and magick of Aleister Crowley.* Ldn: Macdonald, 1971. ix, 413p.
—Rev. ed. Mayflower paperback. 1973.
Crowley climbed in the Alps in the 1890s and was regarded as a promising albeit somwhat erratic climber. He led expeditions to K2 and Kanchenjunga in 1902 and 1905 respectively. He died in 1947.

S209. SYNGE, Patrick M.
Mountains of the moon: an expedition to the Equatorial mountains of Africa. Ldn: Lindsday Drummond, 1937, 1937. xxiv, 221p, 93 plates (2 col), illus, 2 maps (1 fold.). 23cm. 3rd ptg, 1938.
—Special T.B.C. ed. Only 91 plates, no fold. map.
Chiefly walking and botanical exploration. Visits to Mt. Elgon and Mt. Kenya.

T

T01. TALFOURD, Sir Thomas Noon
Vacation rambles and thoughts: comprising the recollections of three continental tours in the vacations of 1841, 1842, and 1843. Ldn: Moxon, 1845. 2v. 22cm.
—2nd ed. 1845.
—3rd ed. 1851.
—Supplement. 1854.
Includes attempt on Mont Blanc.

T02. TARARUA TRAMPING CLUB
Tararua story: jubilee of a mountain club. Edited by B. D. A. Greig. Wellington: Tararua Tramping Club, 1946. 108p, illus, maps. 25cm.
Anniversary publication of a new Zealand climbing club.

T03. TARBUCK, Kenneth
Nylon rope and climbing safety. Edinburgh: British Ropes. [1960]. 35p, illus. 13cm. Two versions seen.
Dynamic belaying; the Tarbuck Knot is now obsolete.

T04. TASKER, Joe (1948-82)
Everest, the cruel way. Ldn: Eyre Methuen, 1981. 166p, 12 plates, illus. 22cm.
Unsuccessful attempt on the west ridge in winter. Tasker and Boardman were later killed attempting the unclimbed north-east ridge of Everest.

T05. TASKER, J.
Savage arena. Ldn: Methuen/N.Y.: St. Martin's, 1982. 270p, 24 plates, illus, maps. 24cm.
Widely acclaimed book which includes his experiences on the Eiger, Dunagiri, Changabang, K2, Kanchenjunga.

T06. TAYLOR, Peter (b.1921)
Coopers Creek to Langtang II. Ldn: Angus & Robertson, 1965. 239p, 24 plates, illus, maps (endpapers). 23cm.
One-man expedition to the Himalaya from Australia.

T07. TAYLOR, Robert
The Breach: Kilimanjaro and the conquest of self. N.Y.: Coward McCann & Geohegan, 1981. 254p, col. illus, map. 24cm.
Account of January 1978 attempt on the Icicle route on Kilimanjaro's south-west Breach Wall. The author was injured, necessitating an arduous rescue.

T08. TAYLOR, William C.
The snows of yesteryear: J. Norman Collie, mountaineer. Toronto: Holt Rinehart & Winston Canada, 1973. [vi], 186p, illus, maps. 24cm.
The only overall account of Collie's life and climbs.

T09. TAZIEFF, Haroun
Craters of fire. Ldn: Hamish Hamilton, 1952.
Includes an account by this Belgian geologist of volcanic eruptions in 1947 near Lake Kivu in Zaire, when he descended into the active crater of Kituro, was chased by a lava flow, etc.

T10. TAZIEFF, H.
Nyiragongo: the forbidden volcano.
—1st U.S. ed. 1979. [4to].
Hazardous descent into the active crater of this African volcano.

T11. TEJADA-FLORES, Lito & STECK, Allen
Wilderness skiing. S.F.: Sierra Club, 1972. 310p, illus. 16cm.
Ski-mountaineering manual, prepared by two leading American climbers.

T12. TEMPLE, John & WALKER, Alan (Editors)
Kirinyaga: a Mount Kenya anthology. Nairobi: Mountain Club of Kenya, [1974]. 61p. 33cm.

T13. TEMPLE, R. Philip (b.1939)
Castles in the air: men and mountains in New Zealand. Edited by . . .Dunedin: John McIndoe, 1973. 168p, illus. 24cm.
Picture history of mountaineering in New Zealand.

T14. TEMPLE, R. P.
Mantle of the skies: the Southern Alps of New Zealand. Christchurch: Whitcombe & Tombs, 1971. 138p, illus (some col), maps.
Photo-album.

T15. TEMPLE, R. P.
Nawok! The New Zealand expedition to New Guinea's highest mountains. Ldn: Dent, 1962. xiv, 189p, 13 plates, illus. 23cm.
—T.B.C. ed.
Attempts on the Carstenz Range.

T16. TEMPLE, R. P.
The sea and the snow: the south Indian Ocean expedition to Heard Island. Melbourne: Cassell Australia, 1966. [xii], 188p, 16 plates, illus. 22cm.
The team sailed to the island in a boat skippered by Tilman, and climbed Big Ben, a massive icy peak.

T17. TEMPLE, R. P.
The world at their feet: the story of New Zealand mountaineers in the great ranges of the world. Christchurch: Whitcombe & Tombs, 1969. 250p, 28 plates (some col), illus, 4 maps. 25cm.
Valuable reference book worthy of an update.

T18. TENZING NORGAY (1914-86)
After Everest: an autobiography. By . . .: as told to Malcolm Barnes. Ldn: Allen & Unwin, 1977. 3-184p, 24 plates (some col), illus, maps. 23cm.

T19. TERRAY, Lionel (1921-65)
Conquistadors of the useless: from the Alps to Annapurna. Trans. [from the French] by Geoffrey Sutton. Ldn: Gollancz, 1963. 351p, 84 plates, illus. 23cm. Also 2nd ptg. From the original: *Les conquérants de l'inutile.* (Paris: Gallimard, 1961)
—U.S. ed. entitled *Borders of the impossible: from the Alps to Annapurna.* N.Y.: Doubleday, 1964. [x], 350p.
Terray was a French climber whose conquests included the Eigerwand, Fitzroy, Annapurna, Makalu and Jannu. He died in a climbing accident.

T20. THOMAS, Lowell
Lowell Thomas' book of the high mountains. N.Y.: Messner, 1964. 512p, illus. 24cm. Softback ed. 1969.
Interesting and wide-ranging survey of mountains and climbing.

T21. THOMAS, M. B. & WALLIS, R. H.
Report on the Royal Navy East Greenland Expedition, 1966. By . . .and members of the expedition. [Plymouth]: The Expedition, [1967]. [64p], plates, illus, maps. 34cm.

T22. THOMPSON, Dorothy Evelyn (1888-1961)
Climbing with Joseph Georges. Kendal: Titus Wilson, 1962. [xii], 159p, 13 plates, illus. 22cm.

Climbing memoirs of a noted British alpinist between the wars. Written as a tribute to her guide, and published posthumously by her friends.

T23. THOMPSON, Margaret
High trails of Glacier National Park. Caldwell, Id, 1938. 167p, plates, illus, fold. map. 23cm. Also 2nd ptg.

T24. THOMSON, Joseph
Travels in the Atlas and southern Morocco: a narrative of exploration. Ldn: George Philip, 1889. xviii, 488p, 31 plates, illus, 2 fold. maps. 20cm.
Contains descriptions of mountain scenery and ascents of Irghalsor, Gadal and Yaurirf.

T25. THOMSON, Thomas
Western Himalaya and Tibet: a narrative of a journey through the mountains of northern India during the years 1847-8. Ldn: Reeve, 1852. xii, 501p, plates (1 fold.), illus, maps. 24cm.
—Reprinted. New Delhi: Manjnsri Pub. House, 1974.
—Another ed. Kathmandu: R. P. Bhandar, 1979. xii, 501p, 14 plates, 2 maps.
Thomson was the first European to cross the Saser and Karakoram passes, and one of the first to describe routes in the Karakoram.

T26. THORINGTON, James Monroe (b.1894)
The glittering mountains of Canada: a record of exploration and pioneer ascents in the Canadian Rockies, 1914-1924. Philadelphia: Lea, 1925. xxii, 310p, 65 plates, illus, maps. 23cm. Also edition of 1500 numbered copies signed by the author.
Thorington was president of the A.A.C., 1941-3, and a fine mountain historian.

T27. THORINGTON, J. M.
Mont Blanc sideshow: the life and times of Albert Smith. Philadelphia: Winston, 1934. xvi, 255p, 19 plates, illus. 23cm.
Refers to Smith's celebrated illustrated lectures of his ascent of Mont Blanc.

T28. THORINGTON, J. M.
The Purcell Range of British Columbia. N.Y.: A.A.C., 1946. [12], 152p, illus, maps (1 in pkt). 24cm.
A classic monograph on this range which includes the Bugaboo Mountains and Snowpatch Spire.

T29. THORINGTON, J. M.
A survey of early American ascents in the Alps in the nineteenth century. N.Y.: A.A.C., 1943. viii, 83p, illus. 23cm.
Excellent record with many extracts from original accounts, diaries, letters etc.

T30. THWAITES, Reuben Gold
A brief history of Rocky Mountain exploration with especial reference to the expedition of Lewis and Clark. N.Y.: Appleton, 1904. xiv, 276p, 7 plates, illus, map. 19cm. (Expansion of the Republic series)

T31. THWAITES, R. G.
Early western travels, 1748-1846. Edited by ...Cleveland, OH: Arthur H. Clark Co., 1905.
Includes expeditions by Pike, Long et al.

T32. TICHY, Herbert
Cho Oyu: by favour of the gods. Trans. [from the German] by Basil Creighton. Ldn: Methuen, 1957. 196p, 36 plates (some col), illus. 23cm. From the original: *Cho Oyu: Gnade der Götter.* (Vienna: Ullstein Verlag, 1955)
This Austrian expedition was the smallest at that time to succeed on a major Himalayan peak.

T33. TICHY, H.
Himalaya. Trans. [from the German] by Richard Rickett and David Streatfeild. N.Y.: Putnam, 1970/Ldn: Hale, 1971. 175p, 61 col. plates, illus, maps. 28cm. From the original: *Himalaya.* (Vienna: Schroll, 1968)
Photo-album of Austrian Himalayan expeditions.

T34. TICHY, H.
Tibetan adventure: travels through Afghanistan, India and Tibet. Trans. from the German by Ian F. D. Morrow and L. M. Sievking. Ldn: Faber & Faber, 1938.

261p, illus, 2 maps. 22cm. From the original: *Zum heiligsten Berg der Welt.* (Vienna: Seidel, 1937)
Tichy disguised himself and joined a pilgrimage to the most holy mountain Kailas.

T35. TILMAN, Harold William (1898-1978)
The ascent of Nanda Devi. Cambridge: University Press/N.Y.: Macmillan, 1937. xiv, 235p, 35 plates, illus, 2 maps (1 fold). 23cm. Some U.S. copies are said to have inferior illustrations.
—R.U./C.U.P. ed. in pictorial boards. Virtually identical with original.
—Guild paperback. 1949.
Account of first ascent by Tilman and Odell, members of the British-American 1936 expedition.

T36. TILMAN, H. W.
China to Chitral. Cambridge: University Press, 1951. xii, 124p, 69 plates, illus, maps. 24cm.
Account of his journey through Chinese Turkestan in 1949. He attempted Bogdo Ola and Chakar Aghil with Shipton.

T37. TILMAN, H. W.
Ice with everything. Sidney, BC: Gray's Pub, 1974. 142p, illus, maps. 22cm.
—U.K. ed. Nautical Pub, 1974.
In later life Tilman spent his time sailing to remote arctic and antarctic locations, landing to do a bit of climbing. This book describes visits to east and west Greenland, 1971-3.

T38. TILMAN, H. W.
In 'Mischief's' wake. 1971
Sailing adventures; 'Michief' was the name of his favourite boat.

T39. TILMAN, H. W.
'Mischief' among the penguins. Ldn: Hart-Davis, 1961. 192p, plates, illus, maps. 23cm.
Voyage to and climbing on Crozet Island in the Indian Ocean.

T40. TILMAN, H. W.
'Mischief' goes south. Ldn: Hollis & Carter, 1968. 190p, illus, maps.
Voyage to South Shetland Islands, 1966-7; circumstances prevented any climbing.

T41. TILMAN, H. W.
'Mischief' in Greenland. Ldn: Hollis & Carter, 1964. 192p, illus, 2 charts.
Expeditions to the west coast of Greenland and Baffin Islands, 1961-2.

T42. TILMAN, H.W.
'Mischief' in Patagonia. Cambridge: University Press, 1957. 185p, illus. 23cm.
—T.B.C. ed.
Traverse of the southern ice-cap from Calvo Fiord eastwards to Lago Argentino, and return; a total of six weeks' arduous travel.

T43. TILMAN, H. W.
Mostly 'Mischief'. Ldn: Hollis & Carter, 1966. 191p, 16 plates, illus, maps. 23cm.
Voyages to the Arctic and Antarctic.

T44. TILMAN H. W.
Mount Everest 1938. Cambridge: University Press, 1948. x, 160p, 36 plates, illus, 2 maps. 23cm. R.P., 1948.
Tilman led this small expedition which included Shipton and Smythe. They reached c.8300m.

T45. TILMAN, H. W.
Nepal Himalaya. Cambridge: University Press, 1952. xi, 272p, 40 plates, illus, maps. 23cm.
Account of three expeditions — Langtang and Ganesh; Annapurna IV and Manaslu; and the Khumba side of Everest, discovering the southern approach.

T46. TILMAN, H. W.
The seven mountain-travel books. Introduction by Jim Perrin. Appendices by Ken Wilson. Ldn: Diadem/Seattle: Mountaineers, 1983. 896p, illus, maps. 23cm.
Reprint of Tilman's climbing books.

T47. TILMAN, H. W.
Snow on the Equator. Ldn: Bell, 1937/N.Y.: Macmillan, 1938. xii, 265p, 20 plates, illus, maps. 23cm.
—T.B.C. ed. 1940. Only 16 plates.
Climbing with Shipton — Mt. Kenya, Kilimanjaro, Ruwenzori.

T48. TILMAN, H. W.

Triumph and tribulation. [U.K.]: Nautical Pub/N.Y.: Ziff-Davis, 1977. 153p, illus, maps. 22cm.
Voyages to Spitsbergen; Disko Island, west Greenland and Angmagssalik, east Greenland.

T49. TILMAN, H. W.

Two mountains and a river. Cambridge: University Press, 1949. xii, 233p, 37 plates, illus, maps. 22cm.
Attempts on Rakaposhi and Muztagh Ata; and a visit to the source of the River Oxus.

T50. TILMAN, H. W.

When men and mountains meet. Cambridge: University Press, 1946. x, 232p, 36 plates illus, maps. 23cm. R.P., 1947.
Exploration in the Assam Himalaya — Zemu Gap, Gori Chen, and adjacent peaks. The second part of the book deals with his wartime experiences with Albanian and Italian partisans. He is honoured annually in the Italian town of Belluno.

T51. TISSOT, Victor

Unknown Switzerland [*reminiscences of travel*]. Trans. from the 12th edition by Mrs Wilson. Ldn: Hodder, 1889. x, 361p. 20cm.
—U.S. ed. N.Y.: A. D. F. Randolph, [1890].
—Another ed. N.Y.: J. Pott, 1900.
—Another ed. N.Y., 1901. 371p, illus, col. fold. map.
Chapter on mountain climbing and glaciers.

T52. TOBIAS, Michael Charles & DRASDO, Harold (Editors)

The mountain spirit. Woodstock, NJ: Overlook Press, 1979/Ldn: Gollancz, 1980. 264p, illus. 26cm.
Explores facets of the influence of mountains from myths and legends to extreme climbing. Tobias is an American climber who has studied comparative literature, philosophy and art-history; Drasdo is a British climber involved in outdoor pursuits.

T53. TOKYO HIMALAYA EXPEDITION

Mountain of White Devil: South Pillar of Dhaulagiri I, 1976 & 1978. Tokyo: The Expedition, 1979. [44], 387p, illus (mostly col), maps. 26cm. In Japanese with English summary. Yak. j. 463.
Six climbers died in the 1976 expedition but the 1978 party were successful.

T54. TOKYO UNIVERSITY KARAKORUM EXPEDITION

Khinyang Chhish 1965. Tokyo: Meikei-dô, 1968. var. pag., illus (some col), maps. 24cm. In Japanese with English summary. Yak. j. 455.

T55. TOKYO UNIVERSITY NEPAL HIMALAYA EXPEDITION

Churen Himal 1971. Tokyo: The Expedition, 1973. var. pag., illus, maps. 26cm. In Japanese with English summary. Yak. j. 456.
Unsuccessful expedition.

T56. TOKYO UNIVERSITY OF AGRICULTURE & TECHNOLOGY ALPINE CLUB

Dhaulagiri II, 1975. Tokyo: The Expedition, 1976. [20], 53p, illus, maps. 26cm. In Japanese with English summary. Yak. j. 462.
Unsuccessful attempt from south side.

T57. TOLL, Roger W.

The mountain peaks of Colorado: containing a list of named points of elevation in the State of Colorado with elevations and topographic details. [Denver]: Colorado Mountain Club, 1923. 59p. 23cm.
This publication served as an early guidebook.

T58. TOLL, R. W.

Mountaineering in the Rocky Mountain National Park. [Compiled] by ...and [edited by] Robert Sterling Yard. Compiled from the records of the Colorado Mountain Club. Washington, DC: Government printing Office, 1919. 106p, plates, illus, 2 maps (1 in pkt). 23cm. Softback ed. 1921.
Served as an early guidebook.

T59. TOMBAZI, N. A.
Account of a photographic expedition to the southern glaciers of Kanchenjunga in the Sikkim Himalaya. Bombay: The Author, 1925. x. 80p, illus, map. 25 × 20cm. Edition of 150 copies.
Their route took them over an eastern spur of Kabru to the Talung Glacier and Zemu Gap.

T60. TOWNSEND, J. H.
The two climbers; a cry from the Alps: a true story. Ldn: Partridge, [1904]. 32p.
Account of an accident to the author's brother on the Dent de Jaman in 1864.

T61. TRANTER, Philip N. L. (1939-66)
No tigers in the Hindu Kush. Edited by Nigel Tranter. Ldn: Hodder, 1968. 155p, 17 plates, illus. 23cm.
—T.B.C. ed. 1969. Only 7 plates.
Account of a four-man Scottish expedition in 1965, written by Tranter's father from diaries after his son was killed in a road accident.

T62. TRENKER, Luis
Brothers of the snow. Trans. from the German by F. H. Lyon. Ldn: Routledge, 1933.
—U.S. ed. N.Y.: Dutton. 1934. 247p.
Trenker was a Tyrolese guide who starred in a number of pre-war mountain film spectaculars, including playing the part of Jean-Antoine Carrel.

T63. TRENTON, Patricia & HASSICK, Peter H.
The Rocky Mountains: a vision for artists in the nineteenth century. Norman: Univ. Oklahoma Press, in assoc. with Buffalo Bill Historical Center, Cody, WY, 1983. xix, 418p, illus (some col), map, bibl. [4to].
Well researched and illustrated presentation of the U.S. Rockies in nineteenth century art.

T64. TRUFFAUT, Roland (b.1911)
From Kenya to Kilimanjaro. Ldn: Hale, 1957. 157p, 24 plates, illus, maps. 23cm. From the original: *Du Kenya au Kilimanjaro.* (Paris: Fulliard, 1953)
Includes account of ascent of the north face of Mt. Kenya.

T65. TUCKER, John William
Kanchenjunga. Ldn: Elek Books/N.Y.: Abelard Schumann, 1955. 224p, 20 plates, illus. 23cm.
—Panther paperback. 1957.
—Another U.S. ed. in boards. 1966.
Reconnaissance expedition in 1954, finding the route for the first ascent in 1955.

T66. [TUCKETT, Elizabeth F.]
How we spent the Summer: or, A 'Voyage en Zigzag' in Switzerland and Tyrol, with some members of the Alpine Club. From the sketch book of one of the party. Ldn: Longmans, 1864. 40 leaves of illus. 27 × 36cm. 2nd ptg, 1864.
—3rd ed. redrawn, 1866. 40p, illus. 27 × 36cm.
—6th ed. 43p, illus. 27 × 37cm.
The author, who was a sister of F. F. Tuckett, produced several delightful Victorian sketchbooks depicting their Alpine travels.

T67. [TUCKETT, E. F.]
Pictures in Tyrol and elswhere: from a family sketchbook, by the author of a 'Voyage en Zigzag'. Ldn: Longmans, 1867. 313p, plates, illus. 21cm.
—2nd ed. 1869.

T68. [TUCKETT, E. F.]
Zigzagging amongst Dolomites. Ldn: Longmans, 1871. [3], 38p of illus, map. 26 × 36cm.

T69. TUCKETT, Francis Fox (1834-1913)
A pioneer in the high Alps: Alpine diaries and letters of F. F. Tuckett, 1856-1874. [Edited by W. A. B. Coolidge] Ldn: Arnold, 1920. xii, 372p, 8 plates, illus, 2 fold. maps. 23cm.
Tuckett climbed extensively in the latter part of the nineteenth century, adopting the scientific approach to mountain travel.

T70. TURNER, Samuel (1869-1929)
The conquest of the New Zealand Alps. Ldn: Fisher Unwin, 1922. 292p, 23 plates, illus. 22cm.
His later climbs in New Zealand, particularly on Mt. Tutuko.

T71. TURNER, S.
My climbing adventures in four continents. Ldn: Fisher Unwin, 1911. 283p, 52 plates, illus. 23cm.
—U.S. ed. N.Y.: Scribners & Unwin, n.d. 283p.
—Cheap ed. Fisher Unwin, 1913. xii, 382p, illus. 21cm.
Turner was a mountaineer whose travels included Siberia, South America and New Zealand. His bombastic style spoils his books and detracts from his not inconsiderable climbing achievements.

T72. TURNER, S.
Siberia: a record of travel, climbing and exploration. Ldn: Fisher Unwin, 1905. xvi, 420p, illus. 22cm.
—U.S. ed. Philadelphia: Jacobs, n.d.
—Cheap ed. Fisher Unwin, 1911. 320p, plates. 21cm.

T73. TURRILL, W. B.
Joseph Dalton Hooker: botanist, explorer and administrator. Ldn: Nelson, 1963. xi, 228p, illus, maps. 20cm.
—Scientific Book Club ed. No ills.
Hooker was the first European to made an almost complete circuit of Kanchenjunga, 1848-9. His adventurous life included an antarctic expedition and travels in the Atlas Mountains of Morocco.

T74. Tyndale, Harry Edmund Guise (1888-1948)
Mountain paths. Ldn: Eyre & Spottiswoode, 1948. x, 208p, illus. 23cm.
Climbing reminiscences; the later chapters deal with Julius Kugy and the Julian Alps. Tyndale was one of Irving's protegés along with Mallory. He edited various mountaineering publications including the *Alpine Journal.*

T75. TYNDALL, John (1820-93)
The glaciers of the Alps: being a narrative of excursions and ascents, an account of the origin and phenomena of glaciers, and an exposition of the physical principles to which they are related. Ldn: Murray, 1860. xxii, 444p, 6 plates, illus. 20cm.
—U.S ed. Boston: Ticknor & Fields, 1861. xx, 446p.
—New [2nd] ed. Ldn: Longmans, 1896. xvii, 445p, 5 plates. 20cm. Prefatory note by Mrs Tyndall, minor textual corrections and improved index.
—New Universal Library ed. Ldn: Routledge, [1905]. xii, 200p. 16cm. Omits Part II (scientific material).
—Silver Library ed. Longmans, 1906. Edited by Mrs Tyndall.
—Everyman's Library ed. Ldn: Dent, [1906]. xiv, 274p. Combined with *Mountaineering in 1861.* R.P., 1911, 1928.
Tyndall is best known for his devotion to science and his first ascent of the Weisshorn. He was also a contender for the first ascent of the Matterhorn.

T76. TYNDALL, J.
Hours of exercise in the Alps. Ldn: Longmans, 1871. xii, 473p, 7 plates, illus. 21cm. R.P., 1871.
—3rd ed. 1873. xiv, 475p.
—4th ed. 1899. xii, 418p, 7 plates. 20cm. With minor textual corrections and an index.
—Silver Library ed. 1906. Edited by Mrs Tyndall.
—6th ed. 1936.
—U.S. editions. N.Y.: Appleton, 1871. Reprints (?), 1872, 1873, 1874, 1875, 1883, 1885.
—Another ed. (reprint?) Appleton, 1895. xii, 473p, 7 plates. 19cm. R.P., 1896, 1897.
—Westminster [4th] ed. Edition of 1000 numbered copies.
Includes his Matterhorn attempts, ascent of the Weisshorn, death of Bennen, and numerous other climbs.

T77. TYNDALL, J.
Mountaineering in 1861: a vacation tour. Ldn: Longmans, 1862. x, 105p, 2 plates. 2cm.
—Also issued under title *Vacation tour in Switzerland.*
—Reissued with *Glaciers of the Alps.* Everyman's Library.
Contains mostly attempts on the Matterhorn.

U

U01. ULLMAN, James Ramsay (1908-71)
Americans on Everest: The official account of the ascent led by Norman G. Dyrenfurth. By . . .and other members of

the expedition. Philadelphia: Lippincott, 1964/Ldn: Michael Joseph, 1965. xxiv, 429p, 56 plates (some col), illus, map (endpapers). 25cm.
Three parties reached the summit, including the first ascent of the west ridge, and descent of south ridge.

U02. ULLMAN, J. R.

High conquest: the story of mountaineering. Philadelphia: Lippincott, 1941. 334p, illus, maps. 24cm. R.P., 1941 twice, 1943.
—T.B.C. ed. 1943.
—Rev. & reissued as *The age of mountaineering.* With a chapter on British mountains by W. H. Murray. Lippincott, 1954. 352p. Ldn: Collins, 1956. 384p, 24 plates. 22cm.

U03. ULLMAN, J. R.

Kingdom of adventure Everest: a chronicle of man's assault on the earth's highest mountain. Narrated by the participants. With an accompanying text by . . .N.Y.: Sloane, 1947. 411p, plates, illus, maps. 22cm.
—U.K. ed. Ldn: Collins, 1948. 320p, 25 plates, illus, maps. 23cm.
Passages from various Everest narratives, linked by Ullman's text.

U04. ULLMAN, J. R.

Straight up: the life and death of John Harlin. N.Y.: Doubleday, 1968. 288p, 32 plates, illus. 24cm.
Biography of this outstanding American climber (1935-66) who was killed during the first direct ascent of the Eigerwand.

U05. ULLMAN J. R.

Tiger of the snows: the autobiography of Tenzing of Everest, written in collaboration with James Ramsay Ullman. N.Y.: Putnam, 1955. xvi, 294p, 19 plates, illus. 23cm. Also 2nd ptg.
—U.K. ed. entitled *Man of Everest: the autobiography of Tenzing.* Ldn: Harrap, 1955. 320p, 36 plates (some col), illus. 21cm. R.P., 1955.
—Reprint Soc. ed. 1956.
—Corgi paperback. 1957.
—Abridged ed. by W. V. Venkat Rao entitled *Tenzing of Everest.* Madras: O.U.P., 1958. Also 1966.
—Another ed. Ldn: Severn House, 1975. 320p, 32 plates, illus. 21cm. Spine title: *Sherpa Tenzing, man of Everest.*

U06. UNDERHILL, Miriam (née **O'Brien**) **(1899-1976)**

Give me the hills. Ldn: Methuen, 1956. 252p, 36 plates (some col), illus. 23cm.
—U.S. ed. Riverside, Co: Chatham Press, in assoc. with Appalachian Mountain Club, 1971. 278p, illus. 24cm. Enlarged edition, adding a final chapter and many more illustrations.
The author was one of the few leading American climbers active in the Alps between the wars. The book also includes climbs in the U.S. Rockies.

U07. UNITED STATES GEOLOGICAL AND GEOGRAPHICAL SURVEYS

Annual reports of the United States Geological and Geographical Survey of the Territories. Washington, D.C.: Government Printing Office, 1875-8. 13v.
The 'Hayden' reports. Volumes covering 1873-5 are relevant to Colorado mountaineering and exploration.

U08. UNITED STATES GEOLOGICAL AND GEOGRAPHICAL SURVEYS

Executive and descriptive report of Lieutenant William L. Marshall, Corps of Engineers, on the operations of Party No. 1, Colorado Section, Field Season of 1875. Washington, D.C.: Government Printing Office, 1876.
Relevance to Colorado mountaineering.

U09. UNITED STATES GEOLOGICAL AND GEOGRAPHICAL SURVEYS

Report upon United States Geographical Surveys west of the One Hundredth Meridian. Washington, D.C.: Government Printing Office, 1889. Vol. 1, Geographical Report.
The 'Wheeler' report; relevance to Colorado mountaineering.

U10. UNITED STATES GEOLOGICAL AND GEOGRAPHICAL SURVEYS

Second expedition to Mount St. Elias, in 1891. By Israel Russell. 13th annual report.

U11. UNIVERSITY COLLEGE OF NORTH WALES MOUNTAINEERING CLUB
Plateriyayoc Expedition Peru, 1968: report. Bangor: The Expedition, [1969?]. 28p, illus.
Climbs in the northern group of the Cordillera Urubamba; and El Misti in south-west Peru.

U12. UNIVERSITY COLLEGE OF NORTH WALES MOUNTAINEERING CLUB
Report of the University College Bangor Andean Expedition, 1966. Bangor: The Expedition, [1967?]. 10p.
Cordillera Real, Bolivia; numerous first ascents in the northern Illampu region.

U13. UNIVERSITY OF BRISTOL MOUNTAINEERING CLUB
Kulu 1976: the report of the University of Bristol Mountaineering Club Himalayan Expedition. Bristol: The Expedition, 1976. 12p, illus, maps. 30cm.

U14. UNIVERSITY OF SOUTHAMPTON
Himalayan Expedition, 1977: report. 248p, illus, maps.
Comprehensive report of expedition to the frontier district of Ladakh; half of the team carried out exploratory mountaineering in the Zanskar range.

U15. UNIVERSITY OF SOUTHAMPTON
Ladakh Expedition, 1976: report. Southampton: The Expedition, 1977. 94p, plates (1 fold.), illus, maps. 30cm.

U16. UNSWORTH, Walter (b.1928)
Because it is there: famous mountaineers, 1840-1940. Ldn: Gollancz, 1968. 144p, 8 plates, illus. 23cm.
Twenty-four biographical sketches.

U17. UNSWORTH, W.
The book of rock climbing. Ldn: Barker, 1968. 112p, illus. 24cm. Also 1974.

U18. UNSWORTH, W.
Classic walks of the world. Sparkford: Oxford Illus. Press, 1985. 160p, illus (some col), maps.
Everest, Peru, Kilimanjaro, Mont Blanc, John Muir Trail, etc.

U19. UNSWORTH, W.
Encyclopædia of mountaineering. Compiled by . . .Ldn: Hale/N.Y.: ?, 1975. 272p, 16 plates, illus, maps. 25cm.
—Penguin paperback. 1977.
Good reference book although weak on American and other foreign entries. The author is well-known in the mountain world, not only through his books but also as a magazine editor and publisher of guideboods.

U20. UNSWORTH, W.
The English outcrops. Ldn: Gollancz, 1964. 192p, plates, illus, maps. 22cm.
Narrative guide to areas such as Harrison's Rocks, Derbyshire gritstone, etc.

U21. UNSWORTH, W.
Everest: [a mountaineering history]. Ldn: Allen Lane/Boston: Houghton Mifflin, 1981. xiv, 578p, plates (some col), illus, bibl. 24cm.
—Penguin paperback. 1982.
Definitive history of Everest climbing.

U22. UNSWORTH, W.
The high fells of Lakeland. Ldn: Hale, 1972. 223p, 24 plates, illus. 22cm.
—2nd ed. Milnthorpe: Cicerone Press, 1982. Softback.

U23. UNSWORTH, W.
Matterhorn man: the life and adventures of Edward Whymper. Ldn: Gollancz, 1965. 127p, 8 plates, illus. 23cm.

U24. UNSWORTH, W.
North face: the second conquest of the Alps. Ldn: Hutchinson [Junior Books], 1969. 160p, 12 plates, illus. 21cm.
Includes — Mummery on the Matterhorn; G. W. Young on the Täschhorn; T. G. Brown on the Brenva face of Mont Blanc, etc.

U25. UNSWORTH, W.
Savage snows: the story of Mont Blanc. Ldn: Hodder, 1986. 192p, 16 plates, illus. 24cm.

U26. UNSWORTH, W.
This climbing game: an anthology of mountain humour. Compiled by

. . .illustrated by Ivan Cumberpatch. Ldn: Viking, 1984. 220p, illus. 23cm.
—Penguin paperback, 1985.
Short stories, extracts and snippets.

U27. UNSWORTH, W.
Tiger in the snow: the life and adventures of A. F. Mummery. Ldn: Gollancz, 1967. 126p, 8 plates, illus. 23cm.

U28. UNSWORTH, W.
Walking and climbing. Ldn: Routledge & Kegan Paul, 1977. [viii], 72p, illus. 24cm. (Local Search series)

U29. UNSWORTH, W.
The young mountaineer. Ldn: Hutchinson, 1959. 191p, illus. 20cm.

U30. UNWIN, David J.
Mountain weather for climbers. Leicester: Cordee, 1978. 60p, illus, maps, bibl. 15cm.

V

V01. VAN DER SLEEN, W. G. N.
Four months' camping in the Himalayas. Trans. [from the Dutch] by M. W. Hoper. Ldn: Philip Allen, 1929. xiv, 213p, 39 plates, illus. 25cm. From the original: *Vier maanden Kampeeren in den Himalaya* (Rotterdam: Nijgh & Van Ditmar, 1927)
Around Kailas in Tibet; mainly geological expedition.

V02. VAN DYKE, John Charles
The mountain: renewed studies in impressions and appearances. Ldn: Werner Laurie/N.Y.: Scribners, 1916. xvi, 234p, plate, illus. 19cm.
Analysis of the beauty of mountain scenery from the plains to the highest peaks.

V03. VERGHESE, B. G.
Himalayan endeavour. Bombay: Times of India, 1962. xii, 155p, 14 plates (some col), illus. 22cm.
Summary of Indian mountaineering; particularly Kamet, Nun, Everest, Annapurna III.

V04. VERWOORN, Aat (b.1945)
Beyond the snowline. Wellington: Reed/Auckland: McIndoe, 1981. [4], 156p, 16 plates, illus. 22cm.
Climbing experiences of a group of friends around the world — New Zealand, Australia, North and South America, Europe and Antarctica. Bruce Jenkinson was one of this circle.

V05. VIAL, A. E. Lockington
Alpine glaciers. Ldn: Batchworth, 1952. viii, 126p, illus. 26cm.
Photo-album.

V06. VICTORIAN BUSHWHACKING AND MOUNTAINCRAFT TRAINING ADVISORY BOARD
Bushwhacking and mountaincraft leadership. Manual of the V.B. & M.T.A.B., 1978.
Australian instruction manual.

V07. [VIDEO FILM]
Barnaj. Chameleon Films Production. 23 minutes. Colour.
Journey overland and ascent of Barnaj in Kishtwar Himalaya.

V08. [VIDEO FILM]
Everest in winter. Chameleon Film Service Production. 55 minutes. Colour.
British 1980-1 attempt via west ridge.

V09. [VIDEO FILM]
Everest the hard way. Barclays Bank International. 75 minutes. Colour.
British 1975 ascent of south-west face.

V10. [VIDEO FILM]
Everest — the last unclimbed ridge. Principal cameraman, Joe Tasker. Jardine Matheson Group Production. 53 minutes. Colour.
Attempt from Tibet, largely filmed by one of the two climbers who disappeared near the top of the north-east ridge.

V11. [VIDEO FILM]
Everest unmasked. Principal cameraman Eric Jones, for Harlech T.V. 52 minutes. Colour.
First ascent without oxygen by Messner and Habeler.

V12. [VIDEO FILM]
From the ocean to the sky. In association with Michael Dillon Enterprises. 55 minutes. Colour.
Hillary's expedition up the Ganges and ascent of Akash Parbat and Nar Parbat.

V13. [VIDEO FILM]
K2–the savage mountain. Allen Jewhurst and Chris Lister. Yorkshire Television. 50 minutes. Colour.
British 1978 attempt on west ridge, and history of the peak.

V14. [VIDEO FILM]
Kongur. Jardine Matheson Group Production. 29 minutes. Colour.
Bonington's 1981 expedition.

V15. [VIDEO FILM]
Matterhorn. Principal cameraman Eric Jones, for Harlech T.V. 52 minutes. Colour.
First filmed ascent of the north face.

V16. [VIDEO FILM]
Out of the shadow into the sun. Filmed by Leo Dickinson. Yorkshire Television. 40 minutes. Colour.
First filmed ascent of the Eigerwand.

V17. [VIDEO FILM]
Trango. Chameleon Films Production. 36 minutes. Colour.
Ascent of the granite spire Trango Tower by Joe Brown in 1976.

V18. VIGNE, Godfrey T.
Travels in Kashmir, Ladak, Iskardo: the countries adjoining the mountain-course of the Indus and the Himalaya, north of the Punjab. Ldn: Colburn, 1842. 2v. plates, illus, map. 20cm.
—2nd ed. 1844.
—New ed. 1981.
Vigne was one of the first Europeans to describe routes into the Karakoram. He made extensive journeys in Kashmir, Ladakh and Baltistan in the years 1835-8, reaching the snout of the Chogo Lungma Glacier, and ascending the Saltoro valley in search of the Saltoro Pass. His book is a classic and was the first comprehensive account of the region, and thus invaluable to the Great Trigonometrical Survey of India a few years later. First reference to Nanga Parbat.

V19. VISSER-HOOFT, Jenny (-1939)
Among the Kara-Korum glaciers in 1925. With contributions by P. C. Visser. Ldn: Arnold, 1926. xii, 303p, 25 plates, illus. 23cm.
Account of the Netherlands 2nd Karakoram expedition, exploring the Batura, Hispar and Shimshal glaciers. Mrs Visser-Hooft accompanied her husband on four Karakoram expeditions in the years 1922-35. Dr. Philips Christiaan Visser (1882-1955) was a distinguished Dutch diplomat and mountain explorer, who unravelled many Karakoram glacier puzzles.

V20. VOINA, V. & MARKELOV, A.
In the mountains of Karachai-Circassia: Teberda-Dombai. Moscow, 1979. 140p, col. illus, panorama. [4to]. Text in English and Russian.
Caucasus.

W

W01. WADDELL, Laurence Austine (1854-1938)
Among the Himalayas. With numerous illustrations by A. D. McCormick, the author and others, and from photographs. Ldn: Constable, 1899. xvi, 452p, illus, fold. map. 25cm.
—2nd ed. Ldn: Constable/Philadelphia: Lippincott, 1900. Cheap ed. xvi, 452p, illus. 22cm.
Waddell made several journeys including one to the Yalung Glacier over the Kang La. His book, praised by Freshfield, is more of interest to ethnologists and folk-lore enthusiasts. His contribution to the discussion of W. W. Graham's claimed ascent of Kabru is still of interest.

W02. WALKER, Bryce S.
The Rocky Mountains. Amsterdam: Time Life Books, 1973. 184p, col. illus. 27cm. (World's Wild Places series)

W03. WALKER, James Hubert
Mountain days in the Highlands and Alps. Ldn: Arnold/NY: Macmillan, 1937. 320p, 64 plates, illus. 23cm.
Climbing reminiscences.

W04. WALKER, J. H.
On hills of the north. Edinburgh: Oliver & Boyd, 1948. xvi, 182p, 24 plates, illus, maps. 22cm.
Walking through the mountains of Scotland; with geological notes.

W05. WALKER J. H.
Walking in the Alps. Edinburgh: Oliver & Boyd, 1951. xii, 274p, 24 plates, illus, maps. 24cm.
Excellent descriptions of high-level routes and circuits.

W06. WALKER, Kevin
Mountain navigation techniques. Ldn; Constable, 1986. 256p. 18cm.

W07. WALL, David
Rondoy: an expedition to the Peruvian Andes. Ldn: Murray, 1965. [14], 176p, 24 plates, illus. 23cm.
Account of a difficult first ascent in the Cordillera Huayhuash; two members of the party were killed while retracing the summit ridge.

W08. WALLER, James
The everlasting hills. Ldn: William Blackwood, 1939. xii, 190p, 64 plates, illus, maps. 23cm.
Climbs in the Karakoram — Saltoro Kangri and Masherbrum — with John Hunt.

W09. WALTON, Elijah (1832-80)
The Bernese Oberland: twelve scenes among its peaks and lakes. With descriptive text by T. G. Bonney. Ldn: W. M. Thompson, 1874. 1v. (chiefly col. illus). 44cm.
Walton was a British artist who delighted in mountain scenery and atmospheric effects; noted for his truthful rendering of rock structure and mountain form.

W10. WALTON, E.
English Lake scenery. With descriptive text by T. G. Bonney. Ldn: W. M. Thompson, 1876. [102] leaves, col. plates, illus. 34cm.

W11. WALTON, E.
The peaks and valleys of the Alps. [Chromolithographed by J. H. Lowes] With descriptive text by T. G. Bonney. Ldn: Day, 1867. Volume of 21 illus. 57cm.
—Reissued. Ldn: Sampson Low, 1868. 42p, 21 col. plates, illus. 56cm.

W12. WALTON, E.
Peaks in pen and pencil for students of alpine scenery. Edited by T. G. Bonney. Ldn: Longmans, 1872. 1v. (chiefly illus). 49cm.

W13. WALTON, E.
Welsh scenery [chiefly in Snowdonia]. With descriptive text by T. G. Bonney. Ldn: W. M. Thompson, 1875. 1v. (chiefly col. illus). 34cm.

W14. WALTON, William Howard Murray
Scrambles in Japan and Formosa. Ldn: Arnold, 1934. 304p, 26 plates, illus, 3 maps. 23cm.
An important contribution to the English-language literature on these areas. The Rev. Walton was a missionary, as was the Rev. Walter Weston, the 'Father' of mountaineering in Japan.

W15. WARBURTON, Lloyd E.
The steepest mountain.: the New Zealand Andes Expedition, 1960. Invercargill: Cuthill, 1964. 136p, illus. [8vo].
First ascent of Nevado Cayesh, a very severe ice pinnacle in the Cordillera Blanca, Peru.

W16. WARD, Frank Kingdon (1885-1958)
Burma's icy mountains. Ldn: Cape, 1949. 287p, 16 plates, illus, 2 fold. maps. 21cm.
Account of two expeditions, 1937-39, into Burma's 20,000 ft mountains, by a famous British plant-hunter.

W17. WARD, F. K.
Modern exploration. Ldn: Cape/R.U., 1945. 124p. 20cm.
—Another ed. 1946.
Reference to the Himalayan 8000-metre peaks.

W18. WARD, Julius H.
The White Mountains; a guide to their interpretation. Boston/N.Y., 1896.
—2nd rev. enlarged ed. Boston: Houghton Mifflin, 1896. ix, 311p, plates (1 fold), illus, map, bibl. 19cm.

W19. WARD, Michael Phelps (b.1925)
In this short span: a mountaineering memoir. Ldn: Gollancz, 1972. 304p, 24 plates, illus, maps (endpapers). 23cm.
Autobiography of British surgeon and mountaineer, who was a member of several Himalayan expeditions — Everest, Ama Dablam, Makalu. He also visited Bhutan.

W20. WARD M. P.
Man at high altitude. 1974.

W21. WARD, M. P.
Mountain medicine: a clinical study of cold and high altitude. Ldn: Crosby Lockwood Staples, 1975. x, 376p, 4 plates, illus, bibl. 23cm.
—U.S. ed. Van Nostrand, 1976.
Authoritative survey of high altitude sickness.

W22. WARD, M.P.
The mountaineer's companion. Edited by ...Ldn: Eyre & Spottiswoode, 1966. 589p, 26 plates (2 col), illus. 23cm.
Fine anthology containing prose and poetry extracted from numerous mountaineering books.

W23. WARWICK, Alan Ross
With Whymper in the Alps. Illustrated by Henry Toothill. Ldn: Muller, 1964. 143p, 12 plates, illus, maps. 19cm.

W24. WASHBURN, Henry Bradford Jr. (b.1910)
Among the Alps with Bradford. N.Y.: Putnam, 1927. xiv, 160p, 42 plates illus. 20cm. Also 2nd ptg.

W25. WASHBURN, H. B.
Bradford on Mount Washington. N.Y.: Putnam, 1928. xii, 123p, 31 plates, illus. 19cm.

W26. WASHBURN, H. B.
Bradford on Mount Fairweather. N.Y.: Putnam, 1930. ix, 127p, 31 plates, illus, maps. 20cm.
The second and not very successful attempt on this Alaskan peak. Washburn is best known as the greatest authority on Mt. McKinley.

W27. WASHBURN, H. B.
The trails and peaks of the Presidential Range of the White Mountains. Worcester. MA: The Author, 1926. 79p, 1 fold. plate, illus, map. 16cm.
New Hampshire section.

W28. WATERMAN, Jonathan
Surviving Denali: a study of accidents on Mount McKinley, 1910-1982. N.Y.: A.A.C., 1983. 192p, illus. 23cm. Softback.

W29. WATSON, Jim
On foot & finger: climbing & walking cartoons. Milnthorpe: Cicerone Press, 1986. [104p]. 12 × 18cm.

W30. WATSON, Sir Norman & KING, Edward J.
Round Mystery Mountain: a ski adventure. Ldn: Arnold, 1935. xii, 246p, 33 plates, illus, maps. 23cm.
First ski crossing of the Coast Range, British Columbia. Mystery Mountain is Mount Waddington.

W31. WEDDERBURN, Ernest Alexander Maclagan (1912-44)
Alpine climbing on foot and with ski. Illustrated by Edo Derzaj. Manchester: Open Air Publications, [1936]. 118p, illus. 17cm.
—Rev. ed. by C. B. Milner. Manchester: Countrygoer Books, 1954. x, 131p, 9 plates, illus, maps. 21cm.

W32. WEIR, Thomas
Camps and climbs in arctic Norway. Ldn: Cassell, 1953. viii, 85p, 41 plates, illus. 23cm.

—T.B.C. ed. with fewer plates.
Climbs in the Lofoten district by a well-known Scottish climber and broadcaster.

W33. WEIR, T.
East of Katmandu. Edinburgh: Oliver & Boyd, 1955. [6], 138p, 49 plates (2 col), illus. 23cm.
—U.S. ed. New Jersey: Essential, 1956. 138p.
—Another ed. Edinburgh: Gordon Wright, [c.1981].
Ascents of several peaks up to 22,000 ft, c.15 miles south-east of Gauri Sankar in 1952.

W34. WEIR, T.
Focus on mountains. Illustrations by Joan Tebbut. Edinburgh: MacDougall, [1965]. 80p, illus. 20cm.

W35. WEIR, T.
Highland days. Ldn: Cassell, 1948. xii, 139p, 23 plates, illus. 23cm.
—Another ed. 1984. xi, 147p, plates, illus, maps. 23cm.
Climbing reminiscences.

W36. WEIR, T.
The ultimate mountains: an account of four months' mountain exploring in the central Himalaya. Ldn: Cassell, 1953. x, 98p, 49 plates, illus, maps. 23cm.
Account of the Scottish Himalayan expedition with W. H. Murray and others.

W37. WELLS, Grant Carveth
Adventure. Garden City, NY: Garden City Publishing Co., 1931. xx, 338p, plates, illus. 22cm.
Includes references to Mt. Baker in the Ruwenzori, and Mt. Kenya.

W38. WELLS, G. C.
In coldest Africa. N.Y.: McBride, 1931. xi, 255p, illus. 21cm.
Travels among the high ranges of Africa; includes some walking and climbing in the Ruwenzori.

W39. WELLS, G. C.
Kapoot: the narrative of a journey from Leningrad to Mount Ararat in search of Noah's Ark. N.Y., 1933. 264p, illus. 21cm.
Includes journey through the Caucasus.

W40. WEST, John B.
Everest: the testing place. N.Y.: McGraw Hill, 1985. 256p.
American Medical Expedition; five climbers reached summit.

W41. WEST, J. B. & LAHIRI, Sukhamay (Editors)
High altitude and man. Bethesda: American Physiological Society, 1984. 199p.
Collection of symposium papers; primarily for physiologists.

W42. WEST, J. B. (Editor)
High altitude physiology. [Pennsylvania]: Hutchinson Ross, 1982. 462p. (Benchmark Collection).
Historical survey of published material.

W43. WEST, Lionel F.
The climbers' pocket book: rock climbing accidents with hints on first aid to the injured, some uses of the rope, methods of rescue and transport. Manchester: Scientific Publishing, [1907]. 76p, illus. 16cm. Limp cloth.
The first British manual on crag rescue.

W44. WESTMORLAND, Horace ['Rusty'] (1886-1984)
Adventures in climbing. Ldn: Pelham Books, 1964. 124p, 8 plates, illus. 20cm.
Part instruction, part reminiscence. The author, who came from a famous Lake District climbing family, spent most of his career soldiering in Canada. He was honoured in both Britain and Canada for services to mountain rescue.

W45. WESTON, Walter (1861-1940)
Mountaineering and exploration in the Japanese alps. Ldn: Murray, 1896. xvi, 346p, 27 plates, illus, 2 fold. maps. 25cm.
Apparently there was also a facsimile reprint.
The Rev. Weston is revered as the 'Father' of mountaineering in Japan.

W46. WESTON, W.
The playground of the Far East. Ldn: Murray, 1918. xiv, 333p, 19 plates, illus, 2 fold. maps. 23cm.
Follow-up to his first book on mountaineering in Japan.

W47. WHEELER, Arthur Oliver (1860-1945)
The Selkirk Range. Ottawa: Government Printing Bureau, 1905-6. 2v. xviii, 459p, 92 plates, illus, 10 maps (some fold.). 24cm. Separate box with 14 maps and plans. Part II deals with travel and exploration; Part IV deals with mountaineering.
Wheeler was the leading spirit in the early days of the Alpine Club of Canada, and supervised their summer camps. He masterminded the exploration and first ascent of Mt. Robson.

W48. WHEELER, Olin D.
Climbing Mount Rainier: descriptive of an ascent of the highest peak in the United States — exclusive of Alaska — where living glaciers are found.
St. Paul, MN: 1901. 68p, illus. 19cm. (Riley's Northern Pacific Monographs, 2).

W49. WHEELOCK, Walt
Ropes, knots and slings for climbers. Illustrated by Ruth Daly. Glendale, CA: La Siesta Press, 1960. 35p, illus.
—Rev. ed. by W. Wheelock & Royal Robbins. La Siesta Press, 1967. 70p.

W50. WHERRY, George Edward (1852-1928)
Alpine notes and the climbing foot. Cambridge: Macmillan & Bowes, 1896. xvi, 174p, illus. 19cm.
The author, who was a surgeon and a mountaineer, made a study of the feet of Alpine guides; one of the curiosities of climbing literature.

W51. WHERRY, G. E.
Notes from a knapsack. Cambridge: Bowes & Bowes, 1909. xii, 312p, illus, map. 19cm.
Miscellaneous essays relating to walking and climbing.

W52. WHILLANS, Donald Desbrow (1933-85) & ORMEROD, Alick
Don Whillans: portrait of a mountaineer. Ldn: Heinemann, 1971. x, 266p, 16 plates, illus. 23cm.
—Penguin paperback ed. 1973. R.P., 1976.
Biography of an outstanding British mountaineer who partnered Joe Brown in the resurgence of British rock-climbing in the 1950s. Later he made many fine climbs in the Alps, Himalaya and South America.

W53. WHILT, James W.
Mountain memories. Illustrated by F. M. Harrow. N.p., [1925]. 104p, illus. 19cm.
Rhymes dedicated to the Rockies.

W54. 'WHIPPLESNAITH' (pseud. of Noel Howard Symington)
The night climbers of Cambridge. Ldn: Chatto & Windus, 1937. vii, 184p, 55 plates, illus. 23cm. R.P., 1937, 1953.
Wall and roof climbing on college buildings is a traditional Cambridge sport.

W55. WHITE, Anne Terry
All about mountains and mountaineering. N.Y.: Random House, [1962]. [viii], 144p, illus. 24cm.

W56. WHITE, J. Claude
Sikkim and Bhutan: twenty-one years on the North-east frontier, 1887-1908. Ldn: Arnold, 1909. xx, 332p, illus, map. 26cm.
—Reprinted. Delhi: Vivek Pub. House, 1971. xix, 332p, illus, map. 24cm.
White travelled extensively in Sikkim and Bhutan. He was mainly responsible for opening up roads and bridges which made access easier for later explorers. In 1890 he crossed the Guicha La to the Talung Glacier south-east of Kanchenjunga and followed the Talung valley to the Tista, being probably the first European to investigate the gorges between Pandim and the Simvu group.

W57. WHITE, Victor H.
The story of Lige Coalman. Sandy, OR: St. Paul's Press, 1972. [4], 160p, 8 plates, illus. 21cm.
Edited autobiography of the man who climbed Mt. Hood 586 times, built the summit look-out, and took part in numerous rescues.

W58. WHITEHEAD, John

Exploration of Mount Kina Balu, North Borneo. Ldn: Gurney & Jackson, 1893. x, 317p, col. plates, illus. 37cm.
The main object of the expedition was ornithological but the book is also a fine mountain travel book with much interesting information on a variety of topics.

W59. WHITNEY, Josiah Dwight

The Yosemite guidebook: a description of the Yosemite Valley and the adjacent region of the Sierra Nevada and the big trees of California. Sacramento: Geological Survey of California, published by authority of the Legislature, 1869. 155p, 8 plates, illus, 2 fold. maps (in pkts). 24cm.
—3rd ptg. 1870.
—Pocket ed. 1871.
—New ed. rev. & corrected. 1874.
Whitney was head of the California Survey; his assistants included William Brewer and Clarence King. His book contains some history of the climbing and exploration of the mountains of the Sierra Nevada.

W60. WHYMPER, Edward (1840-1911)

Chamonix and the range of Mont Blanc: a guide. Ldn: Murray, 1896. xiv, 192p, illus, fold. maps. 19cm. Paper covers. Reissued annually up to 1911.
—Facsimile reprint of 1st ed. Reading: West Col, 1974. Linen covers.

W61. WHYMPER, E.

Episodes from the ascent of the Matterhorn. Illustrated from the author's drawings. Ldn: Harrap, 1928. 192p, illus. 17cm.
Abridged from the author's *Scrambles* for use in schools.

W62. WHYMPER, E.

How to use the aneroid barometer. Ldn: Murray, 1891. 61p. 24cm. Paper covers.
Tables and information based largely on his experiences in the Andes. This monograph is virtually another appendix to his book *Travels.*

W63. WHYMPER, E.

Letter addressed to members of the Alpine Club [on the controversy over a leap by Christian Almer]. [The Author], 1900. 16p, plate, illus. 22cm.
This arose out of a violent argument with Coolidge who maintained that the leap illustrated in *Scrambles* never took place.

W64. WHYMPER, E.

A right royal mountaineer [Duke of the Abruzzi]. Ldn: The Author, 1909. 23p.

W65. WHYMPER E.

Scrambles amongst the Alps in the years 1860-69. Ldn: Murray, 1871. xx, 432p, 23 plates, illus, 5 fold. maps. 24cm. Some copies marked '4th Thousand'.
—2nd ed. [ptg], 1871.
—U.S. ed. Cleveland: Burrows, 1872
—2nd U.S. ed. Philadelphia: Lippincott, 1873. 164p, illus. 24cm.
—3rd ed. abridged and published as *The ascent of the Matterhorn.* Ldn: Murray, 1880.
—4th ed. Ldn: Murray, 1893. xx, 468p. Also de luxe edition bound by Zaehnsdorf. This is regarded as the definitive edition.
—Another U.S. ed., bound with another book *Down the Rhine* by Lady Blanche Murphy. Philadelphia: Lippincott, n.d. [c.1884?]. 164p + 75p, illus. Pictorial cover. Same version apparently republished — Cleveland: Burrows, 1899.
—5th ed. Ldn: Murray, 1900. xviii, 468p.
—Shilling Library ed. Ldn: Nelson, [1908?]. R.P., 1920?
—6th ed. With additional illustrations and material from the author's unpublished diaries. Revised and edited by H. E. G. Tyndale. xxii, 414p. Ldn: Murray/N.Y.: Scribner's, 1936. R.P., (U.S.) 1937?
—Reprinted 1948.
—7th ed. 1965.
—Another ed. reprinted from original 1872 U.S. ed. Berkeley: Ten Speed Press, 1981. R.P. 1985 (softback).
—Another ed. Century Pub. 1985. Softback ed. of 1936 ed.
—Another ed. Exeter: Webb & Bower/ Salt Lake City: Smith, 1986. Facsimile of 6th ed. with col. illus by John Cleare.
The most famous of all mountaineering books. Whymper was a young wood engraver who became obsessed with

making the first ascent of the Matterhorn. The price he had to pay for achieving this was the loss of four of his companions in the most celebrated mountain disaster of all time. His one other great expedition was in 1880 to the Andes of Ecuador. Although his writings and lecturing brought him success his life may be said to have been ruined by the tragedy which followed his moment of triumph.

W66. WHYMPER, E.

Travels amongst the great Andes of the Equator. Ldn: Murray, 1891-2. xxvi, 456p, 20 plates, illus, 4 maps (1 fold. in pkt). With supplementary volume of scientific material. Also numbered and signed edition in 2v. plus volume of maps.
—2nd ed. 1892.
—U.S. ed. N.Y.: Scribner's, 1892. xxiv, 456p, illus, 4 maps (1 in pkt). 24cm. R.P., 1896.
—Smaller cheaper U.S. ed. entitled *In the great Andes of the Equator.* Scribner's, 1892. xxiv, 456p. 1v. including the appendices. (Library of Contemporary Exploration and Adventure)
—Shilling Library ed. Ldn: Nelson. [1911].
—Chiltern Library ed. Ldn: Lehmann, 1949. 272p.
—Another ed. Edited and introduced by Eric Shipton. Ldn: Knight, 1972. xxiv, 214p.
This book was the first of the few great classics of South American mountaineering literature, equalled only by books like De Agostini's *Andes Patagonicos.* It remains essential reading for anyone visiting Ecuador.

W67. WHYMPER, E.

The valley of Zermatt and the Matternorn: a guide. Ldn: Murray, 1987. xiv, 212p, illus, maps. 19cm. Reissued annually up to 1911.
—Facsimile reprint of 1st ed. Reading: West Col, 1974. Linen covers.

W68. WIBBERLEY, Leonard

The epics of Everest. Illustrated by Genevieve Vaughan-Jackson. N.Y.: Farrar Strauss & Young, 1954. viii, 242p, illus. 21cm.
—Another ed. N.Y.: Junior Literary Guild & Ariel Books, 1954.
—U.K. ed. Ldn: Faber, 1955. 217p, illus. 21cm.
—Paperback. N.Y.: Dell, 1966. Revised ed.?
Summary of climbing up to first ascent.

W69. WICKERSHAM, Hon James W.

Old Yukon: tales-trails-and trials. Washington, DC: Washington Law Book Co., 1938. xii, 514p, illus. 24cm.
—Another ed. 1979.
Wickersham was a Federal Judge and later Alaska Territory Delegate to Congress. He made the first climbing attempt on Mt. McKinley in 1903, reaching nearly 10,000 ft (described in pp. 203-320 of his book).

W70. WICKHAM, R. S.

Friendly Adirondacks: a book concerning walking trips among seldom climbed mountains. Adirondack Mountain Club, 1924.

W71. WILCOX, Joe

White winds. Los Alamitos, CA: Hwong Publishing, 1981. 499p, illus, map. 23cm.
Wilcox was leader of an expedition to Mt. McKinley in 1967, when seven out of twelve members died. By an examination of all available data Wilcox provides a convincing and harrowing reconstruction of the probable course of the disaster. For another version of the expedition see Howard Snyder's book, *Hall of the mountain king.*

W72. WILCOX, J.

Reader's guide to the Hall of the mountain king. [Issued with *White winds*]
A 100-page, point by point rebuttal of statements made by Howard Snyder in his book, *Hall of the mountain king.*

W73. WILCOX, Walter Dwight (1869-1949)

Camping in the Canadian Rockies. N.Y.: Putnam, 1896. xiv, 283p, 25 plates, illus. 26cm.
—Revised and enlarged ed. This and subsequent editions entitled *The Rockies of Canada.* Putnam, 1900.
—3rd ed. xii, 300p. Putnam, 1909. This edition largely rewritten, with the

photogravures increased from 25 to 38, more than half of them being different from those in the previous edition. One fold. map in pkt.
—Another ed. 1916. ix, 300p. 24cm.
Wilcox was an original A.A.C. member. He explored the Canadian Rockies in the 1890s to the north of Kicking Horse Pass and south to Mt. Assiniboine.

W74. WILKERSON, James A.
Hypothermia, frostbite and other cold injuries. By ...[and others]. Seattle: Mountaineers, 1986. [xiv], 105p, col. plates, illus.
Companion volume to his *Medicine for mountaineering.*

W75. WILKERSON, J. A. (Editor)
Medicine for mountaineering: a handbook for treatment of accidents and illnesses in remote areas. Seattle: Mountaineers, 1967. xx, 309p, illus. R.P., 1973.
—2nd ed. 1975. 368p. R.P., 1978, 1982.
—3rd ed. 1985. 440p.
Comprehensive expedition handbook.

W76. WILKINS, Thurman
Clarence King: a biography. N.Y.: Macmillan, 1958. ix, 441p, illus. [8vo].

W77. WILLIAMS, Brian
Conquerors of Everest. Ldn: Ward Lock, 1979. 25p, illus, map. 23cm. (Kingfisher Explorer books: history makers)
—Another ed. Pan Books, 1979.
For young readers.

W78. WILLIAMS, Charles
The Alps, Switzerland and the north of Italy. N.Y.: Alex. Montomery, 1854. vi, 633p, illus, map. 28cm.
Includes accounts of early Mont Blanc ascents, reproductions of some of Auldjo's engravings, an account of early ascents of the Jungfrau, selections of mountain poetry, etc.

W79. WILLIAMS, Cicely (-1985)
A church in the Alps: a century of Zermatt and the English. Ldn: Commonwealth and Continental Church Society, 1970. 46p, illus (some col). 19cm.
The English Church in Zermatt opened in 1870; includes the Matterhorn disaster, Alpine Club centenary, etc.

W80. WILLIAMS, C.
Women on the rope: the feminine share in mountain adventure. Ldn: Allen & Unwin, 1973. 240p, 8 plates, illus. 23cm.
Useful history of women's climbing.

W81. WILLIAMS, C.
Zermatt saga. Ldn: Allen & Unwin, 1964. 197p, 9 plates, illus. 23cm.
A history of one of the most famous mountaineering centres in the world.

W82. WILLIAMS, Gwyn
Eastern Turkey. Ldn: Faber, 1972.
Includes an appendix for the alpinist traveller by S. E. P. Nowill.

W83. WILLIAMS, Jenny C.
Cambridge Garhwal Himalaya Expedition, 1977: report. Marlborough: The Expedition, [1978]. 46 leaves, illus, maps. 30cm.

W84. WILLIAMS, John Harvey
The guardians of the Columbia: Mount Hood, Mount Adams and Mount St. Helens. Tacoma, WA: The Author, 1912. 144p, illus (some col). 26cm.
His three books form a matching, finely illustrated set of monographs, giving among other things details of climbing history. Classics of their kind.

W85. WILLIAMS, J. H.
The mountain that was "God": being a little book about the great peak which the Indians named "Tacoma" but which is officially called "Rainier". Tacoma, WA: The Author, 1910. 111p, illus (some col). 26cm. Also produced in de luxe binding and softback?
—2nd rev. ed. enlarged. N.Y.: Putnam, 1911. 144p, illus (some col), maps. 26cm.
—3rd ed. abridged, rewritten and with several different illustrations.

W86. WILLIAMS, J. H.
Yosemite and its high Sierra. Tacoma & S.F.: The Author, 1914. 147p, illus (some col). 26cm. Also in illustrated wrappers.
—2nd rev. ed. enlarged, S.F, 1921. 194p, illus, maps. 26cm.

W87. WILLIAMS, Knox & ARMSTRONG, Betsy
The snowy torrents: avalanche accidents in the United States, 1972-1979. Jackson: Teton, 1984. 221p.
Previous volumes (same general title) — 1910-1966 (by Dale Gallagher); 1967-1971 (by Knox Williams).

W88. WILLIAMS, Paul M.
Rescue leadership. Seattle: The Author, 1977. [iv], 77p.

W89. WILLIAMS, William
My summer in the Alps, 1913. N.Y.: The Author, 1914. 21p, 6 plates, illus. 26cm. Slipcase. Edition of 300 copies on hand-made Dutch paper. Pages only; never bound.

W90. WILLIG, George & BERGMAN, Andrew
Going it alone. N.Y.: Doubleday, 1979. 158p, illus. 27cm.
Autobiography of American climber who soloed the 110-storey South Tower of the World Trade Center, New York City.

W91. WILLIS, Marcia
Jungles, rivers and mountain peaks. Ldn: Aldus, 1971. (Encyclopaedia of Discovery and Exploration)
—Another ed. Ldn: Readers' Digest Assoc., 1979. 191p, illus (some col), maps. 27cm.

W92. WILLS, Sir Alfred (1828-1912)
The ascent of Mont Blanc: together with some remarks on glaciers. Ldn: The Author, 1858. 90p. 18cm.
Presumably the same material that was added to the second edition of *Wandering among the high Alps.*

W93. WILLS, A.
"The Eagle's Nest" in the Valley of Sixt: a summer home among the Alps, together with some excursions among the great glaciers. [Illustrated with coloured lithographs by his wife.] Ldn: Longmans, 1860. xx, 327p, 12 col. plates, illus, 2 fold. maps. 21cm. R.P., 1860.

W94. WILLS, A.
Wandering among the high Alps. Ldn: Bentley, 1856. xx, 384p, 4 col. plates, illus. 20cm. (Also edition de luxe in tooled brown morocco? See *Alpine Journal,* v. 24, p. 602.)
—2nd ed. revised with additional material on Mont Blanc and glaciers. xx, 426p. No plates.
—Abridged ed. omitting 3 chapters and the appendices from the 2nd ed. Oxford: Blackwell, 1937. R.P., 1939.
Alfred Wills was an original Alpine Club member and President, 1864-5. While his ascent of the Wetterhorn was not particularly momentous, it is customarily accepted as ushering in the 'Golden Age' of mountaineering.

W95. WILSON, Andrew
Abode of snow: observations on a journey from Chinese Tibet to the Indian Caucasus, through the upper valleys of the Himalaya. Edinburgh: Blackwood, 1875. xxvi, 476p, illus, map. 21cm.
—2nd ed. 1876. xxviii, 436p, illus, map. 20cm.
—Reprint of 1st ed. Delhi: Manjusri Pub. House, 1971/Kathmandu: R. P. Bhandar, 1979 (Bibliotheca Himalayica, Ser. I-Vol.12)
Wilson journeyed from Simla to Kashmir through Shingo La, Padum, Penze La, Dras and Zoji La in 1873.

W96. WILSON, Claude (1860-1937)
Mountaineering. With illustrations by Ellis Carr. Ldn: Bell, 1893. viii, 208p, illus. 17cm. Also 50 copies were printed on hand-made paper and were not for sale. (All England series)
Instructional: a delightful period piece.

W97. WILSON, C.
An epitome of fifty years' climbing. The Author, 1933. 119p. 22cm. Edition of 125 numbered copies, none of which was for public sale.
Chiefly a list of his climbs.

W98. WILSON, Edward Livingstone
Mountain climbing. By ...[and others]. [N.Y.]: Scribner's/Ldn: Kegan Paul French

Trubner, 1897. xii, 358p, illus. 21cm. Two different bindings seen.
Includes Mt. Aetna, Mt. Ararat, Mt. St. Elias, Mt. Washington.

W99. WILSON, Henry Schütz (1824-1902)
Alpine ascents and adventures: or, Rock and snow sketches. With two illustrations by Marcus Stone and Edward Whymper. Ldn: Sampson Low, 1878. xii, 319p, plate, illus. 19cm. 2nd ed. 1878.

W100. WILSON, James Gilbert (b.1937)
Aorangi: the story of Mount Cook. Christchurch: Whitcombe & Tombs, 1968. 253p, 20 plates (some col), illus, maps, bibl. 22cm.
Climbing history of New Zealand's highest peak.

W101. WILSON, Joseph
A history of mountains, geographical and mineralogical; accompanied by a picturesque view of the principal mountains of the world, in their respective proportions ..., by Robert Andrew Riddell. Ldn: Nicol, 1807-10. 3v. plates, illus. 31cm.
Wilson's work is a remarkable attempt (at this date) to produce a complete gazetteer of the world's mountains, with descriptions of their physical features etc. The sections on Europe, North and South America are covered in considerable detail. New Zealand is also included. The information was obviously obtained from travel books.

W102. WILSON, Ken (b.1941) & GILBERT Richard
The big walks. Compiled by ...Ldn: Diadem Books, 1980. 256p, ill (many col), illus. 28cm.
Describes 55 challenging mountain walks and scrambles in Britain; illustrations, route diagrams and descriptions.

W103. WILSON, K.
Classic rock: great British rock-climbs. Compiled by ...: with editorial assistance from Mike Pearson. Ldn: Granada, 1978. 256p, illus (some col). 29cm.
Classic British rock-climbs with illustrations, route diagrams and descriptions.

W104. WILSON, K. & GILBERT, R.
Classic walks: mountain and moorland walks in Britain and Ireland. Compiled by ...Ldn: Diadem, 1982. 272p, illus (some col). 29cm.
Descriptions, route diagrams and illustrations.

W105. WILSON, K.
Cold climbs: the great snow and ice climbs of the British Isles. Compiled by ...[and others]. Ldn: Diadem, 1983. xv, 279p, illus (some col), maps. 29cm.

W106. WILSON, K. & NEWMAN, B.
Extreme rock. 1986.

W107. WILSON, K.
The Games climbers play. Edited by ...Ldn: Diadem/S.F.: Sierra Club, 1978. 688p, plates, illus. 22cm. R.P., 1981.
Anthology of over 100 articles chosen from contemporary climbing magazines and journals.

W108. WILSON, K.
Hard rock: great British rock-climbs. Compiled by ...with editorial assistance from Mike and Lucy Pearson. Diagrams by Brian Evans. Ldn: Hart-Davis, MacGibbon, 1974. xx, 220p, illus. 29cm. R.P., 1975, 1978. 4 ptgs.
—2nd ed. updated. Ldn: Granada, 1981.
Illustrations, route diagrams and descriptions.

W109. WINDHAM, William (1717-61)
An account of the glacieres or ice alps of Savoy: in two letters, one from an English gentleman to his friend at Geneva: the other from Peter Martel, engineer to the said English gntleman [sic] illustrated with a map, and two views of the place etc. As laid before the Royal Society. Ldn: Peter Martel, 1744. [MDCCXLIV] 28p, [30], 2 fold. plates, map. 29cm.
—2nd ed. Ipswich: W. Craighton, 1747. 34p.
Windham and his friends visited Chamonix in June 1741. They went up to the Montenvers and studied the Mer de

Glace. Windham's account is always linked with that of Pierre Martel, who visited Chamonix the following year. Both their original accounts were written in French and circulated in Geneva in manuscript only. A version (still in French) of the two manuscripts, edited by Leonard Boulacre, was published in *Journal Helvetique,* May-June, 1743.

W110. WINNER, E. & E.
Four thousand meters: the high peaks of the contiguous U.S.
Lists the 653 highest peaks.

W111. WINTER, J. B.
Extracts from my mountaineering journal. 1922.

W112. WOLFE, Linnie Marsh
John of the mountains: unpublished journals of John Muir. Edited by . . .Boston: Houghton Mifflin, 1938. xxiv, 459p, 8 plates, illus. 22cm.

W113. WOLFE, L. M.
Son of the wilderness: the life of John Muir. N.Y.: Knopf, 1945. xvii, 364, xvip, plates, illus. 22cm.
Fascinating biography, commissioned by Muir's elder daughter.

W114. WOLLASTON, Alexander Frederick Richmond (1875-1930)
From Ruwenzori to the Congo: a naturalist's journey across Africa. Ldn: Murray, 1908. xxvi, 315p, plates (1 fold.), illus, maps. 23cm.

W115. WOLLASTON, A. F. R.
Letters and diaries of A. F. R. Wollaston. Selected and edited by Mary Wollaston. Cambridge: University Press, 1933. xiii, 261p, plates, ports. 23cm.
Wollaston's mountaineering exploits included visits to the Ruwenzori, the 1921 Everest expedition, Dutch New Guinea and Colombia.

W116. WOOD, H.
Kara-koram. Explorations in the Eastern Kara-koram and the Upper Yarkand valley. Narrative report of the Survey of India detachment with the de Filippi scientific expedition, 1914. Dehra Dun: Trigonometrical Survey, 1922. iii, 42p, illus, map. 33cm. (Record of the Survey of India, vol. 8-A)

W117. WOOD, H.
Report on the identification and nomenclature of the Himalayan peaks as seen from Katmandu, Nepal. Calcutta: Government Printing Office, 1904. iv, 8, ivp, 3 panoramas, map. 34cm.

W118. WOOD, Robert L.
Across the Olympic Mountains: the Press Expedition, 1889-90. Seattle: Mountaineers & University of Washington Press, 1967. xvi, 220p, illus. 24cm.
—Paperback ed. 1976.
Story of very rough six months' winter crossing of a hitherto unknown area, sponsored by the Seattle *Press.* Written up from members' accounts. The author has over thirty years' experience of the Olympic Mountains.

W119. WOOD, R. L.
Men, mules and mountains. Seattle: Mountaineers, 1976. xx, 507p, illus, maps, bibl. 21cm.
The first detailed exploration of the Olympic Mountains in 1890 by an expedition led by Lieut. P. O'Neil.

W120. WOOD, Walter A. Jr. (b.1907)
History of mountaineering in the St. Elias Mountains. Scarborough: Yukon Alpine Centennial Expedition, [1967]. [ix], 45p, map.
Reproduced in part in Marnie Fisher's book, *Expedition Yukon.*

W121. WOOLSEY, Elizabeth D.
Off the beaten track. Wilson: The Author, 1984. 208p, illus.
The author was with Wiessner and House at the time of the first ascent of Mt. Waddington: she also climbed extensively in the Alps and Tetons, and was an Olympic skier.

W122. WORKMAN, Fanny Bullock (1859-1925) **& WORKMAN, William Hunter** (1847-1937)
The call of the snowy Hispar: a narrative of exploration and mountaineering on the

northern frontier of India. With an appendix by Count Dr. Cesare Calciati and Dr. Mathias Koncza. Ldn: Constable, 1910. xvi, 298p, 86 plates illus, 2 fold. maps. 25cm.
Account of their fourth expedition in 1908. They explored the Hispar Glacier; then descended the Biafo Glacier.

W123. WORKMAN, F. B. & W. H.
Ice-bound heights of the Mustagh: an account of two seasons of pioneer exploration and high climbing in the Baltistan Himalaya. Ldn: Constable/N.Y.: Scribner's, 1908. xvi, 444p, 7 plates (some col), illus, 2 fold. maps. 25cm.
Account of their 1902-3 expedition in Baltistan. They explored the Chogo Lungma Glacier and later reached the Nushik La from the Hoh Lumba Glacier.

W124. WORKMAN, F. B. & W. H.
In the ice-world of Himalaya: among the peaks and passes of Ladakh, Nubra, Suru, and Baltistan. Ldn: Fisher Unwin, 1900/N.Y.: Cassell, [1900]. xvi, 204p, 67 plates, illus, 3 maps. 23cm.
—Cheap ed., 1901, being a reprint omitting 2 portraits and route map.
Account of their first Himalayan expedition, 1898-9, during the course of which they reached the Karakoram Pass and explored tht Biafo Glacier.. The first of several handsome books recounting their travels.

W125. WORKMAN, F. B. & W. H.
Peaks and glaciers of Nun Kun: a record of pioneer exploration and mountaineering in the Punjab Himalaya. Ldn/N.Y: Constable, 1909. xvi, 204p, illus, map. 24cm.
Expedition to the Nun Kun massif in 1906, during which Mrs Workman established a new world height record for women (c.23,000 ft) on the Pinnacle Peak, at the age of forty-seven.

W126. WORKMAN, F. B. & W. H.
Two summers in the ice-wilds of Eastern Karakoram: the exploration of nineteen hundred square miles of mountain and glacier. Ldn: Fisher Unwin, 1917. 296p, 134 plates, illus, 3 maps. 24cm.
Their fifth and last Karakoram expedition, 1911-2. They explored the Hush valley and the Saltoro and Baltoro Glaciers.

W127. [WORLD CLIMBING]
World climbing. Introduction by Terry King. Sheffield: Dark Peak, 1980. 368p, illus. 30cm.
Reference book consisting of the 'INFO' pages of *Mountain* magazine, nos. 1-64 (Jan. 1969-Dec. 1978), being a total of 10 years' information on the major events of mountaineering and rock-climbing worldwide.

W128. WRIGHT, Jeremiah Ernest Bamford (1895-1975)
Mountain days in the Isle of Skye. Edinburgh: Moray Press, 1934. 239p, 63 plates, illus. 23cm. (N.B.: The British Library catalogue wrongly gives his last Christian name as 'Benjamin'.)
Wright was a professional guide, who later founded the Mountaineering Association, a training organization, which sent many young climbers on British and Alpine mountaineering holidays in the 1950s and 1960s.

W129. WRIGHT, J. E. B.
Rock-climbing in Britain. Ldn: Nicholas Kaye (for the Mountaineering Assoc.), 1958. 142p, 31 plates, illus, maps. 22cm.
—Reprinted with revised appendices, 1964.
Description of areas and selected climbs.

W130. WRIGHT, J. E. B.
Technique of mountaineering: a handbook of established methods. With drawings by W. J. Kidd. Published under the auspices of the Mountaineering Association. Ldn: Mountaineering Assoc., 1955. 160p, 21 plates, illus. 21cm.
—Another ed. Ldn: Nicholas Kaye, 1955. 144p, 20 plates, illus. 20cm.
—2nd rev. ed. Kaye, 1958. 191p.
—3rd rev. ed. Kaye, 1964. 192p.

W131. WRIGHT, Nicholas
English mountain summits. By . . .Photographs by Iain Wright. Ldn: Hale, 1974. 208p, 24 plates, illus, maps. 23cm.

W132. WRIGHT, R. I. & HERGER, Robert
The Canadian Rockies.
—2nd ed. Vancouver: Whitecap/ Canmore: High Country Color, 1982. 88p, 78 col. plates.
Over 100 spectacular photographs by some of Canada's leading mountain photographers.

W133. WROE, Stanley
Rock climbing. Oxford: Oxford Illustrated Press, 1979. [vii], 92p, illus. 25cm.

W134. WYATT, Colin
Call of the mountains. Ldn: Thames & Hudson, 1952. 96p, 75 plates, illus. 31cm. R.P., 1962.
—U.S. ed. N.Y.: Beechhurst, 1953.
Photo-album; skier's eye-view of the world's mountains.

W135. WYMER, Norman
Sir John Hunt. Oxford: O.U.P., n.d. [c.1954]. 32p, illus. 19cm. Limp cloth. (Lives of Great Men and Women series).
Biographical sketches for schoolchildren; second half deals with Everest.

W136. WYVILL, Brian & CAMPBELL-KELLY, Ben
British Caledonian Airways Cerro Torre Expedition, 1978. (A Patagonia handbook): report. The Expedition, [1978?].

Y

Y01. YAKUSHI, Yoshimi (Editor)
Exploration in the central Nepal Himalaya, 1965-66. Toyama/Kyoto: Tomari Mountaineering Club Expedition, 1966. 10, 154p, illus, maps. 26cm. In Japanese with English summary. Yak. j. 744.
Reconnaissance expedition to Tilito Himal and exploration in Annapurna Himal, Khumbu Himal, etc.

Y02. YAKUSHI, Y. (Editor)
Gurja Himal: Japanese expedition to Nepal Himalaya, 1969. Toyama: The Expedition, 1970. vi, 168p, plates (1 fold., some col), illus, map. 25cm. In Japanese with English summary. Yak. j. 746.

Y03. YAMADA, Arata
The way to Chogoli: the first ascent of the north face of K2, 1982. Tokyo: Asahi-Shimbun, 1982. 82p, col. illus, maps. In Japanese with English summary and photo captions. Yak. j. 828.

Y04. YAMADA, Keiichi
The Himalaya from the air. Tokyo: Tokyo-Newspaper, 1975. 110p, mostly col. illus, col. fold. map (end pkt). 29cm. Slipcase. In Japanese with English photo-captions. Yak. j. 762.
Aerial pictures taken in 1973 covering the areas of Annapurna, Manaslu, Langtang-Jugal, Rowaling, Khumbu, Ganesh, Dhaulagiri & Kanchenjunga.

Y05. YAMATO, M.
Dhaula Himal Expedition, 1965. Edited by . . ., H. Sugita & M. Oki. Nagoya: Himalayan Committee of the Aichi-ken Mountaineering Union, 1967. 400p, illus (some col), maps. 25cm. In Japanese with English summary. Yak. j. 02.
Official account of 1965 Dhaulagiri II expedition.

Y06. YANG KE-HSIEN
The ascent of the Mustagh-Ata. Trans. [from the Chinese] by Ho Yong-Kong. Peking: Foreign Languages Press, 1959. 60p, illus, map. 19cm. Yak. j. 03.
First ascent by a Sino-Russian expedition.

Y07. YELD, George (1845-1938)
Scrambles in the eastern Graians, 1878-1897. Ldn: Fisher Unwin, 1900. 279p, 20 plates, illus, fold. map. 21cm.
Yeld, one-time editor of the *Alpine Journal,* was an authority on the Graian Alps, and collaborated with Coolidge in the production of the Conway-Coolidge guidebook to the area (i.e. *Mountains of Cogne*).

Y08. YODO, Takayoshi
The ascent of Manaslu in photographs. Tokyo: Mainichi Newspaper, 1956. var.

pag, plates (some col), illus, maps. 30cm. English summary.
Photo-album of the Japanese expeditions, 1952-56 with 186 illustrations.

Y09. [YOMIURI-NEWSPAPER (Editor)]
Everest: the glory of women. Tokyo: Yomiuri-Newspaper, 1975. 128p, col. plates, illus. 29 × 22cm. With English captions. Yak. j. 786.
Photo-album of ascent by Japanese Ladies Expedition in 1975.

Y10. YOMIURI-NEWSPAPER (Editor)
Stood on the summit of Chomolangma. Photo-album of the Japanese Alpine Club expedition to Everest through the Chinese route. Tokyo: The Newspaper, 1980. 134p, illus (some col), maps. 29 × 22cm. Yak. j. 787.

Y11. YOSHIZAWA, Ichiro (Chief Editor)
Mountaineering maps of the world: Himalaya. Tokyo: Gakushûkenyû-sha, 1977. 329p, illus (some col), maps. 37cm. In Japanese. Yak. j. 774.
Includes 52 pages of maps with place names in roman script.

Y12. YOSHIZAWA, I. (Chief Editor)
Mountaineering maps of the world: Karakoram & Hindu Kush. Tokyo: Gakushûkenkyû-sha, 1978. 350p, illus (some col), maps. 37cm. In Japanese. Yak. j. 775.
Includes Pamirs and Tian-Shan; 54 pages of maps. Place names on maps and mountain names under colour illustrations in roman script.

Y13. YOUNG, Eleanor & YOUNG, G. W.
In praise of mountains: an anthology for friends. Compiled by ...Ldn: Muller, 1948. [59p], illus. 14cm. R.P., 1951.

Y14. YOUNG, Geoffrey Winthrop (1876-1958)
April and rain. Ldn: Sidgwick & Jackson, 1923. 64p. 20cm.
Poems.

Y15. YOUNG, G. W.
Collected poems. Ldn: Methuen, 1936. viii, 245p. 23cm.

Y16. YOUNG, G. W.
Freedom. Ldn: Smith, Elder, 1914. viii, 146p. 23cm.
Poems.

Y17. YOUNG, G. W.
The grace of forgetting. Ldn: Country Life, 1953. 352p, plates, illus, maps. 23cm.
Mainly non-mountaineering experiences, including service in an ambulance division in World War I, when he lost a leg.

Y18. YOUNG, G. W.
Influence of mountains upon the development of human intelligence. Glasgow: Jackson, 1957. 30p. 22cm. Softback.
The 17th W. P. Ker Memorial Lecture, 2 May, 1956. Ker was a scholar and mountaineer, whose protegées included Janet Adam Smith and Freya Stark.

Y19. YOUNG, G. W. (Editor)
Mountain craft. Ldn: Methuen/N.Y.: Scribner's, 1920. xx, 603p, 10 plates, illus. 23cm. R.P., 1928, 1934.
—4th ed. rev. Methuen, 1945. R.P., 1946, 1949.
—7th ed. rev. 1949. R.P., 1954.
Long regarded as a classic manual of mountaineering, this book also contains some of Young's finest writing. He was a scholar, as well as a great climber, and one of the most influential figures in twentieth century British climbing.

Y20. YOUNG, G. W.
Mountains with a difference. Ldn: Eyre & Spottiswoode, 1951. xii, 282p, 12 plates, illus. 22cm. (New Alpine Library series)
Account of his Alpine climbs with an artificial leg, after 1918. Includes the dedication of the Fell & Rock war memorial on Great Gable.

Y21. YOUNG, G. W.
On high hills: memories of the Alps. Ldn: Methuen, 1927/N.Y.: Dutton, 1928. xvi, 368p, 24 plates, illus. 23cm. R.P., 1927, 1933, 1944.

—5th ed. 1947. xii, 352p.
This book contains accounts of his great Alpine climbs before 1914, and much of his finest prose.

Y22. YOUNG, G. W.
Snowdon biography. By ..., Geoffrey Sutton and Wilfrid Noyce. Edited by Wilfrid Noyce. Ldn: Dent, 1957. xiv, 194p, 16 plates, illus, map (endpapers). 22cm.
History of climbers' involvement with the Snowdon district; and a section on the associated literature.

Y23. YOUNG, G. W.
Wall and roof climbing. By the author of "The roof-climber's guide to Trinity". Eton College: Spottiswoode, 1905. viii, 109p. 23cm. Softback.
Humorous collection of references in literature to this traditional Cambridge sport.

Y24. YOUNG, G. W.
Wind and hill. Ldn: Smith, Elder, 1909. viii, 106p. 19cm.
Poems.

Y25. YOUNG, Peter
Himalayan holiday: a trans-Himalayan diary, 1939. Ldn: Jenkins, [1945]. 108p, plates (1 fold.), illus, maps. 22cm.
Northern Kashmir, Ladakh and Baltistan.

Y26. YOUNG, Samuel Hall
Alaska days with John Muir. N.Y.: Fleming H. Revell, 1915. 226p, 12 plates, illus, map. 20cm. Several ptgs.
The author, who was a missionary in Alaska, accompanied his friend Muir on some of his Alaskan excursions.

Y27. YOUNGHUSBAND, Sir Francis Edward (1863-1942)
The epic of Mount Everest. Ldn: Arnold, 1926. 319p, 16 plates, illus, map. 21cm. R.P. numerous times, 1926-34.
—Cheap ed. 1947.
—Reissued. Wakefield: E.P. Pub, 1974.
Summary of the first three expeditions. Younghusband was one of the major figures in the organization of early Everest expeditions.

Y28. YOUNGHUSBAND, F. E.
Everest the challenge. Ldn/N.Y.: Nelson, 1936. x, 243p, 16 plates, illus. 23cm.
—2nd ed. 1936. With an account of the 1936 Everest expedition and future prospects.
—Cheap ed. 1941. R.P. several times, 1942-48.
This book deals with Everest and the overall appeal of the Himalaya.

Y29. YOUNGHUSBAND, F. E.
The heart of a continent: a narrative of travels in Manchuria, across the Gobi Desert, through the Himalayas, the Pamirs, and Chitral, 1884-1894. Ldn: Murray, 1896. xx, 409p, 18 plates, illus, 4 fold. maps (1 in pkt). 24cm. R.P., 1896, 4th ptg 1897.
—Abridged ed. entitled *Among the celestials.* Murray, 1898. xi, 261p, plates, illus. 22cm.
—Another ed. Murray, 1904. xvii, 332p, illus, map.
—Rev. ed. with additional material, entitled *Heart of a continent: commemorating the fiftieth anniversary of his journey from Peking to India.* Murray, 1937. xvi, 243p, plates, map. 23cm.
After crossing the Gobi Desert to Yarkand, Younghusband crossed the Mustagh Pass in the Karakoram and descended the Baltoro Glacier. In 1889 he explored the area of the Aghil Pass-Shaksgam River-Gasherbrum and Urdok glaciers. In 1890 he explored the Pamir plateau from Kashgar.

Y30. YOUNGHUSBAND, F. E.
Kashmir. Painted by E. Molyneux. Ldn: Black, 1909. xv, 283p, col. plates (1 fold.), illus, map. 21cm.
—3rd rev. ed. 1924.
—4th ed. 1933. 283p, 32 col. plates, 2 maps.
—Another ed. Delhi: Sagar Pub, 1970.
General work on Kashmir, including mountaineering.

Y31. YOUNGHUSBAND, F. E.
Wonders of the Himalaya. Ldn: Murray/N.Y.: Dutton, 1924. vii, 210p, plate, map. 23cm.
—Another ed. 1929.
—Another ed. 1977.
Memoirs of his Himalayan explorations.

Z

Z01. ZOGG, Hans A.
Cordillera Blanca 1964 Seattle Expedition: ascent of Nevado Huascarán, July 10, 1964. By ...[and others]. Seattle: The Expedition, 1964. 55p, illus, map. 25cm.
—2nd ed. 1965.

Z02. ZUNDEL, Stanley L.
I climb to live: health and transcendency on the mountain. Los Angeles: The Author, 1979. 144p, illus.
Mostly illustrations.

Z03. ZURBRIGGEN, Mathias (-1918)
From the Alps to the Andes: being the autobiography of a mountain guide. [Trans. from the Italian by Miss Mary Alice Vialls.] Ldn: Fisher Unwin, 1899. xvi, 269p, illus. 23cm.
Biography of the guide who accompanied Conway to the Karakoram; and Fitzgerald to New Zealand and the Andes.

Z04. [ZURCHER, Frédéric]
Mountain adventures in the various countries of the world: selected from the narratives of celebrated travellers. Ldn: Seeley Jackson, 1869. viii, 320p, 24 plates, illus. 19cm. Based on *Les ascensions célèbres,* compiled by Frédéric Zurcher and Elie Margollé (Paris, 1867).
—Another ed. Edited and with an introduction and additions by Joel Tyler Headley. N.Y: Scribner's, 1872. 356p.
—Another ed. Scribner Armstrong, 1876. With 39 plates.
Includes stories from Mont Blanc, Pyrenees, Elbruz, Ararat, etc.

CLIMBERS' GUIDEBOOKS

Sub-divisions:

General and England	Nos. 1-190
Wales	201-269
Scotland	301-378
Ireland	401-433
European Alps	501-544
United States of America	601-764
Rest of World	801-898

General

Q01. CLEARE, John
British sea stacks. 1974.

Q02. NEILL, John
The Climbers' Club Bulletin. C.C., 1964. 58p, illus, map. 22cm. (New Climbs series, 1)

Q03. ROGERS, Nigel
New Climbs: C.C., 1966. 74p, illus. 22cm. (New Climbs series, 2)

Q04. ROGERS, N.
New climbs 1967. C.C., 1967. 130p, illus, maps. 22cm. (New Climbs series, 3)

Q05. ROGERS, N.
New climbs 1968. C.C., 1968. 124p, illus, map. 22cm. (New Climbs series, 4)

Q06. ROGERS, N.
New climbs 1969. C.C., [1969]. 118p, illus, maps. 22cm. (New Climbs series, 5)

Q07. ROPER, Ian
New climbs 1970. C.C., [1970]. 120p, illus. 22cm. (New Climbs series, 6)

Lake District

Q08. ANGELL, I. R.
Interim guide to St. Bees Head. The Author, 1970. 12p, illus, map. 30cm.

Q09. ARMSTRONG, D.
Recent developments in the Lake District. By . . ., — . Botterill & P. Whillance. Stockport: F.R.C.C., 1977.

Q10. ARMSTRONG, D. & Whillance, P.
Lakes new climbs, 1981/82. Stockport: FRCC.

Q11. AUSTIN, J. A.
Great Langdale. Stockport: F.R.C.C., 1967. xii, 238p, illus, maps. 16cm.

Q12. AUSTIN, J. A. & VALENTINE, R.
Great Langdale. Stockport: F.R.C.C., 1973. 256p, col. plate, illus, map. 16cm.

Q13. BASTERFIELD, George & THOMPSON, A. R.
Crags for climbing in and around Great Langdale (by George Basterfield) and *Rock climbing in Buttermere* (by A. R. Thomson). Barrow-in-Furness: F.R.C.C., [1926]. 68p, plates (1 fold), illus, map. 21cm.

Q14. BEETHAM, Bentley
Borrowdale. Stockport: F.R.C.C., 1953. 173p, plate, illus. 16cm. R.P., 1960.

Q15. BENNETT, Robert
Climbing in the Wasdale area. 1975.

Q16. BENNETT, R.
Winter climbs in the Lake District. By . . ., W. Birkett & A. Hyslop. Milnthorpe: Cicerone Press, 1979. 80p, illus.
—2nd ed. 1985. By Bennett & Birkett. 90p.

Q17. BERZINS, M.
Recent developments in the Lake District. Stockport: F.R.C.C., 1979.

Q18. BOWER, George S.
Doe Crags and climbs around Coniston: a climbers' guide. Barrow-in-Furness: F.R.C.C., [1922]. 47p, plates, illus. 21cm.

Q19. BURBAGE, M. & YOUNG, W.
Scafell group. Stockport: F.R.C.C., 1974. 201p, col. plate, illus, map. 16cm.

Q20. CLARK, Syd
Borrowdale. Stockport: F.R.C.C., 1978. 257p, col. plate, illus, map. 16cm.

Q21. CLEGG, S.
Lake District North. By . . ., C. Read & R. Wilson. [1978]. (Lakeland Climbers' Guide Books). 124p.
Lake Ditrict South (same compilers) 1979. 132p.

Q22. CLEGG, William
Great Langdale. By . . ., A. R. Dolphin & J. W. Cook. Stockport: F.R.C.C., 1950. 162p, col. plates, illus. 16cm. R.P., 1954.

Q23. COOPER, C. J. Astley
Great Gable, Borrowdale, Buttermere. By . . ., E. Wood-Johnson & L. H. Pollitt. Manchester: F.R.C.C., 1937. 153p, plate, illus. 16cm.

Q24. COOPER, C. J. A.
Great Gable, Green Gable, Kirkfell, Yewbarrow, Buckbarrow. By . . ., W. Peascod & A. P. Rossiter. Manchester: F.R.C.C., 1948. 129p, plate, illus. 16cm.

Q25. CRAM, Alan Geoffrey
Pillar group. Stockport: F.R.C.C., 1968. 148p, col. plate, illus, map. 16cm.

Q26. CRAM, A. G.
Rock climbing in the Lake District: an illustrated guide to selected climbs in the Lake District. By . . ., Chris Bilbeck, Ian Roper. Ldn: Constable, 1975. xiii, 250p, illus, maps. 18cm.

Q27. CRAM, A. G.
St. Bees and new climbs in the Lake District. F.R.C.C., 1972. 66p.

Q28. DRASDO, Harold
Eastern crags. F.R.C.C., 1959. viii, 192p, illus. 16cm. Includes 30p supplenent of new climbs throughout the Lake District, added since the supplement included with the 1957 Dow Crag Guide.
—New ed. 1967 with subtitute supplement to climbs in the Eastern Crags. only by N. J. Soper. viii, 241p, illus. maps. 16cm.

Q29. DRASDO, H. & SOPER, N. J.
Eastern crags. Stockport: F.R.C.C., 1969. 233p, col. plate, illus, maps. 16cm.

Q30. EVANS, R. Brian & UNSWORTH, Walt
The southern Lake District. Part I. Difficult to hard severe. Manchester: Cicerone Press, 1971. 55p, illus, map. 17cm.

Q31. EVANS, R. B.
Scrambles in the Lake District. Milnthorpe: Cicerone Press, 1982. 192p, illus, maps.
Guide to ascents which are not quite rock climbs proper.

Q32. FEARNEHOUGH, Pat L.
Great Gable, Wasdale and Eskdale. Stockport: F.R.C.C., 1969. 151p, col. plate, illus, maps. 16cm.

Q33. GREENOP, Donald
The western Lake District. Part I. Difficult to hard severe. Manchester: Cicerone Press, 1972. 83p, map. 17cm.

Q34. GROSS, H. S. & THOMSON, A. R.
Climbs on Great Gable (by H. S. Gross) and *Rock climbing in Borrowdale* by A. R. Thomson). Barrow-in-Furness: F.R.C.C., [1925]. 63p, plates, illus. 21cm.

Q35. HARGREAVES, A. T.
Dow Crag, Great Langdale and outlying crags. By . . .[and others]. Manchester: F.R.C.C., 1938. 176p, col. plate, illus. 16cm.

Q36. HARGREAVES, A. T.
Dow Crag and other climbs. By . . .[and others]. Stockport: F.R.C.C., 1957. 135p, plate, illus. 16cm.

Q37. HARGREAVES, A. T.
Scafell group. Manchester: F.R.C.C., 1936. 115p, col. plate, illus. 16cm.

Q38. HARGREAVES, A. T.
Scafell group. By . . ., A. R. Dolphin & R. Miller. Stockport: F.R.C.C., 1956. 154p, col. plate, illus. 16cm.

Q39. HASSALL, G. A.
The northern Lake District. Part I. Difficult to hard severe. Manchester: Cicerone Press, 1969. 40p, illus, map. 17cm.

Q40. HOLLAND, C. F.
Climbs on the Scawfell group: a climbers' guide. Barrow-in-Furness: F.R.C.C., [1924]. 66p, plates, illus. 21cm.

Q41. KELLY, H. M.
Pillar Rock and neighbouring climbs: a climbers' guide. Barrow-in-Furness: F.R.C.C., [1923]. 68p, plates, illus. 21cm. —New rev. ed. Manchester: F.R.C.C., 1935. 121p, plate, illus. 16cm. Slight variation in title.

Q42. KELLY, H. M. & PEASCOD, W.
Pillar Rock and neighbourhood. Stockport: F.R.C.C., 1952. 130p, plate, illus. 16cm.

Q43. MARTINDALE, John Robert
Dow Crag area. Stockport: F.R.C.C., 1976. [12], 150p, plate, illus, map. 16cm.

Q44. MILLER, David
Dow Crag area. Stockport: F.R.C.C., 1968. 133p, plate, illus, maps. 16cm.

Q45. MILLER, D. (Editor)
Scafell, Dow and Eskdale. Stockport: F.R.C.C., 1984. iv, 276p, illus, maps.

Q46. MILLER, D. & SOPER, N. J.
75 new climbs in the Lake District, 1964-1965. Stockport: F.R.C.C., 1966. 40p. 16cm.

Q47. MILLER, D. & AUSTIN, J. A.
New climbs in the Lake District, 1966. Stockport: F.R.C.C., 1967. 64p. 16cm.

Q48. MORTIMER, Michael G.
Great Langdale. F.R.C.C., 1980.

Q49. NUNN, Paul J. & WOOLCOCK, O.
Borrowdale. Stockport: F.R.C.C., 1968. 219p, plate, illus, maps. 16cm.

Q50. OLIVER, Geoffrey & GRIFFIN, L. Joe
Scafell group. Stockport: F.R.C.C., 1967. 172p, col. plate, illus, maps. 16cm.

Q51. PEASCOD, William & RUSHWORTH, G.
Buttermere and Newlands area. Manchester: F.R.C.C., 1949. 125p, col. plate, illus. 16cm.

Q52. PHIZACKLEA, Al & KENYON, Ron (Editors)
Recent developments in the Lake District, 1983-84. Stockport: F.R.C.C., 1985.

Q53. ROPER, Ian
Buttermere and Eastern Crags. By . . ., E. M. Grindley & G. N. Higginson. Stockport: F.R.C.C., 1979. 208p, illus. 16cm.

Q54. ROSS, Paul & THOMPSON, Michael
Borrowdale: a climber's guide. The Authors, [1966]. 112p, illus. 17cm.

Q55. SHEFFIELD UNIVERSITY MOUNTAINEERING CLUB
Guide to climbs in Grisedale, Deepdale and Dovedale. By members of . . .Sheffield U.M.C., [1956]. iv, 44p, fold. map. 15cm.

Q56. SOPER, N. J. & ALLINSON, N.
Buttermere and Newlands area. Stockport: F.R.C.C., 1970. 151p, col. plate, illus, maps. 16cm.

Q57. YOUNG, William
New West–new climbs on Gable and Pillar and interim guide to Buckbarrow. Edited by David Miller. Stockport: F.R.C.C., 1985.

South-east England

Q58. [ANONYMOUS]
Harrison Rocks: the climbs. The Author, [c.1952]. i, 23p. 17cm.

Q59. [ANONYMOUS]
Bowles Rocks. [4 pamphlets issued between 1960-69?]

Q60. BRYSON, H. Courtney
Rock climbs round London. [N.p.]: The Author, 1936. 25p, illus, map. 19cm.

Q61. DANIELLS, Tim
Southern sandstone. C.C., 1981. 128p, illus.

Q62. HARTLEY, H. S. & GRAY, O.
Roof climbers' guide to St. John's. Cambridge: Metcalfe, 1921. 31p, illus. 22cm.

Q63. PANTHER, Trevor S.
New rock climbing guide to Harrison's Rocks. The Author, [1967]. 48p, illus, maps. 14cm.
—2nd ed. 1968. 52p, illus, maps. 14cm.

Q64. PYATT, Edward C.
Sandstone climbs in south-east England. Junior Mountaineering Club of Scotland (London Section), 1947. 48p, illus, maps. 22cm.
—Rev. ed. by D. G. Fagan & J. V. Smoker. C.C., 1963. xii, 112p, illus, maps. 16cm.

Q65. PYATT, E. C.
Climber's guide to south-east England. Stockport: C.C., 1956. 100p, plates, illus. 15cm. R.P., 1960.

Q66. PYATT, E. C.
South-east England.
—2nd rev. ed. by L. R. & L. E. Holliwell. Stockport: C.C., 1969. xvi, 147p, illus, bibl. 16cm.

Q67. SMOKER, J. V.
[*Supplement of new routes at High Rocks.*] The Author, [c.1957]. i, 7p. 17cm.

Q68. SMOKER, J. V. & FAGAN, D. G.
Recent developments on south-east England. Sandstone Climbing Club, 1963. [3], 22p, 7 plates. 16cm.

Q69. [WEATHERHEAD?]
Night-climber's guide to Trinity. 1960.

Q70. YOUNG, Geoffrey Winthrop
Roof-climber's guide to Trinity. Cambridge: Spalding, 1900.
—Rev. ed. 1930.

South-west England

Q71. ANDREWS, A. W. & PYATT, Edward C.
Cornwall. Stockport: C.C., 1950. 164p, plates, illus, maps. 16cm.

Q72. ANNETTE, Barrie M.
Limestone climbs on the Dorset coast.
—2nd ed. Southampton: Southampton University Mountaineering Club, 1960. 36 leaves, plate, illus. 21cm. Typescript.
—3rd ed. Cade & Co. Ltd, [1964]. 52p, illus, maps.16cm.

Q73. ARCHER, Clement Hugh
Coastal climbs in north Devon. Minehead: The Author, [1961]. 49p, plates, maps. 25cm.
—Supplement for 1962.
—Supplement for 1963-5.

Q74. BANNER, Hugh I.
Limestone climbs in south-west England. University of Bristol Mountaineering Club, 1954. viii, 52p, illus. 20cm.
—Rev. ed. by B. G. N. Page. U.B.M.C., 1955. 54p, illus. 17cm.

Q75. BIVEN, P. H. & MCDERMOTT, M. B.
Cornwall. Vol. 1. Sidcup: C.C., 1968. xi, 209p, plates (1 fold), illus, maps. 16cm.

Q76. BROOMHEAD, Richard
Cheddar: Cheddar Gorge, Brean Down, the Mendips. Leicester: Cordee, 1977. 96p, illus, maps. 18cm.

Q77. BROWN, D. W.
Lundy: a new climbs supplement. University of Bradford Union M.C., 1967. ii, 17p, 21cm.
—2nd ed. 1969. 24p.

Q78. CALVERT, F. T.
Some Gloucestershire climbs. Gloucestershire Mountaineering Club, 1958. 20p, illus. 22cm.

Q79. CANNINGS, Frank E. R.
Climbing guide to Chudleigh Rocks. Exeter & District Climbing Club, February 1964. 12p, illus. 33cm.

—2nd ed. by ...& P.H. Biven. The Authors, Dec. 1964. 14p, illus. 33cm.
—*Supplement of new climbs.* P. H. Biven & F. E. R. Cannings, Oct. 1965. 4p. 33cm.
—*Chudleigh guide: addendum to supplement.* [1966]. 4p. 33cm.

Q80. CANNINGS, F. E. R.
Rock climbs at the Wyndcliffe: interim guide. The Author, [1970]. i, 11 leaves, maps. 33cm.

Q81. CARVER, Toni
Climbing in Cornwall: a climber's guide to north, south and east Cornwall. Compiled and edited by ...St. Ives: J. Pike, 1973. 84p, illus, maps. 19cm.

Q82. CREWE, Richard J. & SHEPTON, R. L. M.
Dorset. Leicester: R. J. Crewe, 1977. xxi, 232p, illus, maps. 16cm. Revised edition of C.C. guidebook, *Dorset* (1969) by White & Shepton.

Q83. DEARMAN, R. S. & RILEY, D. W.
Climbers' guide to Cheddar Gorge. The Authors, 1970. ii, 39p, illus. 15cm.

Q84. [DENTON, J. W.]
Climbing guide to Dartmoor. The Author, [1955?]. 17p. 40cm.

Q85. DERRY, J. D.
Some rock climbs near Plymouth. The Author, [1951]. 18 leaves, maps. 33cm.
—New ed. Cover title, *Rock climbs.* Dartmouth: Royal Navy College, [1952?]. 51 leaves, maps. 19cm.

Q86. GLOUCESTERSHIRE MOUNTAINEERING CLUB
Rock climbs in the Wye Valley and Cotswolds. The Club, 1962.
—New ed. The Club, 1965. 24p, illus, maps. 22cm.

Q87. GOODIER, R.
Climbing in Corwall 1955: supplement of new climbs. By ...[and others]. C.C., 1955. i, 21p, illus. 33cm.
—Copy of a section of the above: *Climbing on Bosigran Main Face.* By [J. Smith]. Junior Leaders Regiment, [1966]. 26p. 18cm.

Q88. [HONE, John]
Brean Down: a rock climbing guide. The Author, [1960]. 16p, map. 18cm.

Q89. JENKIN, Gordon
Swanage: rock climbs in Dorset.
—3rd ed. Leicester: C.C., 1985. 262p, illus. 17cm.

Q90. KING, R. S.
Climbing report: some sandstone climbs in the Frome Valley at Bristol. Bristol Exploration Club, 1966. 18p, illus, maps. 26cm.

Q91. [LAWDER, K. M.]
Lundy. The Author, [c.1965]. 9 leaves. 33cm.

Q92. LAWDER, K. M. (Editor)
Climbing guide to Dartmoor and south-west Devon. Portsmouth: Royal Navy Ski & Mountaineering Club, [1957]. vi, 70p, plate, illus, map. 16cm.

Q93. LAWRANCE, C. J. & BROWN J. L.
Guide to Main Cliff, Cleeve Hill. Oxford M.C., 1970. 5 leaves, diag. 21cm.

Q94. LITTLEJOHN, Pat R.
South Devon: Chudleigh, Torbay, Torquay, Brixham, Berry Head. By ...in association with Peter Biven. Goring, Reading: West Col Prod., 1971. 172p, illus, maps. 17cm.

Q95. LITTLEJOHN, P. R.
South-west climbs. Ldn: Diadem, 1979. 304p, illus, maps. 18cm.

Q96. LITTLEJOHN, P. R. & O'SULLIVAN, Peter
South Devon & Dartmoor. Leicester: Cordee, 1985.

Q97. MASON, G.
Easier climbs in the Avon Gorge, Bristol. The Author, 1964. ii, 50p. 17cm.

Q98. MONKS, S.
Avon Gorge. Sheffield: Dark Peak, 1980.

Q99. MOULAM, Anthony J. J.
Dartmoor. Goring, Reading: West Col, 1976. 68p, illus, maps. 17cm.

Q100. MOULTON, Robert D.
Rock climbing in Devonshire. Royal Navy Mountaineering Club, 1966. 114p, illus, maps. 16cm.

Q101. MOULTON, R. D. & THOMPSON, T. D.
Chair Ladder and the south coast. Leicester: C.C., 1975. 154p. 17cm.

Q102. MOULTON, R. D.
Lundy rock climbs. Royal Navy Mountaineering Club, 1970. 52p, illus, maps. 16cm.
—2nd ed. Buckhurst Hill: The Author for Royal Navy and Royal Marines M.C., 1974. 122p, illus. 18cm.
—3rd ed. R.N. & R.M.M.C./B.M.C., 1980. 128p, illus, maps.

Q103. MOULTON, R. D. & THOMPSON, T. D.
Cornwall: West Penwith. Stockport: C.C., 1975.

Q104. MOULTON, R. D.
Devon rock climbs. Leicester: Cordee, 1979?

Q105. NIXON, John
Limestone climbs in south-west England. Limestone Climbing Group, 1964. viii, 84p, illus. 16cm.

Q106. NIXON, J.
Climbing guide to the Avon Gorge. Bristol: University of Bristol Mountaineering Club, 1959. 45p, illus. 17cm.

Q107. O'SULLIVAN, Peter
Devon new climbs 1980. R. D. Moulton/Royal Navy & Royal Marines M.C., 1980. 48p, illus. Supplement to Devon guides by Moulton & Littlejohn.

Q108. O'SULLIVAN, P.
Cornwall-West Penwith. C.C., 1984. 240p, illus, maps.

Q109. PENNING, Tony
Wyndcliffe [near Wintours Leap, River Wye]. South Wales Mountaineering Club, 1983. 20p.

Q110. PERRIN, Jim
Wintour's Leap: interim guide. 1971.

Q111. STEVENSON, Vivian N.
Cornwall. Vol. 2. Stockport: C.C., 1966. x, 150p, plates, illus, maps. 16cm.

Q112. WARD-DRUMMOND, Edwin
Gorge, sixty-eight [*Avon Gorge*]. [The Author?], [1968]. 16p. 14cm.

Q113. WARD-DRUMMOND, E.
Extremely severe in the Avon Gorge: [the 1967 guide to the harder climbs]. Bristol: N. Crowhurst, 1967. 30p, illus, map. 21cm.

Q114. WHITE, R. C.
New climbs on the limestone cliffs of East Dorset. Southampton University M.C., 1967. 23p. 27cm.

Q115. WHITE, R. C. & SHEPTON, R. L. M.
Dorset. C.C., 1969. x, 134p, illus, maps. 16cm.

Q116. WILLSON, John & HOPE, David E.
Wye Valley. Vol. 1. Wintour's Leap, Symonds Yat, Western Cliffs. Leicester: Cordee, 1977. 123p, illus, maps. 18cm.

Q117. WILLSON, J. & HOPE, D.
Wye Valley: 1982 supplement. Leicester: Cordee, [1983?]. 32p.

Q118. WYVILL, B.
Rock climbs in the Avon Gorge. Bristol: University of Bristol M.C., n.d.

Midlands

Q119. UNSWORTH, Walt
Climber's guide to Pontesford Rocks. Shrewsbury: Wilding, 1962. 35p, illus. 16cm.

Q120. VICKERS, Kenneth S.
Rock climbs in Leicestershire: interim guide. Leicester: Leicester Association of Mountaineers, 1966. 46p, illus. 18cm.

Q121. VICKERS, K.
Climbs in Leicestershire. 1972.

Peaks, Pennines, North-west England

Q122. AINSWORTH, Les & WATKIN, Phil
Lancashire: guide to rock climbs. Rocksport Magazine, [1969]. 98p, illus, maps. 16cm.

Q123. AINSWORTH, L.
Rock climbs in Lancashire and the north-west. Manchester: Cicerone Press, 1975.
—Supplement, 1979. L. Ainsworth, D. Cronshaw & A. Evans.
—3rd ed. 1983. 360p.

Q124. ALLSOPP, Allan (Editor)
Kinder, Roches and northern areas. (Climbs on gritstone, v. 3) Birkenhead: Willmer, 1951. 153p, plates, illus. 16cm.
—Another ed. 1957. iv, 80p, illus, maps. 16cm. More or less a reprint of part of the 1951 guide.

Q125. ALLSOPP, A.
Cadshaw Rocks. The Author, 1950. 7 leaves. 33cm. With 'notes added 1960'.

Q126. ALLSOPP, A. & EVANS, R. B.
West Yorkshire area. (Climbs on gritstone, v. 5) Birkenhead: Willmer Bros & Haram, 1957. iv, 140p, illus, map. 16cm.

Q127. [ANONYMOUS]
Ravensdale. The Author, [1967?]. 7 leaves. 33cm.

Q128. ASHTON, G. & NEWCOMBE, R.
Guide to Pex Hill. Liverpool District M.C., 1965. 8 leaves, diag. 21cm.

Q129. AUSTIN, J. A.
New climbs–West Yorkshire area. Yorkshire Mountaineering Club, [1965]. 12p. 23cm.

Q130. BALLARD, J. & MARSHALL, E.
Rock climbs in the Peak. Derwent Valley [Gardom's Edge to Milford Crag]. V. 5. Manchester: B.M.C./Leicester: Cordee, 1981. 240p, illus. 17cm.

Q131. BANCROFT, Steve
Rock climbs in the Peak: recent developments. [Manchester]: Peak Committee of B.M.C., 1977. 87p, illus. 17cm.

Q132. BEBBINGTON, M. H.
Yorkshire gritstone: a rock climber's guide. P. Holt & Yorkshire M.C., 1969. vi, 249p, illus, maps. 16cm.
—New ed. 1974. 266p.
—Another ed. [Bradford]: Yorkshire M.C., [1980]. 200p, illus, maps. 17cm.

Q133. BIRTLES, Geoffrey B.
Stoney Middleton dale. [N.p.]: The Author, 1966. [51p]. 18cm. Typescript.

Q134. BLACK, A. B.
Rock climbing guide to the Wilton Quarries. Bolton: Alpine Sports, 1969. 32p, illus. 21cm.

Q135. BROWELL, M.
Climbs in the Peak. Vol. 6 — Staffordshire area. By . . ., S. & B. Dale & N. Longland. Manchester: B.M.C., 1981. 268p, illus.

Q136. No Entry

Q137. BYNE, Eric
Sheffield-Froggatt area. (Rock climbs in the Peak, v. 3) Cade & Co., 1965. vi, 216p, illus, maps. 16cm.

Q138. BYNE. E.
Climbing guide to Brassington Rocks. Birmingham: Midland Association of Mountaineers, 1950. 35p, plates, illus. 14cm.

Q139. BYNE, E. & WHITE, W. B. (Editors)
Further developments in the Peak District. Birkenhead: Willmer & Haram, 1957. iv, 205p, plates, illus. 16cm.

Q140. BYNE, E. (Editor)
The Saddleworth-Chew Valley area. [N.p.]: Cade & Co., [1965]. 210p, plates, illus, bibl. 16cm.

Q141. BYNE, E. (Editor)
Sheffield area: climbs on gritstone, vol. 2. Birkenhead: Willmer Bros, 1951. vi, 172p, illus, maps. 16cm.
—Rev. ed. 1956. 171p, plates, illus, bibl. Practically a reprint.

Q142. BYNE, E. (Editor)
The Sheffield-Stanage area. [N.p.]: Cade & Co., [1963?]. 214p, plates, illus. 16cm.

Q143. BYNE, E.
Bleaklow area: rock climbs in the Peak.
—2nd ed. C.C., 1971. 234p, illus. 16cm.

Q144. BYNE, E.
Chatsworth gritstone area. C.C., 1970.

Q145. BYNE, E.
Froggatt area.
—2nd ed. C.C., 1973. 238p, illus. 16cm.

Q146. CAINE, J. W.
Climber's guide to the Isle of Man. Manx Fell & Rock Club, 1955. 19p, diag. 21cm.
—Reset ed. entitled *Fell walking & climbing guide to the Isle of Man.* Cade & Co., 1961. 24p, diag. 21cm.

Q147. CARSTEN, H. A.
Climbers' guide to Helsby Rocks. Liverpool: Wayfarers' Club, [1946]. 48p, diag. 14cm. Cover title: *Helsby Rocks.*
—Rev. ed. by Hugh Banner. 1957. 32p, diag. 22cm.

Q148. CLARKE, T. M.
Black Rocks and Cratcliffe Tor. The Author, 1970. ii, 30p. 21cm.

Q149. EVANS, A. J.
Interim guide to Stannington Ruffs. Rocksport Magazine, 1969. 16p, illus, map. 13cm. Pull-out supplement to Feb. 1969 issue.

Q150. EVANS, Ray
Guide to Wilton Quarries, Number One and Number Two. Bolton: Alpine Sports, 1966. 12p, illus. 17cm.

Q151. GARTRELL, Geoffrey
Rock climbs — Isle of Man. Manchester: Cicerone Press, [1973]. 50p, illus, maps. 17cm.

Q152. [GRAHAM, Fergus]
Recent developments on gritstone. [By . . .and others]. The Authors, [1924]. xiv, 83p, illus. 16cm.

Q153. GREGORY, David
Froggatt area. Manchester: B.M.C., 1979?

Q154. GRIFFITHS, B. & WRIGHT, A.
Stanage area. C.C., 1976. 208p, illus. 17cm.

Q155. HARDING, P. R. J. & MOULAM, A. J. J.
Guide to Black Rocks and Cratcliffe Tor. Malvern: C.C., 1949. x, 27p, plates, illus, bibl. 22cm.

Q156. HARTLEY, J. A. & LEGGETT, E. N.
Heptonstall Quarry. The Authors, 1962. 16p, 2 fold. plates. 18cm.

Q157. JACKSON, Chris
Northern limestone–rock climbs in the Peak. Vol. 4. Manchester: Peak Committee of B.M.C., 1980. 224p, illus.

Q158. LAYCOCK, John
Some shorter climbs (in Derbyshire and elsewhere). Manchester: Refuge Printing Department, 1913. ix, 116p, plates, illus, bibl. 16cm.
—Another ed. entitled *Some shorter climbs.* Cover title: *Gritstone climbs.* The Author, [1918-23?] iii, 116p, diag. 20cm. Typescript copy of original guide.

Q159. LEE, Martin
Climbers' guide to Helsby Crags. Liverpool: Wayfarers' Club, 1964. iv, 52p, illus. 16cm.

Q160. LEGGETT, E. N. & AMBLER, C. R.
Woodhouse Scar: a climber's guide. The Authors, 1960. 24p, fold. plates, illus. 18cm.

Q161. MILBURN, Geoffrey (Editor)
Stanage Millstone. Manchester: B.M.C., 1983. 336p, illus, maps.

Q162. MITCHELL, Michael A. (Editor)
Climbs on Yorkshire limestone. Clapham, Yorks: Dalesman, 1963. 40p, illus, maps. 22cm.

Q163. NUNN, Paul J.
Southern limestone: rock climbs in the Peak. C.C., 1970. 238p, illus. 16cm.

Q164. NUNN, P. J.
The Kinder area. Manchester: B.M.C., [1974]. 208p, illus, bibl. 16cm.

Q165. NUNN, P. J.
The northern limestone area. Compiled and arranged by . . .Climbers' Club for B.M.C., Peak District Committee, 1969. xiv, 265p, plates, illus, map, bibl. 16cm.

Q166. NUNN, P. J.
Rock climbing in the Peak District: a photographic guide for rockclimbers. Ldn: Constable, 1975. xx, 304p, illus, maps, bibl. 18cm.
—3rd ed. 1983. xx, 328p.

Q167. PARKER, H. C. (Editor)
Laddow area. Birkenhead: Willmer Bros, 1948. 68p, plates, illus, map, bibl. 16cm.

Q168. PEARSON, H.
Guide to Laddow. Carl K. Brunning, [1934]. 32p, illus. 17cm. Reprinted from the *Mountaineering Journal,* Jun-Aug, 1933.

Q169. ROUSE, Alan
Helsby and the Wirral. Manchester: Cicerone Press, 1976. 82p.

Q170. SALT, David
Rock climbs on the Roches & Hen Cloud: a complete guide. North Staffordshire M.C. 1968. iii, 55p, illus, map. 21cm.

Q171. SALT, D.
The Staffordshire gritstone area. Compiled by . . .Manchester: Peak Committee of B.M.C., [1973]. 231p, illus, bibl. 16cm.

Q172. SCOTT, Douglas Keith
Climbs on Derwent Valley limestone. Nottingham Climbers, Club. [1965]. 82p, illus, map. 22cm.

Q173. SHEFFIELD UNIVERSITY MOUNTAINEERING CLUB
Wharncliffe Crags. By members of . . .Carl K. Brunning, [1934]. Reprinted from the *Mountaineering Journal,* Sep-Nov, 1933.

Q174. SIMCOCK, Peter (Editor)
Rock climbs on the North York moors. Leicester: Cordee/Cleveland Mountaineering Club, 1985. 159p.

Q175. SMITH, J.
Climbers' guide to the Staffordshire Roaches and Hen Cloud area. Sheffield: Brian G. Stokes, 1968. vi, 42p, illus. 16cm.

Q176. VICTORY, J.
Interim guide to Frogsmouth Quarry [near Runcorn] N.W.F.A. (abbreviation for ?), [c.1954]. 17 leaves, diag, map. Photocopied MS.

Q177. WEST, G. T. W.
Rock climbs on the mountain limestone of Derbyshire. Cade & Co. [for Manchester Gritstone Climbing Club], [1961]. vi, 152p, illus, maps. 16cm.

Q178. [WEST, G. T. W. ?]
Tintwhistle Knarr Quarry. The Author, [c.1962]. 7 leaves. 33cm.

Q179. WHITTAKER, Robert
Chew Valley area: rock climbs in the Peak. C.C., 1976. 170p, illus. 17cm.

Q180. WILKINSON, Frank (Editor)
Yorkshire limestone: a rock climber's guide. Bradford: Yorkshire Mountaineering Club, 1968. 169p, illus, maps. 16cm.
—Another ed. 1974. 245p.

Q181. WILSON, R. G.
Recent developments on Peakland gritstone. Manchester University Mountaineering Club, [1961]. 30p. 22cm.

Q182. YEOMAN, F. H.
Stancliffe Quarry. Rocksport Magazine, [1970]. 3 leaves. 30cm.

North-east England

Q183. HAIGHTON, N. E.
Northumberland: a rock climbing guide. Northumberland Mountaineering Club, 1971. 254p.
—4th ed. 1979.

Q184. LESNIAK, Eddie (Editor)
Yorkshire gritstone. Yorkshire Mountaineering Club, 1982. xii, 230p, illus.

Q185. MARR, Anthony
North York moors climbers' guide. Goring, Reading: West Col, 1970. 158p, illus, maps. 17cm.

Q186. NORTHUMBRIAN MOUNTAINEERING CLUB
Some Northumbrian rock climbs. By members of the ...Sunderland: Grant Ogilvy & Co. Ltd, 1950. 96p, illus, maps. 17cm.

Q187. NORTHUMBRIAN MOUNTAINEERING CLUB
A rock-climber's guide to Northumberland. Compiled by members of the ...
—2nd ed. Clapham via Lancaster: Dalesman, 1964. 68p, illus. 19cm.

Q188. WILSON, Maurice F. (Editor)
Climbs in Cleveland. Billingham: Cleveland Mountaineering Club, [1956]. 83p, illus. 16cm.

Q189. WILSON, M. F.
Climbs on the North York Moors. Cleveland Mountaineering Club, 1961. iv, 159p, illus, maps. 16cm.

Q190. WILSON, Stewart G. & KENYON, Ronald J.
North of England: Eden Valley, North Lakes limestone, etc. Penrith: Pointer Publications, 1980. 201p, illus, map. 17cm.

WALES

North Wales, Snowdonia

Q201. ASHTON, Steve
Scrambles in Snowdonia. Milnthorpe: Cicerone Press, 1980. 144p, illus.

Q202. BANNER, Hugh I. & CREW, Peter
Clogwyn du'r Arddu. C.C., 1963. ix, 103p, illus, maps. 16cm.
—New ed. C.C., 1967. viii, 144p, illus. 16cm.

Q203. BARFORD, John E. Q.
Three cliffs in Llanberis. C.C., 1944. 24p, illus. 22cm. Reprinted from *Climbers' Club Journal.*

Q204. CARR, Herbert R. C.
Climbers' guide to Snowdon and the Beddgelert district. [N.p.]: C.C., 1926. 143p, plates (3 fold. col), illus, maps, bibl. 16cm.

Q205. CATHCART, Stuart
Clwyd limestone [Llangollen area]. Milnthorpe: Cicerone Press, 128p.

Q206. COX, A. David M. & KRETSCHMER, H. E.
Craig yr Ysfa. C.C., 1943. 36p, illus. 22cm. Reprinted from *Climbers' Club Journal, 1943.*

Q207. CREW, Peter
Craig Gogarth. The Author, 1966. 40p, illus. 17cm.
—Rev. ed. 1967. 40p, illus. 17cm.

Q208. CREW, P.
Anglesey–Gogarth: Craig Gogarth, South Stack, Holyhead Mountain; Gogarth Upper Tier (By Les Holliwell). Goring, Reading: West Col, 1969. 107p, plates, illus, maps. 17cm.

Q209. CREW, P. & ROPER, I.
Cwm Glas.
—2nd ed. Stockport: C.C., 1970. ii, 157p, illus, maps. 16cm.

Q210. CREW, P.
Llanberis south. Stockport: C.C., 1966. ix, 158p, illus, maps. 16cm.

Q211. CREW, P. & HARRIS, Alan
Tremadoc area: Tremadoc Rocks, Craig y Gelli and Carreg Hylldrem. Goring, Reading: West Col, 1970. 106p, 16 plates, illus, map. 17cm.

Q212. DANCE, E. W. & EGGLINTON, G.
Quellyn area: interim guide. Manchester University Mountaineering Club, [1954?]. 42p, illus. 22cm. Reprinted from *M.U.M.C. Journal, 1953-4.*

Q213. DRASDO, Harold
Lliwedd.
—3rd ed. C.C., 1972.

Q214. [DURKIN, Dave]
Holyhead Mountain. The Author, [1967]. 20 leaves. 23cm.

Q215. EDWARDS, J. Menlove & BARFORD, J. E. Q.
Clogwyn du'r Arddu. Manchester: C.C., 1942. 24p, plates, illus, bibl. 22cm. Reprinted from *Climbers' Club Journal, 1942.*

Q216. EDWARDS, J. M. & NOYCE, C. W. F.
Cwm Idwal group. C.C., 1936. viii, 141p, illus, map. 16cm.
—2nd rev. ed. Manchester: C.C., 1940. vii, 145p, plates, illus. 16cm.
—Reprint. 1946.

Q217. EDWARDS, J. M. & NOYCE, C. W. F.
Tryfan group. [N.p.]: C.C., 1937. ix, 122p, plates, illus. 16cm.

Q218. EDWARDS, Rowland
Climbs on North Wales limestone: the Little Orme, the Great Orme, Craig y Forwyn. Leicester: Cordee, 1976. 56p, illus. 18cm.

Q219. HARDING, P. R. J.
Llanberis Pass. Stockport: C.C., 1950. 228p, plates, illus, map. 16cm. R.P., 1955.

Q220. HATTON, Peter
The three cliffs. Manchester: C.C., 1974. x, 140p, illus, maps. 16cm.

Q221. HOLLIWELL, Les
Carneddau. Manchester: C.C., 1975. 151p, illus, maps. 18cm.

Q222. JAMES, Ron
Rockclimbing in Wales. Ldn: Constable, 1970. 241p, illus. 22cm.
—2nd rev. ed. 1975. xiv, 242p.
—3rd ed. 1982. 266p.

Q223. JONES, Trevor & NEILL, John
Snowdon south.
—2nd ed. Stockport: C.C., 1966. x, 142p, illus, maps. 16cm.

Q224. KIRKUS, Colin F.
Glyder Fach group.
—New rev. ed. [N.p.]: C.C., 1937. ix, 113p, plates, illus, map. 16cm.

Q225. LEES, John R.
Moelwynion: an interim guide to the lower crags. [N.p.], 1962. 329-355p. 22cm. Offprint from *Climbers' Club Journal, 1962.*

Q226. LEPPERT, Zdzislaw
Ogwen [Tryfan, Glyder Fach, Cwm Idwal, etc.] C.C., 1982. 208p, illus.

Q227. MCCALLUM, Keith
Eastern Snowdonia: guide to climbing in the Lledr Valley, Carreg Hyll Drem and Carreg y Fran. The Author, 1967. 27 leaves. 21cm.

Q228. [MCCALLUM, K.]
Snowdon West: Cwm Pennant. The Author, [1967]. 4 leaves. 26cm.

Q229. MCCALLUM, K.
Carnedds West: crags in the Sychnant Pass. The Author, [1967]. 3 leaves. 26cm.

Q230. MCCALLUM, K.
Western Snowdonia: guide to climbing at Cwm Silyn and Castell Cidwm. The Author, 1968. 29 leaves, illus. 22cm.

Q231. MCGINLEY, Leigh
Tremadog.
—5th ed. C.C., 1983. 166p, illus.

Q232. MILBURN, Geoffrey
Llanberis Pass. Manchester: C.C., 1978. 160p, illus, maps. 18cm.
—Rev. ed. 1981. 182p.

Q233. MILBURN, G.
Gogarth 1981. C.C., 1981. 54p.

Q234. MORTIMER, Michael
Tremadog and the Moelwyns. C.C., 1979?

Q235. MOULAM, A. J. J.
The Carneddau. Stockport: C.C., [1950]. 123p, plates, illus, map. 16cm.
—2nd ed. 1966.

Q236. MOULAM, A. J. J.
Cwm Idwal.
—New ed. Stockport: C.C., 1958. ix, 126p, plates, illus. 16cm.
—Rev. ed. 1964.
—Another ed. 1967. x, 154p.

Q237. MOULAM, A. J. J.
Snowdon east. Stockport: C.C., 1970. vii, 191p, illus, maps. 16cm.

Q238. MOULAM, A. J. J.
Tryfan and Glyder Fach. Stockport: C.C., 1956. xi, 153p, plates, illus. 16cm. R.P., 1959.
—Another ed. C.C., 1966. x, 159p.

Q239. NEILL, John
Cwm Silyn and Tremadoc. C.C., 1955. 40p, illus. 22cm. Reprinted from the *Climbers' Club Journal, 1956.*
—*Tremadoc supplement.* 16p. 22cm. Reprint from journal.

Q240. NEILL, J. & JONES, Trevor
Snowdon south. Stockport: C.C., 1960. xii, 109p, plates, illus. 16cm.

Q241. NEWCOMBE, Rick
Winter climbs in North Wales [Ogwen area to the Arans]. Cicerone Press, 1974. R.P., 1977, 1979.
—2nd rev. ed. 1980. 104p.

Q242. NOYCE, C. Wilfrid F. & EDWARDS, J. Menlove
Lliwedd group.
—New rev. ed. C.C., 1939. xii, 173p, plates, illus, map. 16cm.

Q243. POLLITT, Andrew
North Wales: new climbs. C.C./B.M.C., 1983. 70p, illus.

Q244. POLLITT, A.
North Wales limestone [new climbs]. C.C., 1984. 32p.

Q245. ROSCOE, Donald Thomas
Llanberis north. Stockport: C.C., 1961. 108p, plates, illus. 16cm.
—Another ed. 1964. viii, 126p. R.P., 1966.

Q246. STYLES, Showell
Climbs on Moel y Gest. The Author, [1950?]. 8p, illus. 23cm.

Q247. THOMSON, James Merriman Archer & ANDREWS, A. W.
The climbs on Lliwedd; issued by the Climbers' Club. Ldn: Arnold, 1909. xv, 99p, plates, illus. 16cm.

Q248. THOMSON, J. M. A.
Climbing in the Ogwen district; [issued by the Climbers' Club]. Ldn: Arnold, 1910. xx, 124p, plates, illus. 16cm.
—Appendix, containing accounts of many new climbs: by H. E. L. Porter. Arnold, 1921. N.B.: There are three forms of the appendix:
(a) Pages 125-154 only;
(b) Pages 125-162, the additional pages describing climbs on Carnedd y Filiast. Llech Ddu, and new ascents 1915-21;
(c) As (b) plus 8-page 'Special appendix of ten years' climbs' by W. Henry Lewin.

Q249. WILLIAMS, Paul
Snowdonia rock climbs. Extreme Books & Design/Cordee, 1982. 299p, illus.

Q250. WILSON, Ken & LEPPERT, Z.
Cwm Idwal.
—3rd ed. C.C., 1974. iii, 197p, illus, maps. 16cm.

Q251. YATES, M. & PERRIN, Jim
Cwm Silyn and Cwellyn. Stockport: C.C., 1971. xiii, 173p, illus, maps. 16cm.

Central and South Wales

Q252. ARMY MOUNTAINEERING ASSOCIATION
Pandy Rocks.

Q253. BENNETT, Roger J. F.
Llanymynech Crags: interim guide to the rockclimbing. The Author, 1970. i, 32 leaves, illus. 16cm.

Q254. [BRADLEY, J. H.]
Brecon Beacons National Park: interim guide to rock climbing. Brecon Beacons National Park Joint Advisory Committee, 1967. 10p. 33cm.
—2nd ed. 1970. 8p. 33cm.

Q255. DANFORD, Mike & PENNING, Tony
Gower and South East Wales. South Wales Mountaineering Club, 1983. 192p, illus, maps.

Q256. FOSS, Adrian & PARSONS, Lynn
Interim rockclimbing guide to South Wales. South Wales Mountaineering Club & Y.H.A. South Wales Region, 1969. i, 30p. 21cm.

Q257. HORSFIELD, J. C.
Interim guide to Craig Cefn Coed. South Wales M.C., [1970]. i, 9p, illus. 33 cm. Preceded by anonymous typescript edition.

Q258. LAMBE, R. E.
Craig Cowarch: a guide to the rock climbs on the crags of Craig Cowarch. Stafford: The Mountain Club, 1958. v, 72p, plates, illus. 17 × 21cm.

Q259. LAMBE, R. E. & KNOX, A. B.
Guide to Craig Cowarch and other mid-Wales crags. Stafford: The Mountain Club, 1964. iv, 85p, illus. 17cm.

Q260. LEYSHON, Peter & JONES, Cledwyn
Taff Fechan. Ldn: B.M.C., 1969. 24p, illus. 22cm. Issued as a free supplement to the Spring 1969 issue of the B.M.C. journal *Mountaineering.*

Q261. LITTLEJOHN, Pat & HARBER, Michael
Pembroke. C.C., 1981. 269p, illus, maps. 17cm.
—2nd ed. Leicester: C.C., 1985.

Q262. MONTJOYE, Jon de & HARBER, M.
Pembroke–1982 supplement. C.C., 1982. 68p.

Q263. MORTLOCK, Colin
Rock climbing in Pembrokeshire. Tenby: H. G. Walters, 1974. 160p, maps. 19cm.

Q264. PENNING, Tony
New climbs in South-east Wales and the Gower. Reading: West Col, 1981. 44p, illus. 16cm.

Q265. SOUTH WALES MOUNTAINEERING CLUB
South-east Wales — a guide to rock climbing. 1973.

Q266. SUMNER, J.
Central Wales: Craig Cowarch and the Arans. Goring, Reading: West Col, 1973. 153p, plates, illus, maps. 17cm.

Q267. SUMNER, J.
Dolgellau area: Cader Idris and the Rhinog Range. Goring, Reading: West Col, 1975. 139p, illus, map. 17cm.

Q268. SUMNER, J.
Aran–Cader Idris climber's guide supplement 1980. Goring, Reading: West Col, 1980. 64p, illus.

Q269. TALBOT, J. O.
Gower peninsula: Caswell Bay to Worms Head, Burry Holms to Tor Gro. Goring, Reading: West Col, 1970. 160p, plates, illus, maps. 17cm.

SCOTLAND

Q301. ALEXANDER, Sir Henry
The Cairngorms. Edinburgh: S.M.C., 1928. viii, 218p, plates (some fold), illus, map, bibl. 23cm. R.P., 1931.
—2nd ed. 1938. x, 236p. Appendix by G. R. Symmers on new climbs on Lochnagar, etc.
—3rd ed. 1950. Revised by W. A. Ewen.
—4th ed. 1968. Revised by Adam Watson and others.
—5th ed. 1975. Revised by Adam Watson.

Q302. ANDREW, K. M. & THRIPPLETON, A. A.
The southern uplands. Edinburgh: S.M.T., 1972. 231p, plates, illus, bibl. 22cm.

Q303. BENNET, Donald
Southern Highlands. Edinburgh: S.M.T., 1972.

Q304. BENNET, D.
The Munros: the Scottish Mountaineering Club hillwalkers' guide. Edinburgh: S.M.T., 1985.

Q305. BENNET, D.
The western Highlands. Edinburgh: S.M.T., 1983. xii, 180p, illus, maps.

Q306. BROWN, Hamish M.
The Island of Rhum: a national nature reserve. Manchester: Cicerone Press, 1972. 64p, illus, maps. 17cm.
Half of the book is devoted to rock climbs.

Q307. BULL, S. P.
Black Cuillin ridge-scrambler's guide. Edinburgh: S.M.T., 1980. 112p, illus.

Q308. [CAITHNESS MOUNTAINEERING AND SKI CLUB]
Rockclimbing guide to West Dunnet Cliffs. [The Club], [1970?]. 6 leaves, illus. 33cm.

Q309. CLOUGH, Ian
Guide to winter climbs: Ben Nevis and Glencoe. Manchester: Cicerone Press, 1969. 50p, illus. 19cm.
—2nd ptg with 2 extra pages. 1969.
—Rev. ed. 1971. By ...& Hamish McInnes, entitled *Ben Nevis and Glencoe: guide to winter climbs.* 65p.
—Another ed. 1978.

Q310. CRAVEN, W. H. & S. A.
Guide to the Island of Rhum. Horbury: Junior M.C. of Yorkshire, [1946]. 16p, illus. 18cm.

Q311. CROCKETT, Ken V.
The western outcrops [Glasgow area]. Nevisport, 1975.

Q312. CROCKETT, K. V.
Glencoe and Glen Etive–rock and ice climbs. Edinburgh: S.M.T., 1980. 264p, illus, maps.

Q313. CULLEN, J. M.
Guide to rock climbs at the Whangie. By ...with C. Vigano & I. McBain. The Authors, 1951. 8p, illus. 21cm. Preceded by provisional edition, November 1950.

Q314. CUNNINGHAM, J.
Cairngorms, Lochnagar and Creag Meaghaidh: guide to winter climbs. Manchester/Milnthorpe: Cicerone Press, 1973. 59p, illus, maps.
—Another ed. 1976.
—Another ed. 1978.
—Rev. ed. with additional material by Allen Fyffe. 1981. 112p.

Q315. CUTHBERTSON, David
Creag Dubh and Craig-a-Barns. Edinburgh: S.M.T., 1983. 142p, illus.

Q316. CUTHBERTSON, D.
Rock climbs in Glen Nevis.

Q317. DUNCAN, David
Rock climbing guide to the north-east coastline of Scotland. [Aberdeen]: Etchachan Club, 1969. 68p, illus. 20cm.

Q318. DUTTON, G. J.
Shorter guide to Arthur's Seat. By ...[and others]. Edinburgh University M.C., 1947. 12 leaves. 26cm.

Q319. [ETCHACHAN CLUB]
Rock climbing guide to the cliffs of the north-east coast of Scotland. Aberdeen: The Club, 1960. 112p, illus (2 fold), map. 21cm.

Q320. FLEMING, M.
Climber's guide to Creag Dubh and the eastern outcrops. By ...[and others]. Fort William?: Graham Tiso, 1967. xvi, 117p, illus. 16cm.

Q321. FRERE, Richard
Rock climbs: guide to the crags in the neighbourhood of Inverness. Inverness:

Northern Chronicle, 1938. 70p, illus. 19cm. Reprinted at original column width from articles in the newspaper.

Q322. FYFFE, Allen F.
Cairngorms area. Vol. 5. South-east Cairngorms, Creag an Dubh-Loch, Glen Clova. Edinburgh: S.M.T., 1971. 113p, illus, map. 17cm.

Q323. FYFFE, A. & NISBET, Andrew (Editors)
Climbers' guide to the Cairngorms. Edinburgh: S.M.T., 1985. 364p.

Q324. GRINDLEY, Ed
Ben Nevis and Glencoe: winter climbs. Milnthorpe: Cicerone Press, 1981. 112p, illus. Update of guidebook by Ian Clough, revised by H. MacInnes.

Q325. GRINDLEY, E. (Editor)
Rock climbs: Glen Nevis and the Lochaber outcrops. Milnthorpe: Cicerone Press, 1985. 120p.

Q326. HIGHRANGE SPORTS (Editor)
Glasgow outcrops. Highrange sports, 1976.

Q327. HINDE, J.
Climbs on Mica Ridge, Loch Duntelchaig. R.A.F. Mountaineering Association, 1965. 3p, illus. 23cm.

Q328. HODGE, Edmund W.
The northern Highlands.
—3rd ed. Edinburgh: S.M.C., 1953. 162p, plates (1 fold), illus, maps. 23cm.

Q329. HODGKISS, Peter
The central Highlands. Edinburgh: S.M.T., 1984. xiv, 210p, illus, map. Completely revised edition.

Q330. HOUSTON, J. R.
Arrochar. Edinburgh: S.M.T., 1970. 103p, illus. 18cm. Cover title: *Climbers' guide to Arrochar.*

Q331. HUMBLE, Ben H. & NIMLIN, J. B.
Rock climbs at Arrochar. Edinburgh: S.M.C., 1954. 64p, illus. 16cm.

Q332. JOHNSTONE, G. Scott
Western Highlands. Edinburgh: S.M.T., 1973.

Q333. JOHNSTONE, J. M.
Rock climbs in Arran. Edinburgh: S.M.C., 1958. 84p, illus, map. 16cm.
—New ed. with appendix of new climbs. S.M.T., 1963. 95p.

Q334. LING, W. N.
The northern Highlands. Edinburgh: S.M.C., 1932. 87p, plates (some fold., some col), illus, maps. 22cm.
—2nd rev. ed. by W. N. Ling & J. R. Corbett, 1936.

Q335. LOVAT, L. S.
Climbers' guide to Glencoe and Ardgour. Vol. 1. Buchaille Etive Mor.
—2nd ed. Edinburgh: S.M.C., 1959. xvii, 99p, illus, map. 16cm.

Q336. LOVAT, L. S.
Climbers' guide to Glencoe and Ardgour. Vol. 2: Glencoe, Beinn Trilleachan and Garbh Bheinn. Edinburgh: S.M.T., 1965. xxii, 160p, illus. 16cm. With *Addendum: new climbs in Glencoe* by J. R. Marshall.

Q337. LOW, T.
Rock climbs on Dumyat, Ben Ledi, Lochan An Eirianach. Ochils Mountaineering Club, [c.1961]. 20 leaves, fold. plate, illus. 17cm.

Q338. MACINNES, Hamish
Scottish climbs: a mountaineer's pictorial guide to climbing in Scotland. Ldn: Constable, 1971. 2v., illus, maps, bibl. 18cm.
—3rd ed. 1981.

Q339. MACINNES, H.
Scottish winter climbs. Ldn: Constable, 1982. 480p, illus.

Q340. MCKEITH, A.
Coire Ardair, Creag Meaghaidh: winter. The author, [1966?]. ii, 20p, illus. 20cm.

Q341. MACKENZIE, J. R.
Rock and ice climbs in Skye. Edinburgh: S.M.T., 1982. 206p, illus, maps.

Q342. MACKENZIE, W. M. (Editor)
Climbing guide to the Cuillin of Skye. Edinburgh: S.M.C., 1958. 160p, illus, map. 17cm.

Q343. MACPHEE, C. Graham (Editor)
Ben Nevis.
—Rev. ed. 1936. viii, 101p, plates (some fold), illus. 22cm.

C344. MACPHEE, C. G.
Climbers' guide to Ben Nevis. Edinburgh: S.M.C., 1954. xii, 156p, illus, maps. 16cm.

Q345. MACROBERT, Harry (Editor)
Ben Nevis. Edinburgh: S.M.C., 1920. 42p, plates (some fold), illus, map. 23cm.

Q346. MACROBERT, H. (Editor)
The central Highlands. Edinburgh: S.M.C., 1934. 158p, plates (2 fold. col), illus, maps. 22cm.
—2nd ed. 1952.

Q347. MARCH, William
Cairngorms. Vol. 1. Loch Avon horseshoe . . .Edinburgh: S.M.T., 1973.

Q348. MARSHALL, J. R.
Ben Nevis. Edinburgh: S.M.T., 1969. 224p, illus. 17cm.
—Rev. ed. with supplement 1979. 256p.

Q349. MARSHALL, William
Sea cliff climbs in the Aberdeen area. Aberdeen: Etchachan Club, [1977?].

Q350. MUNRO, Sir Hugh
Munro's tables of the 3000-feet mountains of Scotland, and other tables of lesser heights. Originally published with the S.M.C. general guidebook.
—New ed. Edinburgh: S.M.C., [1953]. 80p. 23cm.
—Rev. ed. by J. C. Donaldson & W. L. Coats. S.M.T., 1969. 96p.
—Metric ed. edited and revised by J. C. Donaldson, 1974.
—Rev. ed. by J. C. Donaldson & H. M. Brown. S.M.T., 1981. x, 104p.
—Rev. ed. by J. C. Donaldson. 1984.

Q351. MURRAY, William H.
Rock climbs: Glencoe and Ardgour. Edinburgh: S.M.C., 1949. 164p, illus, maps. 17cm.

Q352. NAISMITH, W. W. (Editor)
The islands of Scotland (excluding Skye). Edinburgh: S.M.C., 1934. 135p, plates (some fold, some col), illus, maps, bibl. 23cm.

Q353. NIMLIN, J. B.
Rock climbs on the Cobbler: a symposium. By . . ., B. H. Humble & G. C. Williams. Edinburgh: S.M.C., [1940]. 16p, illus. 22cm. Offprint from *S.M.C. Journal.*

Q354. O'HARA, M. J.
Carn More: interim guide to the district north of Loch Maree. Cambridge University M.C., [1958]. 40p, illus. 22cm. Offprint from *C.U.M.C. Journal.*

Q355. PARK, A. R. M. & TRANTER, Philip N. L.
Interim guide to Easter Ross. Corriemulzie Mountaineering Club, 1966. i, 43p, illus, map. 21cm. cover title: *Rock and ice guide to Easter Ross.*
—*Foinavan supplement to the C.M.C.* . . .28p, illus, map. 19cm.

Q356. PARKER, J. A.
The western Highlands. Edinburgh: S.M.C., 1931. vi, 133p, plates (1 fold), illus, bibl. 22cm.
—3rd rev. ed. 1947.
—4th rev. ed. by G. Scott Johnstone. 1964.

Q357. PARKER, J. Wilson
Scrambles in Skye. Milnthorpe: Cicerone Press, 1983. 144p, illus, maps. (Plus separate 4-colour map)

Q358. PARKER, J. W.
The Munros: a list and general map. The Author, 1981.

Q359. ROWE, I. G.
Northern Highlands area. Vol. 1. Letterewe and Easter Ross. Edinburgh: S.M.T., 1969. 192p, illus, maps. 17cm.

Q360. SCHWARTZ, Klaus & Blyth, D. S.
Rock climbs in Glen Nevis: the Polldubh crags. Lochaber Mountain Rescue Association, 1970. iv, 138p, illus (1 fold). 17cm.

Q361. SCHWARTZ, K.
Rock climbs in Glen Nevis–Polldubh and other crags. Nevis-print, 1979?

Q362. SIMPSON, J. W.
Cuillin of Skye.
—3rd ed. Edinburgh: S.M.T., 1969. 2v., illus, maps. 17cm.

Q363. SKIDMORE, W.
Rock climbs at Creag Liath (Loch Eck). The Author, [1965]. 6 leaves, fold. plate. 19cm. Photocopied MS.

Q364. SKIDMORE, W.
Rock climbing guide to Largs: the Quadrocks. The Author, [1966]. 6p, illus. 21cm. Photocopied MS.

Q365. SLESSER, Malcolm
The Island of Skye. Edinburgh: S.M.T., 1970. 176p, 52 plates, illus, maps, bibl. 22cm.
—2nd ed. 1975. 192p.

Q366. SMITH, Malcolm
Climbers' guide to the Cairngorms area. Edinburgh: S.M.C., 1961-62. 2v., illus, maps. 16cm.

Q367. STEAD, C. & MARSHALL, J. R.
Rock and ice climbs in Lochaber and Badenoch. Edinburgh: S.M.T., 1981.

Q368. STEEPLE, E. W.
Island of Skye. Edited by . . ., G. Barlow & H. MacRobert. Edinburgh: S.M.C., 1923. 126p, plates (some fold), illus, map (in pkt). 23cm.
—2nd rev. ed. 1948.
—3rd ed. 1954.

Q369. STEVEN, Campbell R.
Central Highlands. Edinburgh: S.M.T., 1968. 191p, illus, maps. 22cm.

Q370. STRANG, Tom
The northern Highlands. Edinburgh: S.M.T., 1970. 222p, plates, illus, maps, bibl. 22cm.
—2nd ed. 1975.

Q371. STRANGE, G. S.
Cairngorms. Vol. 2, Ben Macdhui . . .Edinburgh: S.M.T., 1973.

Q372. STRANGE, G. S. & DINWOODIE, D. S.
Climbers' guide to the Cairngorms area. Vol IV/V/Lochnagar, Creag an Dubh Loch [and outlying cliffs]. Edinburgh: S.M.T., 1978. 171p, illus.

Q373. TENNENT, Norman
The islands of Scotland. Edinburgh: S.M.T., 1971. 172p, plates (1 fold), illus. 22cm.

Q374. TURNBULL, D. G. & R. W. L.
Northern Highlands area. Vol. 2: Torridon . . .Edinburgh: S.M.T., 1973.

Q375. WALLACE, W. M. M.
Arran. Edinburgh: S.M.T., 1970. 160p, illus, map. 18cm.
—Rev. ed. 1979 with supplement by W. Skidmore. 184p.

Q376. WILSON, J. D. B. (Editor)
The southern Highlands: including an appendix on the rock climbs in the Arrochar district by B. H. Humble & J. B. Nimlin. Edinburgh: S.M.C., 1949. xi, 204p, plates, illus, map. 23cm.

Q377. YOUNG, James Reid (Editor)
Scottish Mountaineering Club guide. Vol. 1 Section A [general volume]. Edinburgh: S.M.C., 1921. 144p, plates, illus. 23cm.
—New ed. revised to 1933 entitled: *General guide-book.* Includes Munro's tables.

Q378. WILLIAMS, Noel
Scrambles in Lochaber. Milnthorpe: Cicerone Press, 1985. 144p.

N.B.: Three other pamphlets listed in Bridge's bibliography are: Traprain Law; Craig y Barns; Ben A'an. No details.

IRELAND

Q401. BRIMS, C.
Cliff climbs. The Author, 1966

Q402. COLEMAN, J. C.
Climbing in Ireland. [N.p.]: Irish Tourist Bureau, n.d. 14p, illus, map. 23cm.

Q403. COLEMAN, J. C.
The mountains of Killarney. Dundalk: Dundalgan Press, 1948. iv, 60p, illus, maps. 18cm.
—Another ed. Dublin, 1975.

Q404. CURRAN, Mick
Antrim coast rockclimbs: interim guide. Edited by . . .; additional information by Calvin Torrans. Dublin: F.M.C.I., 1975. 32p, maps. 16cm.

Q405. FEDERATION OF MOUNTAINEERING CLUBS OF IRELAND
New climbs. Dublin: F.M.C.I., 1973. [Published annually]. 15-22cm.
—1976. 34p.
—1977. 50p.
—1978. 40p.
—1981. By Dawson Stelfox.
—1982. By Tom Ryan. 96p.

Q406. FORSYTHE, John & MERRICK, Robin
Guide to Mourne rock climbs. The Authors, [1968]. 41 leaves. 33cm.

Q407. FORSYTHE, J. (Editor)
Mourne rock-climbs. Dublin: F.M.C.I., 1973. 88p, illus, map. 16cm.

Q408. FORSYTHE, J.
Rock climbs in Donegal. New University of Ulster Mountaineering Club, [1973].

Q409. GRIBBON, P. W. F.
Mourne rock climbs. Northern Ireland Tourist Board/Belfast Section, Irish Mountaineering Club, [1957]. 48p, illus. 16cm.
—Appendix by Ivan Firth. [1962?]. i, 27p. 17cm.
—Supplement. [1964?]. 12p. 21cm.

Q410. HIGGS, Kenneth (Editor)
Wicklow rock climbs. Dublin: F.M.C.I., 1982. 128p, illus, map.

Q411. IRISH MOUNTAINEERING CLUB
Rock-climber's guide to Glendalough. Dublin: I.M.C., 1957. 38p, illus. 13cm.

Q412. IRISH MOUNTAINEERING CLUB
Rock-climber's guide to Donegal. Dublin: I.M.C., 1962. 56p, illus, map. 14cm.

Q413. [IRISH MOUNTAINEERING CLUB?]
Ben Corr rock climbs [Glen Inagh]. I.M.C. (?), [1966]. 4 leaves. 33cm.

Q414. [JOHNSON, Harold C.]
Some climbs in the Scalp. By H.C.J. The Author, 1958. 3 leaves. 21cm.

Q415. JOHNSON, R. R.
Mourne rock climbs. The Author, 1949.

Q416. KENNY, Peter
Guide to the rock climbs of Dalkey Quarry. Dublin: I.M.C., 1959. 64p. Typescript, cyclostyled, card covers.
—2nd ed. Edited by Barry O'Flynn. Dublin: I.M.C., 1964. 48p, illus, map. 13cm.

Q417. LEONARD, Jim
Malinbeg and other sea cliffs. Dublin: F.M.C.I., 1979. 45p, illus, maps. South-west Donegal.

Q418. LYNAM, Joss P. O'F.
Ben Corr rock-climbs. [Dublin]: I.M.C., 1951. 29p, illus, map. 13cm.

Q419. LYNAM, J.
Bray Head. [Dublin]: I.M.C., 1951. 23p, illus. 13cm.

Q420. LYNAM, J. & CONVERY, Liam
Bray Head and minor crags around Dublin. Dublin: F. M. C. I., 1978. 81p, illus, maps.

Q421. LYNAM, J. & PERROTT, W. R.
Guide to Dalkey Quarry. [Dublin]: I.M.C., 1949. 14 leaves, diag. 23cm.

Q422. LYNAM, J.
Interim rock-climbing guide to Coum Gowlaun and other sandstone climbs in Galway and South Mayo. [N.p.]: [I.M.C.?], 1969. ii, 12p, illus. 15cm.

Q423. LYNAM, J.
Twelve Bens. [Dublin]: I.M.C., 1953. 29p, illus, bibl. 13cm.
—New ed. [Dublin]: F.M.C.I., 1971. 29p.

Q424. O'LEARY, Paddy
Interim climbing guides: Playground, Co. Cavan and Antrim Coast. Spillikin Club, 1967. 6 leaves, illus. 21cm.

Q425. PERROTT, W. R.
Luggala. [Dublin]: I.M.C., 1950. i, 24p, diag. 26cm.
—New ed. entitled *Climber's guide to Luggala.* [Cover title, *Lugala rock climbs.*] I.M.C., 1967. 32p, fold. plate. 17cm.

Q426. RICHMOND, Pat (Editor)
Wicklow rock-climbs (Glendalough and Luggala). Dublin: F.M.C.I., 1973. 86p, illus. 16cm.

Q427. ROTHERY, Sean & LYNAM, Joss
Selected climbs on Ben Corr. [Dublin]: I.M.C., 1967. 18p, fold. plate. 17cm.

Q428. RYAN, Tom
Burren Seacliff [North-west Clare]. Dublin: F.M.C.I., 1978. 32p, illus, maps.

Q429. TORRANS, Calvin & SHERIDAN, Clare
Antrim coast. Dublin: F.M.C.I., 1981. 92p, illus.

Q430. TORRANS, Calvin & STELFOX, Dawson
Rock climbing in Ireland. Ldn: Constable, 1984. 260p, illus, maps. 18cm.

Q431. WALL, Claud W.
Mountaineering in Ireland for the hill-walker and the rock-climber. With and introduction by Dr. Robert Lloyd Praeger. Dublin: Irish Tourist Association, 1939. 88p, illus, map. 18cm. R.P., 1944.
—New ed. revised by Joss Lynam. Dublin: F.M.C.I., 1976. 111p, map, bibl.

Q432. [WATHEN, R. J.]
Interim guide to Donegal. Part I. The Poisoned Glen. by R.J.W. [Dublin]: I.M.C., [1958?]. 7 leaves. 33cm.

Q433. YOUNG, Stephen
Dalkey rock-climbs. Dublin: F.M.C.I., 1974.
—Another ed. 1979. 111p, illus, maps.

EUROPEAN ALPS

Q501. ALPINE CLIMBING GROUP
Selected climbs in the range of Mont Blanc. Ldn: A.C.G., [1954]. 1v (loose-leaf), illus. 23cm.

Q502. ALPINE CLIMBING GROUP
Selected climbs in the range of Mont Blanc; trans. and adapted by the . . .from the Guide Vallot and other sources; edited by E. A. Wrangham. Ldn: Allen & Unwin, 1957. 224p, illus, map. 17cm.

Q503. ANDERSON, Michael
Brenta Dolomites: scramblers' guide. Goring, Reading: West Col, 1982. 56p, maps.

Q504. ANDERSON, M.
Karwendel. Goring, Reading: West Col, 1971. 56p, illus, map. 19cm. (Pilot alpine guides)

Q505. ANDERSON, M.
Mittel Switzerland. Goring, Reading: West Col, 1974. 51p, illus, maps. 18cm. (Pilot alpine guides)

Q506. BRAILSFORD, John
Dolomites East: . . .selected climbs; adapted . . .and compiled with additional information by . . .Ldn: Alpine Club, 1970. 247p, plates, illus, maps, bibl. 17cm.

Q507. BRAILSFORD, J.
Dolomites West: . . .selected climbs; adapted . . .and compiled with additional information by . . .Ldn: Alpine Club, 1970. 176p, illus, maps, bibl. 17cm.

Q508. COLLOMB, Robin Gabriel
Bernese Alps central. Compiled and edited by . . .Ldn: Alpine Club, 1978. 199p, illus. 17cm.

Q509. COLLOMB, R. G.
Bernese Alps east. Compiled and edited by . . .Ldn: Alpine Club, 1978. 174p, illus. 17cm.

Q510. COLLOMB, R. G.
Bernese Alps west: . . .a selection of popular walking and climbing routes. Compiled by . . .Goring, Reading: West Col, 1970. 73p, plates, illus, map. 17cm.

Q511. COLLOMB, R. G.
Selected climbs in the Bernese Alps. Compiled . . .and adapted with additional material by . . .Ldn: Alpine Club, 1968. 223p, illus, bibl. 16cm.

Q511a. COLLOMB, R. G.
Bernina Alps: selection of climbs.
—2nd ed. Goring, Reading: West Col, 1976. 127p, illus, map. 17cm.

Q512. COLLOMB, R. G.
Bregaglia east: . . .a selection of climbs. Compiled and edited by . . .Goring, Reading: West Col, 1971. 120p, illus, map, bibl. 17cm.

Q513. COLLOMB, R. G. & CREW, Peter
Bregaglia west: a selection of popular and recommended climbs. Compiled by . . .Goring, Reading: West Col, 1967. 86p, illus, maps, bibl. 17cm.
—2nd ed. by R. G. Collomb, 1974.

Q514. COLLOMB, R. G.
Chamonix–Mont Blanc. Ldn: Constable, 1969.

Q515. COLLOMB, R. G.
Graians east: Gran Paradiso area: a selection of popular and recommended climbs. Compiled by . . .Goring, Reading: West Col, 1969. 84p, plates, illus, map, bibl. 17cm.

Q516. COLLOMB, R. G.
Graians west: Tarentaise and Maurienne: a selection of popular and recommended climbs. Compiled by . . .Goring, Reading: West Col, 1967. 128p, illus, map, bibl. 16cm.

Q517. COLLOMB, R. G.
Julian Alps: mountain walking and outline climbing guide. Compiled by . . .; assisted by M. Anderson. Goring, Reading: West Col, 1978. 136p, illus, maps, bibl. 18cm.

Q518. COLLOMB, R. G.
Maritime Alps: . . .a selection of popular and recommended climbs. Compiled by . . .; based on the works of Vincent Paschetta. Goring, Reading: West Col, 1968. 100p, illus, map, bibl. 17cm.

Q519. COLLOMB, R. G. & O'CONNOR, W. H.
Mont Blanc range. Vol. 1. Trélatête, Mont Blanc, Maudit, Tacul, Brenva. Ldn: Alpine Club, 1976. 221p, illus, bibl. 16cm.

Q520. COLLOMB, R. G.
Mountains of the Alps: tables of summits over 3500 metres with geographical and historical notes and tables of selected lesser heights. Vol. 1. Western Alps. Goring, Reading: West Col, 1971. 96p, illus. 23cm.

Q521. COLLOMB, R. G.
Pennine Alps central. Compiled and edited by . . .Ldn: Alpine Club, 1975. 373p, illus, map, bibl. 17cm.

Q522. COLLOMB, R. G.
Pennine Alps east. Compiled and edited by . . .Ldn: Alpine Club, 1975. 169p, illus, bibl. 17cm.

Q523. COLLOMB, R. G.
Pennine Alps west. Compiled and edited by . . .Ldn: Alpine Club, 1979. 232p, illus. 17cm.

Q524. COLLOMB, R. G. & CREW, P.
Selected climbs in the Mont Blanc range. Vol. 1. (Col de la Seigne to Col du Géant). Trans. and adapted . . .and compiled with additional material by . . .Ldn: Alpine Club, 1967. 241p, illus, maps, bibl. 16cm.

Q525. COLLOMB, R. G.
*Selected climbs in the Pennine Alps. Vol. 2 (Col du Gé*ant to Petit Col Ferret and Fenêtre d'Arpette). Trans. and adapted . . .and compiled with additional material by . . .Ldn: Alpine Club, 1967. 185p, illus. 16cm.

Q526. COLLOMB, R. G.
Zermatt and district, including Saas Fee. Ldn: Constable, 1969. xiv, 242p, illus, maps, bibl. 21cm.
—2nd ed. Reading: West Col, 1984. 144p, illus, maps.

Q527. CREW, Peter
Selected climbs in the Dolomites. Edited by . . .; diagrams by R. B. Evans. Ldn: Alpine Club, 1863. 214p, illus, maps, bibl. 16cm.

Q528. [DAVIES, Cecil]
Via Ferrata: scrambles in the Dolomites. Trans. from the German by . . .Milnthorpe: Cicerone Press, 1982. 176p, plate, illus, maps.

Q529. GRIFFIN, Lindsay N.
Mont Blanc range. Vol. 2. Chamonix Aiguilles, Rochefort, Jorasses, Leschaux. Compiled by . . .Ldn: Alpine Club, 1978. 219p, illus, bibl. 17cm.

Q530. GRIFFIN, L. N.
Mont Blanc range. Vol. 3. Triolet, Vert/Drus, Argentière, Chardonnet, Trient. Compiled by . . .Ldn: Alpine Club, 1980. 228p, illus. 17cm.

Q531. GYGER, W. J.
Guide to climbs in the Upper Engadine. —3rd ed. Sameden, St. Moritz: Engadin Press, 1925. 101p, illus, maps. 17cm.

Q532. Neill, John
Selected climbs in the Pennine Alps. Edited by . . .Ldn: Alpine Club, 1962. 246p, illus, bibl. 16cm.

Q533. PIOLA, Michel
Topo guide to the rock climbs of the Mont Blanc area. Milan: Melograno, 1986. 160p, illus, maps.

Q534. ROBERTS, Eric
High-level Route Chamonix-Zermatt-Saas: ski mountaineering in the Mont Blanc Range and Pennine Alps. Goring, Reading: West Col, 1973. 136p, plates, illus, maps. 19cm.
—Rev. ed. 1984. 148p, illus, maps.

Q535. ROBERTS, E.
Glockner region. Goring, Reading: West Col, 1976. 135p, plates, illus, map, bibl. 17cm.

Q536. ROBERTS, E.
Stubai Alps: a survey of popular walking and climbing routes. Compiled by . . .Goring, Reading: West Col, 1972. 156p, illus, map, bibl. 17cm.
—Reprinted with supplement. 1981.

Q537. ROBERTS, E.
Zillertal Alps. By . . .and R. Collomb. Reading: West Col, 1980. 94p, plates, illus, map. 18cm.

Q538. TALBOT, Jeremy O.
Central Switzerland: Grimsel, Furka, Susten: a guide for walkers and climbers. Goring, Reading: West Col, 1969. 181p, illus, maps, bibl. 16cm.

Q539. TALBOT, J. O.
Engelhörner and Salbitschijen; including Wellhörner and Scheidegg-Wetterhorn: a selection of popular and recommended climbs. Compiled by . . .Goring, Reading: West Col, 1968. 107p, illus, map, bibl. 17cm.

Q540. TALBOT, J. O.
Kaisergebirge: a selection of climbs. Compiled by . . .Goring, Reading: West Col, 1971. 96p, illus, map, bibl. 17cm.

Q541. THOMPSON, Arthur J.
Ortler Alps: . . .a selection of popular and recommended climbs. Compiled by . . .Goring, Reading: West Col, 1968. 98p, illus, map, bibl. 17cm.

Q542. UNSWORTH, Walter
Oetztal Alps. Reading: West Col, 1969.

Q543. WEST COL PRODUCTIONS
Dents du Midi region: an interim guide. Goring, Reading: West Col Productions, 1967.

Q544. WRANGHAM, E. A. & BRAILSFORD, J.
Selected climbs in the Dauphiné Alps and Vercours. Trans. . . .and adapted . . .by Ldn: Alpine Club, 1967. 176p, illus, map. 16cm.

UNITED STATES OF AMERICA

General

Q601. BRADLEY, Dwight & PFEFFER, Tad
Obscure crags guide to cliffs in Maine, Vermont and New Hampshire. Randolph, NH: The Authors.

Q602. COLE, P. & WILCOX, R.
Shades of blue (New England ice routes). E.M.S., 1976. 73p, illus.

Q603. HALL, Chris
Southern rock: a climber's guide. Charlotte: East Woods Press, 1981. 143p, illus, diag, maps.
Covers five States; selected climbs only.

Q604. HARLIN, John III
Climber's guide to North America. Vol. 1 West Coast rock climbs. Denver: Chockstone Press, 1984. 358p, illus, diag, maps, bibl.
Describes over 500 climbs in 16 major areas.

Q605. HARLIN, J.
Climber's guide to North America. Vol. 2 Rocky Mountain rock climbs. Denver: Chockstone Press, 1986. 400p, illus, 25 maps.
Approximately 500 routes in 19 areas, from Montana through Colorado to Arizona.

Q606. HARLIN, J.
Climber's guide to North America. Vol. 3 East Coast rock climbs. Denver: Chockstone Press, 1986.

Q607. WILCOX, Rick
Ice climber's guide to northern New England. North Conway, NH: International Mountain Equipment, 1982. 225p, illus, diag, 4 maps.

Alaska

Q608. COWALS, Dennis (Editor)
Mount McKinley climber's guide. Anchorage: Alaska Alpine Co., 1976.
Guide-map showing 4 principal routes. 34″ × 22″.

Q609. HOEMAN, J. Vincent
Alaska mountain guide. [c.1971]

Q610. RANDALL, Glenn
Mt. McKinley climber's handbook. Talkeetna: Genet Expeditions, 1984. 152p.
Guide to the usual west buttress route.

Q611. WASHBURN, Bradford
Tourist guide to Mount McKinley: story of 'Denali' — 'The Great One', the record of McKinley climbs. Anchorage: Alaska Northwest, 1971. 79p, plates, illus, maps. R.P., 1976.
—4th rev. ed. 1980. 80p.
Includes list of first 100 ascents.

Arizona

Q612. LOVEJOY, David
Granite Mountain: a pocket guide to rock climbing in Granite Basin, Prescott National Forest, Arizona. Prescott, AS: Published on a grant from The Prescott Institutions, 1973. 120p, illus.

Q613. MEZRA, J.
The Dells. [Mimeograph route guide to rocks near Prescott, Arizona.] 1976. 15p.

Q614. TREIBER, Larry & GRUBBS, Bruce
Central Arizona climbing guide. [Phoenix: Desert Mountain Sports?]

Q615. WAUGH, Jim.
Topo guide to Granite Mountain, Prescott, Arizona. Glendale, AS: Polar Designs, 1982.

California

Q616. [AUTHOR?]
Day climber's guide to Santa Clara Valley. Starr Craig Pub.

Q617. BECK, Erick
Climber's guide to Lake Tahoe and Donner summit. Tahoe: City Department of Parks & Recreation.

Q618. DEXTER, G.
Climber's guide to the Lake Tahoe region. By ...[and others]. Modesto, CA: Mountain Letters, 1976.

Q619. DRAKE, Gene
Guide to Lover's Leap.

Q620. FRESNO BIG WALL SOCIETY
Climber's guide to Tollhouse Rock. Fresno: [Robbins Mountain Shop?]

Q621. GAGNER, Paul G.
Rock climber's guide to Pinnacles National Monument. Fort Collins: Taylor-Powell Ptg, 1983. 146p, illus, maps.

Q622. HELLWEG, Paul & FISHER, Donald B.
Stoney Point guide [Los Angeles area]. Glendale, CA, 1982. 70p.

Q623. HOOD, Ron
Sierras: topographic reference guide to the Sierra Nevada mountain range and portions of the Mt. San Gorgonio and Mt. San Jacinto wilderness areas. Northridge, [1975]. 32p text, 60 full-page maps. 28cm.

Q624. JENKEWITZ-MEYTRAS, Christine
Tahoe rock climbs [Donner Summit, Sugarloaf, Lovers' Leap, Tahoe]. Denver: Chockstone Press, 1986.

Q625. LANTRY, Werner
Climber's guide to Mission Gorge.

Q626. LEADABRAND, Russ
Guidebook to the San Bernadino Mountains of California. Los Angeles: Ward Ritchie Press, 1964.

Q627. LEADABRAND, R.
Guidebook to the San Gabriel Mountains of California. Los Angeles: Ward Ritchie Press, 1964.

Q628. LEADABRAND, R.
Guidebook to the Sunset Ranges of southern California. Los Angeles: Ward Ritchie Press, 1965.

Q629. MESSICK, Tim
Rock climbs of Tahquitz and Suicide Rocks. 1985. 80p, illus.

Q630. MEYERS, George
Yosemite climbs: a rock climbing guide to Yosemite Valley. Denver: Chockstone Press, 1982. 260p, illus, maps.

Q631. MEYERS, G.
Yosemite climbs: topographic drawings of the best rock climbing routes in Yosemite Valley. Modesto, CA: Mountain Letters, [1977]. 114p, 15 plates, illus. 22 × 28cm.

Q632. NICOL, Dave (Editor)
Rock-climbs in Yosemite — topographical diagrams of selected routes. Portinscale, Cumbria: The Author, [1975]. 50p, illus. [4to]. Looseleaf.

Q633. REID, Don & FALKENSTEIN, Chris
Rock climbs of Tuolumne Meadows. Denver: Chockstone Press, 1983. 120p, plates, illus, maps.
—2nd rev. ed. 1986.

Q634. ROBBINS, Royal
Guide to the Hinterlands.

Q635. ROBINSON, John W.
Camping and climbing in Baja. Glendale, CA: La Siesta Press, 1967. 96p, illus, map.
—3rd ed. 1972.

Q636. ROBINSON, J. W.
San Bernardino Mountain trails: 100 wilderness hikes. Berkeley, CA: Wilderness Press, 1972.
—2nd rev. ed. Berkeley, [1975]. 258p. 20cm.

Q637. ROPER, Steve
Climber's guide to the High Sierra. S.F.: Sierra Club, 1976. 380p, illus.

Q638. ROPER, S.
Climber's guide to Pinnacles National Monument. Berkeley, CA: The Ski Hut, 1966. 69p, illus, maps.
—Another ed. 1971.
—Another ed. 1974. By Ralph Webb. 128p, illus.

Q639. ROPER, S.
Climber's guide to Yosemite Valley. S.F.: Sierra Club, 1964. 190p, illus.
—Another ed. 1971. 305p, illus. R.P., 1975.

Q640. [SIERRA CLUB]
Climber's guide to the High Sierra. Preliminary edition (Parts 1-6). S.F.: William Shand Memorial Fund, Sierra Club, 1949.

Q641. STECK, Allen
Guide to Mount Shasta.

Q642. VOGE, Hervey H. & SMATKO, Andrew J.
Mountaineer's guide to the High Sierra. S.F.: Sierra Club, 1972. 356p, illus. 16cm.

Q643. VOGEL, Randy
Joshua Tree rock climbing guide. Denver: Chockstone Press, 1986.

Q644. VOGEL, R.
Orange County hunk guide.
—2nd ed. Laguna Beach: Bonehead Press, 1982. 63p, illus, map.

Q645. VOGEL, R.
Topo guide to Tahquitz and Suicide. Laguna Beach Bonehead Press, 1980. 80p, illus, maps. Ring bound.

Q646. VOGEL, R.
Rock climbs of Tahquitz and Suicide Rocks. Denver: Chockstone Press, 1985.

Q647. WHEELOCK, Walt & CONDON, Tom
Climbing Mount Whitney.
—2nd ed. Glendale, CA: La Siesta Press, 1978. 36p, maps.

Q648. WHEELOCK, W.
Desert peaks guide: Part 1 (southern California).
—Rev. ed. Glendale, CA: La Siesta Press, 1964.
—Another ed. 1971. 40p, illus.

Q649. WHEELOCK, W.
Desert peaks guide: Part 2 (Death Valley country). Glendale, CA: La Siesta Press, 1975. 48p, illus.

Q650. WHEELOCK, W.
Southern California peaks. Glendale, CA: La Siesta Press, 1973. 48p, illus. 22cm. Walking routes up 112 peaks in the San Gabriel, San Bernardino, San Jacinto and neighbouring mountains.

Q651. WHITE, Douglas
Crags and boulders of San Diego County.

Q652. WILTS, Chuck
Climber's guide to Tahquitz and Suicide Rocks. N.Y.: A.A.C., 1968.
—6th ed. 1979. 208p, illus, maps.

Q653. WOLFE, John & DOMINICK,?
Climber's guide to Joshua Tree National Monument. San Jacinto, CA: Arrow Ptg Co., 1976.
—Supplement to 1976 ed. 192p.
—Another ed. 1979.

Colorado

Q654. AMENT, Pat & MCCARTHY, Cleveland
High over Boulder.
—2nd rev. ed. Boulder: Pruett, 1970. 368p, illus, maps.

Q655. AMENT, P. & ERICKSON, J.
5.10. Upgraded supplement to *High over Boulder.*

Q656. AMENT, P.
Eldorado: a climber's route guide. Paddock, 1975. 148p, illus.

Q657. BORNEMANN, Walter R. & LAMPERT, Lyndon J.
Climbing guide to Colorado's Fourteeners. Boulder: Pruett, 1978. 238p, illus, maps. 22cm.

Q658. BORNEMANN, W. R.
Colorado's other mountains: a climbing guide to selected peaks under 14,000 feet. Evergreen: Cordillera, 1984. 160p, illus, 32 maps.

Q659. DORNAN, David
Rock climbing guide to the Boulder, Colorado area. Boulder: Outdoors, 1961.

Q660. ERICKSON, James S.
Rocky heights: a guide to Boulder free climbs 1980. The Author, 1980. 280p, illus.

Q661. FRICKE, Walter W. Jr.
Climber's guide to the Rocky Mountain National Park area. Boulder: Paddock Pub, 1971. 225p, illus.

Q662. GARRATT, Mike & MARTIN, Bob
Colorado's high thirteens: a climbing and hiking guide. Evergreen: Cordillera, 1984. 246p, illus.
Includes route descriptions for 169 peaks, and list of the 741 highest summits in Colorado.

Q663. KIMBALL, Scott
Longs Peak free-climber.

Q664. KIMBALL, S.
Rock climbs of Lumpy Ridge and the Estes Park area. [Longs Peak, Spearhead, Diamond.] Denver: Chockstone Press, 1986.

Q665. KINGERY, Elinor Eppich
Climber's guide to the high Colorado peaks. Denver: Colorado Mountain Club, 1931.

Q666. LAVENDER, Dwight & LONG, Carleton
San Juan Mountaineers' climber's guide to southwestern Colorado. Typescript, 1932. Held in Colorado Mountain Club Library.

Q667. MCCHRISTAL, J.
Rock climber's guide to the Garden of the Gods. Denver: Colorado Mountain Club, 1975. 64p.

Q668. NESBIT, Paul W.
Longs Peak: its story and climbing guide. Colorado Springs: The Author, 1946. 47p, illus, map. 23cm.
—5th rev.ed. enlarged. 1963. 64p, illus. 23cm.

Q669. ORMES, Robert M.
Guide to the Colorado Mountains. Denver: Sage Books, 1952. 239p, plates (some col), illus, maps. 16cm.
—6th rev. ed. Chicago: Swallow Press, 1974.

Q670. RICHARDS, S.
Colorado Fourteens (a condensed guide). Denver: Colorado Mountain Club, 1978. 24p, illus.

Q671. ROSEBROUGH, Robert F.
San Juan Mountains: a climbing and hiking guide. Evergreen: Cordillera, 1986. 274p, illus, maps.

Q672. ROSSITER, R.
Boulder climbs: a pictorial guide. 1985. 175p.
Topo guide to the Boulder area.

Q673. SALAUN, Chip & KIMBALL, S.
Thath-aa-ai-atah: a rock climber's and scrambler's guide to the Lumpy Ridge area. The Authors, 1980. 192p, illus, maps.

Connecticut

Q674. NICHOLS, Ken
Traprock: Connecticut rock climbs. N.Y.: A.A.C., 1982. 479p, illus, sketches, maps.

Q675. YALE MOUNTAINEERING CLUB
Climber's guide to Ragged Mountain.
—Supplement. By Ken Nichols.

Illinois

Q676. KOLOCOTRONIS, J. (?)
Guide to the Mississippi Palisades. [South Ohioville?]
—New ed. 1965 with addendum. 24p.

Q677. NICODEMUS, M. & A.
Climber's guide to Kankaku River State Park. 1979. 23p.

Indiana

Q678. ZVENGROWSKI, Pete
Portland Arch Guide. [Urbana: Simian Outing Society, Univ. Illinois?]

Iowa

Q679. FURGUSON, J.
Climber's guide to Palisades Kepler State Park. 1978. 127p, illus.

Kentucky

Q680. IRONS, G.
Climber's guide to Pilot Rock. 1979. 32p.

Maine

(See also under *General.*)

Q681. [AUTHOR?]
Mountain climbing in Maine. Augusta, ME, 1959. 56p, illus. 19cm.

Q682. ELLISON, Leslie
Clifton rock climbs. Orno, ME: Maine Outing Club.

Massachusetts

Q683. [BERKSHIRE SCHOOL]
Guide to Black Rock. Sheffield, MA: Outing Club, Berkshire School.

Q684. CROWTHER, William R. & THOMPSON, Anthony W.
Climber's guide to the Quincy Quarries. Cambridge, MA: M.I.T. Outing Club, 1968.

Q685. HENDRICKS, Steve & STRIEBERT, Sam
Climbing in Eastern Massachusetts. Milgamex Co., 1975. 76p, illus.

Q686. REPPY, — & STRIEBERT, S.
Guide to Crow Hill.

Q687. WILLIAMS OUTING CLUB
The Mountains of Eph: a guidebook of the Williams Outing Club. Williamstown, MA: W.O.C. Trail Commission 1927. 55p, plates (some fold.), illus, maps. 18cm.

Michigan

Q688. [AUTHOR?]
Climber's guide to Taylor's Falls. Minneapolis, MI: Midwest Mountaineering.

Q689. BRIGHT, K. Bruce & VAN LAAR, J.
Climber's guide to Grand Ledge. Spartan Village, East Lansing, MI: The Authors, 1969.

Montana

Q690. [AUTHOR?]
Montana rock climbs in the Mission Range.

Q691. EDWARDS, J. Gordon
Climber's guide to Glacier National Park. S.F.: Sierra Club, 1960. 142p, 48 plates, illus, maps.
—Another ed. Mountain Press, 1976. 192p, illus.

Nevada

Q692. DAFOE, Carmie R. Jr.
Guide to Nevada's Rocky and East Humboldt Mountains. 1971.

Q693. URIOSTE, Joanne
Red rocks of southern Nevada. N.Y.: A.A.C., 1984. 252p, illus, diag, maps.

New Hampshire

(See also under *General.*)

Q694. BALDWIN, Henry I. (Editor)
Monadnock Guide. Concord, NH: Society for Protection of New Hampshire Forests, 1970. 128p, illus, diag, 3 maps.

Q695. COTE, Joseph & Karen
Climber's guide to Cathedral and White Horse Ledges. The Authors, 1968.

Q696. COTE, J.
Climber's guide to Mount Washington Valley. Topsfield, MA: Fox Run Press, 1972. 95p, illus.
—Supplement by Henry Barber. 1973. 17p.

Q697. PETERSON, Howard
Cannon: a climber's guide. South Lancaster, MA: Three Owls Productions, 1975.

Q698. PORTER, John
Guide for climbers: Cannon. By . . . [and others]. South Lancaster, MA: Three Owls Productions.
—2nd ed. c.1973. Entitled *Climber's guide to Cannon Cliff.* Three Owls. 62p, illus.

Q699. ROSS, Paul & ELLMS, Chris
Cannon, Cathedral, Humphrey's & White Horse, a rock climber's guide. North Conway, NH: International Mountain Climbing School, 1978. 157p, illus, diag, sketch maps.
—Rev. ed. 1982.

Q700. WEBSTER, Edward
Rock climbs in the White Mountains of New Hampshire. Conway, NH: Mountain Imagery, 1982. 294p, illus, diag, bibl. 15cm.

New Mexico

Q701. HILL, Mike
Hikers and climbers guide to the Sandias. Albuquerque: Univ. New Mexico Press, 1983. xii, 234p, illus, diag, charts, map, bibl.

Q702. KYRLACH, Bob
Guide to the Sandia Mountains.
—New ed. 1970 by Lawrence G. Kline?

Q703. UNGNADE, Herbert E.
Guide to the New Mexico mountains. Albuquerque: Univ. New Mexico Press, 1965.

New York

Q704. DU MAIS, Richard
Shawangunk rock climbing. Denver: Chockstone Press, 1985. 120p, illus (mostly col).

Q705. GRAN, Arthur
Climber's guide to the Shawangunks. N.Y: A.A.C. with Appalachian Mountain Club, 1964. ix, 155p, illus, maps. 17cm.

Q706. HEALY, Trudy
Climber's Guide to the Adirondacks: rock and slide climbs. 1967.
—2nd rev. ed. Adirondack Mountain Club, 1972. 108p.

Q707. MELLOR, Don
Climbing in the Adirondacks. Lake Placid: Lake Placid Climbing School/Sundog Ski & Sports, 1983. 178p, illus.

Q708. SWAIN, Todd
Gunks guide. Rock climbs in the Shawangunks of New York. New Paltz: Alpine Diversions, 1986. 320p, illus.

Q709. [STORM KING SCHOOL?]
Student's guide to Storm King Mountain. [Storm King School?]

Q710. WILLIAMS, Richard C.
Shawangunk rock climbs. N.Y.: A.A.C., 1972. 136p, illus, maps.
—Another ed. 1980. 463p, illus, appendices.

North & South Carolina

Q711. HOLDEN, Alex
Carolina crags.

Q712. WILLIAMS, Art
Climber's guide to the Carolinas. Greenville, SC.

Ohio

Q713. DE GUISEPPI, J.
Climber's guide to Clifton Gorge. RG Press, 1979. 76p, illus.

Oregon

Q714. DODGE, Nicholas A.
Climbing guide to Oregon. Portland: Mazamas & Beattie & Co., 1968. viii, 154p, illus, maps.
—2nd ed. Beaverton: Touchstone, 1975. 160p, illus, maps.

Q715. THOMAS, Jeff
Oregon rock: a climber's guide [Beacon, Smith Rock, Stein's Pillar]. Seattle, [1983]. 136p, illus.

Pennsylvania

Q716. JIRAK, Ivan L.
Pittsburgh area. Pittsburgh, PA, 1971. 61p, illus.

South Dakota

Q717. KAMPS, Bob
Climber's guide to the Needles of the Black Hills of South Dakota. N.Y.: A.A.C., 1971.

Q718. MCGEE, Dingus
Poorperson's guidebook: selected free climbs of the Black Hills Needles. Devils Tower: Poorperson's, 1981.

Q719. MARRIOTT, Hollis & HORNING, Dennis
Black Hills Needles: selected free climbs. —Rev. ed. Custer: Poorperson's, 1984. 20p, illus, maps.

Q720. PIANA, Paul
Touch the sky: the Needles in the Black Hills of South Dakota. N.Y.: A.A.C., 1983. 304p, illus, separate maps.

Tennessee

Q721. ROBINSON, Robert
Southern sandstone: a climber's guide to Chattanooga, Tennessee. Nashville: Concord, 1985. 144p, illus, maps.

Utah

Q722. ELLISON, Les & SMOOT, Brian
Wasatch rock climbs. N.Y.: A.A.C., 1984. 302p, illus, maps.

Q723. KELSEY, Michael R.
Utah mountaineering guide (and the best canyon hikes). Springville: The Author, 1983. 160p, illus, maps.

Q724. SMITH, Dave
Wasatch granite (a rock climbing guide to some great Utah rock: the smooth and polished granite of Little Cottonwood Canyon and other areas). 96p.

Q725. [WASATCH PUBLISHERS?]
Climber's guide to the Salt Lake granite. Salt Lake City: Starlight & Storm/Wasatch Publishers?

Q726. [ZION NATIONAL PARK]
Climbing reports in Zion National Park files. (1930 onwards)

Vermont

(See under General.)

Virginia

Q727. [AUTHOR?]
Climber's guide to Great Falls Park. 1975. 31p.

Q728. GREGORY, J.
Climber's guide to Carderock. 1980. 56p.

Washington

Q729. BECKEY, Fred
Climber's guide to the Cascade and Olympic Mountains of Washington. N.Y.: A.A.C., 1949. 271p.
—Supplement, 1953.
—Rev. ed. 1961. by G. R. Sainsbury.

Q730. BECKEY, F.
Cascade alpine guides, climbing and high routes: Columbia River to Stevens Pass. Seattle: Mountaineers, 1973. 354p, illus, maps. 18 × 22cm.

Q731. BECKEY, F.
Cascade alpine guides, climbing and high routes: Stevens Pass to Rainy Pass. Seattle: Mountaineers, 1977. 354p, illus, maps. 18 × 22cm.

Q732. BECKEY, F.
Cascade alpine guides, climbing and high routes: Rainy Pass to Fraser River. Seattle: Mountaineers, 1981. 328p, illus, maps. 18 × 22cm.

Q733. BECKEY, F.
Darrington and Index: rockclimbing guide. Seattle: Mountaineers, 1976. 63p, illus. 22cm.

Q734. BECKEY, F. & BJORNSTAD, Eric
Guide to Leavenworth rock climbing areas. Seattle: Mountaineers, 1985. 86p, illus, maps. 21cm.

Q735. BROOKS, D.
Climber's guide to Washington rock (Index, Darrington, Leavenworth,

Peshastin, Castle & Midnight Rocks, Tumwater Canyon and Snow Creak Wall). Seattle, 1982. 176p.

Q736. CARLSBAD, R. & BROOKS, D.
Rock climbing, Leavenworth & Index. Signpost Publications, 1976. 91p, illus.

Q737. CROWDER, D. F. & TABOR, R. W.
Routes and rocks in the Mt. Challenger Quadrangle. Seattle: Mountaineers, 1968. 47p, plates (1 fold. col), illus, maps (1 in pkt), bibl. 19cm.

Q738. KLOKE, Dallas M.
Boulders and cliffs: a climber's guide to lowland rock in Skagit and Whatcome Counties. Signpost publications, ?. 80p, illus, maps.

Q739. MOLENAAR, Dee
Climbing history and routes of Mount Rainier.

Q740. OLYMPIC MOUNTAIN RESCUE
Climber's guide to the Olympic Mountains. Seattle: Mountaineers, 1972. 225p, illus, 4 maps.
—Another ed. 1979.

Q741. SMUTEK, Ray
Mount St. Helens Washington: a climber's guide. Renton: Off Belay, 1969. Broadsheet, illus, maps. 23cm.

Q742. WASHINGTON STATE UNIVERSITY ALPINE CLUB
Granite Point guide.

West Virginia

Q743. CLARK, A.
Climbing guide to Cooper's Rocks. [Morgantown: Pathfinders of West Virginia?]

Q744. ROBINSON, F. R. (Editor)
Climber's guide to Seneca Rocks. Potomac Appalachian Trail Club, Mountaineering Section, 1971. 122p.

Q745. WEBSTER, Bill
Seneca Rocks West Virginia: a climber's guide.
—Rev. ed. Chapel Hill: Earthbound, 1980.

Wisconsin

Q746. HERMACINSKI, Leo
Extremist's guide to Devil's Lake new climbs. Taped Squirrel Productions, 1985.

Q747. SMITH, David & ZIMMERMAN, Roger
Climber's and hiker's guide to Devil's Lake. [Madison, WI: Hoofer Mountaineers Memorial Union, Univ. Wisconsin Press?], 1970. 97p.

Q748. WIDULE, William & SWARTLING, Sven Olof
Climber's guide to Devil's Lake. Madison, WI: Univ. Wisconsin Press [for Chicago Mountaineering Club], 1979. 198p, illus, maps. 16cm.

Wyoming

Q749. BONNEY, Orrin Hanning & Lorraine
Bonney's guide to Jackson's Hole and Grand Teton National Park. Ord, NE, 1961.

Q750. BONNEY, O. H. & L.
Field book – the Absaroka Range and Yellowstone Park. 1963.

Q751. BONNEY, O. H. & L.
Field book — Yellowstone Park and the Absaroka Range (including North Absaroka, Washakie & Teton wilderness areas). Climbing routes and back country.
—2nd ed. 1977.

Q752. BONNEY, O. H. & L.
Field book — the Teton Range and Gros Ventre Range. 1963.

Q753. BONNEY, O. H. & L.
Field book — the Wind River Range (including Bridger, Glacier and Popo Ague wilderness areas, and Wind River reservation). 1962.
—2nd rev. ed. Houston: Bonney & Bonney, 1968. 195p, illus, maps.

Q754. BONNEY, O. H. & L.
Guide to the Wyoming mountains and wilderness areas. Denver: Sage Books, 1960. 389p, illus, maps, bibl. 25cm.
—2nd rev. ed. 1965. 528p, illus, maps. 25cm. Comprises the three field books.
—3rd rev. ed. 1977.

Q755. COULTER, Henry & MCLANE, Merrill F.
Mountain climbing guide to the Grand Tetons. Hanover, NH: Dartmouth Mountaineering Club, 1947. 67p, fold. plate, illus, map. 18cm.

Q756. FRYXELL, Fritiof N.
The Medicine Bow Mountains of Wyoming. S.F., 1926.

Q757. GARDINER, Steve & GUILMETTE, Dick
Devil's Tower National Monument: a climber's guide. Seattle: Mountaineers, 1986.

Q758. HALFPENNY, Jim
Guide to south east Wyoming.

Q759. JACQUOT, Ray G. & HOGG, R. O.
Climber's guide to the Snowy Range of Wyoming. 1970.

Q760. KELSEY, Joe
Climbing and hiking in the Wind River Mountains. S.F.: Sierra Club, 1980. 400p, illus, maps, bibl.

Q761. MCGEE, Dingus
Free climbs of Devil's Tower. By ...and the Last Pioneer Woman.
—5th ed. Devil's Tower: Poorperson's, 1979. 12p, illus, maps.
—Another ed. 1981.

Q762. ORTENBURGER, Leigh
Climber's guide to the Teton Range. S.F.: Sierra Club, 1956. [xii], 159p, illus, maps. 19cm.
—Another ed. 1962.
—Rev. ed. 1965. xiii, 336p, 24 plates, illus, maps.
—Condensed ed. Palo Alto, CA, 1979. 144p.

Q763. RYPKEMA, Terry & HAIRE, Curt
Climber's guide to Devil's Tower. The Authors, 1977. 80p, illus.

Q764. SUBLET, Jerry
Vedavoo climbs. By ...[and others].

REST OF WORLD

Sub-sections:
General
Africa
Asia
Australia
Canada
Europe
Latin America
New Zealand

General

Q801. KELSEY, Michael R.
Climbers and hikers guide to the world's mountains. Springville, UT: Kelsey Publishing Co., 1981. 679p, maps. 19cm.
—2nd rev. ed. enlarged. Springville, UT: The Author/Sparkford: Oxford Illustrated Press, 1984. 800p, illus, maps. 27cm.
Useful guide to selected peaks around the world.

Africa

Q802. BRISTOW, David & WARD, Clive
Mountains of southern Africa. Cape Town: Struick, 1986. 144p, col. pl.

Q803. CAPE PENINSULAR PUBLICITY ASSOCIATION
Table Mountain: some easy climbs to the summit. Cape Town: Cape Peninsular Publicity Assoc., 1914.

Q804. CLOAT, Tom
A hundred boulders. [Salisbury?]: Mountain Club of Rhodesia, 1978. n.p., fold. maps, diag.
Guide to climbs at Epworth Balancing Rocks.

Q805. COLLOMB, Robin Gabriel
Atlas Mountains of Morocco. Reading: West Col, 1980. 131p.
Tobkal massif and lesser known areas.

Q806. FIELD, Edgar Stanley & PELLS, Edward G.
A mountaineer's paradise: a guide to the mountains of the Worcester district. Cape Town: Mountain Club of South Africa, [1925]. 130p, illus. 20cm.
Covers 80 peaks and 200 routes.

Q807. GAY, A. C.
Some notes on mountaineering in the High Atlas. Duplicated typescript, 1968. 17p.

Q808. MOUNTAIN CLUB OF KENYA
Guide to Mount Kenya and Kilimanjaro.
—2nd ed. completely revised. 1963. 192p, illus, map. 16cm.
—3rd ed. completely revised. 1971. Edited by John Mitchell. 240p, illus, maps. 16cm.
—4th ed. 1981. By Iain Allan. 288p, illus, maps.

Q809. MOUNTAIN CLUB OF SOUTH AFRICA (Cape Town Section)
Table Mountain guide: walks and easy climbs on Table Mountain, Devil's Peak, with 2 contour maps. Cape Town: Stewart Ptg Co., 1944.
—3rd ed., 1966 entitled *Table Mountain, Devil's Peak and Lion's Head.*

Q810. OSMASTON, Henry A. & PASTEUR, David
Guide to the Ruwenzori: the mountains of the Moon. Kampala: Mountain Club of Uganda/Goring, Reading: West Col, 1972. 200p, illus, maps, bibl. 18cm.

Q811. POWELL, Colin G.
Guide to Ndeiya.
—2nd ed. Nairobi: Mountain Club of Kenya, [1968]. 84p, illus. 11 × 17cm.

Q812. POWELL, C. G.
Outlying crags. [Nairobi?]: The Author, [1970?]. 29p, col. plates, illus. 33cm.
Kenya, Kilimanjaro region.

Q813. REID, Ian C. (Editor)
Guide book to Mount Kenya and Kilimanjaro. Duplicated typescript, 1959.

Q814. ROBSON, Peter
Mountains of Kenya. Nairobi: East African Publ. House for Mountain Club of Kenya, 1969. 80p, col. plates, illus, maps, bibl. 23cm.

Asia

Q815. BEZRUCHKA, Stephen
Guide to trekking in Nepal. Kathmandu: Sahayogi Prekashan, 1972. [4], 204p. illus, maps. 19cm.
—2nd ed. 1974.
—3rd ed. 1976. x, 230p.
—4th ed. Leicester: Cordee/Kathmandu: Sahayogi Press, 1981. 256p, illus, 10 maps. 22cm.
—5th ed. rev. 1985. 352p.

Q816. BUNNELL, J. F.
Rock climbing guide to Hong Kong. Hong Kong: Cathay Press, 1959. 65p, plates, illus. 16cm.
—Another version by D. C. Reeve, with new routes added.

Q817. HIMALAYAN CLUB
Climber's guide to Sonamarg, Kashmir. [By C. W. F. Noyce]. Delhi: Himalayan Club, [1945]. vii, 51p, plates (1 fold.), illus, map. 23cm.

Q818. JACCARD, Pierre & VITTOZ, Pierre
Ladakh: for travellers, climbers and Tibetan culture lovers. Geneva: Artou, 1976. Yak. J. 01.

Q819. JACKSON, John Angelo
Climbing and trekking guide for Sonamarg, Kashmir. Srinagar, 1976. 56p, illus, maps. 22cm. Paperback.

Q820. KOHLI, M. S.
Himalayan treks and climbs. Bombay: Air-India, [1971?]. 48p, plates, illus. 23cm. Not in Yakushi. Copy in Alpine Club library.

Q821. KOHLI, M. S.
The Himalayas: playgrounds of the gods. (Trekking-climbing-adventures for mountaineers and trekkers). Delhi: Vikas Pub. House, 1983. 244p, col. illus, maps.

Q822. SWIFT, Hugh
Trekker's guide to the Himalaya and Karakoram. S.F. & Ldn, 1982. ix, 342p, illus, maps. 22cm.

Q823. WARD, Alexander
Climbing and mountain walking in Mauritius. Port Louis: P. Mackay, 196?

Australia

Q824. BAXTER, Chris & DEWHURST, C.
Rock climbing guide to Victoria. Melbourne: Victoria Climbing Club, 1967.

Q825. BAXTER, C.
Central Grampians. Melbourne: Victoria Climbing Club, [1977?].

Q826. BAXTER, C.
Central Victoria. 1974.

Q827. EWBANK, John M.
Rock climbs in the Blue Mountains. Sydney, 1964.

Q828. GRANDAGE, J. & TAYLOR, R.
Rock climbing guide to the Grampians. Melbourne: Victoria Climbing Club, ?

Q829. MCMAHON, & LINDOFF,
Wonderland Range. 1975.

Q830. ROBINSON, P.
Climbers guide to Frenchmans Cap. Climbers Club of Tasmania, 1979.

Q831. STONE, M. & SPEEDIE, I.
Mount Arapiles. Melbourne: Victoria Climbing Club, 1965.

Q832. SYDNEY ROCK-CLIMBING CLUB
The rock-climbs of New South Wales. Compiled by members of the . . .Sydney: S.R.C.C., [1963]. 112p, illus. 26cm.

Q833. UNIVERSITY OF NEW ENGLAND MOUNTAINEERING CLUB
New England tablelands. Armidale, N.S.W., 1971. 3rd ed.

Canada

Q834. ALPINE CLUB OF CANADA
Mountaineering around Montreal (an unofficial and preliminary attempt at a local guidebook for rockclimbing, mountain climbing . . .). By the Montreal Section of the A.C. of C. & Le Club de Montagne Canadien. Point Claire, Quebec: A.C. of C., 1964. 351p. 22cm.

Q835. BRITISH COLUMBIA MOUNTAIN CLUB
Northern cordillera. B.C.M.C., 1913.

Q836. CAMPBELL, Jim
Squamish rock climbs. The Author, 1985.

Q837. CULBERT, Dick
Alpine guide to south-western British Columbia. Vancouver: The Author, 1974. 441p, illus (some col), bibl. 17cm.

Q838. CULBERT, D.
A climber's guide to the Coastal Ranges of British Columbia (International border to Nass River). [Banff]: Alpine Club of Canada, [1965]. [vi], 312p, plates, illus. maps.
—2nd ed. Vancouver: A.C. of C., 1969. vi, 426p, plates (some fold.), illus, maps. 18cm.

Q839. GREENWOOD, Brian & KALLEN, Urs
Climber's guide to Yamuska. 1970.
—2nd ed. by Urs Kallen. [Calgary?]: [The Authors?], 1977. 43p, illus. 14 × 22cm. Calgary area, east of main Rockies.

Q840. KRUSZYNA, Robert & PUTNAM, William Lowell
Climber's guide to the interior ranges of British Columbia South.
—6th ed. [N.Y.]: A.A.C., 1977. 226p, illus, maps. 17cm.

Q841. MARSH, James
Climbing in southern Ontario. Toronto: Section of A.C. of C., 1980. 157p, illus, maps.

Q842. OUROM, Anders
Climber's guide to the Squamish Chief. Vancouver: British Columbia Mountaineering Club, 1980. 101p, plates, illus, maps.

Q843. PALMER, Howard & THORINGTON, James Monroe
Climber's guide to the Rocky Mountains of Canada. N.Y.: Knickbocker Press for A.A.C., 1921. xvii, 183p, plates (some fold), illus, maps, bibl. 18cm.
—2nd ed. 1930.
—3rd ed. 1940.
—3rd ed., 2nd ptg, 1943. Corrected to January, 1943. 250 copies only.
—Rev. ed. by J. M. Thorington. A.A.C., 1953.
—6th ed. by J. M. Thorington & W. L. Putnam. A.A.C., 1966. xx, 381p.

Q844. PUTNAM, William Lowell
Climber's guide to the interior ranges of British Columbia.
—4th ed. N.Y.: A.A.C., 1963.
—5th ed. N.Y.: A.A.C., 1971. 323p, plates, illus, maps, bibl. 17cm.
—6th ed. N.Y.: A.A.C., 1975. 210p. Northern section only.

Q845. PUTNAM, W. L.
Climber's guide to the Rocky Mountains of Canada North, 1974. By . . ., Chris Jones & R. Kruszyna.
—Being the 6th ed. of this guide now split into North and South sections. Based on previous editions by J. M. Thorington. [N.Y.]: A.A.C., 1974. 289p.
—Another ed. 1975.
—Another ed. 1979.

Q846. PUTNAM, W. L. & BOLESL Glen W.
Climber's guide to the Rocky Mountains of Canada South.
—Being the 6th ed. of this guide now split into North and South sections. Based on earlier editions by J. M. Thorington. [N.Y.]: A.A.C., 1973. 330p,
—Another ed. 1979. 473p.

Q847. SMAILL, Gordon
Squamish Chief guide. Vancouver: B. Lupul & M. Smaill, 1975. 114p, illus (some fold.). 19cm.

Q848. SOLE, Albi
Waterfall ice: climbs in the Canadian Rockies. Calgary: Rocky Mountain Books, 1980. iv, 92p, illus, maps.

Q849. SPOHR, Gregory
Selected climbs in the Carnmore area. Banff: A.C. of C., 1976. 37p, illus, map. 15cm.

Q850. THORINGTON, James Monroe
Climber's guide to the interior ranges of British Columbia. N.Y.: A.A.C., 1937. xii, 149p, plate, map, bibl. 17cm. 250 copies.
—2nd ed. 1947. xii, 170p.

Q851. WHEELER, Arthur Oliver
The Selkirk mountains: a guide for mountain climbers and pilgrims. Information by . . .[Text by Mrs H. J. Parker.] Winnipeg: Stovel Co., 1912. 199p, plates (some fold.), illus, maps, bibl. 20cm. Paper-bound.

Q852. WORDSWORTH, Glen
Climber's guide to the Squamish Chief and surrounding area. 1967.

Europe

Q853. ADAMEC, V. & ROUBAL, R.
High Tatras: a tourist's guide. Bratislava, 1974. 210p, illus, maps. Excursions, alpinism, skiing.

Q854. BATTAGEL, Arthur
Pyrenees east: a guide to the mountains for walkers and climbers. Goring, Reading: Gastons-West Col, 1975. 144p, illus, map, bibl. 17cm.

Q855. BATTAGEL, A.
Pyrenees west: a guide to the mountains for walkers and climbers. Goring, Reading: Gastons-West Col, 1975. 136p, illus, maps, bibl. 17cm.

Q856. BATTAGEL, A.
Pyrenees, Andorra, Cerdagne: a guide to the mountains for walkers and climbers. Goring, Reading: West Col, 1980. 88p, illus, map.

Q857. BENNET, Donald J.
Staunings Alps–Greenland: Scoresby Land and Nathorsts Land. Reading: Gastons-West Col, 1972. 120p, plates (2 fold), illus, maps (loose), bibl. 20cm.

Q858. BOUVIER, Jean-Pierre
Rock-climbing in France. Trans. from the French by Claudie Dunn. Ldn: Diadem, 1984. 72p, maps.
Location and description of 279 crags all over France.

Q859. COLLOMB, Robin Gabriel
Corsica Mountains. Reading: West Col, 1982. 95p, illus, maps.

Q860. COLLOMB, R. G.
Picos de Europa (northern Spain). Reading: West Col, 1983. 144p, illus, maps.

Q861. COPELAND, Fanny S. & DEBELAKOVA, M. M.
Short guide to the Slovene Alps [Jugoslavia] for British and American tourists. Ljubljana: Kleinmayr & Bamberg, 1936. 128p, plates (2 fold.), illus, map. 16cm.

Q862. GRAHAM, J. D.
Rock climbing in Malta. Goring, Reading: West Col, [1970]. v, 103p, illus. 17cm.

Q863. GUNNING, Asbjorn & SCHLYTTER, Boye
Climbs in the Horungtinder, Norway. Edited [for] Norsk Tindeklub by . . .Oslo: Grndahl, 1933. 23p, 1 fold. col. plate, illus, map (in pkt). 23cm. Paperback. From the original: *Fører for Bestigninger i Horungtindene.*

Q864. HASSE, Dietrich & STUTTE, Heinz Lothar
Meteora–Griechenland. [1985?] 102p, illus (some col). Text in English and German.

Q865. HOWARD, Tony
Selected climbs in Romsdal. 1965.

Q866. HOWARD, T.
Walks and climbs in Romsdal, Norway. Manchester: Cicerone Press, 1970. 174p, illus, maps (endpapers). 16cm.
—Another ed. 1979. 208p.

Q867. KLINAR, S.
How to climb Triglav. Ljubljana, 1979. 64p, illus, map.

Q868. LIVESEY, Peter
French rock-climbs: a selection of fine free rock-climbs chosen from outside the Alps area. Leicester: Cordee, 1980. 101p, illus. Fontainbleau, Saussois, Verdon, etc.

Q869. MARSDEN, A. D.
Climbing guide to Gibraltar. Yeovil: D. M. Haynes for the Joint Services Mountaineering Assoc., [1965]. 82p, illus. 21cm.

Q870. NORWAY TRAVEL ASSOCIATION
Rock climbs in Norway [Jotunheimen/Nordmore/Lofoten/Sunnmore/Romsdal]. Ldn: Norway Travel Assoc., [1953]. 5v in one, 1 fold. plate, illus, map. 21cm.

Q871. REYNOLDS, Kev
Walks and climbs in the Pyrenees. Milnthorpe: Cicerone Press, 1978. 127p, illus, maps. 19cm.
—2nd rev. & expanded ed. 1983. 208p.

Q872. SPIKAS, G.
The mountains of Greece. Athens Efstathiadis, 1982. 204p, illus (some col), maps.
Comprehensive guide, celebrating the 50th anniversary of the Greek Alpine Club of Athens.

Q873. SPILSBURY, Harry & AGAR, C. R.
First impressions of Norway and some notes on the Sunnmore Alps and the Horungtinder. Norwegian Travel Bureau, [1936[. 16p, plates, map. Printed card covers.

Q874. STYLES, Showell
Walks and climbs in Malta. The Author, 1944.

Q875. VÉRON, Georges
Pyrenees high level route: Atlantic to Mediterranean; mountain walking and trekking guide for a complete traverse of the range in 45 day stages with 50 easier or harder alternatives and variations. Goring, Reading: Gastons-West Col, 1981. 136p, maps.

Q876. WELLE-STRAND, Erling
Mountain touring holidays in Norway. Compiled and edited by ...Oslo: Nortrabooks (Norway Travel Assoc.), 1974. 96p, illus, maps. 21cm.

Latin America

Q877. BARTLE, Jim
Trails of the Cordilleras Blanca and Huayhuash. Lima: The Author, 1980. [In 2 parts?]
—2nd ed. Healdsburg, CA: The Author, 1981. 159p, col. plates, illus, fold. map (in pkt). 18cm.

Q878. BRADT, Hilary & George
Backpacking and trekking in Peru and Bolivia. Boston, MA & Chalfont St. Peter, Bucks: Bradt Enterprises, 1975.
—2nd ed. 1977.
—3rd ed. 1980. [8], 135p, illus, maps. 22cm.

Q879. BRADT, H. & PILKINGTON, John
Backpacking in Chile and Argentina (plus the Falkland Islands). Boston, MA & Chalfont St. Peter, Bucks: Bradt Enterprises, 1979. 128p, illus, maps. 22cm.

Q880. BRADT, H. & RACHOWIECKI, R.
Backpacking in Mexico & central America. Bradt Enterprises. 2nd ed.
Includes climbing guide to Mexico's major volcanoes.

Q881. BRADT, H. & G.
Backpacking in Venezuela, Colombia and Ecuador: treks in the northern Andes. Boston, MA & Chalfont St. Peter, Bucks: Bradt Enterprises, 1979. 128p, illus, maps. 22cm.

Q882. FOURTOT, W. & SEIGNEUR, Y.
30 days in Peru/30 jours au Pérou/30 dias en el Perú. 1984. 131p, illus (some col), maps. Text in English, French and Spanish.
Guidebook for the Cordillera Blanca for small groups of climbers; most informative.

Q883. KOERNER, Michael
The fool's guide to Ecuador and Peru. Birmingham, MI: Buzzard Mountaineering, 1976. ix, 92p, maps. 18cm. Paper-bound.
Despite the jokey presentation (e.g. there is nothing about Peru) this is a proper guidebook packed with information.

Q884. MORALES ARNAO, César
Huascarán climbing guide. [Lima?]: Ediciones Turismo Andino, [1981?]. 21p, plates, illus, maps. 22cm. Text in English and Spanish.

Q885. PARRA, L. A.
Practical guide and routes of ascension to Mount Aconcagua. 2nd ed. Trans. from the Spanish by Ruth Alice Epiphanovitch. Mendoza, Argentina: The Author, 1985. 24p, 4 route diag, map.

Q886. PECHER, R. & SCHMIEMANN, W.
Southern Cordillera Real: a guide for mountaineers, skiers and walkers. Trans. from the German by Ewald Osus. Chur (Switz.): Plata Publishing, 197. 57p, plates, illus, maps. 20cm.
Selected climbs and ski runs.

Q887. RACHOWIEKI, Rob
Climbing and hiking in Ecuador. Chalfont St. Peter, Bucks/Cambridge, MA: Bradt Enterprises, 1984. 160p, illus, maps. 21cm.

Q888. RICKER, John F.
Yuraq Janka: guide to the Peruvian Andes Part I; Cordilleras Blanca and Rosko. Banff: Alpine Club of Canada/N.Y.: A.A.C., 1977. xi, 180p, plates (some fold.), illus. 2 col. fold. maps (loose). 23cm.
—2nd ed. Banff, 1981. 180p.
Definitive guidebook; climbs to 1975.

Q889. SECOR, R. J.
Mexico's volcanoes: a climbing guide. Seattle: Mountaineers, 1981. 120p,

New Zealand

Q890. BISHOP, G.
The Mount Aspiring region. Christchurch: New Zealand Alpine Club, 1974. 59p, illus, maps.
—New ed. Dunedin, 1976. 68p.
—Rev. ed. 1981. 69p.

Q891. HALL-JONES, Gerard (Editor)
Moir's guidebook: southern section. Hollyford Southwards. Christchurch: New Zealand Alpine Club, 1979. 5th ed. [xvii], 136p, plates, illus, maps.

Q892. HALL-JONES, G. (Editor)
Moir's guidebook ...Otago and Southland: southern section. Edited by G. Hall-Jones. Christchurch: Whitcombe & Tombs, 1959.

Q893. HEWITT, L. Rodney & DAVIDSON, Mavis M.
The Southern Alps. Part 2. Mount Cook alpine regions. Christchurch: Pegasus Press, 1953. 56p, plates, illus. 18cm. (New Zealand holiday guides, 8)
—Another ed. 1972. 72p.

Q894. KENNEDY, L. D. (Editor)
Moir's guide book: northern section. Route Burn Track and Lake Wakatipu Watershed to Lake Ohau Watershed. Christchurch: New Zealand Alpine Club, 1984. 5th ed. [xv], 103p, plates, illus, maps.

Q895. LOGAN, Hugh
The Mount Cook guidebook: a climber's guide to the Mt. Cook region. Christchurch: New Zealand Alpine Club, 1982. 132p, plates, illus, maps.

Q896. MOIR, G. M.
Guidebook to the great southern lakes and fiords of western Otago. 1925.
—Rev. ed. enlarged. 1948.
Very successful book and a major influence in the growth of tramping and climbing.

Q897. ODELL, R. S.
Handbook of the Arthur's Pass National Park. 1935.
Useful information; similar to Moir's guidebook.

Q898. PASCOE, John Dobree
The Southern Alps. Part I. From the Kaikouras to the Rangitata. Christchurch: Pegasus Press, 1951. 96p, 8 plates, illus, maps. 18cm. (New Zealand holiday guides, 3).

Facing page:
Hemis, Ladakh

FICTION
(Novels, Short Stories, Drama)

N.B.: This listing has been built up from published sources, correspondence with collectors and personal knowledge. A good many items are very tenuous; some are unverified.

X01. AITMATOV, Chingiz & MUKHAMEDZHANOV, Kaltai
The ascent of Mount Fuji. N.Y.: Farrer Strauss & Giroux, 1975. 212p. 20cm.
Stage drama.

X02. ALBRAND, Martha
A call from Austria. Ldn: Hodder, 1963.

X03. ALBRAND, M.
None shall know. N.Y.: Little Brown, 1945.

X04. ALDOUS, Allan
McGowan climbs a mountain. O.U.P., 1945.
Young adult adventure story set in the Himalaya.

X05. ALEXANDER, Mrs (pseud. Annie French Hector)
A second life. Ldn: Bentley, 1885. 3v.
—Another ed. Ldn: Hutchinson, [1904]. 189p. [8vo].
Heroine fakes death in a crevasse on the Mer de Glace to escape from her husband.

X06. ALLAN, Mabel Esther
Shadow over the Alps. Ldn: Hutchinson, 1960.

X07. ALVAREZ, Al
Hers. Ldn: Weidenfeld & Nicholson, 1974.
Short chapter on climbing in eternal triangle story.

X08. ANDERSON, Hans Christian
The ice maiden. 1846?
—Another ed. Ldn: Bentley, 1863.
Swiss fairy tale.

X09. ANDREW, Jim
Bar-room mountaineers. Ldn: Cassell, 1965. [6], 215p. 21cm.
Passing references to climbing in story of juvenile delinquency.

X10. [ANONYMOUS]
An alpine tale. By the author of 'Tales from Switzerland'. Ldn: Westley, 1823. 3v. 19cm.

X11. [ANONYMOUS]
Château of Leaspach: or, The stranger in Switzerland: a tale. Ldn: Newman, 1827. 3v. 20cm.

X12. [ANONYMOUS]
Continental adventures: a novel. Ldn: Hurst Robinson, 1826. 3v. 20cm.

X13. ARTHUR, Elizabeth (b.1953)
Beyond the mountain. N.Y.: Harper Row, 1983. ix, 211p. 22cm.
Story of guilt, desire and passion. A woman climber's odyssey on a Himalayan peak.

X14. ATWATER, Montgomery
Ski-patrol. Ldn: Faber, 1945. 162p. 20cm.

X15. ATWATER, M.
Ski lodge mystery.
Climax on mountain peak.

X16. ATWATER, M.
Snow rangers of the Andes. N.Y.: Random House, 1967.
Young adult story of espionage and romance.

X17. AUDEN, Wystan Hugh (1907-73) & ISHERWOOD, Christopher
The ascent of F6: a tragedy in two acts. Ldn: Faber, 1936. 123p. 23cm. Also 2nd ed and reprints.
—U.S. ed. N.Y.: Random House, 1937.
—Another ed. issued with *On the frontier.* Faber paperback, 1958.
Satirical verse drama, first performed February 26, 1937 at the Mercury Theatre, London.

X18. BAGLEY, Desmond
High citadel. N.Y.: Doubleday, 1965.
—U.K. ed.
—Paperback ed.
Thriller. Two men escape over a high pass in the Andes.

X19. BAGLEY, D.
Snowtiger. Ldn: Collins/N.Y.: Doubleday, 1975. 287p. 21cm.
—B.C.A. ed.
Thriller. A powder-snow avalanche is started with terrible consequences.

X20. BAKER, Olaf
Shasta of the wolves. Ldn: Harrap, [1921]. 276p, illus. 21cm.
Volume of children's fiction about the mountains around Shasta.

X21. BALLANTYNE, Robert Michael (1825-94)
Freaks on the fells. Ldn: Nelson, n.d. 346p. 19cm.
By a a famous Scottish writer of boys' stories

X22. BALLANTYNE, R. M.
Rivers of ice: a tale illustrative of alpine adventure and glacier action. Nisbet, 1875. vii, 430p, plates, illus. 18cm.

X23. BALLANTYNE, R. M.
The rover of the Andes: a tale of adventure in South America. Nisbet, 1885. viii, 431p, plates, illus. 18cm.

X24. BARTROPP, John
Barbarian: a tale of the Roman Wall. Ldn: Chambers, 1933. 320p. 20cm.
Chapter on cliff-climbing at night.

X25. BATES, Peter
The Red Mountain. Ldn: Hale, 1966. 176p. 21cm.
Thriller. Prisoners of war escaping over the Alps to Switzerland at the end.

X26. BATES, Ralph (1899-)
Sirocco. N.Y.: Random House, 1939.
Written by an English novelist who lived much of his life abroad.

X27. BATES, R.
The miraculous horde. Ldn: Cape, ?.
A piece called 'Wailing precipice' may be extracted from this or perhaps from his book *43rd Division,* a story of patrol actions in the Pyrenees during the Spanish Civil War.

X28. BAUM, Vicki
Marion alive. Ldn: Michael Joseph, 1943. 452p. 19cm.
At one point the heroine falls into a crevasse, loses her ice axe and breaks her ankle.

X29. BELL, Margaret E.
Danger on Old Baldy. N.Y.: Morrow, 1944. 224p.

X30. BENNETT, Robert Ames
Avalanche gulch. Ldn: Collins, 1937.
—New ed.

X31. BENSON, Irene Elliott
Campfire girls mountaineering: or, Overcoming all obstacles. N.Y.: Doubleday, 1918. 212p, illus.

X32. BENSON, Monsignor Robert Hugh (1871-1914)
The coward. Ldn: Hutchinson, 1912. 392p. 20cm.
Includes short Alpine episode. The author had climbed with his brothers, hence his realistic mountain descriptions.

X33. BENTON, Kenneth
Craig and the Jaguar. Ldn: Macmillan/N.Y.: Walker, 1973. 223p.
Thriller set against background of the Cordillera Blanca, Peru. The Jaguar is a peak.

X34. BLACKBURN, John
Bound to kill/Blue Octavo. N.Y.: M.S. Mill/Ldn: Cape, 1963.

X35. BLACKWOOD, Algernon
Pan's garden: a volume of nature stories. Ldn: Macmillan, 1912. vii, 530p.
Fantastic tales of the power of nature over man's mind, including 'The Glamour of the Snow', etc.

X36. BORDEAUX, Henry
Footprints in/beneath the snow. Ldn: Fisher Unwin/N.Y.: Duffield, 1913. From the original: *La neige sur les pas* (Paris: Plon-Nourrit, [1911])

X37. BORDEAUX, H.
The house that died /House of the dead. Ldn: Fisher Unwin, [1923]. 270p. 19cm.
Gloomy tale of the Maurienne (Maritime Alps); chamois hunting but no proper climbing.

X38. BOTTOME, Phyllis (1884-1963)
Masks and faces. Ldn: Faber, 1940.
Includes short story, 'A Splendid Fellow', by an Anglo-American author whose study of psychology helped to shape her fiction.

X39. BOWMAN, William E. (-1984)
Ascent of Rum Doodle. Ldn: Parrish, 1956. 141p, 16 plates, illus. 22cm.
—U.S. ed. N.Y.: Vanguard, 1956. 113p, plates, illus.
—Paperback ed. Sheffield: Dark Peak, 1979.
—Arrow paperback. 1983.
Satirizes Himalayan expedition books. The illustrations are mostly taken from nineteenth century magazines.

X40. BOYLE, Kay (b.1903)
His human majesty. N.Y.: McGraw-Hill, 1949. 295p. 20cm.
—Another ed. Whillesey, 1949.
Story told against background of training mountain troops in Colorado.

X41. BOYLE, K.
1939. N.Y.: Simon & Schuster, 1948.
Nothing known. (Source-Pokorny)

X42. BOYLE, K.
Avalanche. N.Y.: Simon & Schuster, 1944. 209p.
—U.K. ed. Ldn: Faber, 1945. 154p. 19cm.
Romance, espionage and adventure in the French Alps during World War II. Climbing episodes.

X43. BOYLE, K.
Thirty stories. N.Y.: Simon & Schuster, 1946.
Includes short climbing story, 'Maiden, Maiden'.

X44. BOZMAN, Ernest Franklin (1895-1968)
'X plus Y': the story of two unknown quantities. Ldn: Dent, 1936. 282p. 20cm.
Includes climbing episodes, that of a 4000-metre peak in the Graian Alps, at the end of the story being the most descriptive.

X45. BRANDIS, Madeleine
The little Swiss wood carver. N.Y.?: Grosset & Dunlap, [1929]. 160p, illus. [8vo].
Small climbing incident in this story set in the Alps.

X46. BRAY, Claude
Ivanda: or, The pilgrim's quest: a tale [of Tibet]. Ldn: Warne, 1894. 355p, plates, illus. 21cm.

X47. BRECK, Vivian
High trail. Garden City, NY, 1948. 214p.

X48. BRIDGES, Constance
Thin air. N.Y.: Brewer & Warren, 1930.

X49. BRIDGES, Woodrow (pseud. William Woodbridge)
Shooting skyward. Tacoma, WA: Smith-Kinney, 1912. 63p, 8 plates, illus.
Includes satirical account of ascent of Mt. Rainier.

X50. BROCK, Emma
High in the mountains: Robi and Hanni in the Swiss Alps. N.Y.?: Whitman, 1938. ?p, col. illus. [4to].
Climbing scenes in children's story set in the Alps.

X51. BROWN, E.
Dark rainbow.

X52. BUCHAN, John
John McNab.
Exciting deer-stalking in Scottish Highlands, etc.

X53. BUCHAN, J.
Mountain meadow. Literary Guild, 1940.
—Another ed. Boston: Houghton Mifflin, [1941]. [xlix], 277p.

X54. BUCHAN, J.
Mr. Standfast. Ldn: 1919/N.Y: Doran, 1919.

—Another ed. Ldn: Nelson, n.d. 384p. 16cm.
—Penguin paperback
Includes Alpine climbing episodes.

X55. BUCHAN, J.
Prester John. 1910.
Hero escapes from a cave by means of a dangerous rock climb.

X56. BUCHAN, J.
The three hostages. Ldn: 1924/Boston: Houghton Mifflin, 1924.
—Another ed. Ldn: Nelson, n.d. 379p. 16cm.
Ends with exciting man-hunt and rock-climb in Scottish Highlands.

X57. BUCK, Pearl
Other gods: an American legend. 1938.
—Another ed. N.Y.?: World Books, [1947]. 381p. [8vo].
Mountaineering background.

X58. BURGBACHER, K.
White hell: a story of the search and rescue service in the Alps. Ldn: Methuen, 1963. 208p, illus. 20cm.

X59. BUTLER, Samuel
Erewhon. 1872.
The opening chapters accurately portray Bulter's mountain exploration in New Zealand. The descent into Erewhon is based on the Val Ticino.

X60. BUTTERFIELD, F.
The crevasse: a dramatic study. Oxford: Parker, 1903. 39p. [8vo].
A macabre monologue with melodramatic plot.

X61. CANNAN, Joanna
Ithuriel's hour. Ldn: Hodder, 1931. 320p. 20cm. R.P., 1931, 1933 (3rd).
—Reissued as *Hour of the angel.* Pan Books, 1949.
Ambition to succeed on a Himalayan peak leads to manslaughter.

X62. CANNAN, J.
The hills sleep on. Ldn: Hodder, 1935. 317p. 20cm.
Thriller. Starts in the Alpine Club and climaxes in Tibet.

X63. CANNAN, J.
The lady of the heights. 1931.

X64. CANNON, Le Grand Jr.
Look to the mountain. Ldn: Cassell, 1943. 410p, map. 20cm.
New Hampshire setting.

X65. CARR, Glyn (pseud. Showell Styles)
Corpse at Camp Two. Ldn: Bles, 1955. 256p.
All these stories are thrillers and most involve a fair amount of climbing. The principal character is an amateur detective called Abercrombie Lewker.

X66. CARR, G.
Corpse in the crevasse. 1952.

X67. CARR, G.
Death finds a foothold. Ldn: Bles, 1961.

X68. CARR, G.
Death of a weirdy. Ldn: Bles, 1965. 223p.

X69. CARR, G.
Death on Milestone Buttress. Ldn: Bles, 1951.
—Paperback ed.
—Large print ed. Bath: Chivers, 1980.
Milestone Buttress is a well-known crag in Snowdonia.

X70. CARR, G.
Death under Snowdon. Ldn: Bles, 1954. 239p. 19cm.
—Paperback ed.

X71. CARR, G.
Fat man's agony. Ldn: Bles, 1969. 224p. 19cm.
Title is name of fictitious rock-climb.

X72. CARR, G.
Holiday with murder. Ldn: Bles, 1960.

X73. CARR, G.
Ice-axe murders. Ldn: Bles, 1958. 256p.

X74. CARR, G.
Lewker in Norway. 1963.

X75. CARR, G.
Lewker in Tyrol. Ldn: Bles, 1967. 223p. 19cm.

X76. CARR, G.
Murder of an owl. Ldn: Bles, 1956. 287p.
Set in Cwm Idwal, Snowdonia.

X77. CARR, G.
Murder on the Matterhorn. Ldn: Bles, 1951.
—U.S. ed. N.Y.: Dutton, 1953. 244p.

X78. CARR, G.
Swing away climber. Ldn: Bles/N.Y.: Washburn, 1959. 256p. 19cm.
Set on Dinas Cromlech, a famous hard crag in Snowdonia.

X79. CARR, G.
Youth hostel murders. Ldn: Bles, 1952.
—U.S. ed. N.Y.: Dutton, 1953. 224p.

X80. CASOLORO, D.
The ice king. Ardmore: Whitmore, 1981.

X81. CHARLES, R.
Sun virgin.
Setting–Sangay in Ecuadorian Andes.

X82. CLARKE, Isobel Constance
In an alpine valley. Ldn: Longmans, 1937.

X83. CLEARY, Jon
Pulse of danger. N.Y.: Morrow, 1966.

X84. CLEEVE, Roger
The toad beneath the harrow. Ldn: Allen & Unwin, 1969.

X85. CLEMENTS, E. H.
High tension. Ldn: Hodder, 1959.
Thriller.

X86. 'CLIMBER & CLUTCH'
Hobbs and Larkins in North Wales. Drawn by Climber, written by Clutch. c.1880.
Skit on amateur climbing in Wales.

X87. COLLINS, Barry
The ice chimney.
Stage-play about Maurice Wilson on Everest. First produced at the Edinburgh Festival. New version played at Lyric Theatre, Hammersmith in 1980.

X88. COOK, Victor
Anton of the Alps. Ldn: Methuen, 1912.
Climax on top of Alpine peak.

X89. COOPER, Edward H.
The Monk wins out. Ldn: Duckworth, 1900. 351p. 20cm.
Horseracing and mountaineering.

X90. CORNWALL, Nellie
Hallvard Halvorsen: or, The avalanche: a story of the Fjeld fjord and Fos. Ldn: Partridge, [1888]. 316p, illus. 20cm.

X91. COUCH, Stata A.
In the shadow of the peaks: a novel. Ldn: Greening, 1909. 320p, plates, illus. 20cm.
Scenes in the valley of Cuernavaca, Mexico; description of ascent of Popacatapetl.

X92. COVINGTON, Lynn
A mountain tale. N.Y.: Carlton Press, 1963.

X93. COXHEAD, Elizabeth (1904-79)
One green bottle. Ldn: Faber, 1951. 3-281p. 19cm.
—U.S. ed. Philadelphia: Lippincott, 1951. 254p.
—Fontana paperback. 1955.
—Portway reprint. Bath: Chivers, 1973.
Romance, climbing and character-building, set in Snowdonia. Still a leading contender as the finest climbing novel ever written.

X94. COXHEAD, E.
June in Skye: a novel. Ldn: Cassell, 1938. 292p. 20cm.

X95. COXHEAD, E.
Figure in the mist. Ldn: Collins, 1955. 256p.

X96. CROCKETT, Samuel Rutherford (1860-1914)
Lone march.
—3rd ed. Ldn: Hodder, 1899. xii, 419p, plates, illus. 21cm.

—U.S. ed. N.Y.: Dodd Mead, 1900.
One chapter includes a rather absurd climbing episode supposedly set on and around the Eiger. The book was originally brought out in magazine form as *A woman of fortune.*

X97. CROFT-COOKE, Rupert
The white mountain. [U.S.A.]: Cosmopolis, 1933.
—U.K. ed. Ldn: Falcon, 1949.
By well-known British writer.

X98. CROFT-COOKE, R.
Escape to the Andes. N.Y.: Messner, 1938.

X99. CRONIN, A. J.
Enchanted snow.
Skiing thriller.

X100. CURTIS, Monica
Landslide. Ldn: Gollancz, 1934. 286p. 19cm.
Climbing episodes in a story about an imaginary Fascist State of Europe.

X101. DAUDET, Alphonse (1840-97)
Tartarin on the Alps. Ldn: 1885.
—Other editions. 1887, 1888, 1892.
—Another ed. Ldn: Dent 1902. 368p.
—Everyman's Library ed. with *Tartarin of Tarascon.* Ldn: Dent, 1910.
The second of the Tartarin novels. An example of humour turning on the depiction of character. Includes ascents of the Rigi, Jungfrau and Mont Blanc. A classic.

X102. D'AULAIRE, Ingri & Edgar
The magic meadow. N.Y.: Doubleday, [1958]. 55p, col. illus. [4to].
Children's picture book set in the Alps; several climbing illustrations and incidents.

X103. DAUMAL, René (1908-44)
Mount Analogue: a novel of symbolically authentic non-Euclidean adventures in mountain-climbing. By ...Trans. [from the French] and introduction by Roger Shattuck. Postface by Véra Daumal. Ldn: Vincent Stuart Pub, 1959. [6], 106p. 23cm. From the original: *Mont Analogue* (Lib. Gallimard, 1952)
—Another ed. Baltimore: Penguin Metaphysical Library, 1968. R.P., 1974.
—Another ed. S.F.: City Lights Books, 1972.
Unfinished allegorical novel. Daumal was a student of G. I. Gurdjieff. Fascinating.

X104. DAVIDSON, Lionel
The rose of Tibet. Ldn: Gollancz, 1962. 320p. R.P., 1963.
—Companion B.C. ed. 1963. 320p. 19cm.
—Penguin paperback. 1964. 314p. 19cm.
Secret mission into Chinese-occupied Tibet.

X105. DIBBEN, J. V.
Mountain adventure. Ldn: Epworth, 1947.

X106. DISNEY, Walt
Mountaineering Mickey. Ldn: Collins, 1937.

X107. DOLBIER, Maurice (b.1912)
Nowhere near Everest? Illustrated by Virgil F. Partch. N.Y.: Knopf, 1955. vi, 56p, illus, 25cm.
Almost a satire on Bowman's *Rum Doodle.*

X108. DOWNIE, John
High fidelity. Bristol: July Fox, 1980. 48p. 22cm.
One-act play. The scene is a mountain top, possibly in the Himalaya. Lack of oxygen begins to affect the two climbers, with some surprising revelations.

X109. DRUMMOND, June
Cable car. Ldn: Gollancz, 1965.
—U.S. ed. N.Y.: Reinhart, 1967.
Thriller set in fictional mid-European state, involving international intrigue.

X110. DUCKWORTH, F. R. G.
Swiss fantasy. Ldn: Benn, 1948. 128p, plates, illus. 19cm.

X111. DUFF, Douglas V.
On the world's roof. Ldn: Peal Press, [c.1950?]. 5-223p. 19cm.
—Another ed. Ldn: Abbey Rewards, n.d. N.pag. 20cm. Pictorial boards.
Young adult adventure story set in Tibet, from whence fugitive Nazis are planning to conquer the world with a secret weapon.

X112. DUFFIELD, Anne
Glittering heights.
—New ed. Ldn: Cassell, 1937.

X113. DUNDAS, L.
He liked them murderous.
Thriller set in the Andes.

X114. DUNSTAN, Mary
Jagged skyline. Ldn: Constable, 1935. xiv, 386p. 19cm.
Ski-mountaineering and superstition in the Alps.

X115. DUNSTAN, M.
He climbed alone. Ldn: Heinemann, 1948. 253p. 20cm.
Romance and climbing in the Alps.

X116. DUTTON, G. J. F.
The ridiculous mountains: tales of the Doctor and his friends in the Scottish Highlands. Ldn: Diadem, 1984. 158p. 23cm.
Humorous short stories; classic.

X117. EKVALL, R. B.
Tents against the sky. N.Y.: Farrar Strauss Young, 1954. 264p.
A novel of Tibet. Yak. E. 28.

X118. ENGELHARD, Georgia
Peterli and the mountain. Philadelphia: Lippincott, 1954. 40p, illus. 23cm.
Based on the true story of a cat which climbed the Matterhorn. The real cat, a 10-month old kitten, followed some climbers up the Hörnli Ridge, bivouaced in the Solvay Hut and arrived on top next day. Being too tired to continue he was carried down into Italy by other climbers.

X119. EVARTS, Hal G.
The secret of the Himalayas. N.Y.: Scribner's, 1962.

X120. EYRE, Donald C.
John Sikander. Ldn: Hale, 1954. 224p. 20cm.
Search for a mysterious heir leads halfway up a peak in the Himalaya.

X121. FAUST, R.
Snowkill. N.Y.: Leisure books, Nordon Pub, 1974. 201p. 18cm. Softback.
An American journalist is drawn into a treacherous Alpine man-hunt for a Nazi war criminal.

X122. FAUST, R.
Tombs of blue ice. N.Y.: Bobbs-Merrill, 1974. 210p.
—U.K. ed. 1976.
Thriller.

X123. FAUST, R.
Wolf in the clouds. N.Y.: Bobbs-Merrill, 1977.

X124. FENN, George Manville (1831-1909)
The crystal hunters: a boy's adventure in the higher Alps. 1892.
—Another ed. Ldn: Partridge, [c.1900]. 415p.
Tale of mountain climbing, avalanches and alpine adventures, by a famous writer of boys' stories.

X125. FENN, G. M.
In an Alpine valley. Ldn: Hurst & Blackett, 1894. 3v. 20cm.
Alpine scenery and climbing described.

X126. FENNER, Phyllis R.
Perilous ascent: stories of mountain climbing. N.Y.: Morrow, 1970. 190p, illus.
Anthology: authors include David Lavender, Don Knowlton, J. R. Ullman, Robert Murphy, Edwin Muller.

X127. FIRBANK, Thomas
Bride to the mountain: a romance. Ldn: Harrap, 1940. 256p, sketch-map. 19cm.
Supposedly set in the Welsh hills of Aran and Cader; a story of sheep-stealing, murder and romance. Climbing episodes. By the author of *I bought a mountain.*

X128. FITZGERALD, Kevin
It's different in July. 1955.
A 'Feston' story. The central character is the huge and amiable Commander Feston, a modern Bulldog Drummond, with his Siamese cat, Mr. Cheng-Foo. Partly set in Snowdonia.

X129. FITZGERALD, K.
It's safe in England. Ldn: Heinemann, 1949.

A 'Feston' story. Murderous treasure-hunt where the action moves between Cumbria and East Anglia. No climbing as such.

X130. FITZGERALD, K.
Not so quickly. [Pre-1949]

X131. FITZGERALD, K.
Throne of bayonets. Ldn: Heinemann, 1952.
A 'Feston' story. Partly set in Snowdonia. Thrilling shoot-out on top of Lliwedd.

X132. FORSTER, D. K.
Twin giants. Hammond, 1952.
Himalayan setting.

X133. FORBES, Colin
Heights of Zervos. Ldn: Collins, 1970.
—Pan paperback. 1972. R.P., 1973.
War story; battle for a monastery on top of a Greek mountain.

X134. FRISON-ROCHE, Roger
First on the rope. Ldn: Methuen, 1949. 268p.
—U.S. ed. N.Y.: Prentice-Hall, 1950. 246p.
—Limited edition of 750 copies. Ldn: Brun, [1952]. [xi], 268p.
—Four Square paperback. 1959.
Climbing around Chamonix between the wars. The author was a professional guide.

X135. FRISON-ROCHE, R.
Grand crevasse. New Jersey: Prentice-Hall, 1951. 243p.
—U.K. ed. entitled *Last crevasse.* Ldn: Methuen, 1952. 224p. 19cm.
Climbing around Chamonix between the wars.

X136. FRISON-ROCHE, R.
Return to the mountains. Trans. by Hugo Charteris. Ldn: Methuen, 1961. 239p. 20cm.
Sequel to *Grand crevasse.*

X137. GAIR, Malcolm
Snowjob. N.Y.: Doubleday, 1962/Ldn: Collins, 1962.
—Pan paperback, 1965.
Skiing thriller; Swiss Alps.

X138. GALSWORTHY, John
The little dream; an allegory in six scenes. Ldn: Duckworth, [1911]. 38p. 18cm. Also in collected editions of his plays.
Sadly symbolic and metaphyisical stage-play set in an Alpine hut. The characters are Seelchen, a young girl, and a mountaineer.

X139. GANPAT (pseud. M. L. A. Gompertz)
High snow. N.Y.: Doubleday/Ldn: Hodder, 1927.

X140. GANPAT
Mirror of dreams. N.Y.: Doubleday, 1928.

X141. GANPAT
Snow rubies. Edinburgh: Blackwood/Boston: Houghton Mifflin, 1925. viii, 335p. 19cm.
Adventure story set in the mountains of Kashmir. The heroes get caught by a weird tribe of cave-dwellers.

X142. GANPAT
The voice of Dashin: a romance of wild mountains.

X143. GARVE, Andrew
Ascent of D.13. N.Y.: Harper Row, 1968. 187p.
—Thriller B.C., 1969. 191p. 19cm.
—Pan paperback
—Another ed. Ldn: Collins, 1970.
Race to find secret weapon in crashed aeroplane. Climbing and espionage on the Turko-Russian border.

X144. GASTON, Bill
Death crag. Ldn: Hammond, 1965.

X145. GAYLE, Newton
Sinister Crag. Ldn: Gollancz, 1938.
—U.S. ed. N.Y.: Scribner's, 1939. 288p.
Murder thriller about a gang in a Lake District inn.

X146. GEDDIE, John
Beyond the Himalayas; a story of travel and adventure in the wilds of Tibet. Ldn: Nelson, 1882. viii, 256p, 8 plates, illus. 19cm. Yak. G. 24.

X147. GILBEY, Geoffrey
She's and skis. Ldn: Hutchinson, [1937]. 51 illustrations by J. H. Ronson. 288p, illus. 19cm.
Light romantic humour about skiing and après-ski.

X148. GILLESPIE, S.
Himalayan view. Ldn: Bles, 1947.
Yak. G. 58.

X149. GILLMAN, F. R.
Max of the mountains. Ldn: Univ. London, 1937. Softback.

X150. GLYN, Anthony
Kick turn. Ldn: Hutchinson, 1963. 336p. 20cm.

X151. GODDEN, Rumer
Black narcissus. Boston: Little Brown, 1939.
—Penguin paperback.
Story about nuns in a Himalayan convent; one falls in love with an Indian prince. Made into a vivid technicolor picture.

X152. GOS, Charles
Song of the high hills. Ldn: Allen & Unwin, 1949. 224p. 21cm.
Haunting and wistful tale of romance and climbing around Zermatt. Good climbing episodes.

X153. GOWER, Janet
Snow in Austria. 1935.

X154. GRATRIX, Dawson
He and Ski. Ldn: Jenkins, [1929]. 312p. 20cm.

X155. GRAY, Berkeley
Lost world of Everest. Ldn: Children's Press, [1950]. 256p, plate. 21cm.
Several editions.
Story of cave dwellers inside the mountain.

X156. GREY, Rowland
In sunny Switzerland: a story of six weeks. Ldn: Kegan Paul, 1884. ix, 274p. [8vo].
Story centring on Zermatt.

X157. GROGGER, Paula
The door in the Grimming. N.Y.: Putnam, 1936.

X158. GROVES, Paul
The climber. Ldn: Hutchinson, 1977. Softback.

X159. HALE, M.
Empire in Arumac.
Thriller set in the Andes.

X160. HALLIDAY, L.
Top secret.
Thriller.

X161. HAMILTON, Cosmo
The mountain climber. 1905.
Farce in 3 acts. Opened in London at the Comedy Theatre, November 21, 1905.

X162. HAMMOND, Marc
Killer mountain. Futura Publications, 1980. 320p. Softback.
Thriller involving fugitives and a crashed aeroplane in the mountains of Jugoslavia.

X163. HAN SUYIN (pseud. Elizabeth Comber)
The mountain is young. Ldn: Cape, 1958. 578p. 20cm.
—Another ed. 1976.
Early chapters gossip about the Kathmandu political arena. Chapter in the mountains.

X164. HARDING, G.
Sky trap.
Thriller set in the Drakensberg.

X165. HARDY, Ronald
The face of Jalanath. Ldn: Cassell/N.Y.: Putnam, 1973. 200p. 21cm.
—Sphere paperback, 1974.
—Another ed. N.Y.: Pyramid Books, 1976. 254p. Softback.
Secret mission from Kashmir Himalaya into Chinese territory; good climbing episodes.

X166. HARPER, Frank
Night climb: the story of the Skiing 10th. Ldn/N.Y.: Longmans, 1946. [6], 216p. 22cm.
Fictional account, based on fact, of U.S. mountain troops fighting in Europe during World War II.

X167. HARRADEN, Beatrice
Out of the wreck I rise. Ldn: Nelson/ : Stokes, 1912. 383p.
The central character, a swindler, kills himself by getting caught in an avalanche.

X168. HART-DAVIS, Duff
Heights of Rimring. Ldn: Cape, 1980. 332p. 23cm.
Spy thriller set in Nepal involving Tibetan exiles and the Dalai Lama's treasure.

X169. HARTLEY, Norman
The viking process. Ldn: Collins, 1976. 225p.
Thriller with some climbing background.

X170. HARVESTER, Simon
Forgotten road. N.Y.: Walker, 1974. 190p.
Espionage in the Hindu Kush.

X171. HASTON, Dougal
Calculated risk. Ldn: Diadem, 1979. 190p. 23cm.
Climbing in Scotland and the Alps. Unfinished, posthumously published novel.

X172. HEALEY, Larry
The hoard of the Himalayas. N.Y.: Dodd Mead, 1981.

X173. HEALY, Ben
The Millstone men. Ldn: Hale, 1966.

X174. HERZOG, Gérard
Jackson's way. Trans. from the French by Hilary Davis. N.Y.: Farrar Strauss & Giroux, 1978. 281p.
—U.K. ed. entitled *The Jackson route.* Ldn: Collins, 1978. 252p. 22cm.
Alpine climbing story apparently based on the disaster on the Pillar of Frêney on the south side of Mont Blanc.

X175. HEWITT, Douglas
Mountain rescue. Ldn: Eyre & Spottiswoode, 1950.
—Another ed. Eyre & Spottiswoode, 1956. 251p.
North Wales setting. An escaped German prisoner of war is helped by a climber in a 3-day man-hunt.

X176. HILL, Peter
The enthusiast. Boston: Houghton Mifflin, 1979.

X177. HILTON, James (1900-54)
Lost horizon. 1933.
Famous story about a mysterious Tibetan monastery called Shangri La.

X178. HJORTSBERG, William
Alp: a comedy. N.Y.: Simon & Schuster, 1969.
—U.K. ed. Barrie & Jenkins, 1970.
—Another ed. N.Y.: Ballantyne Books, 1971.
Humorous and mildly pornographic story set in the Alps. First ascent of the north face of 'Juggernaut'. Black comedy, very appealing to climbers conversant with mountaineering literature.

X179. HOCKING, Silas Kitto (1850-1935)
The great hazard. Ldn: Fisher Unwin, 1915. 383p. 20cm.
Novel with some Alpine climbing in it. Author very popular in his heyday.

X180. HOGG, Garry
Climbers' glory. Ldn: Bodley Head, 1961. 157p. 19cm. (Earlham Library series)
Romance and rock-climbing in North Wales.

X181. HOLME, Daryl
The young mountaineer: or, Frank Miller's lot in life: the story of a Swiss boy. Ldn: Nimmo, 1874. vi, 282p, plates, illus. 18cm.

X182. HUBANK, Roger
North wall. Ldn: Hutchinson, 1977. [4], 191p, 21cm.
—U.S. ed. N.Y.: Viking, 1978. 198p.
—Another ed. N.Y.: Avon, 1979. 191p. 18cm. Softback.
Imaginary Alpine big-wall climb. One climber wants to die, the other doesn't.

X183. HUNTER, Alan
Gently to the summit. Ldn: Cassell, 1961. [8], 197p. 19cm.
A 'Gently' thriller. Superintendent Gently solves the mystery of a death on Snowdon.

X184. HURSTON, Zoro
The man of the mountain. Ldn: Dent, 1941. 319p. 19cm.

X185. INNES, Hammond
The lonely skier. Ldn: Collins, 1947.
—Fontana paperback ed. 1957. Numerous ptgs.
Thriller set in the Dolomites.

X186. JOHNSTON, Marjorie
The mountain speaks. Ldn: Cassell, 1938. v, 272p. 20cm.
Romance and climbing episodes in the Alps. Incidental climbing, with the inevitable rescue.

X187. JOHNSTON, M.
Pilgrim and the phoenix. Ldn: Hamilton, 1940. 303p. 19cm.

X188. JUDSON, W.
Winter kill. 1970. Adirondacks.

X189. KATZ, Robert
The spoils of Ararat. Boston: Houghton Mifflin, 1978.

X190. KEMBLE, Fanny [Francis Anne]
The adventures of Mr. Timothy Homespun in Switzerland. Ldn: 1889.

X191. KENT, Nora
Summer pilgrimage. Ldn: Macdonald, 1963. 190p.
The emotional entanglements of a Lake District walking party; scenery well described.

X192. KENT, N.
Twilight of Hester Lorimer. Ldn: Macdonald, 1965. 160p.
Murderous passions and climbing around Zermatt.

X193. KEROUAC, Jack
The Dharma bums. N.Y.: 1958.
—U.K. ed. Ldn: Deutsch, 1959.
—Panther paperback, 1972. R.P., 1974, 1977, 1980, 1982.
Two young men in search of Zen investigate the solitude of the high Sierras of California . By a famous novelist.

X194. KLIER, Henry
A summer gone. Ldn: Bles, 1959. 255p. 21cm.
Climbing near Innsbruck and on the north face of the Matterhorn.

X195. KNITTEL, John
Via mala. Stokes, 1935.

X196. KOSTKA, Matthew
Climb to the top. N.Y.: Doubleday, [1960]. 142p, illus.

X197. LAMBERT, D.
Kites of war.
Himalayan setting.

X198. LANG, P. S.
Where the soldanella grows. Ldn: Heath, Cranton & Ouseley, [1908]. 318p. 21cm.

X199. LANG, S.
The iron tooth/claw: a thrilling story of mystery and adventure in the Alps. Ldn: Henderson, [1906]. 64p.
Curious 'penny dreadful' describing the mountaineering exploits of two District Messenger boys in pursuit of criminals.

X200. LANGLEY, Bob
East of Everest. Ldn: Michael Joseph, 1984. [4], 252p. 23cm.
Spy thriller set against background of the highest and most remote mountains in the world.

X201. LANGLEY, B.
Traverse of the gods. Ldn: Michael Joseph, 1980. 251p.
—Sphere paperback, 1982. 242p.
Excellent thriller set on the Jungfrau and north face of the Eiger.

X202. LATHEN, Emma
Pick up sticks. N.Y.: Simon & Schuster, 1970. 192p.
—U.K. ed. Ldn: Gollancz, 1971.
—Arrow paperback. 1972. 224p.
Murder thriller which starts on the Appalachian Trail.

X203. LEADER, C.
Frontier of violence.
Himalayan setting.

X204. LE BLOND, Mrs Aubrey
The story of an Alpine winter. Ldn: Bell, 1907. vii, 289p. 19cm. R.P., 1914.
Romance and winter sports at St. Moritz and Davos.

X205. LEFEBURE, Molly
Scratch & Co.: the great cat expedition. Ldn: Gollancz, 1968. 158p, illus. 21cm.
—U.S. ed. N.Y.: Meredith, 1969. 183p, illus.
Delightful children's story of ascent of Scafell Pike in the Lake District, told in the style of an expedition book. Classic foil to Bowman's *Rum Doodle.*

X206. LERNER, L. A.
A free man. Ldn: Chatto & Windus, 1968.
Iceland setting.

X207. LEVER, Charles
The Dodd family abroad. Ldn: Chapman & Hall, 1859. 2v., plates, illus. 21cm.

X208. LLOYD, Marjorie
Fell Farm campers. Harmondsworth: Penguin Books. (Puffin paperback)
Children's series set in Lake district.

X209. LLOYD, M.
Fell Farm for Christmas. Harmondsworth: Penguin Books. (Puffin paperback)

X210. LLOYD, M.
Fell Farm holiday. Harmondsworth: Penguin Books, 1971. (Puffin paperback)
Camping and climbing in the Lake District.

X211. LLOYD, M.
Fell trek. Ldn: Hutchinson, ?

X212. LONGFELLOW, Henry Wadsworth
Hyperion: a romance. 1839.
—Another ed. Ldn: Walter Scott, 1857.
Included in *Prose writings of Longfellow.* (Camelot series). Pp. 1-206.
Alpine background.

X213. LUNN, Arnold H. M.
Family name. Ldn: Methuen, 1931.
Some Alpine climbing episodes; also some skiing.

X214. LUNN, Peter
Evil in high places. Ldn: Methuen, 1947. 255p. 20cm.
Thriller involving skiing.

X215. MACDONALD, Alexander
Through the heart of Tibet.

X216. MACHARDY, Charles
The ice mirror. Ldn: Collins, 1971.
—Fontana paperback. 1973.
Climbing story set in Scotland and on Eiger North Face.

X217. MACINNES, Hamish
Death reel. Ldn: Hodder, 1976. 192p.
Climax on a sea-stack off the rocky coast of the West Highlands of Scotland.

X218. MACINNES, Helen
Horizon. Ldn: Harrap, 1945. 168p.
—U.S. ed. N.Y.: Little Brown, 1946. 213p.
—Another ed. Severn House, 1975.
Thriller set in war-time Austrian Tyrol.

X219. MACKENZIE, N.
Seven days to death.
Thriller; Himalayan setting.

X220. MCLAREN, Amy
From a Davos balcony. Ldn: Duckworth, 1903. 307p. 20cm.

X221. MACLEAN, Alistair
Guns of Navarone.
Cliff climbing episode at beginning.

X222. MACLEOD, Robert (pseud. Bill Knox)
Path of ghosts. Long, 1971. 184p.
Thriller. Some climbing at end.

X223. MACNEIL, Duncan
Sadhu on the mountain peak. Ldn: Hodder, 1971. 286p.
A 'James Ogilvie' story. Set on the North-west Frontier, Khyber Pass and Afghan hills in the days of the British Raj.

X224. MCNEIL, Janet
Search party. Ldn: Hodder, 1959. 189p.
Much 'soul-searching' takes place while people are waiting for a search party to return. Set in Mountains of Mourne, Northern Ireland.

X225. MAIR, G. B.
Goddesses never die.
Thriller set in the Himalaya.

X226. MANFRED, K. M.
Peelah: or, The bewitched maiden of Nepal. Ldn: Swan Sonnenschein, 1904. 312p. [8vo]. Yak. M. 71.
Story about a mesmerized Anglo-Nepalese girl abducted from England to the forests of Nepal, and her escape.

X227. MANNIN, Ethel Edith (b.1900)
Late have I loved thee. Ldn: Jarrolds, 1948. 350p. 20cm.
—U.S. ed. N.Y.: Putnam, 1948.
—Another ed. Ldn: Hutchinson, 1949.
—Paperback.
Lengthy climbing section in Austrian Alps. Basically a novel about the Catholic faith.

X228. MANNIN, E. E.
Men are unwise. Ldn: Jarrolds, 1934. 287p.
—Paperback ed.
—New ed. Ldn: Severn House, 1976. 3-288p. 21cm.
Story of a man's desire to climb and the terrible consequences when he does.

X229. MANNIN, E. E.
Ragged banners. Ldn: Jarrolds, ?. 319p. 19cm.
—U.S. ed. N.Y.: Knopf, 1931.
—Penguin paperback.

X230. MANNING, Anne
An idyl of the Alps. Ldn: Hall, 1876. vi, 312p. 20cm.

X231. MANNING, A.
The year nine: a tale of the Tyrol. Ldn: Hall, Virtue, 1858. iv, 282p, plates, illus. 21cm.

X232. MANSFIELD, Ernest
Astria, the ice maiden. Ldn: Lonsdale Press, [1910]. 157p.
A romance of Spitzbergen.

X233. MASEFIELD, John
Sard Harker.
Hallucinatory climbing episode, crossing imaginary range in central America.

X234. MASON, Alfred Edward Woodley
The broken road. Ldn: Smith Elder, 1907.
—2nd ed. 1908. vi, 352p. 21cm.
Passing references to climbing in Dauphiné Alps. Basically a story set in India.

X235. MASON, A. E. W.
A romance of Wastdale. 1895.
—Another ed. Ldn: Hodder, [1914]. 160p, plates, illus. 16cm.
Jealousy and murder in the Lake District mountains. His first book and quite good although Mason considered it his worst.

X236. MASON, A. E. W.
Running water. Ldn: Hodder/N.Y: Century, 1907. 352p. 20cm.
—Another ed. Ldn: Collins, n.d. 282p, col. plates, illus. 16cm.
One of the most famous climbing novels, involving a murder plot on the Brenva ice-ridge on Mont Blanc.

X237. MASON, F. van Wyck
Himalayan assignment: a Colonel North novel. N.Y.: Doubleday, 1952. 282p.
—U.K. ed. Ldn: Hale, 1953. 287p. 20cm.
The wiles of two women and a desperate chase through a Himalyan blizzard.

X238. MASON, Richard Lakin
The fever tree. Ldn: Collins, 1962. 320p. Yak. M. 106.
Himalayan setting.

X239. MASTERS, John (1914-83)
Far, far the mountain peak. Ldn: Michael Joseph, 1957. 415p. 20cm.
—U.S. ed. N.Y.: Viking, 1957. 471p.
—Penguin paperback, 1961.
Obsessive ambition to reach the summit of a Himalayan peak. Includes an ascent of the Zmutt Ridge of the Matterhorn.

X240. MASTERS, J.
Himalayan concert/orchestra. Garden City, NY: Doubleday, 1976. 374p. Yak. M. 112.
Background interest.

X241. MASTERSON, W.
Man on a nylon string. Ldn: W. H. Allen/N.Y.: Dodd Mead, 1963. 223p.

—Mayflower paperback 1969.
—Pinnacle paperback 1975.
Thriller in Eigerwand-type setting. Fair amount of climbing.

X242. MATHER, Berkeley
The break in the line. Ldn: Collins, 1970.
—U.S. ed. entitled *The break.* N.Y.: Scribner's, 1970.
Thriller; climax in Himalaya.

X243. MATHER, B.
The pass beyond Kashmir. Ldn: Collins/N.Y.: Scribner's, 1969. 256p.
Spy thriller; climax in Chinese Tibet.

X244. MATHIESON, Eric
Mountain month. Ldn: Hamilton, 1965. 158p.
Story of boys' adventure course in the Lake District. Some climbing and a rescue.

X245. MAYHEW, Henry (1812-87) & Athol
Mont Blanc: a comedy in three acts. First produced at the Threatre Royal, Haymarket, Whit Monday, May 25, 1874. Ldn: The Authors, 1874. 61p. [8vo]. Adapted from: *Le voyage de Monsieur Perrichon* by Eugène Labiche and Edouard Martin (Paris, 1860).
The production ran for three weeks. Henry Mayhew, an English humorist, was one of the originators of *Punch* magazine in 1841.

X246. MEADER, Stephen
Behind the rangers. N.Y.: Harcourt Brace, 1947.
Young adult adventure story set in the Olympic Mountains, Washington State.

X247. MERRICK, Hugh (pseud. Harold A. Meyer) (1898-1980)
Andreas at sundown. Ldn: Hale, 1944. 320p.
An Alpine guide sits in the evening sunshine and retrospects on his life, loves and climbs. Merrick's most charming and plausible novel.

X248. MERRICK, H.
The breaking strain. Ldn: Constable, 1950. 312p.
An incompetent climber leads his party into disaster on an Alpine peak.

X249. MERRICK, H.
Out of the night. Ldn: Hale, 1957. 158p.
An ageing climber embarks on his last Alpine climb with fatal consequences.

X250. MERRICK, H.
Pillar of the sky. Ldn: Eyre & Spottiswoode, 1941. R.P., 1942.
Romance, adventure and a search for a mysterious Himalayan peak. Starts in the Lake District.

X251. MERRICK, H.
Savoy episode. Ldn: Hale, 1946. 192p, 32 plates, illus. 22cm.
This book is supposed to be fiction but is not recognizable as such.

X252. MERRIMAN, Henry Seaton (pseud. Hugh Stowell Scott) (1862-1903)
The slave of the lamp. Ldn: Murray, 1892.
—New ed. Smith, Elder, 1905. 354.
—Another ed. 1916. 327p.
Semi-thriller; includes a climb on a sea-cliff. His first real success as a writer.

X253. MEYERS, Patrick
K2. N.Y.: Dramatists Play Service Inc., 1983. 45p, plate, illus. 20cm.
Stage-play.

X254. MOFFAT, Gwen
Corpse road. Ldn: Gollancz, 1974. 224p. 21cm.
Thriller set in northern Pennines; includes skiing, etc. The author was a professional mountain guide.

X255. MOFFAT, G.
Deviant death. Ldn: Gollancz, 1973. 21p. R.P., 1974.
Thriller set in Derbyshire dales; caving etc.

X256. MOFFAT, G.
Die like a dog. Ldn: Gollancz, 1982. 160p. 21cm.
Thriller set in Snowdonia.

X257. MOFFAT, G.
Grizzly trail.
A 'Miss Pink' thriller. Miss Pink is the author's tough, middle-aged spinster detective.

X258. MOFFAT, G.
Hard option. Ldn: Gollancz, 1975. 222p. 21cm.
An ageing mountain rescue team leader is reluctantly forced to accept that he is no longer capable of great flights of love and rock-climbing; set in Wales.

X259. MOFFAT, G.
Lady with a cool eye. Ldn: Gollancz, 1973. 192p. 21cm. Also 2nd ptg.
Her first novel. Thriller set in North Wales, introducing her amateur detective Miss Pink.

X260. MOFFAT, G.
Miss Pink at the edge of the world. Ldn: Gollancz/N.Y.: Scribner's, 1975. 206p. 21cm.
Thriller set in Scotland; climbs on a sea-stack.

X261. MOFFAT, G.
Over the sea to death. Ldn: Gollancz/N.Y.: Scribner's, 1976. 192p, map. 21cm.
Thriller set in an imaginary valley near the Cuillin mountains in Skye.

X262. MOFFAT, G.
Persons unknown. Ldn: Gollancz, 1978. 174p. 21cm.
Thriller set in west Wales.

X263. MOFFAT, G.
Short time to live. 1977.

X264. MOHR, Max
Philip Glen. Ldn: Sedgwick & Jackson, [1932].
Alpine climbing and skiing.

X265. MONCRIEFF, Ascott Robert Hope
Seeing the world: adventures of a young mountaineer. Ldn: Wells Gardner Darton, 1909. vii, 296p. 22cm.

X266. MONTAGUE, C. E.
Action and other stories. Ldn: Chatto & Windus, 1928.
Alpine ice climbing in short story called 'Action'.

X267. MONTAGUE, C. E.
Fiery particles. Ldn: Chatto & Windus, 1923.
Includes the most famous of all climbing short stories, 'In Hanging Garden Gully'.

X268. MONTAGUE, C. E.
The morning's war. Ldn: Methuen, 1913. 308p. 21cm.
Said to have two good chapters on Alpine climbing.

X269. MONTGOMERY, Elizabeth Rider
Three miles an hour. N.Y.: Dodd Mead, 1952. 245p.
Young adult story set in the Olympic Mountains, Pacific North-west.

X270. MONTOLIEU, Isabelle, Baronne de
The avalanche; or, The old man of the Alps: a tale. Trans. from the French. Ldn: H. N. Batten, 1829. 78p, plates, illus. 18cm.

X271. MOODY, Laurence
The young kings. Ldn: Davies, 1960.

X272. MORGAN, Joan
He lives amid clouds. Ldn: Chapman & Hall, 1947. 199p.

X273. MUIR, Ward
The amazing mutes: their week in lovely Lucerne. Ldn: Simpkin Marshall, [1919]. 189p. 19cm.

X274. MUNDY, Talbot
Ramsden. Ldn: Hutchinson, [1926].
Climbing, etc. in the Himalaya.

X275. MUNROE, Kirk
Rick Dale. N.Y.: Harpers, 1896.
—U.K. ed. Ldn: Arnold, [1896]. viii, 333p, illus.
Includes description of imaginary ascent of Mount Rainier.

X276. MURPHY, Tom
Aspen incident. N.Y.: St. Martin's, 1978.

X277. MURRAY, Jane W.
Walk the high horizon. Philadelphia: Westminster, 1979. 144p.

X278. MURRAY, William Hutchinson (b.1913)
Dark rose the phoenix. Ldn: Secker & Warburg, 1965. 223p.
—U.S. ed. N.Y.: Mackay, 1965.

X279. MURRAY, W. H.
Five frontiers; appointment in Tibet. Ldn: Dent, 1959.
—U.S. ed. entitled *Appointment in Tibet.* N.Y.: Putnams, 1959. 284p, maps. 21cm.
Spy thriller ranging from the Hebrides, to the Maritime Alps, & to Nepal.

X280. MURRAY, W. H.
Maelstrom. Ldn: Secker & Warburg, 1962. 253p. 19cm.
More sailing than climbing; set in the Western Highlands.

X281. MURRAY, W. H.
Spurs of Troodos. Ldn: Dent, 1960. 203p, map.
Thriller mostly set in Cyprus; sequel to *Five frontiers.*

X282. NAILLEN, A. van der
On the heights of the Himalay. N.Y.: Fenno, 1900. 272p. 20cm.

X283. NEWMAN, Terry
No more a brother. Ldn: Cassell, 1958. 208p.
Climax involves mountain accident to hero's brother; passing references to climbing throughout. Alpine.

X284. NICOLAYSEN, Bruce
Perilous passage. Chicago: Playboy, 1976.

X285. NOEL, Sybille
Magic bird of Chomo-Lung-Ma: tales of Mount Everest, the Turquoise Peak. Illustrated by A. Avinoff. Garden City, NY: Doubleday Doran, 1931. [10], 310p, 6 plates, illus. 24cm. Not in Yakushi.

X286. NOYCE, Wilfrid
The gods are angry. Ldn: Heinemann/Cleveland, NY: World Pub, 1957. 198p.
Ascent of a Himalayan peak. A story portraying varying reactions of the climbers — to the mountain, their families, jobs and the Sherpas.

X287. OPPENHEIM, Edwin Camillo
Some peaks. Ldn: Fisher Unwin, 1898.

X288. OWEN, Richard
Eye of the gods. N.Y.: Dutton, 1978.

X289. OXENHAM, John (1852-1941)
Quest for the golden rose. Ldn: Methuen, 1912.
—9th ed. 1919. 294p.

X290. OXENHAM, J.
Their high adventure. Ldn: Hodder, [1910]. 319p.

X291. PEMBERTON, Max (1863-1950)
White motley. Ldn: Cassell, 1913. 340p, plate.
Story of flying over the Alps, crime and romance.

X292. PETERS, E.
Piper on the mountains. Ldn: Collins, 1966.
Thriller set in the Low Tatras. Daughter sets out to discover how and why her father died.

X293. PHELPS, G.
Winter people.
Andes setting.

X294. PHILLIPPS-WOLLEY, Clive
Snap: a legend of the Lone Mountain. Ldn: Longmans, 1889. [x], 310p, 11 plates, illus. 19cm.
—New ptg. 1899.
Some climbing episodes. The author was a travel writer.

X295. PLEYDELL, Susan
Brighouse Hotel. Ldn: Collins, 1977. 221p.
Romance, climbing and mountain rescue, set in Scotland.

X296. POPE, Marion Manville
Up the Matterhorn in a boat. N.Y.: Century, 1897. x, 199p, illus.
Ballooning story; also appeared in magazine form.

X297. POPHAM, Hugh
Beyond the eagle's rage. Ldn: Bodley Head, 1951.

X298. PURSLOW, Richard
Sleep till noonday. Ldn: Heinemann, [1963]. 221p, map. 21cm.
Rock-climbing in North Wales; big climax on Clogwyn du'r Arddu.

X299. RAMUZ, Charles-Ferdinand
When the mountain fell. N.Y.: Pantheon, 1947.
—U.K. ed. Ldn: Eyre & Spottiswoode, 1949. 221p. 19cm. From the original: *Derborence* (Paris: Grasset, 1936).
Two men buried alive in a landslide.

X300. RAMUZ, C.-F.
Terror on the mountain. N.Y.: Harcourt Brace, 1967. From the original: *La grande peur dans la montagne* (Paris: Grasset, 1925).

X301. RAYMOND, Diana
The climb. Ldn: Cassell, 1962. [6], 217p. 21cm.
Eigerwand-type story.

X302. RAYMOND, D.
The dark journey. Ldn: Cassell, 1978. 146p.

X303. RAYMOND, Ernest
Five sons of Le Faber. c.1948.
—Ldn: Book Club, 1948. 296p.
Passing references to climbing in the Lake District.

X304. RAYMOND, E.
The mountain farm. Ldn: Cassell, 1966. 280p. 21cm.
Romance and climbing in the Lake District.

X305. RAYMOND, E.
Nameless places. Ldn: Cassell, 1954. [6], 282p. 21cm.
Pseudo-Lake District setting; main story nothing to do with climbing.

X306. RAYMOND, George
The lone hut: or, A legend of Mont Blanc. A drama in two acts. as represented at the Theatre Royal, Lyceum. Ldn: Olivier, 1842. 38p.

X307. RECHER, Robert
Rudi of the mountains. Edinburgh: Oliver & Boyd, 1964. 160p.
Young adult story about some children and a young alpine guide.

X308. REES, Lucy & HARRIS, Al
Take it to the limit. Ldn: Diadem, 1981. 197p. 23cm.
Sex and climbing in North Wales; climax on a Yosemite climb.

X309. REID, Mayne
The cliff-climbers: or, The lone home in the Himalayas. Sequel to the 'Plant Hunters'. Boston: Tichnor Fields, 1865. 304p, illus. 18cm.
—Another ed. Boston: Osgood, 1871.
—Another ed. N.Y.: Miller, 1880.

X310. REID, M.
The plant hunters: or, Adventures among the Himalayas. Ldn: J. & C. Brown, 1858. vii, 482p, 12 plates, illus. 17cm.
—Another ed. Ldn & N.Y.: Routledge, 1890. vii, 482p, illus. 17cm. Yak. R. 79.

X311. RENAULT, Mary
North face. Ldn: Longmans, 1949. 318p.
—U.S. ed. N.Y.: Morrow, 1949?
Slight references to climbing.

X312. RIDEING, William H.
Boys in the mountains and on the plains. N.Y.: Appleton, 1882.

X313. RIDER, A.
Light affliction.
Himalaya setting.

X314. RITA (pseud. Eliza Margaret Humphreys) (-1938)
Edelweiss, a romance. Ldn: Spencer Blackett, 1890. 160p. 19cm.

X315. ROBERTS, David
Like water and like wind. S.F.: Sierra Club, 1980. Published as pp. 105-166 of *Ascent 1980.*
Alaskan mountaineering. A climber claims an ascent he feels morally entitled to, with terrible consequences.

X316. ROOKE, Daphne
Boy on the mountain. Ldn: Gollancz, 1969. 192p. 21cm.
Story of a group of young people growing up, set in Westland, New Zealand. Includes climbing in imaginary setting.

X317. RUMNEY, A. Wren
The dalesman. Kendal: Titus Wilson, 1911. 219p, plates, illus. 24cm.

X318. RUMSEY, Marian
Danger on Shadow Mountain. N.Y.: Morrow, 1970. 160p, illus.

X319. SALTER, James
Solo faces. Boston: Little Brown, 1979/Ldn: Collins, 1980. 220p.
Climbing in the Alps around Chamonix. Starts in California. Modern classic.

X320. SANDBERG, Peter Lars
Wolf Mountain. Chicago: Playboy Press/Ldn: Arthur Barker, 1975. 311p. 21cm.
Two psychotic killers terrorize a party of schoolgirls in a mountain hut. Set in Colorado Rockies; some climbing.

X321. SANDERS, Lawrence
The first deadly sin. N.Y.: Putnam's, 1973. —Paperback ed. 18th ptg. 1974. 576p.
Starts and ends with rock-climbing sequences. Murder, sex and perversion in the life of a New York City climber.

X322. SAYERS, Dorothy
Five red herrings. Ldn: Gollancz, 1931.
Crime and climbing in Scotland. A 'Lord Peter Wimsey' story.

X323. SCHMIDTMAN, Waldemar
Devil, the life story of a chamois. N.Y.: Century, (1926 or 1936?)

X324. SCHULTZE-SMIDT, B.
A madonna of the Alps. Boston: Little Brown, 1895. 207p, plate.

X325. SCOTT, J. M.
Other half of the orange. Ldn: Heinemann/N.Y.: Dutton, 1955. [4], 241p.
Mystery and romance, searching for a man believed dead. Climbing in Mont Blanc range.

X326. SCOTT, J. M.
Other side of the moon. Ldn: Hodder, 1946.

X327. SCOTT, J. M.
The silver land. Ldn: Hodder, 1937.

X328. SCOTT, J. M.
Touch of the nettle. Ldn: Hodder, 1951. 255p. 20cm.
Thriller set in the Italian Alps. Climax on storm-swept summits pursued by armed enemies.

X329. SCOTT, J. M.
The will and the way. Ldn: Hodder/N.Y.: Dutton, 1949. 251p.
A complicated literary Alpine treasure-hunt on and around Monte Rosa involving a group of beneficiaries to a will.

X330. 'SCRAMBLE, Edward'
Whimpers amongst the Alps. Ldn, 1923. 226p, plates, illus. 22 × 15cm, tapering to 10cm at top.
Ill-fated attempt on the 'Maulwurfshaufen' (Molehill).

X331. SHAW, Robin
Running. Ldn: Gollancz, 1974?
An ex-convict and a bored poetry professor plan the perfect crime whilst climbing together in Maine.

X332. SMITH, Albert Richard (1816-60)
Struggles and adventures of Christopher Tadpole at home and abroad. Ldn: Willoughby, 1848.
Chapter 39, 'Mrs Hamper wishes to ascend Mont Blanc'.

X333. SMITH, Chris Judge & HUTCHINSON, J. Maxwell
The ascent of Wilberforce III (The White Hell of Iffish Adorabad). Originally commissioned for the Traverse Theatre, Edinburgh and put on later in altered form at the Lyric Studio, Hammersmith, during January, 1982.

A high altitude musical extravaganza. Satire on politically motivated mountaineering expeditions.

X334. SMYTHE, Frank
Secret mission. Ldn: Hodder, 1942. 256p. 19cm.
A 'ripping yarn' set in the Himalaya, involving a British scientist, his beautiful daughter and Nazi thugs.

X335. SNEYD-KYNNERSLEY, E. M.
A snail's wooing: story of an Alpine courtship. Ldn: Macmillan, 1910. 344p.
Climbing and life around Zermatt before World War I.

X336. SNOW, Charles H.
The seven peaks. Wright, 1936.

X337. SPILKEN, Aron & O'LEARY, Ed
Burning moon. Chicago: Playboy Press, 1979.

X338. SPYRI, Johanna
Heidi. [Numerous editions]
Story of an orphan girl left with her grandfather to live a lonely life high up in the Alps. Well-known children's book.

X339. STABLES, William Gordon (1840-1910)
In regions of perpetual snow. Ldn: Ward Lock, 1904. viii, 316p, col. illus.
Story of adventure on the glaciers of the Himalaya by well-known Scottish writer of boys' books.

X340. STAPP, Arthur D.
Mountain tamer. N.Y.: Morrow, 1948. 220p, plate.

X341. STEIN, Aaron Marc
Alp murder. N.Y.: Doubleday, 1970. 159p.

X342. STEWART, Cochrane
Windslab. Ldn: Hodder, 1952. 253p, 3 maps.
Set in an Austrian mountain hut, soon after the end of the war. The occupants are threatened by a cornice and slope of windslab snow.

X343. STEWART, Mary
Wildfire at midnight. Ldn: Hodder, 1956. 224p, map. 21cm.
—Paperback ed.
Thriller set in Skye; climbing episodes.

X344. STIMSON, F. J.
Mrs Knollys and other stories. N.Y., 1897.

X345. STRATZ, Rudolph
Where snow is sovereign: a romance of the glaciers. Trans. from the German by Mary Safford. N.Y.: Dodd Mead, 1909. 282p, 12 plates, illus. 19cm.
Focuses on women climbing with guides.

X346. STRAWBRIDGE, Anne W.
Above the rainbow. Stackpole, 1938.
Psychological novel with mountaineering episodes.

X347. STRAWBRIDGE, A. W.
Dawn after danger. N.Y.: Coward McCann, 1934.
Mountaineering episodes.

X348. STYLES, Showell
The camp in the hills. Ldn: Benn, 1964.

X349. STYLES, S.
Journey with a secret. Meredith Press,
—Reissued as *Mystery of the fleeing girl.* N.Y.: Scholastic Book Services, 1970. 190p. Paperback.
Young adult story of a chase across Welsh hills avoiding both police and spies.

X350. STYLES, S.
Kami the Sherpa. Leicester: Brockhampton Press, 1957. 144p. 22cm.
A teenage English boy and a young Sherpa attempt to rescue members of a Himalayan climbing party.

X351. STYLES, S.
Ladder of snow. Ldn: Gollancz/N.Y.: Vanguard, 1962. 189p. 21cm.
—Paperback ed.
Second 'Hughes' story; climbing in the Swiss Alps.

X352. STYLES, S.
The lost glacier. Ldn: Hart-Davis, 1955. 158p.
—U.S. ed. N.Y.: Vanguard, 1956. 192p.
Thriller; climbing in the Himalayas.

X353. STYLES, S.
Lost pothole. Leicester Brockhampton Press, 1961.
—Book club ed.
Two boys hunt for an ancient pothole which contains treasure.

X354. STYLES, S.
Necklace of glaciers. Ldn: Gollancz, 1963.
—Paperback ed.
Third 'Hughes' story; climbing in the Austrian Tyrol. Thriller.

X355. STYLES, S.
Pass of morning. Ldn: Gollancz, 1966. 128p, map.
—U.S. ed. N.Y.: Washburn, 1966. 119p.
—Paperback ed.
Fourth 'Hughes' story; set in Norway. Thriller.

X356. STYLES, S.
Shadow Buttress. Ldn: Faber, 1959. 255p.
A Scottish guide goes blind but wins his way back to the mountains.

X357. STYLES, S.
Sherpa adventure. Illustrated from the author's sketches by Matvyn Wright. N.Y.: Vanguard, 1860. 191p, illus. 21cm. Yak. S. 384.
Story of a youth's conquest of fear, set in the snows and silences of the Himalayas. [Same as X350?]

X358. STYLES, S.
Shop in the mountains. Ldn: Gollancz, 1961. 191p, illus, map. 21cm.
—Paperback ed.
The first story about Simon and Mag Hughes; climbing in North Wales.

X359. STYLES, S.
Snowdon rangers. Ldn: Faber, 1970.
Young adult story of rock-climbing in North Wales.

X360. STYLES, S.
A tent on top. 1971.

X361. STYLES, S.
Tiger Patrol. c.1960.
—New ed. Ldn: Collins, 1966.
Story about a party of Boy Scouts; includes a little climbing.

X362. STYLES, S.
Tiger Patrol presses on. Ldn: Collins, 1961.
Sequel to *Tiger patrol.*

X363. STYLES, S.
Traitor's mountain. N.Y.: Macmillan, 1946. 311p. 19cm.
First appearance of detective Lewker (see books by 'Glyn Carr') in fast-moving spy thriller.

X364. SUTCLIFFE, Constance
Our Lady of the ice: a story of the Alps. Ldn: Greening, 1901. 260p.
—Another ed. Greening, 1909. 128p. 22cm.
An Alpine guide loses his client, then dies saving the brother.

X365. SUTTON, Graham
Damnation of Mr. Zinkler. Ldn: Cape, 1935. 347p.
Clever story of an injured climber's ascent out of Hades, back to life. Classic.

X366. SUTTON, G.
Fell days. 1948.
Mixture of essays and fictional stories; mostly Lake District related.

X367. SYMONDS, Margaret
A child of the Alps. Ldn: Fisher Unwin, 1920. 364p. 20cm. (First novel library series)
Story of a girl's mingled artistic and peasant nature.

X368. TALBOT, Daniel (Editor)
A treasury of mountaineering stories. N.Y.: Putnam, 1954. 337p. 21cm. R.P., 1956.
—U.K. ed. Ldn: Peter Davies, 1955. x, 282p. 21cm.
Volume of chiefly fictional mountain and climbing stories and extracts.

X369. TATHAM, H. F. W.
The footprints in the snow and other tales: with a memoir by A. C. Benson. Ldn: Macmillan, 1910. xxvii, 187p, plates, illus. 22cm.

X370. TAYLOR, Gordon
Place of the dawn.
—Paperback ed. Avon Books, 1975.
Romance and adventure set in mountains of eastern Turkey. A woman archaeologist on a pleasure climb is hunted by villagers seeking revenge.

X371. THORNE, Guy
The greater power: [a story of the present campaign in Italy]. Ldn: Gale & Polden, [1915]. vii, 184p. 19cm.
Refers to World War I in Italy, including hauling big guns up precipices.

X372. TOBIAS, Michael Charles
Deva. San Diego: Avant Books, 1982. 182p, illus. Softback.
Three young climbers pursue the ultimate ascent.

X373. TODD, Ruthven
Over the mountain. Ldn: Harrap, 1939. 218p.
—Another ed. Falcon Press, 1939.
Mountaineering allegory about democracy and fascism.

X374. TOWNEND, Paul
Man on the end of the rope. Ldn: Collins/N.Y.: Dutton, 1960. 256p.
—Fontana paperback 1962.
Eigerwand story; thriller.

X375. TOWNEND, P.
Died O'Wednesday. Ldn, 1959.
—U.S. ed. N.Y.: Walker, 1962.

X376. TRACY, Louis
The silent barrier. Ldn: Ward Lock, [1908?]. 320p, illus.
Love, climbing and attempted crime; set in the Upper Engadine of the Swiss Alps.

X377. TRANTER, Nigel
Cable from Kabul. Ldn: Hodder, 1968. 188p. 21cm.
Thriller set in the Hindu Kush-Karakoram.

X378. TRANTER, N.
Rio d'Oro.
Andes setting.

X379. TREVANIAN
Eiger sanction. N.Y.: Crown, 1972. 316p. Several ptgs.
—U.K. ed. Ldn: Heinemann, 1973. 229p.
—Panther paperback.
Secret service killings. Climbs and climax on Eigerwand. Filmed with Clint Eastwood.

X380. TROYAT, Henri
The mountain. Trans. from the French by Constantine Fitzgibbon. 1953.
—U.S. ed. N.Y.: Simon & Schuster, 1953. 122p.
—Paperback ed.
Two Alpine guides, brothers of vastly different character, set out to rescue survivors of an aeroplane crash. Filmed with Spencer Tracy.

X381. TUGWELL, George
On the mountain, being the Welsh experiences of Abraham Black and Jonas White, Esquires, moralists, photographers, fishermen, and botanists. Ldn: R. Bentley, 1862. viii, 262p, col. plates, illus. 20cm.

X382. TUSHKAN, Georgi
The hunter of the Pamirs: a novel of adventure in Soviet Central Asia. Trans. from the Russian by Gerard Shelley. Ldn: Hutchinson, [1944]. 372p. 26cm. Yak. T. 143.

X383. TWAIN, Mark (pseud. Samuel Langhorne Clemens) (1835-1910)
A tramp abroad. Hartford, 1879.
—U.K. ed. Ldn: Chatto, 1880.
—New ed. 1889. 564p.
—New ed. 1896.
Tongue-in-cheek semi-fictional account of travel in Europe, with mountaineering episodes. Classic.

X384. ULLMAN, James Ramsay
And not to yield. N.Y: Doubleday/Ldn: Collins, 1970. 444p. 22cm.
Long discursive story set against the background of a Himalayan peak.

X385. ULLMAN, J. R.
Banner in the sky. Philadelphia: Lippincott, 1954. 252p.
—U.K. ed. Ldn: Collins, 1955. 254p. 20cm.
—Fontana paperback, 1958.
—Special edition for children, 1959.
—Abridged version 1961 entitled *Third man on the mountain.* Filmed under this title with Michael Rennie.
—Peacock paperback, 1963.
—Puffin paperback, 1968.
—Another ed. Evergreen edition, 1969.
Young adult story loosely based on the first ascent of the Matterhorn.

X386. ULLMAN, J. R.
Sands of Karakoram: a fable. Philadelphia: Lippincott/Ldn: Collins, 1953. 256p. 20cm.
—Another ed. N.Y.: Bantam Books, 1955. 151p. 18cm.
Set in an area north of the Altai Mountains, north-west of the Gobi Desert.

X387. ULLMAN, J. R.
The White Tower. Philadelphia: Lippincott, 1945. 479p, illus (endpapers). 21cm. Also 2nd ptg.
—U.K. ed. Ldn: Collins, 1946. 479p. 21cm.
—Fontana paperback, 1954.
—Mayflower/Dell paperback, 1966.
—Another ed. 1973.
Story of climbers ascending an Alpine peak of Himalayan proportions for nationalistic motives.

X388. VAIDYA, Suresh
Kailas. Queensway Press, 1937.

X389. VAUGHAN, Owen
Vronina: a tale of the Welsh mountains.
—Reissued. Ldn: Duckworth, [1912]. viii, 309p. 19cm.
Good description of mountain scenery and the enjoyment of it; a little climbing.

X390. VIGNANT, Jean-François
The Alpine affair. N.Y.: Chelsea House Pub, 1970.

X391. WALES, Hubert
The thirty days. Ldn: Cassell, [1915]. 312p. 19cm.
Thriller; starts with an ascent of Mont Blanc. A tale of spiritualism.

X392. WALSH, Maurice (1879-1964)
The hill is mine: a tale of the Cairngorms. Ldn: Chambers, 1940. 351p. 18cm.

X393. WALSH, M.
The key above the door. Ldn: Chambers, 1923. Various editions.
His best known book. Slight references to Skye; general Scottish background.

X394. WARD E. M.
Alpine rose. Ldn: Methuen, 1934.
Alpine background story.

X395. WARD, E. M.
Dancing Ghyll. Ldn: Methuen, 1937.
Lake District background story.

X396. WARD, E. M.
Mountain water.
Background only.

X397. WARDEN, Gertrude
The crime in the Alps. Ldn: White, 1908. vii, 311p. 21cm.
Thriller with a booby-trapped pocket barometer set to explode at a certain height.

X398. WATKINS, Olga
Tales from the Tyrol. Edinburgh: Blackwood, 1935. 331p. 21cm.

X399. WELLS, Herbert George (1866-1946)
Ann Veronica. 1909.
—Another ed. Ldn: Newnes, [1913]. 318p, plates. 23cm.
—Everyman Library ed. Ldn: Dent.
One chapter on climbing in Switzerland.

X400. WESTALL, William
Her two millions. 1887. 3v.
—N.Y.: Harpers, 1887.
—Ldn: Ward & Downey, [c.1890]. 388p.
Story set mainly in Switzerland and partly on the Mont Blanc range. Husband pushes his wife into a crevasse.

X401. WEVERKA, Robert
Avalanche. Based on the screenplay by Claude Pola. N.Y.: Bantam Books, 1978. 181p. 18cm. Paperback.
A major motion picture starring Rock Hudson and Mia Farrow.

X402. WHITE, Jon Manchip
Nightclimber. Ldn: Chatto & Windus, 1968.
—U.S. ed. N.Y.: Morrow, 1970.
A Cambridge nightclimber and art historian turns thief to satisfy his passion for collecting and is blackmailed into investigating a mysterious cave which has an evil secret.

X403. WILLIAMSON, C. N. & A. M.
The Princess Virginia. Ldn: Methuen, [1913]. 219p.
Starts with a climbing adventure.

X404. WILSON, Leigh
Do you go back dismayed? Ldn: Methuen, 1949. [6], 202p. 19cm.
Climber masters his fear and returns to Himalayas to seek friend taken prisoner by savage tribesmen.

X405. WINGATE, John
Avalanche. Ldn: Weidenfeld & Nicolson, 1977. 153p, map. 23cm.
Thriller set in the Tyrol; comparatively slight mountaineering interest.

X406. WISE, Harold
Mountain man. Ldn: Skeffington, 1934.

X407. WOLPERT, Stanley
The expedition. Ldn: Cassell, 1967.
—U.S. ed. Boston: Little Brown, 1968. 337p.
Long lead up to a yeti hunt at the end of the book.

X408. YATES, Elizabeth
High holiday: a story of the Swiss Alps. Ldn: Black, 1938.
—2nd ed. 1945. [6], 129p, illus. 23cm.
Pleasant young adult story of Alpine climbing.

X409. YATES, E.
Climbing higher. Ldn: Black, 1939.

X410. YONGE, Charlotte M.
The dove in the eagle's nest. Ldn: Macmillan, 1866. 2v.
—2nd ed. 1869. 1v. R.P., 1871-79 (6 times) with illustrations.
—Reprinted 1890-1907 (11 times)
—Shilling ed. 1908. 293p, plate. 18cm.
A tale of mediaeval Germany with mountain references (e.g. Theuerdank; see G16).

X411.
Adventure stories for boys. Ldn: Hamlyn, 1967. Several ptgs. Pp.107-169. 'High quest'.
Two young men re-enact their grandfathers' climb, to find out what happened.

JOURNALS

Africa

j01. *Mount Kenya Monthly Magazine.* Nanyuki: The Magazine. 33cm. No. 1, 1936-?

j02. **MOUNTAIN CLUB OF EAST AFRICA**
Ice-cap: being the journal of the Mountain Club of East Africa. Moshi: The Club. 26cm. No.1, 1932-?

j03. **MOUNTAIN CLUB OF EAST AFRICA (Kenya Section)**
Bulletin. Nairobi: The Section. 25-36cm. No. 1, 1946-No. 10, 1949. Continued by: Bulletin of Mountain Club of Kenya.

j04. **MOUNTAIN CLUB OF KENYA**
Bulletin. Nairobi: The Club. 21-25cm. No. 11, June 1949-? Frequency varies. Continues: Bulletin of Mountain Club of East Africa (Kenya Section).

j05. **MOUNTAIN CLUB OF NATAL**
Annual. Maritzburg: The Club. 23-24cm. No. 1, 1920-?

j06. **MOUNTAIN CLUB OF RHODESIA**
Mountain Club of Rhodesia Journal. Salisbury: The Club. 22cm. Issues irregular. V.2, 1960?; v.5, 1970; v.6, 1972; v.7, 1974-5.

j07. **MOUNTAIN CLUB OF SOUTH AFRICA**
Annual of the M.C. of S.A. Cape Town: Cape Town Section. 25cm. No. 1, 1894-No. 33, 1930. Continued by: Journal of M.C. of S.A.

j08. **MOUNTAIN CLUB OF SOUTH AFRICA**
Journal of M.C. of S.A. Cape Town Section. 23cm. No. 34, 1931 — in progress. Annual issues. Continues: Annual of M.C. of S.A. Index; v.1-71, 1894-1968.

j09. **MOUNTAIN CLUB OF UGANDA**
Bulletin. Kampala: The Club. 21cm.

j10. **MULANJE MOUNTAIN CLUB**
Journal. Blantyre: The Club. 25cm.

j11. **UMTALI MOUNTAIN AND OUTDOOR CLUB**
Mountain View: official journal. Umtali: The Club. 21cm.

Asia

j12. **CLIMBERS CLUB (Bombay)**
Bulletin. Bombay: The Club. 26cm. No. 1, 1962. 2 issues p.a?

j13. **HIMALAYAN ASSOCIATION**
Journal. Calcutta: The Association. 22-25cm.

j14. **HIMALAYAN CLUB**
Himalayan Journal. Calcutta: The Club. 23cm. Vol. 1, 1929 — in progress. Annual. Indexes: v.1-21, 1929-58; v.22-32, 1959-73; v.33, 1973-74; v.34, 1974-75.

j15. **HIMALAYAN CLUB**
Newsletter. Bombay: The Club. 29cm.

j16. **HIMALAYAN FEDERATION**
Himavanta. Calcutta: The Federation. 22-29cm. 1970? — . Monthly.

j17. **HIMALAYAN MOUNTAINEERING INSTITUTE**
Himalayan Mountaineering Journal. Darjeeling: The Institute. 23cm. Annual.

j18. **HIMALAYAN MOUNTAINEERING INSTITUTE**
Newsletter. Darjeeling: The Institute. 20-22cm. 2 issues p.a.

j19. *Indian Mountaineer*
New Delhi. 2 issues p.a. (May & November)

j20. **JAPANESE ALPINE CLUB**
Sangaku: journal of the J.A.C. Tokyo: The Club. 22-27cm. Vol. 1, 1906 — in progress. In Japanese with English summaries of principal items.

j21. NAINI TAL MOUNTAINEERING CLUB

Nanda: news bulletin. Naini Tal: The Club. 29cm. Vol. 1, no. 1, 1979-?

j22. *The Iwa To Yuki*

Tokyo: Yama-Kei. 26cm. In Japanese with English summaries. 6 issues p.a.

Australia

j23. *Rucksack Magazine*

Waverton, N.S.W.: The Magazine. 24cm.

j24. *Thrutch:* The Australian Climbing Magazine

Annandale, N.S.W.: The Magazine. 25-27cm. 1963 — Quarterly.

j25. VICTORIAN CLIMBING CLUB

Rock. Brighton, Vict: The Club. 30cm. No. 1, 1978 — Annual.

j26. *Wild Magazine*

P.O. Box 415, Prahran, Victoria 3181. Quarterly.

British Isles

j27. ALPINE CLIMBING GROUP

Alpine Climbing: bulletin of the A.C.G. The Group. 30cm. 1954 — ? Now incorporated into the Alpine Journal. Annual. Not published for 1960, 1961.

j28. ALPINE CLUB

Alpine Annual: adapted from the Alpine Journal. Ldn: Dent. 23cm. Vol. 1, 1950-Vol. 2, 1951. No more issues.

J29. ALPINE CLUB

Alpine Journal: a record of mountain adventure and scientific observation. Alpine Club. 23cm. Vol. 1, 1863 — in progress. Annual. Indexes: vols. 1-15, 1863-91; 16-38, 1892-1926; 39-58, 1927-52; 59-73, 1953-68.

j30. ASSOCIATION OF BRITISH MEMBERS OF THE SWISS ALPINE CLUB

Annual report, accounts, balance sheet, list of members, office bearers. 1909-1961/62. 18cm. Title varies, i.e. 1960/61-1961/62 Yearbook and report. Continued by: ABMSAC Journal.

j31. ASSOCIATION OF BRITISH MEMBERS OF THE SWISS ALPINE CLUB

Journal of the A.B.M.S.A.C. 21cm. 1962/63 — in progress. Annual. Continues: Yearbook and report.

j32. BRITISH MOUNTAINEERING COUNCIL

Annual report. Manchester: B.M.C. Size varies. 1968 — in progress.

j33. BRITISH MOUNTAINEERING COUNCIL

Handbook. Manchester: B.M.C. 1971/72 — Alternate years.

j34. BRITISH MOUNTAINEERING COUNCIL

Mountain Life & Rocksport: official magazine of the British Mountaineering Council. Richmond, Surrey: The Magazine. 30cm. No. 1, April 1972 — Dec/Jan., 1976 (23 issues). 6 issues p.a. Continues: Mountaineering. Amalgamated with: Climber & Rambler.

j35. BRITISH MOUNTAINEERING COUNCIL

Mountaineering: official journal of the British Mountaineering Council. Ldn: B.M.C. 22cm. Vol. 1, June 1947 — vol. 6, no. 5, 1971. Frequency varies. Subtitle varies. Continued by: Mountain Life.

j36. C.H.A. MOUNTAINEERING CLUB

The Journal of the C.H.A. [Countrywide Holidays Association] *Mountaineering Club.* The Club. 23cm. vol. 1, no. 1 1931. Continues as: Journal of the Tricouni Club.

j37. CAIRNGORM CLUB

Cairngorm Club Journal. Aberdeen: The Club. 23cm. Vol. 1, no. 1, 1893 — Frequency varies.

j.38. CAMBRIDGE UNIVERSITY MOUNTAINEERING CLUB

Cambridge Mountaineering: journal of the C.U.M.C. Cambridge: The Club. 23cm. 1925/6 in progress. Annual.

j39. CARLISLE MOUNTAINEERING CLUB

Annual Journal of the Carlisle Mountaineering Club. Carlisle: The Club. 22cm. Vol. 1, no. 1. 1954 —

j40. CLEVELAND MOUNTAINEERING CLUB

Newsletter. Cleveland: The Club. 26cm. No. 1, Jan. 1959. Annual.

j41. *The Climber:*

the national monthly magazine for hill and fell-walkers, rock climbers and all mountaineers. Castle Douglas: G. Outram. 25cm. Vol. 1, Nov. 1962 — 1968/Monthly. Continues as: Climber & Rambler.

j42. *Climber*

Glasgow: Holmes McDougall. 30cm. April 1986 — in progress 12 issues p.a. Continues: Climber and Rambler.

j43. *Climber & Rambler:*

journal of the British Mountaineering Council. Edinburgh: Holmes McDougall. 30cm. 1969-86 Monthly. Continues: The Climber. Incorporates: Mountain Life. Continues as: Climber.

j44. CLIMBERS' CLUB

Climbers' Club Bulletin. Old series. 1911 —

j45. CLIMBERS' CLUB

Bulletin. New series. Oxford: Hollywell Press. 26cm. Vol. 1, no. 1, Aug. 1924 — no. 26, May, 1931. Frequency varies. Continued as: New climbs (see GUIDEBOOKS)

j46. CLIMBERS' CLUB

Climbers' Club Journal. The Club. 26cm. Old series. Vol. 1, no. 1, Aug., 1898-vol. 13, nos. 49/50, Sept/Dec., 1910. Quarterly. New series. No. 1, Feb. 1912 — in progress. Annual.

j47. CLIMBERS' CLUB

Rules, list of members and officers. 1900-1912. 21-25cm. Irregularly issued.

j48. *Crags*

Sheffield: Dark Peak. 30cm. No. 1, March, 1976 — no. 33. 6 issues p.a. Ceased publication.

j49. FEDERATION OF MOUNTAINEERING CLUBS OF IRELAND

Mountain Log: F.M.C.I. newsletter. Dublin: F.M.C.I. 21cm. No. 1, 1978 — Quarterly.

j50. FELL AND ROCK CLIMBING CLUB OF THE ENGLISH LAKE DISTRICT

Chronicle [i.e. newsletter] The Club. 30cm. 2 issues p.a.

j51. FELL AND ROCK CLIMBING CLUB

Handbook. Annual.

j52. FELL AND ROCK CLIMBING CLUB

Journal of the Fell and Rock Climbing Club of the English Lake District. The Club. 1907. Frequency varies.

j53. *Footloose*

[Commercial magazine.]

j54. GLOUCESTERSHIRE MOUNTAINEERING CLUB

Rope: the official journal of the Gloucestershire Mountaineering Club. Cheltenham: The Club. 20cm. Vol. 1, no. 1, 1957.

j55. GRAMPIAN CLUB

Grampian Club Journal. Dundee: The Club. 22cm. Vol. 1, no. 1, 1937 —

j56. *Great Outdoors*

Glasgow: Holmes McDougall. 30cm. No. 1, Jan. 1978—in progress. 12 issues p.a.

j57. GRITSTONE CLUB

Gritstone Club Journal. Bradford: The Club. 26cm. 1922 —

j58. *High Magazine*

[for hill-walkers and climbers]: the official magazine of the British Mountaineering Council. Sheffield: The Magazine. 30cm. No. 1, Dec. 1982-in progress. 12 issues p.a.

j59. *International Mountain Year 1980*
Edited by Nigel Gifford. Newcastle-upon-Tyne: KSA, [1980]. 136p, illus. 21cm. Single issue only.

j60. IRISH MOUNTAINEERING CLUB
Irish Mountaineering: journal of the Irish Mountaineering Club. [Dublin]: The Club. 22cm. Vol. 1, no. 1, Aug., 1950 — in progress. Frequency varies. Under different title prior to 1958.

j61. KARABINER MOUNTAINEERING CLUB
Journal of the Karabiner Mountaineering Club. Manchester: The Club. 25cm. Vol. 1, 1950. Continues: Newsletter.

j62. KARABINER MOUNTAINEERING CLUB
Newsletter. [No. 4, July, 1946] — no. 9, Feb., 1948. 33cm. Frequency varies. Continued by: Journal.

j63. LADIES' ALPINE CLUB
[*Report*] The Club. 19cm. 1925 — Annual. Continued by: Yearbook.

j64. LADIES' ALPINE CLUB
[*Yearbook*] The Club. 22cm. 1927-1960. Continues: Report. Continued as: Journal.

j65. LADIES' ALPINE CLUB
Journal. The Club. 23cm. 1961-1975. Annual. Ceased publication. Continues: Yearbook. Amalgamated with: Alpine journal. [Following merger of Ladies' Alpine Club with Alpine Club.]

j66. LADIES' SCOTTISH CLIMBING CLUB
Ladies' Scottish Climbing Club Annual Record. 1907 —

j67. LADIES' SCOTTISH CLIMBING CLUB
Ladies' Scottish Climbing Club Journal. Howgate, Falkirk: The Club. 23cm. No. 1, 1929 — in progress. Frequency varies. No. 1, 1929; 2, 1938; 3, 1952; 4, 1959; 5, 1968; 6, 1978; ?

j68. LANCASHIRE CAVING AND CLIMBING CLUB
Journal. Chorley: The Club. Vol. 1, 1949 — 1968? Annual. Continues: News Bulletin.

j69. LANCASHIRE CAVING AND CLIMBING CLUB
News Bulletin. Bolton: The Club. 22cm. Vol. 1, 1946? — vol. 1, no. 3, Spring, 1947. Continued by: Journal.

j70. LEEDS UNIVERSITY UNION CLIMBING CLUB
Journal. Leeds: The Club. 24cm.

j71. MANCHESTER UNIVERSITY MOUNTAINEERING CLUB
Journal. Manchester: The Club. 27cm. 1929 —

j72. MIDLAND ASSOCIATION OF MOUNTAINEERS
Bulletin. Birmingham: The Association. 22cm. No. 1, 1933 — no. 6, 1939. Annual. Continued by: Journal.

j73. MIDLAND ASSOCIATION OF MOUNTAINEERS
Journal. Birmingham: The Association. 22cm. 1947? — Alternate years. Continues: Bulletin.

j74. MIDLAND ASSOCIATION OF MOUNTAINEERS
Reports. [1920s]

j75. MORAY MOUNTAINEERING CLUB
Moray Mountaineering Club Journal. Elgin: The Club. 23cm. Vol. 1, no. 1, 1935 — Irregularly issued. Jubilee (1931-1981) edition, 1982. 48p.

j76. *Mountain*
Ldn/Sheffield: Mountain Magazine. 32cm. No. 1., 1969 — in progress. 6 issues p.a. Continues: Mountain craft [Published by the Mountaineering Association.] N.B.: Nos. 1-26 published by Y.H.A. (England & Wales)

j77. MOUNTAIN RESCUE COMMITTEE

Mountain and Cave Rescue: with lists of official teams and posts: handbook of the Mountain Rescue Committee. Buxton, Derbyshire: The Committee. 18cm. 1947 — in progress. Title, size and frequency vary. For publications prior to 1947 see main bibliography under First Aid Committee of Mountaineering Clubs.

j78. *Mountain World [Berge der Welt]*

Ldn: Allen & Unwin/Chicago: Rand McNally for Swiss Foundation for Alpine Research. 25cm. 1953-1968/9. 10 volumes. Ceased publication.

j79. *Mountain World:*

climbing, backpacking, skiing, caving, expeditions and allied activities

Edited by Nigel Gifford. Sidcup, Kent: Stone Industrial Publications. 41cm. April, 1980 — Monthly. Ceased publication. Tabloid newspaper format. Each issue approximately 20p with colour illustrations.

j80. *Mountain Year*

Perth: Holmes McDougall. 30cm. No. 1 (Sep. 1975-Sep. 1976). No. 2 (Sep. 1976-Sep.1977). Ceased publication.

j81. MOUNTAINEERING ASSOCIATION

Mountaincraft. Ldn: Mountaineering Association. 22-34cm. 1948-Autumn, 1968, no. 8. Continued by: Mountain.

j82. *Mountaineering Journal*

Edited by Karl Brunning. Birkenhead: Willmer. 26cm. Vol. 1, no. 1, June 1932 — vol. 6, no. 1, Dec. 1937/Jan-Feb., 1938. Quarterly. Ceased publication. N.B.: Vol. 1, no. 1 entitled: The British Mountaineering Journal.

j83. NOTTINGHAM UNIVERSITY MOUNTAINEERING CLUB

Journal. Nottingham: The Club. 26cm.

j84. OXFORD UNIVERSITY MOUNTAINEERING CLUB

Oxford Mountaineerng: journal of the Oxford University Mountaineering Club. Oxford: O.U.M.C. 21cm. 1935 — in progress. Frequency varies.

j85. *Oxford and Cambridge Mountaineering*

1921-1928/9. Subsequently split into the journals published by each university club.

j86. PEAK CLIMBING CLUB

Peak Climbing Club Journal. Vol. 1, no. 1, 1950-

j87. PINNACLE CLUB

Pinnacle Club Journal. Scunthorpe: The Club. 22cm. No. 1, 1924 — in progress. Frequency varies.

j88. PRESTON MOUNTAINEERING CLUB

Journal. Preston: The Club. 27cm. 1937 –. [No. 3, 1947/8; no. 4, 1949]

j89. PUBLIC SCHOOLS ALPINE SPORTS CLUB

Year book. The Club. 19cm. 1907-30.

j90. RAMBLERS' ASSOCIATION

Rucksack.

j91. RIMMON MOUNTAINEERING CLUB

Rimmon Journal. Oldham: The Club. 26cm. Vol. 1, no. 1, Dec. 1962.

j92. *Rock Action*

Stockton-on-Tees. No. 1, Feb. 1983. Ceased publication.

j93. *Rocksport*

Nottingham: P. Grainger. 30cm. Oct/Nov. 1969 — [1973?]. 6 issues p.a. Incorporated into: Mountain life.

j94. ROYAL NAVY SKI AND MOUNTAINEERING CLUB

Year Book. The Club. 22cm. 1961/2 —

j95. RUCKSACK CLUB

Report. 24cm. 1st, 1903 — 3rd, 1905. Annual. Continued by: Rucksack Club Journal.

j96. RUCKSACK CLUB

Rucksack Club Journal. Manchester: The Club 22cm. Vol. no. 1, 1907 — in progress. Annual. Continues: Report.

j97. SCOTTISH MOUNTAINEERING CLUB

Scottish Mountaineering Club Journal. Edinburgh: S.M.C. 23cm. Vol. 1, no. 1, 1890 — in progress. Annual. Indexes: vol. 1-10, 1890-1909; vol. 11-20, 1910-35;

j98. SHEFFIELD UNIVERSITY MOUNTAINEERING CLUB

Journal. Sheffield: The Club. 21cm.

j99. TRICOUNI CLUB

Journal. Ilford: The Club. 23cm. 1935 — Frequency varies. Replaces: Journal of C.H.A. Mountaineering Club.

j100. TUESDAY CLIMBING CLUB

Arête: Tuesday Climbing Club news. Ldn: The Club. 33cm. Vol. 1, 1961-1970. Ceased publication. Continued as club newsletter (same title).

j101. UNIVERSITY COLLEGE OF NORTH WALES MOUNTAINEERING CLUB

Clogwyn: University College of North Wales Mountaineering Club journal. Bangor: The Club. 24cm. 1967? — Annual.

j102. UNIVERSITY OF BIRMINGHAM MOUNTAINEERING CLUB

Journal. Birmingham: The Club. 21cm. [No. 2, 1960 — no. 6, 1964] Annual. Title varies.

j103. WAYFARERS' CLUB

Wayfarers' Bulletin. Liverpool: The Club. Bridges the gap between Wayfarers' Journal, 6 (1939) and 7 (1945).

j104. WAYFARERS' CLUB

Wayfarers' Journal. Liverpool: The Club. 23cm. 1928 — in progress. Frequency varies.

j105. WELLINGBOROUGH MOUNTAINEERING CLUB

Snaplink: Wellingborough Mountaineering Club journal. Wellingborough: The Club. 27cm.

J106. YORKSHIRE MOUNTAINEERING CLUB

Journal. [Bradford]: The Club. 21cm. 1955 — Frequency varies.

j107. YORKSHIRE RAMBLERS' CLUB

Annual report, rules, list of members, etc. Leeds: The Club. 24cm. [1892/3-1897/8.]

j108. YORKSHIRE RAMBLERS' CLUB

Syllabus. 24cm. [1896/7—1898/9)

j109. YORKSHIRE RAMBLERS' CLUB

Yorkshire Ramblers' Club Journal. Leeds: The Club. 24cm. Vol. 1, 1899 — in progress. Frequency varies.

N.B.: references have been noted to other British publications called: Climb; Lam; Plexus; Serac; Tor.

Canada

j110. ALPINE CLUB OF CANADA

Canadian Alpine Journal. Banff: The Club. 24-28cm. Vol. 1, no. 1, 1907 — in progress. Annual.

j111. ALPINE CLUB OF CANADA

Gazette. Banff: The Club. 24cm. No. 1, 1921- Frequency varies.

j112. ALPINE CLUB OF CANADA (Kootenay Section)

Kootenay Karabiner: journal of the Kootenay Section. Kootenay: The Section. 22-28cm. 1964?- 2 issues p.a.

j113. BRITISH COLUMBIA MOUNTAINEERING CLUB

The British Columbia Mountaineer: official organ. Vancouver:: The Club. 23cm. Monthly.

j114. *Crag and Canyon and National Park Gazette*

Banff Hot Springs: I. Byers. 28cm. Vol. 1, 1900— Weekly.

New Zealand

j115. ALPINE SPORTS CLUB (Auckland Branch)

Alpine Sport. Auckland: Alpine Sports Club. 27cm. Vol. 1, no. 1, 1930- Frequency varies.

j116. CANTERBURY MOUNTAINEERING CLUB

The Canterbury Mountaineer: journal of the Canterbury Mountaineering Club. Christchurch: The Club. 23-25cm. No. 1, 1931/2 — in progress. Annual.

j117. FEDERATED MOUNTAIN CLUBS OF NEW ZEALAND

Federated Mountain Clubs Bulletin. Wellington: The Federation. 21cm.

j118. NEW ZEALAND ALPINE CLUB

Bulletin. Wellington: The Club. 21-28cm. 2 issues p.a.

j119. NEW ZEALAND ALPINE CLUB

New Zealand Alpine Journal. Dunedin: The Club. 22-25cm. Vol. 1, no. 1, 1892 — in progress. Annual. Vols. 1 & 2 reprinted in 1976.

j120. TARARUA TRAMPING CLUB

Tararua. Wellington: The Club. 22-28cm. 1947- Annual.

j121. TARARUA TRAMPING CLUB

Tararua Tramper. Wellington: The Club. 21cm. Monthly.

j122. WELLINGTON TRAMPING AND MOUNTAINEERING CLUB

Tramping and Mountaineering. Wellington: The Club. 28cm. Vol. 1, 1948- 3 issues p.a.

South America

j123. SOUTH AMERICAN EXPLORERS CLUB

South American Explorer. Lima, Peru & Denver, CO: The Club. 27-34cm. Vol. 1, no. 1, Oct. 1977 — in progress (no. 13, July, 1986). Frequency varies.

United States of America

j124. ALPINE ROAMERS, WENATCHEE

Alpine Roamers. Mimeographed annuals.

j125. AMERICAN ALPINE CLUB

American Alpine Journal. N.Y.: The Club. 24cm. Vol. 1, no. 1, 1929 — in progress. Annual. Index: vols. 1-20, 1929-1976; annual indexes thereafter.

j126. AMERICAN ALPINE CLUB

Accidents in North American mountaineering including Canada and the United States: report of the Safety Committee of the American Alpine Club. N.Y.: A.A.C. 23cm. No. 1, 1948 (?) — in progress. Annual. Joint publication with Alpine Club of Canada from issues 31 (1978) onwards.

j127. APPALACHIAN MOUNTAIN CLUB

Appalachia: bulletin of the Appalachian Mountain Club. Boston: The Club. 21-27cm. Vol., no. 1, 1907 — in progress. 11 issues p.a.

j128. APPALACHIAN MOUNTAIN CLUB

Appalachia: journal of the Appalachian Mountain Club. 24cm. Vol. 1, no. 1, 1876 — in progress. Frequency varies. Indexes: vols. 1-10, 1876—1904; 11-25, 1905-45; annual indexes from 1966-67.

j129. APPALACHIAN MOUNTAIN CLUB

Appalachia: register of the Appalachian mountain Club. Boston: The Club. 16-20cm. 1890 — vol. 22, no. 3, 1934. New series vol. 1, 1935 —

j130. ASSOCIATED MOUNTAINEERING CLUBS OF NORTH AMERICA

Bulletin. N.Y.: The Clubs. 17cm. [1916-19?]

j131. ASSOCIATED OUTDOOR CLUBS OF AMERICA

Mountain Magazine. Pleasantville, NY: The Association & Adirondack Mountain Club. 27cm. c.1920 — Quarterly.

j132. *Backpacker*
N.Y.: The Magazine. 28cm. 6 issues p.a.

j133. **CALIFORNIA ALPINE CLUB**
[*Journal*]

j134. **CASCADIANS**
Cascadian. Yakima, WA: The Cascadians. Mimeographed annuals.

j135. **CHICAGO MOUNTAINEERING CLUB**
Chicago Mountaineers. Chicago: The Club. 22cm.

j136. **CHICAGO MOUNTAINEERING CLUB**
Newsletter. Chicago: The Club. 29cm. 6 issues p.a.

j137. *CLimbing*
Aspen, CO: Mountain States Communication. 28cm. No. 1, May, 1970- 6 issues p.a.

j138. **COLORADO MOUNTAIN CLUB**
Trail and Timberline. Denver: The Club. 23-25cm. Monthly.

j139. **DARTMOUTH MOUNTAINEERING CLUB**
Dartmouth Mountaineering Journal. Hanover, NH: The Club. 24cm.

j140. *The Eastern Trade*
Edited by John Stannard. Tillson, NY: ? Irregularly published [Newsletter concentrating on the Shawangunk area.]

j141. **HARVARD MOUNTAINEERING CLUB**
Bulletin. Cambridge, MA: The Club. 26cm. Monthly.

j142. **HARVARD MOUNTAINEERING CLUB**
Harvard Mountaineering. Cambridge, MA: The Club. 23-26cm. Vol., no. 1, 1927-

j143 **IOWA MOUNTAINEERS**
Iowa Climber. Iowa: The Club. 24-26cm. Quarterly.

j144. **IOWA MOUNTAINEERS**
Iowa Mountaineers Journal. Iowa: The Club. 26cm. Frequency varies.

j145. **MAZAMAS**
Mazama: a record of mountaineering in the Pacific Northwest. Portland: The Club. 26cm. Vol. 1, no. 1, 1896 — in progress. Annual.

j146. *Mountain Gazette*
Boulder, CO: Write On Publishing. 37cm. ? — no. 76/7, 1978/9. 11 issues p.a. Ceased publication.

j147. **MOUNTAINEERS**
The Mountaineer. Seattle: The Club. 23-29cm. Vol. 1, no. 1, 1907 — in progress. Annual.

j148. **MOUNT WHITNEY CLUB**
Mount Whitney Club Journal. Visalia, CA: The Club. 26cm. V. 1, no. 1, 1902— Annual.

j149. *North American Climber*
Providence, RI:

J150. *Off Belay:* the mountain magazine
Renton, WA: Off Belay. 26cm. No. 1, 1972- ? 6 issues p.a. Ceased publication.

j151. **SIERRA CLUB**
Ascent: Sierra Club mountaineering journal. S.F.: The Club. 28cm. 1967 — in progress. Frequency varies.

j152. **SIERRA CLUB**
Sierra Club Bulletin /Sierra. S.F.: The Club. V.1, no. 1, 1893 — in progress. Retitled in 1964: Sierra.

j153. **STANFORD ALPINE CLUB**
Stanford Alpine Club Journal. [California]

j154. *Summit*
Huntington Park/Big Bear Lake, CA: The Magazine. 29cm. Vol. 1, Nov. 1955 — in progress. (May, 1959 not issued) 6 issues p.a.

j155. *Vulgarian Digest*

BIBLIOGRAPHIES

b01. ALPINE CLUB
Catalogue of books in the Library of the A.C., 1880. 36p. 23cm.
—Catalogue of books. 1888.
—Catalogue of books. 1889.
—[Lists of additions to the Alpine Club Library, 1903-17]
—[List for Nov. 1932], by A. J. Macintosh. 1932.

b02. ALPINE CLUB
Alpine Club Library Catalogue — Books and Periodicals. Vol. 1. Ldn: Heinemann, 1982. Var. pag. 30cm. Softback.

b03. ASSOCIATION OF ASSISTANT LIBRARIANS
Cumulated Fiction Index, 1945-60. Compiled by G. B. Cotton and Alan Glencross. Ldn: Assoc. of Assistant Librarians, 1960. Similar volumes covering the years 1960-69; 1970-74; 1975-78.

b04. BARKER, Clive S.
Bibliography of exploration, mountaineering, travel, history and nomenclature of the Gilgit-Hunza River watershed, Haramosh Range and Basha River watershed in the eastern Hindu Kush and western Karakoram. Wellington: The Author, 1965-75. 3 parts. 34cm.
List of Periodical articles. Typescript. Copy in A.C., Library.

b05. BENT, Allen Herbert
Bibliography of the White Mountains. Boston: Published for Appalachian Mountain Club by Houghton Mifflin, 1911. vii, 114p, illus. 23cm. And supplement.

b06. BRIDGE, George
Rock climbing in the British Isles, 1894-1970: a bibliography of guidebooks. Reading: West Col, 1971. 40p, illus. 22cm. Softback.
Lists 303 items including pamphlets and private press publications. Gives more detail than shown in this bibliography.

b07. CAIRNGORM CLUB
Cairngorm Club Library: catalogue of books. Compiled by Jean A. Callander. Cairngorm Club, 1975. 10p.

b08. CAMPBELL, J. I.
Bibliography of mountains and mountaineering in Africa. Compiled by .... Cape Town: School of Librarianship, University of Cape Town, 1945. [5], 48p. 33cm.
Lists 406 items, chiefly articles published in the *Annual of the Mountain Club of South Africa.* One of the bibliographical series prepared by students studying for the Diploma in Librarianship.

b09. COOLIDGE, William Augustus Brevoort
List of the writings (not being reviews of books) dating from 1868 to 1912 and relating to the Alps or Switzerland of W. A. B. Coolidge. Grindlewald: Jakober-Peter, 1912. 37p.

b10. COX, James R.
Classics in the literature of mountaineering and mountain travel from the Francis P. Farquhar collection of mountaineering literature. An annotated bibliography compiled and edited by ..., Annotations and introductory essay by Nicholas B. Clinch, James R. Cox, and Muir Dawson. Los Angeles: Univ. California Library, 1980. iii-xxiv, 58p, illus. 28cm. Limited edition of 500 copies.

b11. FARQUHAR, Francis Peloubet & ASHLEY, Mildred P.
List of publications relating to the mountains of Alaska. N.Y.: A.A.C., 1934. 37p.
Includes references to newspaper and magazine articles.

b12. FARQUHAR, F. P.
Yosemite, the Big Trees and the High Sierra: a selective bibliography. Berkley: Univ. California Press, 1948. xii, 104p, facsims, ports. 28cm.

b13. FARQUHAR, F. P.
Published writings of Francis Peloubet Farquhar. Together with an introduction

to 'F P.F.' by Susanna Bryant Dakin. S.F.: Privately printed by K. K. Bechtel, 1954. xii, 17p. 26cm.

b14. FELL AND ROCK CLIMBING CLUB (of the English Lake District)
Catalogue of the Library. Compiled by Muriel Files. Lancaster: The Club (at the University), 1972. vi, 81p. 25cm. Members' catalogue. A limited edition of 250 copies with a different introductory section (pp. i-vi) was placed on sale to libraries and the public.
—Supplement. Additions June 1972-May 1975.
—Supplement. Additions June 1975-March 1979.
—Section IV (Maps) of the catalogue, 1978.
Classified order with author index.

b15. FISHER, Joel Ellis
Bibliography of American mountain ascents. N.Y.: A.A.C. Research Fund, 1946. 299p. 22cm.
Peak index by State/country/region with relevant articles to end-1945 from leading mountaineering journals (chiefly American). Includes North and South America.

b16. GOODMAN, E. J.
The exploration of South America: an annotated bibliography. N.Y.: Garland, 1983. xx, 174p. 23cm. (Themes in European expansion: exploration, colonization, and the impact of Empire, 4)
Lists 915 items covering the period of discovery and exploration from the 15th century onwards.

b17. GUPTA, Raj Kumar
Bibliography of the Himalayas. Gurgaon, Haryana: India Documentation Service, 1981. xxxviii, 375p. 22cm.
Includes 4772 items: books and articles (travel, climate, geology, etc).

b18. HIMALAYAN CLUB
Library: classified catalogue of books with alphabetical list of authors. Simla: Himalayan Club, 1936. 69p. Supplements 1936-38

b19. HOCKEN, T. M.
Bibliography of the literature relating to New Zealand. 1909. Continued by A. G. Bagnall of the National Library Service, Wellington.
Invaluable basis for historical research.

b20. JEFFERS, Le Roy
Selected list of books on mountaineering. Compiled by ...N.Y.: New York Public Library, 1914. 15p. 15cm.

b21. KAMBARA, Tatsu (Editor)
Nepal bibliography. Tokyo: The Author, 1959. vi, 121p, errata and addenda. 21cm. Includes 510 books and articles on Nepal. Mimeograph.

b22. KIMES, William F. & Maynie B.
John Muir: a reading bibliography. Chronologically compiled and annotated by ...Foreword by Lawrence Clark Powell. Palo Alto: The Authors, 1977. xviii, 211p, 29cm. Limited edition of 300 copies signed by the authors and the printer Grant Dahlstrom.

b23. KRAMARSIC, Joseph D.
Bibliography of Colorado mountain ascents, 1863-1976. Dillon: The Author, 1979. x, 258p. 28cm. Softback.
Journal articles only.

b24. KRAMARSIC, J. D.
Bibliography of Colorado rock climbs and ice climbs, 1863-1976. Dillon: The Author, 1983. x, 98p. 28cm. Softback.
Journal articles.

b25. KRAWCZYK, Chess
Mountaineering: a bibliography of books in English to 1974. Metuchen, N.J.: Scarecrow Press, 1977. xii, 180p. 23cm.
Lists 1141 references of all sorts, with short title index and brief subject index.

b26. LIBRARY ASSOCIATION
Readers' guide to books on mountaineering. Ldn: Library Assoc., 1962. 27p. 19cm.
—2nd ed. 1972. 39p. 19cm.

b27. MALLA, Khadga Man
Bibliography of Nepal. Compiled by ...Kathmandu: Royal Nepal Academy, 1975. viii, xv, 529p. 29cm.
Contains details of 8327 books and articles on Nepal.

b28. MARSHALL, Julie G.
Britain and Tibet, 1765-1947. The background to the India-China dispute. A select annotated bibliography of printed material in European languages. Bundoora, Melbourne: La Trobe Univ. Library, 1977. xxiv, 372p. 25cm. (La Trobe Univ. Library, Library Publication, 10)

b29. MECKLY, Eugene P.
'Bibliography of privately printed mountaineering books', in *The Alpine Annual: 2*. Ldn: Dent (for Alpine Club), 1951. Pp. 111-6. Reprinted from the *Alpine Journal.*

b30. MONTAGNIER, Henry F.
Bibliography of the ascents of Mont Blanc from 1786-1853. Ldn: Spottiswoode, 1911. 35p. 22cm. Reprinted from the *Alpine Journal.*

b31. MONTAGNIER, H. F.
Further contribution to the bibliography of Mont Blanc, 1786-1853. Ldn: Spottiswoode, 1916. 25p, 3 plates, ports. 22cm. Reprinted from the *Alpine Journal.*

b32. NATIONAL LIBRARY OF SCOTLAND.
Shelf catalogue of the Lloyd collection of Alpine books. Boston, MA: G. K. Hall, 1964. vi, 94p. 26cm.
Lists 1600 items, including some non-Alpine, in several languages. Many duplications and not in any sort of order.

b33. NEATE, William Ronald
Mountaineering and its literature: a descriptive bibliography of selected works published in the English language, 1744-1976. Milnthorpe: Cicerone Press, 1978. 165p, illus. 25cm.

b34. NEATE, W. R.
'Mountaineering fiction', in *Sporting Fictions* (Proceedings of a workshop held at the University of Birmingham in September, 1981, jointly organized and sponsored by the Department of Physical Education and the Centre for Contemporary Cultural Studies). Pp. 414-37. 30cm.

b35. [PAN AMERICAN UNION. Columbus Memorial Library]
Index to Latin American periodical literature, 1929-1960. Compiled in the Columbus Memorial Library of the Pan American Union. Several volumes. Boston: G. K. Hall & Co., 1962.
Lists articles including many in foreign languages.

b36. PORTER, Edward C.
Books on mountaineering: library of mountaineering and exploration and travel: both true and in fiction, history, science, technique, philosophy, art etc. Chicago, 1959. 74p. 25cm.
Lists 750 items.

b37. READ, Brian J.
Mountaineering, the literature in English: a classified bibliography, and an introductory essay. Unpublished, 1975. Librarian's thesis. Copy of typescript in Fell & Rock Library.

b38. SCHAPPERT, Linda G.
Sikkim, 1800-1968: an annotated bibliography. Honolulu: East-West Center, 1968. viii, 69p. 28cm. Mimeograph. (Occasional Papers of East-West Center Library, University of Hawaii, 10)

b39. SMITH, Janet Adam
Mountaineering. Cambridge: Univ. Press for National Book League, 1955. 24p. (Reader's Guides, 2nd series, 1)

b40. THORINGTON, James Monroe
Mountains and mountaineering: a list of the writings (1917-1947) of J. Monroe Thorington. The Author, 1947. 12p. 23cm. Only 150 copies.

b41. THORINGTON, J. M.
Mountains and mountaineering: bibliography of 50 years (1917-67). Alpine writings of J. M. Thorington.

b42. WAGNER, Henry R.

The plains and the Rockies: a bibliography of original narratives of travel. S.F., 1921. [v], 193p. 26cm.
List of works and notes thereon concerned with the early exploration of the Rocky Mountains. Includes, among others, Lewis and Clark; Alexander Henry; David Thompson; Ross Cox; David Douglas; Wilkes; Fremont; Palliser.

b43. WALKER, Bruce

Bibliography of books on Tibet published in English. Laurel, MS: The Author, 1968. 46 leaves.

b44. WARIKOO, Kulbhushan

Jammu, Kashmir and Ladakh: a classified and comprehensive bibliography. Delhi: Sterling Pub., 1976. xxxv, 555p. 22cm.
Most useful bibliography containing 7684 titles of books and articles.

b45. WASHBURN, H. Bradford

Mount McKinley and the Alaska Range in literature: a descriptive bibliography. Boston: Museum of Science, 1951. 88p. 23cm.
Lists 264 items with valuable comments on each. Published at the request of the University of Alaska for distribution at the Alaska Science Conference, 1951.

b46. WOOD, Hugh B.

Nepal bibliography. Eugene, OR: American-Nepal Education Foundation, 1959. 108p. 24cm.
Lists 304 books, 762 magazine articles, 50 newspapers, and 143 unpublished items.

b47. WRIGHT, Walter W.

The White Mountains: an annotated bibliography, 1918-1947. Compiled by ...[Boston], 1948. 205-223p, plates, illus. 22cm. Offprint from *Appalachia,* Dec. 1948.

b48. YAKUSHI, Yoshimi

Catalogue of Himalayan literature. Tokyo: The Author, 1972. 343p. Edition of 500 copies. Lists over 2000 items in various European languages and Japanese. —2nd rev. ed. Tokyo: Hakusuisha Pub., 1984. 759p,. 27cm. Lists 3752 books in European languages and 855 books in Japanese (some with English summaries).

b49. YORKSHIRE RAMBLERS' CLUB

Yorkshire Ramblers' Club Library [catalogue], 1959. Compiled by A. B. Craven. Leeds: Y.R.C. & Leeds Public Libraries, 1959. 154p. 25cm.
Details of the Club Library and mountaineering collection of Leeds Central Library.

ADDENDA

a01. ACADEMIC ALPINE CLUB OF HOKKAIDO
Dhaulagiri I. 8167m. 211p, illus, maps. In Japanese with English summary.
Account of ascent in mid-winter 1982.

a02. BIRKETT, Bill
Classic rock climbs in Great Britain. Sparkford: Oxford Illustrated Press, 1986. 171p, illus (some col). 26cm.

a03. BONINGTON, Chris
The Everest years: a climber's life. Ldn: Hodder, 1986. 256p, illus (some col), maps. 26cm.

a04. BROWN, Hamish
The great walking adventure. Sparkford: Oxford Illus. Press, 1986. 232p, col. illus, maps. 22cm.

a05. CAFFREY, Pat
Climber's guide to Montana. Missoula: Mountain, 1986. 237p, maps.

a06. CROCKET, Ken
Ben Nevis, Britain's highest mountain. Edinburgh: S.M.T., 1986. [xiv], 320p, illus, maps. 24cm.

a07. DESROY, Graham (Ed.)
Yorkshire limestone. Yorkshire M.C., 1985. 320p, illus, maps.

a08. DEUTSCHLE, Phil
The two-year mountain. N.Y.: Universe, 1986. 278p, plates, illus.
Concludes with a solo attempt on Parchamo (20,580′).

a09. DINWOODIE, D. (Ed.)
North-east outcrops of Scotland. Edinburgh: S.M.T., 1984. 284p, maps.

a10. DRAPER
Rockcraft. [1986?]
B.M.C. rock-climbing manual.

a11. DRUMMOND, Ed
A dream of white horses. [1986?]
Articles and poems.

a12. [EXPEDITION ADVISORY CENTRE]
Expedition yearbook. Edited by Nigel and Shane Winser. Ldn: Expedition Advisory Centre. Var. pag., illus. 30cm. Spiral bound.
Annual volumes; summarizes numerous mountain related expeditions, with sketch maps and other illustrations. The Expedition Advisory Centre is jointly administered by the Royal Geographical Society and the Young Explorers' Trust.

a13. FAIRLEY, Bruce
Guide to climbing and hiking in southwestern British Columbia. West Vancouver: Soules, 1986. [xviii], 385p, maps.
Update of 1974 Culbert guide.

a14. FAWCETT, Ron
Climbing. By . . ., Jeff Lowe, Paul Nunn, Alan Rouse. Edited by Audrey Salkeld. Ldn: Bell & Hyman, 1986. 255p, illus (somc col). 28cm.

a15. FINLAY, Winifred
Peril in Lakeland. Ldn: Harrap, 1953. 200p, col. plate, map. 20cm.
Fiction. Young adult adventure story set in the central fells of the Lake District.

a16. FREEMAN, Roger & Ethel
Exploring Vancouver's North Shore mountains. Vancouver: Federation of Mountain Clubs of British Columbia, 1985. 270p, 5 fold. maps. Softbound in slipcase.

a17. GIBBONS, Robert & ASHFORD, Robert
The Himalayan kingdoms: Nepal, Bhutan and Sikkim. Ldn: Batsford, 1983. 157p, plates, illus, maps.

a18. GREIG, Andrew
Kingdoms of experience: Everest the unclimbed ridge. Ldn: Hutchinson, 1986. [iv], 249p, col. illus, maps. 24cm.

a19. GREIG, A.
Summit fever: the story of an armchair climber on the 1984 Mustagh Tower Expedition. Ldn: Hutchinson, 1985. 281p, col. illus. 23cm.

a20. GURUNG, Harka
Maps of Nepal: inventory and evaluation. Bangkok: Orchid Press, 1983.
Well produced reference book on all kinds of maps of Nepal.

a21. HASTENWRATH, Stefan
The glaciers of Equatorial East Africa. [Cape Town?]: D. Reidel Pub. Co., 1984. xxiv, 354p, illus, maps.

a22. HOLZEL, Tom & SALKELD, Audrey Mary (b.1936)
The mystery of Mallory and Irvine. Ldn: Cape, 1986. xi, 322p, plates, illus. 24cm.

a23. JENKINS, Peter
Across China. N.Y.: Morrow/Sweet Springs, 1986. 351p, col. plates, illus, maps.
Account of successful American ascent of Everest North Face in 1984.

a24. JONES, Trevor & MILBURN, Geoff
Welsh rock: 100 years of climbing in North Wales. Glossop: Pic, 1986. 318p, illus (some col). Also limited edition of 300 numbered and signed copies.
History of rock-climbing in North Wales from earliest times.

a25. KAWAGUCHI, Kunio
The Tateyama: beautiful northern Japan alps. Tokyo: Graphic-sha, 1986. 103p, col. plates, illus, map. Captions and epilogue in English.
Photo-album: Tateyama is a 3015m peak on the island of Honshu.

a26. LEVY, Jaynee
Everyone's guide to trailing & mountaineering in southern Africa. Cape Town: Struik, 1982. 392p, col. plates, illus, maps. (R.P., 2nd, 3rd)

a27. MARSH, Terry
The mountains of Wales. Ldn: Hodder, 1985. 256p, illus, map.

a28. MILBURN, Geoff (Ed.)
Derwent gritstone, Manchester: B.M.C., 1985. 264p, illus, (some col), maps. (Peak District climbs, 4th series, vol. 2)

a29. MIZUKOSHI, Takeshi
The Hodaka: radiance and wind in the Japanese alps. Tokyo: Graphic-sha, 1986. 107p, plates, illus. Text and captions in English and Japanese.

a30. MORROW, Pat
Beyond Everest: quest for the seven summits. Camden East: Camden, 1986. 175p, col. plates, illus. Softbound.
Climbing the highest mountain of each of the seven continents; by an outstanding Canadian mountain photographer and climber.

a31. MURRAY
Scotland's mountains. [1986?]

a32. PATEL, Jashbhai
The Garhwal Kumaon Himalayas. Bombay: The Author [distributed by the Himalayan Club], 1985. 248p, illus, maps.
Useful reference book, mainly for trekkers.

a33. PAYNE, Jenifer
Yi Un Sang: epic poet. 1985. Text in English and French.
Poems by a president of the Korean Alpine Club.

a34. POUCHER, W. A.
Ireland. Ldn: Constable, 1986. col. illus.
Photo-album.

a35. PUTNAM, William Lowell
Joe Dodge: one New Hampshire institution. Canaan, NH: Phoenix Publishing, 1986. 184p, illus.
Story of a famous White Mountain personality.

a36. PYATT, Edward C.
The passage of the Alps. Ldn: Hale, 1984. 256p, illus, maps.

a37. REESE, Rick
Montana mountain ranges.
—Rev. ed. Helena, MT: American Geographic, 1985. 104p, col. plates, illus.
Interesting text and illustrations.

a38. RIVOLIER, J.
High altitude deterioration. By ...[and others]. N.Y.: Karger, 1985. 227p, illus.

a39. ROWELL, Galen
Mountain light. S.F.: Sierra Club, 1986. 240p, col. plates, illus.
Compilation of twenty years' of the author's favourite photographs and essays; Himalaya, Alaska, China, Patagonia, Yosemite, etc.

a40. SOMERS, Paul
The shivering mountain. Ldn: Collins, 1959.
—Fontana p/back, 1962. 192p.
Fiction. Kidnapped scientist: potholing climax in Derbyshire.

a41. STEELQUIST, Robert U.
Washington mountain ranges. Helena, MT: American Geographic, 1986. 104p, col. plates, illus.
Fine photography; narratives of early ascents, Ptarmigan Traverse, etc.

a42. TILMAN, H. W.
Adventures under sail: selected writings, edited by Libby Purves. Ldn: Gollancz, 1982. 254p, plates, illus, maps. (Also R.P.)

a43. TULLIS, Julie (-1986)
Clouds from both sides. 1986.
Memoirs of leading British woman climber who died on K2.

a44. VENABLES, Stephen
The painted mountains. 1986.

a45. WIELOCHOSKI, A.
East Africa international mountain guide: Kenya, Tanzania, Uganda, Zaire, including Mount Kenya, Kilimanjaro and the Ruwenzori. Reading: West Col, 1986. 145p, illus.
Expeditions, rock climbs, treks and caving.

a46. WUERTHNER, George
Idaho mountain ranges. Helena, MT: American Geographic, 1986. 104p, col. plates, illus.
Fine photography; list of peaks over 10,000 feet.

INDEXES

SHORT TITLE INDEX

Guidebooks: In view of the sameness of wording, e.g. 'Climbers' guide to ...', most guidebooks are listed under place-names; also items with only minor variations of title have been lumped together.

GENERAL INDEX

Accidents, Search & Rescue

Africa

Alaska

Albania

Alpine Club

Alps

Andes & South America

Avalanches & Snow Safety

Bibliographies

Big Wall Climbing

Biography

(Individual)

Biography

(Collective)

Board Games

Bouldering & Outcrop Climbing

British Isles

Hong Kong

Humour

Indian Mountaineering Foundation

Ireland

Japan & Korea

Journals

Jugoslavia
(Including Julian Alps)

Karakoram

Literature & Art

Malta

Mauritius

Mexico

Mountain Medicine & Physiology

Mountain Navigation

Mountain Weather & Climate

Mountaineering Clubs & Organizations
(See also Alpine Club)

Mysticism

Myth & Symbolism

New Guinea

New Zealand